Odessa Recollected
The Port and the People

Ukrainian Research Institute
Harvard University

Ukrainian Studies

Series Editor: Vitaly Chernetsky (University of Kansas)

Odessa Recollected
The Port and the People

PATRICIA HERLIHY

Boston
2018

Library of Congress Cataloging-in-Publication Data:

The bibliographic data for this title is available from the Library of Congress.

ISBN 978-1-61811-736-6 (hardback)
ISBN 978-1-61811-737-3 (electronic)

Published by the Ukrainian Research Institute, Harvard University, with Academic Studies Press.

Book design by Kryon Publishing Services (P) Ltd.
www.kryonpublishing.com

Cover design by Ivan Grave.

Published by Academic Studies Press in 2018
28 Montfern Avenue
Brighton, MA 02135, USA
press@academicstudiespress.com
www.academicstudiespress.com

To the Memory of David Herlihy, 1930–1991

Table of Contents

Acknowledgments	vii
Introduction	viii

PART ONE
Culture — 1

1. The Persuasive Power of the Odessa Myth — 2
2. Odessa Memories — 27
3. How Ukrainian Is Odesa? From Odessa to Odesa — 74
4. Jewish Writers of Odessa — 83

PART TWO
Community — 99

5. Death in Odessa: A Study of Population Movements in a Nineteenth-Century City — 100
6. The Ethnic Composition of Odessa in the Nineteenth Century — 117
7. Greek Merchants in Odessa in the Nineteenth Century — 137
8. The Greek Community in Odessa, 1861–1917 — 154

PART THREE
Commerce — 169

9. Odessa: Staple Trade and Urbanization in New Russia — 170
10. Commerce and Architecture in Odessa in Late Imperial Russia — 182
11. Port Jews of Odessa and Trieste: A Tale of Two Cities — 196
12. Russian Wheat and the Port of Livorno, 1794–1865 — 209
13. South Ukraine as an Economic Region in the Nineteenth Century — 226

Index — 246

Acknowledgments

Many various archives and libraries in Italy, France, the United Kingdom, Soviet Union, Ukraine, and the United States deserve my gratitude for their help during more than fifty years of research. Obliging directors, knowledgeable archivists, and helpful librarians were essential to finding source material. My late husband David Herlihy read and critiqued the articles published before his death in 1991. It would be impossible to name all the others who assisted me during such a length of time along a circuitous research route.

It would be remiss of me, however, not to thank my coauthor Oleh Hubar (Oleg Gubar') for our joint essay and for sharing with me his extraordinary knowledge of Odessa's past. In addition, I would like to thank other Odessites who hosted, sustained, entertained, and enlightened me about their city's past: Valeria Kukharenko, Alexander Manin, Irina Nemchenko, Elena Igina, and Hobart Earle.

Others who have read or edited various recent pieces are Maxim Shrayer, Ken Frieden, Steven Zipperstein, Guido Hausmann, Stella Ghervas, Irene Herlihy, and Sarah Tracy. Natalie Grishina, Irina Nemchenko, and Helen Schmierer provided indispensable bibliographic assistance. A team—Kathleen McBride, Megan Hurst, Jeffrey White, and Irene Herlihy—helped to format the material.

Essential to publication was the support of Serhii Plokhii, director, and Marika Whaley, publications manager, of the Harvard Ukrainian Research Institute. I owe much to the talented people currently or formerly at Academic Studies Press: Oleh Kotsyuba, Faith Wilson Stein, Kira Nemirovsky, Eileen Wolfberg, and Rebekah Slonim. To the unnamed people who made it possible for me to produce these articles, I offer gratitude; to my children—Maurice, Christopher, David, Felix, Gregory, and Irene—I am thankful for their encouragement and emotional support.

Patricia Herlihy

Introduction

It was in the Florentine *Archivio di Stato* in 1961 that I first discovered Odessa (in Ukrainian, Odesa). As part of my doctoral dissertation, I was examining documents that tracked the export of grain in the nineteenth century from Russian ports on the Black Sea to Mediterranean ports. Naturally, Odessa figured as the principal port of export. The more I read the Tuscan consuls' reports on Odessa, the more I was reminded of my native city of San Francisco, California. Both were boomtowns in the nineteenth century—one attracted adventurers after the discovery of gold and the other attracted commercial entrepreneurs by industrializing Western Europe's voracious demand for grain. Hilly terrain situated on the fringe of their respective countries offered commanding views of the sea in both cities, which enjoyed a Mediterranean-style climate and bloomed into colorful cosmopolitan urban sites. I was determined to find out more about this attractive city, but I could find no general history of Odessa. I soon learned that urban history did not fall within the Marxist paradigm of meaningful historical research, although luckily local imperial Russian historians did write valuable articles about Odessa's history. For Marxists, class struggle within a city was worthy of examination, but a biography of a city itself was not a legitimate field of inquiry.

More than a dozen years and a half dozen children later, I made my first visit to Odessa by sea in the summer of 1974. The Soviet ship had sailed from Alexandria and stopped (inexplicably twenty-four hours late) at Varna, where I excitedly boarded. I remained on deck all night making sure I would miss not a moment of surveying the Black Sea, nor a first glimpse of the city I had by then studied for fourteen years. To my delight, the sea approach was the same romantic one taken by most of the hundred or so foreign travelers whose nineteenth-century accounts I had read. I was greeted at the pier by a member of Intourist, a young woman from Leningrad married to a local sailor. She took me on an obligatory tour of the city. Although her knowledge of its history was a bit shaky, I was careful not to correct her since I was allowed there only as a tourist. I had just given a paper on Black Sea trade at an international economic history conference in Bucharest. I took a train to Varna.

To my surprise a *refusenik* family was already waiting in my room at the Londonskaia Hotel when I arrived. The son, a professor of philosophy, who had managed to emigrate to Boston with his wife and child, had given me a suitcase to deliver to them. He had asked that I not write their names and address but memorize them and that I go surreptitiously to their home on Gogol Street. Their courage surprised me and their hospitality amazed me even more. One of the members, a university student, smuggled books out of the university library, mostly about the grain trade, and brought them to the hotel where I furiously copied excerpts on my Olivetti portable typewriter.

En route by rail back to Bucharest, a train conductor sat with me—the car was nearly empty—to lecture me on the Soviet success in agriculture, even presenting me with a Marxist–Leninist textbook. When we arrived at the border city of Ungheni at midnight, we had to change trains as the gauge of the tracks differed. The Soviet border guards seized my innocuous notes. I put up an enormous fuss, rattling them to such an extent that they returned them to me and exchanged more dollars for my rubles than I was entitled to.

My next, but far from last, trip to Odessa was in 1981, when I was supported by an IREX (International Research and Exchanges Board) grant as the first American exchange professor to do research in Odessa. I was not allowed to see students at the Odessa I. I. Mechnikov University, but that suited me since it gave me more time for research. As the oldest inhabitant (except for the director) in a university dormitory, I made friends among the Soviet and Cuban students, and even with a gorgeous graduate student named Liuda who was planted across the hall to spy on me. I spent my mornings at the Oblast Archives, afternoons at the University Library, and Sundays at the Gogol Public Library. Although food was scarce, I still regard that period as one of the most fulfilling of my life. In short, it was the moment when I became an Odessite at heart. In 1991, I returned to Odessa. It was then that I met Oleh Hubar, the leading historian of the city. I returned to the Oblast Archives. The staff presented me with a bouquet of flowers and showed me the catalog, which oddly had not existed a decade earlier. I realized that they were only obeying orders from on high in 1981. I returned to Odessa again to attend a conference on Ukrainian history and presented the Ukrainian translation (Krytyka Press) of my book *Odessa: A History, 1794–1914* (Harvard University Press) to the University library. In 2002, I was inducted into the World-Wide Club of Odessites as an honorary life member. In 2004, I was awarded the International Deribas Prize for Studies on the Black Sea. It seemed that the city I adopted had adopted me as well. This collection of articles is testimony to my abiding interest in Odessa's history.

Located on the northwest littoral of the Black Sea, Odessa remains of strategic significance in contemporary geopolitical affairs. As a part of Novorossiia and a gateway to Crimea, its location in Ukraine likewise has assumed increased importance. Changing regimes, shifting economic interests, periodic ethnic tensions, and threats of international crises have always marked Odessa's history. Pogroms, revolutionary violence, and the horrors of the Holocaust have left their ugly stains on the annals of the city. But fascinating, cosmopolitan, unique Odessa and its residents' cultural achievements, dry humor, joie de vivre, and fierce independent attitude offer historians still more riches to discover. Fortunately, many able younger scholars are now skillfully unearthing the city's alluring past.

May its future be stable and bright.

Part One
Culture

CHAPTER 1

The Persuasive Power of the Odessa Myth

The citizens of Odessa have cherished their ethnic diversity and vibrant economy since Catherine II officially founded the city in 1794.[1] She took a remote, sparsely populated Turkish fortress and then set out to attract settlers who could defend it.[2] She sent notices throughout Europe offering emigrants land, tax exemptions, and religious freedom. In addition to a nucleus of Russian officials, Polish landlords, and Ukrainians, many non-Slavs responded to her call. Among the early settlers of Odessa were Greek and Italian merchants, Bulgarians, Albanians, Tatars, Swiss, Germans, the French, and even a few English people. Many Jews, notably from Galicia and Poland, took legal residence there.[3] Serfs were not officially invited, of course, but the local authorities, eager to build a population base, often turned a blind eye to the arrival of fugitives. Some of these settlers were eager to acquire a homestead, while others were drawn by the economic opportunities afforded by the new and growing city.

ORIGINS OF THE MYTH

Early visitors from Europe, the United States, and Russia as well as early Odessites began to issue flattering reports, sparking the "myth of Odessa," a magical place where one could instantly become rich simply by setting one's foot in the city. As Menachem-Mendl puts it in a letter to his wife around the turn of the twentieth century, "I want you to know it is simply not in my power to describe the city of Odessa—how big and beautiful it is—the people here, so wonderful; and good-hearted, and the terrific business one can do here."[4] In the early 1820s, N. Chizhov, a naval cadet and friend of the poet Alexander Pushkin and a future Decembrist, writes lyrically of Odessa:

> Imagine that everyone gathers here [in the garden] to enjoy the cool evening and aromatic fragrance of flowers. The tall Turk offers you a tasty Asian drink, while a pretty Italian woman sitting under the dense shade of an elm brought over from the shores of the Volga, proffers ice cream in a cut-glass tumbler... A fellow citizen of the great Washington walks alongside the bearded inhabitants of Cairo and Alexandria; the ancient descendants

---

Originally published as Patricia Herlihy and Oleg Gubar, "The Persuasive Power of the Odessa Myth," in *Cities after the Fall of Communism: Reshaping Cultural Landscapes and European Identity*, ed. John Czaplicka, Nida Gelazis, Blair A. Ruble (Baltimore, MD: Johns Hopkins University Press, 2009), 137–65.

Figure 1.1 The monument to Catherine II and to the other founders of Odessa. Sculptor: Boris Eduards. The monument was erected in 1900 and destroyed in 1920. It was reconstructed by Oleh Chernoivanov and unveiled in October 2007. Photograph by Ivan Cherevatenko.

> of the Normans from the steep cliffs of Norway, the splendid Spaniard from the shores of Guadalquivir, residents of Albion, Provence and Sicily gather, it seems, in order to represent here an abridgment of the universe. It can be said that nowhere in Russia is there another place where you might find such a spectacle.[5]

Throughout the nineteenth and early twentieth centuries, local historians, filmmakers, poets, novelists, journalists, and memoirists universally extolled Odessa as a multiethnic, energetic oasis of freedom and beauty and elaborated the Odessa myth.[6]

The legend of the "golden city" was not without some foundation. In its first half century, young Odessa was the largest exporter of grain in the world, even in the years of the Continental Blockade.[7] A typical Mediterranean port in appearance and function—cosmopolitan, energetic, with an independent character—emerged improbably on the *dikoe pole* (wild field) at the border of a subdued and servile Russia. Persuaded that they were indeed exceptional, Odessites embraced the image projected on them by outsiders. As a result, some might charge that they generated in themselves superciliousness, arrogance, and an augmented self-esteem completed by a certain narcissism and infantilism. The self-image of the Odessites guaranteed them a priori a special quality, one that lent them moral dividends. The Odessite derived as

Figure 1.2 Cafe Fankoni, showing the cosmopolitan liveliness of Odessa. Postcard from the early twentieth century.

Figure 1.3 A view of Odessa Harbor. Lithograph from the middle nineteenth century.

much self-satisfaction from urban citizenship as from a certain perception of Odessa's historical past. The popular singer and bandleader Leonid Utesov expresses this pride in the first lines of his memoirs, "I was born in Odessa. You think I am bragging? But it is really true.

Many people would like to have been born in Odessa, but not everyone manages to."[8] Or more recently, Anatolii Kazik, a cinematographer, notes that whenever one informs others that he or she was born in Odessa, they smile and mention, "Odessa humor, Odessa songs, Odessa jokes and the characteristic Odessa speech, an Odessite is without fail merry, witty, sharp; he is never despondent, petty; he has a superior fascinating personality."[9]

THE SOVIET APPROPRIATION OF THE MYTH

During the Soviet era, the authorities celebrated whatever elements of the myth that suited their ideology. For example, the new Soviet regime, hungry for heroes and national treasures, rapturously accepted the axiom of the exceptionalism of Odessa. Long before the Great Patriotic War (World War II), before the heroic defense in the summer and fall of 1941, Odessa was considered not simply golden but Soviet golden. In Odessa, "by the bluest Black Sea in the world," diggers, pilots, reindeer breeders, builders of DniproHES and Magnitogorsk, and "swineherdesses and shepherds" took refuge from their heavy labors.[10] Here these vacationers met Odessites, reputedly the most hospitable, the merriest, the most fascinating, and the wittiest citizens in the world. Multinational Odessa was a miniature "new historical community—the Soviet people."

The Soviet view of Odessa and the image conveyed in the belles lettres of Pushkin, Batiushkov and Tumanskii, Babel', Paustovskii and Il'f and Petrov were of a carefree and harmonious Odessa.[11] Yet a few "renegades" or "dissidents" looked around and noted that not all was affable, hospitable, or funny. Citizens of various ages and professions strolled around, but they were not really jovial. Even though they all had pleasant expressions on their faces and they would look at you and listen, they did not truly want to hear or understand what you were saying, but only used your remarks as a pretext to joke, pun, or banter. And that is exactly the synthesis of Odessan and Soviet ideology—an excising of the very substance of meaning, leaving only the exotic aesthetic of humor. This stereotype is the source of the never-ending masks, images of the happy heroes of films such as *Happy-Go-Lucky Guys, Two Soldiers*, and other artistic personages composed of "100 percent Odessites."

Soviet Odessa served a special function as a supplier of satire and humor, as a home for funny shows and witty punning, as a haven for outspoken Jews. Limited criticism of Soviet reality spiced up Odessan irony and was not only tolerated but also even encouraged from time to time. In a sense, Odessa was conferred the privilege of being an urban "Holy Fool," a harmless character who could speak the truth under the cover of feigned madness. This veneer of affability to a certain extent protected Odessa from being as thoroughly "Sovietized" as other cities. Simple neglect prevented massive substitutions of Soviet buildings for the older European styles. The Soviet regime needed only to be assured that there were sufficient sanatoria and camps for workers from all over the Soviet Union, but it cared little for the housing needs of the city's residents.

Odessa was content to carry out its role of reveling in its own importance and uniqueness, being able to show its readiness to doubt and disagree without openly challenging the authorities. After all, it has always shown "more color, spunk, and irreverence than other cities in the former Soviet Union."[12] The Club of the Merry and Witty (KVN) has been functioning from the mid-1960s and won the All-Soviet-Union humor championship four times. The important Odessa "Iumorina," the All-Union First of April holiday of humor with elements of carnival, has been celebrated since 1973. The Golden Duke Film Festival, the annual international jazz festival, the festival of contemporary art, the first Literary Museum in the Soviet Union, the International Club of Odessites, and other groups and activities also mark the celebratory inclinations of the natives.

Although now part of an independent Ukraine, Odessa has largely retained its historical-cultural baggage. To be sure, Communist Party ideologues at first tried to recolor the biography of the city to fit the new stereotypes. Soon this latter-day Bolshevik zeal abated, however, as authorities in the capital Kyiv realized that Odessa's traditional image was still attractive. The designations of the "southern Palmyra" or the "capital of humor" thus remained as before. Nevertheless, the city began to reflect on its dried-up moral and material resources.

During the time of the Soviet Union, the economy of the city fell into complete decline; its housing stock became dismally dilapidated, and a large part of the municipal and cultural monuments as well as the entire urban transportation system sank into a

Figure 1.4 The Vorontsov Palace on Prymors'kyi Boulevard. Architect: F. Boffo, 1826–28.

catastrophic situation. At the collapse of the Soviet Union, the process of privatization in Odessa and the first accumulation of capital proceeded chaotically and barbarically, a far cry from democratic ideals.

When the matter arose concerning the monuments of history and culture, the responsible government department often acted the dog in the manger. Instead of leasing these buildings for a modest rent for an extended term requiring simple maintenance, officials burdened investors with the requirement of reconstruction as a condition of low rent. The policy has produced a sharp worsening of the structural condition of the buildings. Historical buildings such as the Odessa branch of the Russian Technical Society, the Palace of Sailors, and even the Vorontsov Palace were without owners for years because of such exactions. The "star of Odessa," the academic Theater of Opera and Ballet, was in the midst of restoration for many years.

Odessa's arrogance, encouraged by the high and the low, has in the end played a nasty joke on the citizenry. Odessa's delusions of its worth extended so far that it never once during the Soviet regime turned to UNESCO with a list of city monuments or statues to ask for assistance with preservation. Such apparent foolishness can be explained not only by patriotic blindness but also by the isolation of the Soviet people for many years from the outside world, from the living city-legends of Europe and from the planet. In comparison with other cities in Russia, Ukraine, and the USSR, Odessa actually is something outstanding both with regard to its society and to its architecture.[13] In this judgment, world opinion was in accord with that of the Odessites. When they were finally solicited, however, the experts of UNESCO concluded that Odessa's historical-cultural monuments did not possess conspicuous cultural value.[14] Perhaps the single truly attractive feature of Odessa's urban design rests on the fact that its historic center was shaped by a single general plan as brilliant as it was simple.

SHAPING THE CITY

One could say that Odessa sits on a high precipice, with its legs hung over to the basin of the Bay of Odessa. François de Wollant—a colleague of one of the main founders of Odessa, Joseph de Ribas, and a military engineer from Holland—planned the street design, having in mind above all the importance of the port for the future city.[15] Aiming to make his design conform to the natural contours of the terrain, de Wollant planned a system of straight perpendicular streets, the direction of which conformed to the orientation of the deep ravines cutting through the high Odessa plateau. The ravines served as natural steep descents to the shore and to the Quarantine and Practical harbors. To the west of the rectangular streets was planned another grid of blocks, lying at a forty-seven-degree angle in relation to the first. Every street led to the sea.

The transition from this general plan to the specific details was accomplished by the architects primarily of Mediterranean origin: Francesco and Giovanni Frapolli, Giordano Toricelli, Francesco Boffo, Gaetano Dall'Aqua, Giovanni Scudieri, Luigi Cambiaggio, and Francesco Morandi, whose best work coincided with the governance of Richelieu, Koble, Langeron, and Vorontsov. As a direct descendant of the ancient Greek colonies of the Northern Black

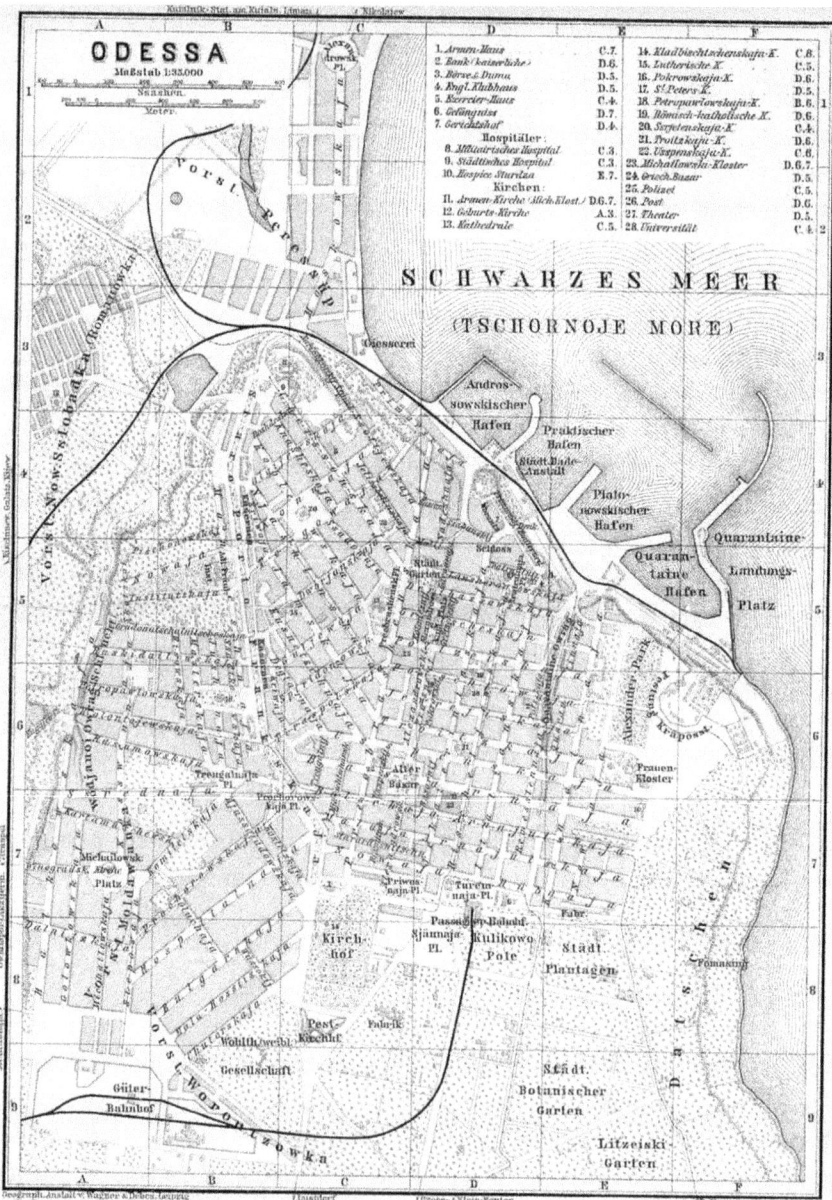

Figure 1.5 A plan of Odessa, 1892. Published in Leipzig.

Sea—mythology was embedded into the very birth of the city—Odessa replicated their design. The social centers were formed basically around three market squares: the Old Bazaar (Free Market), the Greek Bazaar (Northern or Oleksandrivs'ka Square), and the New Bazaar (Khersons'ka Square).[16] These squares lying alongside the transportation arteries imitated the ancient agora and were bordered exclusively by buildings earmarked for trade and decorated with stone arcades and porticos. In the rear of these imposing facades were built the modest houses of the Greek commercial elite.[17]

Figure 1.6 Kateryny ns'ka Square. Lithograph from the end of the nineteenth century.

Figure 1.7 A view of the Practical Harbor of the Odessa Port and the Vorontsov Palace. Lithograph.

The style of their one- and two-story houses, with deeply vaulted cellars and isolated internal courtyards to ensure privacy, confirmed the tradition of "my house is my castle." The only demand made by homeowners of the Italian architects was functionality. The natives of Southern Italy and France, South Slavic countries, and Anatolia also incorporated the essentials of their native ways of life into their new residences in Odessa. Imposing houses

Figure 1.8 Fruktovyi Commercial Row at the Pryvoz market. Architect: Fedir Nesturkh, 1913

Figure 1.9 The monument to the Duc de Richelieu on Prymors'kyi Boulevard. Postcard from the beginning of the twentieth century.

were relatively rare at the turn of the nineteenth century, but there were a few: the house of M. Kramarev on Preobrazhens'ka Street, of F. de Ribas on Derybasivs'ka Street and of L. Lashkarev on Hrets'ka Street. Later a series of mansions appeared, among which were the palatial country house of Vorontsov, the State Stock Exchange, and various offices. Then came stone bridges, the Boulevard Staircase, and the monument to the Duc de Richelieu. Even in later years of deliberate beautification, functionality nonetheless always dominated Odessa's approach to urban planning. For example, the colossal storehouses of Sabanski and Papudov played an important role during the period of the Free Port from 1819 to 1857. After the Crimean War, which was disastrous for Russia and the Odessan grain trade, the storehouses were transformed into expensive rental properties while the gigantic grain storage place of Rafalovich was reconstructed into the Russian Theater.

For almost the entire second half of the nineteenth century, the real estate market in the city experienced an enormous boom in rental property. The precipitous growth of the population, the development of the stylish sea health-resorts, the building of railroads, the creation of the Russian Society of Shipping and Trade, the Voluntary Fleet, private shipping companies, the growth of export-import operations, the strengthening of the regional money market—each of these factors inflated prices for real estate and correspondingly for rents. A new army of landlords was more concerned about exacting profits than in erecting pompous outward appearances. Dozens of such monotonous buildings from that time survive to this day.

A fortunate exception is the few private residences and offices belonging to the generation of sons, that is, the descendants of the patriarchs of grain exporters and traders (Marazli, Abaza, Rodokanaki, Ralli, Mavrokordato, Papudov, and Sevastopulo), who received European educations with corresponding polish. These youths had a predilection for buildings not with patina and antiquity, imitating the picturesque ruins of Ol'via and Pantikapea, but for buildings like those of European capitals. Even the nouveaux riches rooted in Odessa, such as Anatra, Ashkenazi, Dement'ev, Efrusi, Liban, Mendelevich, Russov, and Fal'ts-Fein, rose to the new European standard with their buildings. These moguls competed to simulate Western Europe so that the patriarchal architecture of ancient Odessa and of the Southern Palmyra gradually dissolved and Odessa metamorphosed into "Little Paris." Unlike their frugal fathers, the sons learned how to put on airs and to master pretentiousness. By about 1830, Odessa presented a unified architectural ensemble, one that was a successful mirror of an ancient city; by the middle of the nineteenth century, however, eclecticism, but to be sure of a European style, had become a dominant characteristic of the city scene. Even the scattered oriental motifs echo European predilections for the exotic, such as the arch at the entrance to Otrada on Frantsuz'kyi Boulevard, the spa on the corner of Shchepkin'ska and Preobrazhens'ka Streets, and the arabesque decoration on the facade of the Vorontsov Palace.

Little by little, the porticos along the length of the thoroughfare Oleksandrivs'kyi Prospekt were closed. Instead of facades with Ionian and Doric columns, there remained mostly decorative pilasters. And the Prospekt itself lost importance. It was closed on one side by the Derybasivs'ka Street houses built by the city architect, G. I. Toricelli. And in the middle of the Greek market arose the round house of A. I. Maiorov, along with the no less extensive home of the beer king I. A. Ansel'm. From the 1870s, profitable houses replaced buildings of classical design. The building boom at the turn of the twentieth century led to the formation of a kind of metaphorical modern museum under the sky, while sometimes destroying the best of the classical models—for example, the house of Kramerev (now the Passage), the guardhouse (the house of Libman), and the house of Marini (the Hotel Bol'shaia Moskovskaia).

The making of the architectural fabric of the city in the late nineteenth century became completely pragmatic, with no one casting a glance at the past. Today, no one would find controversial the then-modern designs of the prominent architects Alexander Bernardazzi, Lev Vlodek, Eduard Mesner, Valer'ian Shmidt, Felix Gąsiorowski, and Wilhelm Kabiolski, who worked between 1880 and 1910. Simply put, life's demands had to be met and people had to put up with it.

In later years, the Bolshevik state joyfully squeezed common workers and countless Communist Party and Soviet institutions into the spacious rental houses and into the luxurious single homes of the destroyed nobility. Sturdy as were those buildings, they could not last forever, and after seventy heroic years they were in a sorry condition. The highest achievement of the years from 1930 to 1950 was the Stalinist imperial style, a form of housing that proved its worth in building for the "radiant future." Nonetheless, later Odessites rejoiced in Khrushchev-style houses, where hundreds of people lived like worker bees in individual cells to await the soon-to-arrive fully communistic society.[18]

The inevitability of change is supremely evident, but not to the Odessite, an inveterate municipal patriot, who, famously gesticulating, tries to convince the visitor that the local theater is the third in the world according to its beauty or that this or that house has the longest balcony in Europe, that the Potemkin Steps are the eighth wonder of the world and so on. Odessa, it must be said, when it comes to formal art criticism, lives with its head turned backward. In resisting change, regional experts invoke memoirs, and anecdotes by regional historians or by their dilettante analogues, to support the notion of the purported harmonious architectural beauty of the past.[19]

Odessa is simultaneously seized by two mutually exclusive realities. One is an active, sometimes too frenetic attempt to inscribe the city into a new historical context. The second is a convulsive, rather hysterical, grasp for the past, one that is putatively heroic. Those who wish to justify bulldozed attacks on the old houses grope for some kind of ideological basis, although progress for itself need not be based on theory. New buildings and structures thrust through the turf suddenly as though they were mushrooms. Everything gives evidence that the city has a "primitive accumulation of capital" sufficient for massive construction projects, even making allowances for mammoth corruption. As Mikhail Gorbachev put it, "The process has started and it cannot be stopped."

THE ONCE AND FUTURE MYTH

The peculiarities of Odessa—that is, the aspects of the Odessa myth, particularly the city's multiethnic composition—dictate policy at all levels, including that of the local administration in shaping the construction process. Investors and their shadowy protectors and comrades in arms, the officials, demonstrate constant loyalty to the idea of a multiethnic city, with stress on generously financing the building of cultural and educational centers, churches, and memorial complexes representing various religions and ethnic groups. The construction of new buildings, not only as a battle for spheres of influence and an instrument to launder money but also as an opportunity to pay reverence to the Odessa mentality to invoke an element of the Odessa myth insofar as this myth is profitable, serves the purpose of manipulating social consciousness, providing regional and material surrogates for bread and circuses.

The Rabelaisian model of the carnivalesque city (once inhabited by Mikhail Bakhtin) remains real. Odessites continue to pose with alacrity as mutes donning masks corresponding to their assumed identity, preferring even fake holidays to monotonous provincial vegetation. This is a struggle in which all the intellectual efforts of the municipal patriots oddly coincide with the goals of business people, who pragmatically exploit the Odessa myth to extract money from it.

Despite the expressed doubts concerning the durability of the Odessa myth, the recent election of the president of Ukraine only demonstrates its lasting power. During the elections of 2004, Odessa behaved exactly as it did in 1917–18; it did not take sides. During the Civil War, the choice was between Petrograd and Kyiv, between the Petrograd Soviet and the Central Rada. In 2004, the choice was between Donets'k and L'viv. So, wrapped up in the myth of its uniqueness, Odessa as before attempted to creep by Scylla and Charybdis. Already at the time of perestroika, Odessa nurtured radical ideas of becoming a free city, or a city-state, based on a series of precedents, among which was the historical experiment of Odessa as a *porto-franco* (1819–57). At the time of Gorbachev, no one could predict to what degree the USSR would collapse, or if a free city would be permitted, resembling something like those of the Hanseatic League. This invaluable experience with the powerful myth of a free city does not register with contemporary masters of public relations. With the building, in part by German investors, of a superhighway from Odessa to Kyiv, Odessa will be tethered more tightly to its capital, thus thwarting its inclination to float by the sea as an independent entity. Ukraine has also declared its intention to use the Odessa-Brody pipeline, not to carry Russian oil, but to transfer Caspian oil to Plock and Gdansk in Poland for further transshipment to Europe, especially to Germany.[20] Thus, Odessa's name is linked, willy-nilly, with a westward thrust of Ukraine's foreign policy.

At the same time that the prestige of Odessa and the region is decaying and declining and there is no possibility of political separation, Odessa impetuously sees its golden, separate future. Believing in the Odessa myth, municipal ideologues proclaim, "We are not Russians, nor Ukrainians, nor Jews, nor Americans, nor Bushmen, nor Chinese, we are Odessites!" The centralizing power must understand, respect, and, if worse comes to worst, tolerate regional mentalities, perhaps even going so far as to form a federal government. Only the blind do not see the difference between Odessa and Ivano-Frankivs'k, Donets'k and L'viv, Ternopil' and Kharkiv, and Chernivtsi and Sevastopol'. Attempts at a totalitarian leveling of regional ideologies that are based on historical and cultural traditions, even the most absurd and paradoxical ones, are perceived as only leading to the strengthening of centrifugal forces. Another conundrum: The more independent Odessa becomes (and not it alone), the more it will become a Ukrainian city.

As Ukraine is being drawn closer to the orbit of European power (it is already on its way to joining NATO), it will of course take its major seaport with it, although the smug Odessa myth insists that the city, despite its Turkish roots, has been European in its architecture, in its cosmopolitan nature, and in its climate since its birth. To the extent that Western Ukraine (e.g., L'viv) can boast of its European roots in Austrian Galicia, so too Ukraine's "window to the South" relies on its European foundational myths to assert its unique European genesis.

Odessa no longer attracts foreigners as settlers, as it did in the nineteenth century, but it harbors the notion that it is multinational by catering to the descendants of foreigners. Various ethnic and religious communities contributed to the establishment of many societies and churches. Funds from expatriates helped to rebuild Catholic and Protestant churches and to restore synagogues. In recent years, cultural institutions of various faiths and ethnic groups have either been rebuilt or created anew, namely, a series of Orthodox churches such as the Cathedral of the Transfiguration, the Church of Saint Gregory the Theologian, the port church named for Saint Nicholas of Myra, the Alexander Church, the Archangel Michael women's monastery, the Church of Sturdza Charitable Community, and the Church of Sts. Adrian and Natalia. Other confessions are also well represented. Examples are the Armenian Apostolic Church of Saint Gregory the Teacher, the main Catholic church on Katerynyns'ka Street, the Church of Saint Gregory the Illuminator, the renovated Main Synagogue on Rishel'ievs'ka Street, the synagogues on Remisnycha

Figure 1.10 Cathedral Square.

Figure 1.11 The steeple of the Cathedral of the Transfiguration of the Savior. The cathedral was built in 1837, destroyed in the mid-1930s, and restored in 2001.

(now Osypova) and Mala Arnauts'ka streets, the rectory of the Evangelical Lutheran Church on Novosel's'koho Street, the Reformed Church on Pastera Street (Khersons'ka), the Evangelical churches of Balkovs'ka and Kartamyshevs'ka Streets, the Arab Cultural Center on Rishel'ievs'ka Street, built largely through the generosity of Adnan Kivan, a Muslim entrepreneur. Suddenly, the city boasts Greek, Bulgarian, French, Italian, and other cultural associations, as well as a variety of Jewish cultural educational organizations and societies for the approximately 36,000 Jews in a city of 1.2 million. Most of these institutions either own their property within the city or in the region (oblast), or they are in the process of acquiring the property. A few Westerners do emigrate to Odessa, such as

Figure 1.12 The Church of Saint Nicolas of Myra on the wharf at the Black Sea port, built 1993–94. Architect: Volodymyr Kalinin.

Hobart Earle, an American, who for the past dozen years has been the conductor of the Odessa Philharmonic Orchestra, which performs in an ornate early Italian Renaissance-style building that once served as the Stock Exchange.

It is telling that the creators of many of these new buildings of culture, indeed the new constructions in general, give little heed to the surrounding architecture and are not overly concerned with visual or city-planning harmony. The hastily assembled contemporary architecture reminds one of the cloak of a dervish with his multicolored pieces of splendid brocade and cashmere sewn together with homespun linen and sacking. The words of a Czech journalist, observing Times Square with its vibrant coloration, likewise apply to Odessa: "The colors completely do not match one another, and as the saying goes, there is here neither rhyme nor reason, and yet this motley collection unexpectedly creates a thing of beauty."[21] In odd and inexplicable ways, the seemingly unsuitable buildings in terms of scale, chronology, style, function, and structure in the historic center of Odessa convey a sense of harmony. Whatever attempts have been made to regulate this flow of construction and to direct it into some artistic channel have, as a rule, ended in failure. The usual view of chaos clearly needs revision.

Possessing only some formal "general plans" for the development of the city, Odessa is oblivious to the direction in which it should move, or where to perch and how it should

Figure 1.13 The Armenian Apostolic Church of Saint Gregory the Teacher.

develop. It ponders, "Does preservation sterilize creativity and innovation? But if there is no preservation will it not then deprive us of roots and indispensable memories needed for innovation?"[22] If Odessa chooses the direction of becoming a tourist and resort city, then it would be expedient to reconstruct memorial buildings in the historic center in the genre of "green archaeology," by removing the chief transport lines, one by one, to the periphery, and leaving the city as a "museum under the open sky," exclusively for pedestrians and bicyclists, ice cream vendors, street musicians, beggars, and prostitutes. To live up to its glory as a strong industrial and commercial center, the city has restored historical facades and, in some cases, added on a story or two and large plate glass windows. Although the Municipality of Odessa has a city Architectural Commission, which offers advice on the city's building needs and their architectural merit, the City Council has the final determination on what is built and where.

What standards will be adopted for Odessa's revival—those of the period before the memorable prewar year 1913, or before a year such as 1894, the year of the one-hundredth anniversary of Odessa? Or should it be those before 1854, in the era when the city wore the crown as the world's leading exporter of grain? No one answers these questions because some answers might suggest a return to cesspools, heating by stove, kerosene lighting, hauled or rain water for drinking and household needs, and transport by carts. This is how the mythmaking of the glorious past functions in the civic consciousness of Odessites, who avoid the logical

Figure 1.14 The Arab Cultural Center on Rishel'ievs'ka Street, 2002. Architect: Dmytro Povstaniuk.

consequences of returning to the past. Though romanticizing Odessa of old, Odessites do not want anything to do with shriveled acacias or privies. Odessites have become accustomed to the fact that nothing depends on them; they take no initiative but treasure paperweight mementos and picturesque ruins.

Not a single city in Ukraine and in all probability in all the former USSR can boast of such an abundance of monuments, memorial plaques, and other "street furniture" per capita as can Odessa. Suffice to say that on one day alone, September 2, 2004, the anniversary of Odessa's 210 years, four new monuments were unveiled: the first to the romantic Polish poet, Adam Mickiewicz; the second to the former Greek city head, Grigorii Marazli; the third to the founder of the Greek independence society, Filiki Eteria; and the fourth to the orange. This last is instructive. As the nineteenth century began, Odessan Greeks on behalf of the citizens sent oranges to Saint Petersburg to Emperor Paul I. An orange was an exotic item in those years, especially in the winter, and all the more so in the north of Russia. The reason for the gift was that the new emperor jealously sought to destroy all the projects undertaken by his mother Catherine II, among which was her pride and joy—Odessa. Paul I had refused, therefore, to finance the budget of young southern Odessa, so the building of the city and port declined in consequence, and it was in danger of never being completed. Quick-thinking Odessites resorted to a time-proven method—the bribe. Paul took the gift and immediately became more receptive to Odessa, restoring credits and privileges. After two hundred years, the citizenry decided to honor this curious historical fact with a monument, *The Orange That Saved Odessa*, by the sculptor Oleksandr Tokarev. Literally a couple of months later, "the Orange Revolution" laid claim to the color of this monument as its own symbol. It can be no coincidence that in December 2004, the opponents of Viktor Yushchenko hurled oranges at his supporters when he was speaking at an election rally in Odessa.[23]

Memorials of literary figures in the Sculpture Garden of the Literary Museum lie a few meters from *The Orange*.[24] Outdoor monuments to the citizens' favorite writers, their literary heroes, and figures of the city's folklore have been planted in the Sculpture Garden each year beginning in 1995, on April 1. There can be seen the personages of Il'f and Petrov, Kuprin and Kozachinsky; the heroes of the Jewish anecdotes of Rabinovich; the writer Kvanetsky, "the future Odessan genius"; the text of the song from the film *Two Soldiers* and phrases from "Odessa Mama" embodied in bronze and marble. The *Monument to the Reader* by the Kyivan sculptor Oleh Chernoivanenko took its place in the Literary Museum Sculpture Garden on April 1, 2005. It is a miniature replica of the original enormous monument in Catherine Square dedicated to Catherine II, which was torn down by the Bolsheviks. As before, the empress is surrounded by her four favorites: de Ribas, de Wollant, Potemkin, and Zubov. But in this new version, the men are holding books in their hands; one is reading Babel', another is reading Il'f and

Figure 1.15 The monument to Rabinovich (a character from Jewish jokes) in the Sculpture Garden of the Literary Museum.

Petrov, another is perusing Zhvanetsky, and de Wollant, the city's planner, is reading a guidebook to Odessa. The empress herself studies a Russian-Ukrainian phrase book. Apparently the city has changed physically beyond the city's planner comprehension and Catherine is searching for the new basis of her Imperial power—Ukraine.

The difference in distance between *The Orange* and the Sculpture Garden is just about the same degree as that between the latter and the city duma, where stands the prerevolutionary monument to Pushkin. Shoulder to shoulder with *The Orange* stands the old and durable Italian copy of Laocoön. Conversely, the classic Prymors'kyi Boulevard and Katerynyns'ka Square have long had monuments side by side of differing quality: the refined bronze monument of the first Odessa governor, the Duc de Richelieu (1828), is twinned with the granite block of the sailors of the battleship *Potemkin* (1965), nicknamed *The Iron* by Odessites. On the eve of the fall of the Soviet Union, it was possible for Soviets to write, "Perestroika and democratization in all spheres of life in our nation opened the broad possibility to exploit monuments to create human consciousness and humanistic ideas."[25] In Odessa, the prescription meant turning from the heroic to the humorous.

In celebration of the two-hundredth anniversary of Pushkin's birth, a new, modernized version of the poet sculpted by Oleksandr Tokarev was installed and awaits photograph opportunities a mere two blocks from the classic Pushkin monument erected in 1899. Suddenly,

Figure 1.16 The new monument to Alexander Pushkin on Pushkins'ka Street. Sculptor: Oleksandr Tokarev.

Figure 1.17 The monument to one of the main founders of Odessa, Joseph de Ribas, placed on Derybasivs'ka Street in 1994 for the two-hundredth anniversary of the founding of the city. Sculptor: Oleksandr Kniazyk.

Figure 1.18 The monument to the aviator Serhii Utochkin on Derybasivs'ka Street. Sculptor: Oleksandr Tokarev, 2000.

the revered Duc de Richelieu, clad in a toga, overlooking the grand staircase, reappears in another statue as a twenty-first-century dude in jeans. On Derybasivs'ka Street have been placed monuments to Joseph de Ribas; to the legendary balloonist and sportsman Serhii Utochkin, who is portrayed as about to launch a paper airplane; to the founder of Soviet Jazz, Leonid Utesov; and to a bronze chair from Il'f's and Petrov's best-selling book *The Twelve Chairs*.[26]

On Preobrazhens'ka Street stands an outdoor monument to the film star Vira Kholodna and nearby a much earlier sculpture had been placed of "Petia and Gavrik," personages in another best seller, *White Sails Gleam* by Valentin Kataev. At the sea terminal stands the controversial monument *Golden Child*, the work of Ernst Neizvestny symbolizing the city and port. And at the ninth sea station, Large Fountain, on the outskirts of the city, one finds the sculpture complex *The Rape of Europe*.

Somber recollections of the darker moments of the recent past are the monuments to the Odessan victims of Chornobyl, to the victims of the Afghanistan War, to sailors lost at sea, to a sailor's wife, to the fighter pilots of World War II, to the heroes of the U-boat fleets of both world wars, to the second Jewish Cemetery destroyed in the 1970s, to the massacre of 25,000 Jews by Romanians in 1941, and to the Jews who were annihilated after they were sent on the Road of Death to the Nazi concentration camps.[27]

What, then, does one see? One sees that the historical, literary, and folklore heroes are all abandoning the confines of museums in droves to dot the landscape, and in dominating the terrain, they intensify and strengthen the Odessa myth in the consciousness of Odessites as they go about their ordinary daily business. With each monument, it becomes more and more difficult to find suitable space for another. Currently, only a handful of sculptors—such as Oleksandr Tokarev, Mykola Stepanov, Volodymyr Traskov, Oleksandr Kniazyk, and Taisia Sud'ina—create all these monuments. Especially distinctive is the statue of the Otaman Holovatyi, one of the leaders of the Black Sea Cossack Host, which joined the Russian regular army. This monument was erected to please contemporary nationalist patriots who probably

Figure 1.19 The monument to film star Vira Kholodna on Preobrazhens'ka Street. Sculptor: Oleksandr Tokarev, 2003.

do not understand that their hero was a mercenary, an active participant of the bloody conquest of the Caucasus and, it must be said, a rather curious precedent to current events.

Of course, aging Odessa maintains its pretensions and claims to originality for the way it decorates itself, for how it applies makeup to prepare for its role. The majority of the monuments of the city, whether international or European, of local significance or not, are becoming decrepit and neglected. The contrast between the old homes and the new elements of architecture and decoration is striking. As a rebellious and independent-minded city under the tsars, Odessa lost favor with the powers that could have helped maintain the city; as a Soviet spa, the city's central structures and infrastructures were neglected. Now as a city with a distinctive Russian culture serving as the major port of Ukraine, it is attempting to adjust the myth to suit new realities.

Today, Odessa has great difficulty in representing itself as a soubrette. On the contrary, it more often inspires pity and sympathy, and itself to be debased and scorned. Rejuvenation cannot, however, be done piecemeal. Steps must be taken for a makeover. First, Odessa must cease to engage in self-delusion—fasting will not be followed immediately by feasting. No noble benefactors will appear to support the carnival. Odessites themselves must lend their own time and efforts to the project of self-realization. Only under these conditions will the Odessa myth be strengthened, nourishing itself with new affirmation.

Notwithstanding the ephemeral nature of the Odessa myth, it remains and continues to be a powerful ideological factor. To be sure, the old architecture and new monuments draw attention to the past, but the shape and symbolism of the new monuments and buildings force Odessites to confront their future. With earnest effort and honest direction, this Black Sea port may well have commenced creating a new legend for itself.

Notes

1 For a general history of the city, see Patricia Herlihy, *Odessa: A History, 1794–1914* (Cambridge, MA: Harvard University Press, 1986).
2 Roger P. Bartlett, *Human Capital: The Settlement of Foreigners in Russia, 1762–1804* (Cambridge: Cambridge University Press, 1979), 135–42, 210–12.
3 Steven J. Zipperstein, *The Jews of Odessa: A Cultural History, 1794–1881* (Stanford, CA: Stanford University Press, 1985); Patricia Herlihy, "Port Jews of Odessa and Trieste: A Tale of Two Cities," *Jahrbuch des Simon-Dubnow-Instituts* vol. 2 (2003): 183–98.
4 Menachem-Mendl is Sholem Aleichem's fictional character in his *The Adventures of Menachem-Mendl* (New York: Putnam, 1979), 10.
5 N. A. Chizhov, "My vkhodim v sad," *Syn Otechestva* 2 (1823). Other Russian travelers also commented favorably: N. S. Vsevolozhskii, "Walking around the city I was happy, I delighted in the activity, concern, novelty, liveliness, which one almost always meets in merchant cities on the sea. I saw here people of all nations: Greeks, Italians, Germans, French, Jews (there are many here), Armenians and a crowd of Ukrainians, resting between oxen and their carts on the squares. The latter only come to unload their wheat. In general the various pictures of the sea, the completely European, magnificent city is astonishingly attractive." N. S. Vsevolozhskii, *Puteshestvie cherez Iuzhnuiu Rossiiu, Krym i Odessu v Konstantinopol', Maluiu Aziiu, Severnuiu Afriku* (Moscow: Tip. Avgusta Semena 1839), 42. And O. P. Pushkin, "Sometimes I think I am in a foreign land alone among foreigners, but Russian

speech, Russian uniforms remind me that I am indeed in Russia and I am all the more delighted, walking and resting with the elite society under the beautiful southern sky in the evening coolness." O. P. Pushkin, *Zametki i vospominaniia russkoi puteshestvennitsy po Rossii v 1845 gody*, part 2 (Saint Petersburg, 1848), 32.

6   For a sampling of foreigners' reports before 1830, see Thomas Alcock, *Travels in Russia, Persia, Turkey, and Greece, 1829* (London: E. Clarke, 1831); Ignace Antoine Anthoine, *Essai historique sur le commerce et la navigation de la Mer-Noire* (Paris: H. and Ve. Agasse, 1805 and 1820); T. B. Armstrong, *Journals of Travel in the Seat of War; during the Last Two Campaigns of Russia and Turkey* (London: A. Seguin, 1831); G. de Castelnau, *Essai sur l'histoire ancienne et moderne de la Nouvelle Russie*, 3 vols. (Paris: Rey et Gravier, 1820); Edward Daniel Clarke, *Travels in Russia, Tartary and Turkey*, 2 vols. (Edinburgh: William and Robert Chambers, 1839); Josiah Conder, *Modern Traveller; Russia*, vol. 10 (London: J. Duncan, 1830); Henry S. Dearborn, *A Memoir on the Commerce and Navigation of the Black Sea*, 2 vols. (Boston: Wells and Lilly, 1819); Charles B. Elliott, *Travels in the Three Great Empires of Austria, Russia and Turkey*, 2 vols. (Philadelphia: Lea and Blanchard, 1839); W. Eton, *A Concise Account of the Commerce and Navigation of the Black Sea* (London: T. Cadell and W. Davies, 1805); Jean Françoise Gamba, *Voyage dans la Russie méridionale* (Paris: C. J. Trouvé, 1826); Maria Guthrie, *Lettres sur la Crimée, Odessa et La Mer d'Azov* (Moscow: Bouvat, 1810); Ebenezer Henderson, *Biblical Researches and Travels in Russia* (London: J. Nisbet, 1826); Mary Holderness, *New Russia: Journey from Riga to the Crimea by Way of Kiev* (London: Sherwood, Jones and Co., 1823); Comte de La Garde-Chambonas, *Voyage de Moscou à Vienne, par Kow, Odessa, Constantinople, Bucharest et Hermanstadt* (Paris: Treuttel et Wuertz, 1824); Robert Lyall, *Travels in Russia, the Krimea, the Caucasus, and Georgia*, 2 vols. (London: T. Cadell and W. Blackwood, 1825); Edward Morton, *Travels in Russia and a Residence at St. Petersburg and Odessa in the Years 1827–1829* (London: Longman, Rees, Orme, Brown and Green, 1830); Robert Stevens, *An Account of Odessa* (Newport: William Simons, 1819); and James Webster, *Travels through the Crimea, Turkey and Egypt*, 2 vols. (London: H. Colburn and R. Bentley, 1830).

7   Patricia Herlihy, "Odessa, Staple Trade and Urbanization in New Russia," *Jahrbücher für Geschichte Osteuropas* 21 (1974): 121–37.

8   Cited by Robert A. Rothstein, "How It Was Sung in Odessa: At the Intersection of Russian and Jewish Culture," *Slavic Review* 60 (Winter 2001): 788.

9   Anatolii F. Kozak, *Odessa zdes' bol'she ne zhivet* (Samara: Tarbut, 1997), 139.

10 "Bluest Black Sea" is a refrain from the popular song, "He Who Was Born by the Sea," from the Khrushchev era film *A Sailor from the Kometa*; "Swineherdesses and Shepherds" is from the Stalinist film of that name extolling the multinational composition of the Soviet Union.

11 A. S. Pushkin, 1799–1837; K. N. Batiuskov, 1787–1855; V. I. Tumanskii, 1800–1860; I. E. Babel', 1894–1940; K. G. Paustovskii, 1892–1968; Ilia Il'f (I. A. Fainzilberg), 1897–1937; and Evgenii Petrov (E. P. Kataev), 1903–42.

12 http://www.theodessaguide.com/index.htm.

13 For architecture, Oleg Gubar', *Odessa: Pale-Roial', Illiustrirovannyi Al'bom* (Odessa: Letopis' i K., 2003); and Patricia Herlihy, "Commerce and Architecture in Odessa in Late Imperial Russia," in *Commerce in Russian Urban Culture 1861–1914*, ed. William Craft Brumfield, Boris V. Anan'ich, and Yuri A. Petrov (Baltimore: Johns Hopkins University Press, 2001), 80–94. For civil society, Guido Hausmann, *Universität und städtische Gesellschaft in Odessa 1865–1817* (Stuttgart: F. Steiner, 1998).

14 "Vysotkami po staroi Odesse," *Migdal'* 50 (August–September 2004): 14–18.

15 François De Wollant, *Ocherk moei sluzhby v Rossii, 1787–1811* (Odessa: Optimum, 1999).

16 For the connection between Odessa and the Ancient Greek colonies, Neal Ascherson, *The Black Sea* (New York: Hill and Wang, 1995), 7–84; and Charles King, *The Black Sea: A History* (Oxford: Oxford University Press, 2004), 25–61.

17. Patricia Herlihy, "Greek Merchants in Odessa in the Nineteenth Century," *Harvard Ukrainian Studies* 3–4 (1979–80): 399–420; and Patricia Herlihy, "The Greek Community in Odessa, 1861–1917," *Journal of Modern Greek Studies* 7 (1989): 235–52.
18. Oleg Gubar', "Kamennaia letopis' Odessy," in *Odessa v novykh pamiatnikakh, memorial'nykh doskakh i zdaniiakh* (Odessa: Optimum, 2004), 8–14.
19. Oleg Gubar', "Bez ansamblia, sam," *Or sameakh* 28 (September 2004).
20. Laurence Mackin, "Poland Tapping Up Ukraine for Oil," *Warsaw Business Journal*, March 29, 2005.
21. Liudvik Ashkenazi, *Bab'e leto* (Moscow: Izdatel'stvoi inostrannoi literatury, 1958), 2.
22. Alois Riegl, *Le culte moderne des monuments: Son essence et son genèse* (Paris: Paris-Villemin École d'Architecture, 1984).
23. http://webmail.east.cox.net/agent/mobmain?mobmain=1.
24. Oleg Gubar', *Odessa v novykh pamiatnikakh, memorial 'nykh doskakh i zdaniiakh* (Odessa: Optimum, 2004).
25. M. A. Poliakov and E. A. Shulepov, ed. *Voprosy okhrany i ispol'zovaniia pamiatnikov istorii i kul'tury* (Moscow: Nauchno-issledovatel'skiiv institut kul'tury, 1990), 4.
26. For a discussion of Utochkin, Patricia Herlihy, "Odessa Memories," in *Odessa Memories*, ed. Nicholas Iljine (Seattle: University of Washington Press, 2003), 31–32; and Oleg Gubar' and Alexander Rozenboim, "Daily Life in Odessa," in *Odessa Memories*, 98.
27. Gubar', *Odessa v novykh pamiatnikakh*, 43–55.

CHAPTER 2

Odessa Memories

Odessa as a new town, as a boomtown, as a frontier city, attracted the best and the worst of Russian society. People with daring, entrepreneurial skills and high hopes for freedom flocked there to find an El Dorado, or as the Yiddish saying promised, "to live like God in Odessa."[1] Others were already fugitives from the law, saw the commercial entrepôt as a potential for criminal activity, and sought their fortunes dishonestly. While many considered Odessites amoral as well as apolitical, most conceded that there were also many creative spirits in literature and the arts, sincere patriots, zealous reformers, good mothers and fathers. As Jabotinsky wrote, "Odessa was one of those few cities which created their own type of people."[2] Just as the city presents physical contrasts—the flatness of the steppes and the steepness of the bluffs, land and sea, sun and fog—Odessa's history presents light and dark passages.

Nature and history have conspired to create a singular, enchanting city by the sea—Odessa. The very name with its soft frame of vowels, its whispering sibilants, vaguely Greek, or perhaps Italian in origin, definitely not Slavic, is only the first of the city's many mysteries. Legends, not documents, say that the empress founder, Catherine II, gave a verbal order to name the city for the Greek epic hero Odysseus, but to render the word in the feminine gender. There are also tales that there had once been a Greek colony by that name in the vicinity, so that this was to be the second Odessa. The ancient Greek colony of Odessa, however, had been located in Bulgaria, many miles away.[3]

Odessa, easily pronounced by all tongues, was a kind of Esperanto city, or more accurately a Tower of Babel, reflecting the dozens of ethnic groups who carved out space within its capacious embrace, each speaking its own language, with Italian becoming the first lingua franca of the seaport. Only later did the Russian language predominate, but still twenty or more languages could be heard on the city's streets. An evocative place, Odessa has elicited stories, journals, histories, paintings, photographs, films, poetry, jokes, and songs across its two-hundred-year history from the famous and unknown to commemorate and even celebrate their experiences there.

Mysterious, magical, and majestic sitting on a high bluff overlooking the Black Sea, Odessa was also the scene of abject poverty, brutality, and violence. A popular Jewish song, "Odessa Mama," bespeaks the affection of the city's residents, but mothers can be cruel as well as kind. The unique mix of peoples in Odessa served as a matrix for creating wealth and art, but

---

Originally published as Patricia Herlihy, "Odessa Memories," in *Odessa Memories*, ed. V. Iljine (Seattle: University of Washington Press, 2003), 3–37.

Spa advertisement.

it was also a volatile mixture that sporadically erupted in dreadful pogroms and revolutions, as its darker pages of history record.

The city's very genesis was in violence, the forcible taking of the Turkish site by the Russian military in 1789. And from the start, foreigners formed part of the city's history. Don Joseph de Ribas, a soldier of fortune born in Naples of Spanish and Irish stock and one of the many adventurers in Catherine II's service, stormed the fortress and helped to secure it in September 1789. The Turks conceded the territory to Russia in 1792, by the Treaty of Jassy, where de Ribas was one of the three negotiators for Russia. Two years later began the transformation of the Turkish fort, Yeni-Dünya (New World), on the site of the former village Khadzhibei, into Odessa.

Another foreigner, the Flemish François de Wollant, was charged with building the new Russian fort. Having entered Catherine's service in 1787 from The Hague, he served in both the Russian imperial army and navy and was promoted to lieutenant-colonel engineer in 1791. The following year he was entrusted with the building of Odessa's port, stores, temporary quarantine buildings, and barracks. He is the first known resident of Odessa to leave his memoirs, which were not discovered until 1997.[4] Together with de Ribas, he drew up a plan for the city and construction began under the supervision of Prince Platon Zubov, the governor-general of the province of New Russia (Novorossiia) of which Odessa now formed a part. Because of the ravines dividing the city, d Wollant laid out two gridirons intersecting at a forty-five-degree angle. To preserve uniform rectangularity in the city blocks, the principal gridiron had to be set at an angle to the shore. The plan provided for spacious streets one hundred feet wide. An esplanade separated the old Turkish fort from the residential area, forming a stately space overlooking the bluff to the water.

With the rapid rise of the new town on the southern fringe of the Russian Empire, young and beautiful Odessa appeared to emerge like Aphrodite from the foam of the Black Sea. One writer remarked, "Salt spray as stiff as whipped-up white of egg blew off the crest of the waves, and froth billowed and quivered on the beach; it was easy to believe the Greeks that it had given birth to Aphrodite."[5] Isaac Babel' lovingly described his city as being on "the sun-drenched steppes washed by the sea."[6] Although Catherine had said she thought that the capital of Russia should be on the Black Sea, not in Northern Russia, she never saw her creation, for she died in 1796, only two years after the official birthday of the city. She chose her architect and engineer well, however, in selecting de Wollant and de Ribas. No doubt there were capable Russian engineers, but these two adventuresome and imaginative foreigners had participated in the conquest of the area and had an interest in its future.

De Ribas, effectively the head of the emerging city after 1793, became its first official *gradonachal'nik* (city chief) in January 1797. After the death of his patroness, Catherine, he was dismissed from his office, returned to St. Petersburg, became embroiled with the plot to assassinate Catherine's son, Paul I, and died in 1801, the same year as the murdered tsar.

Meanwhile, his younger brother Felix followed him into the Russian army, married a Polish woman, and after leaving the military, became a landowner, grain merchant, and entrepreneur by building a pasta factory in Odessa. Not wishing to become a Russian subject, he sought and received in 1807 the title of Odessa Consul for Sicily, then under Bourbon rule. For twenty years he sent commercial and political reports as well as personal letters to Naples, which, in a way, also represent the diary of his life in Odessa. One of the highlights of his official life was the visit of Queen Maria Carolina of Sicily to Odessa in 1813. But even this royal personage was subjected to a stay in the Quarantine, because the plague had visited Odessa the year before. As soon as she got out of Quarantine, she attended the Odessa theater.

Although Felix fell on hard times financially toward the end of his long life, he groomed his oldest son Michael to carry on the role of Consul for Sicily by training him in the Italian, French, Russian, and German languages. But the government of the Two Sicilies never gave him the coveted position. Young Michael had to be content with being appointed by his father as an unpaid vice-consul. Unlike his father, who was a merchant and industrialist, scholarly Michael composed the first short history of Odessa in 1834 in Italian. He later wrote various articles on geography and even a short story, but he admitted that he could not fully identify himself as either Neapolitan or Russian, only as an Odessite. As an Italian journalist once wrote, "In Odessa Russians feel a bit foreign and foreigners feel a bit Russian."[7] Michael de Ribas did finally become a Russian subject, a member of the city's Society for History and Antiquity, as well as the editor of one of Odessa's first newspapers, the *Journal d'Odessa*, published in French and Russian. Eventually, he became a bibliographer in Odessa's library.[8]

One of the de Ribas descendants, Alexander, fully acculturated as a Russian in Odessa, published in 1913 a history of the city and his own memoirs in Russian entitled *Old Odessa*.[9] As the writer Yuri Olesha recorded in his memoirs, "Alexander Mikhailovich de Ribas was a respected man in Odessa, an expert on the city and its history, who had lived there a long time, and who, moreover, was the director of the Public Library. He was a tall old man with a long white beard, and when speaking, he shaped his lips in a manner that betrayed his provenance: he was French."[10] This vignette of the lives of the de Ribas family shows how this Spanish (not French) family from Naples became true Odessites and how they contributed to the conquest, building, commerce, wealth, and intellectual life of the city of their adoption.

Many other foreigners came to Odessa to make a fortune in exporting the golden grain from the steppes. The most visible of these were the Greek émigrés who answered the siren call of the seaport. Within four years of the establishment of the city, at least forty Greek families resided in Odessa, which one Greek described as the land of "milk and honey" because trade flourished and the rule was mild. These prosperous families soon built their own Greek theater, commercial school, and benevolent societies. The Ralli, Rodokanaki, Scaramanga, Serafino, Mavrokordato, Iannopulo, Christodoulou, Mavros, Papudov, Zarifi, Paleologos, Inglesi, and Marazli families were among the pioneers in the grain trade. They took advantage of far-flung family members in Mediterranean and European seaports, Venice, Trieste, Livorno, Marseille and others for commercial intelligence and help in selling Russian grain to be transformed into French bread and Italian pasta. By 1832 most of the forty export firms in Odessa were in Greek hands, some worth as much as a million rubles, but most valued between 50,000 and 100,000 rubles.

Many of these wealthy Greeks enhanced Odessa's civic and cultural life.[11] Dmitrios Inglesi was mayor of the city from 1818 until 1821, and Grigorii Marazli became mayor in 1879, serving for nearly a quarter of a century. During that period, he established forty social and educational institutions and made many municipal improvements. He shifted his family's commercial wealth into real estate and industry, a sign of the family's long-term commitment to the city. The tax register of 1873 shows that he owned more than a dozen pieces of choice real estate worth then about 300,000 rubles, or about 0.7 percent of the value of all the private buildings in Odessa. In 1899, he and several others, including Edmund G. Harris, an English engineer, applied to set up a joint-stock company in the construction business with offices in Odessa, Kherson, Bessarabia, Podillia, Katerynoslav, and Taurida. Thanks to the success of his

Aviation school advertisement.

many business ventures, he was able to indulge his generous impulses, such as subsidizing the publication of many books on Odessa's history. As mayor, he attempted to introduce electric lights into the city. With his own money, he built a chapel in the Christian cemetery. He gave the city a neoclassical palace, built in 1828, by architect Francesco Buffo for Lev Aleksandrovich Naryshkin, which is now a museum of art. Marazli also donated to the city another showplace, a French neoclassical mansion built in 1856 for the rich merchant Abaza. Since 1920, it has housed the Western and Eastern Arts Museum.

In 1883, Marazli engaged the architect Felix Gąsiorowski to build a huge public library on Exchange Square, the first building constructed in Odessa specifically for public use. Today this

Palladian palace houses the Archeological Museum. In 1892, Marazli built another enormous public reading room in the Greek revival style with two public schools attached, designed by Iu. M. Dmytrenko also a gift to the city. These libraries served until 1904, when the city built a neoclassical library (now named for Maxim Gorky) on Pastera Street. Marazli gave one of his dachas, located about four kilometers from the city, to the Odessa branch of the Imperial Horticultural Society, which was founded in 1884. Marazli's interest in science was reflected in his equipping the bacteriological laboratory in the city. This was the first of its kind in the empire; there, the Nobel Prize–winning scientist I. Mechnikov made his valuable experiments in microbiology. Today Odessa University is named for Mechnikov.

Marazli built a children's park in the Duc de Richelieu's Gardens for the poor children of the Moldavanka and Slobidka-Romanivka districts. He paid for an addition to the Sturdza Almshouse for children. In 1870, in memory of his mother, Zoia Fedorivna, he contributed five thousand rubles to support girls living in the Maria Theodorovna Orphanage. In 1892, he not only financed a retirement home for veterans but also donated a large shelter for the homeless. Among his many charities were large subventions to the City Theater, especially to support Italian opera. Grateful to the "pearl of the Black Sea" that had conveyed wealth to the family, Marazli in turn enriched and adorned the city.

In addition to the riches promised by the "happy marriage" between the black earth grain-producing region and the Black Sea port, foreigners were attracted to Odessa because of its progressive administration. After valiant service fighting in the Russian army, the much-beloved Frenchman Armand Emmanuel, Duc de Richelieu, related to the famous cardinal, ruled benignly and efficiently over the city from 1803 until his return to Paris as French foreign minister in 1814. Modest in his demeanor and in his material demands, hardworking, and devoted to the city, he carried the population through the plague in 1812 and fostered the grain trade in Odessa. His kindness and compassion enabled him to bring social harmony to the disparate people coming to live in the "Little Paris," so that both Nogai Tatars and local Jews regarded him as a father. Clad in a toga atop a pedestal, the Duc's statue stands above the giant staircase overlooking the harbor, a continuing reminder of the genial governor-general who gave the city such a favorable start.

Richelieu was Odessa's "Johnny Appleseed." To anyone who promised to plant and tend them, he gave acacia trees, which he imported from Vienna and paid for himself. To colonists, he gave land if they promised to plant three hundred trees. Although the cliffs and seashore of Odessa were covered with broom and presented a lovely yellow face to the sailor, the terrain lacked trees. One of the duke's legacies, the Prymors'kyi Boulevard, an esplanade paralleling the sea cliff, is especially cool under the shade of acacias and inviting to strollers and those who would sit on benches to read, relax, or eye the passing promenaders.

Richelieu was succeeded by his friend and military companion, Louis Alexandre, Comte de Langeron, who headed the city's and region's administration until 1822. He was able to extract from the tsar free-port status for Odessa so that imports did not bear Russian tariffs. Writing back to France, he said, "All the territory entrusted to me is as large as all of France and is populated by ten different nationalities and by many foreigners. There are to be found also ten different religions and all ten are practiced freely. One can judge the work which burdens me and the absolute impossibility of my doing it all."[12] He must have been overworked or extremely absentminded because when Tsar Alexander I, his patron, came to visit him and the city founded by the tsar's grandmother, Langeron inadvertently locked the tsar in the house. Apparently, this mishap did not discourage Alexander's youngest brother Nicholas, the future Nicholas I, from spending four days with Langeron in Odessa; he was impressed by the vibrant city. Langeron passed his retirement in St. Petersburg, where he died of cholera in 1831. It was said that as long as he was in Odessa, he never learned the Russian language, although he married a Russian princess, Trubetskaya.

Another noble presided over the city's growth and fortunes for over thirty years, Count Mikhail S. Vorontsov, who was appointed governor-general of New Russia in 1823. Although he spent his youth in London, where his father was Russian ambassador to the Court of St. James and one of his contemporaries sniffed, "he is more an English lord than a Russian dignitary," he was a Russian. Dedicated to his work as caretaker of the city and region, honest and liberal, he was also, like the Duc de Richelieu, tolerant of all the ethnic groups and religious groups he governed. Jews hailed him as their benefactor. Under his guidance the Archeological Museum opened in 1825. In 1828, he founded the Imperial Agricultural Society for Southern Russia in the city, and about a decade later, he helped to found the Imperial Odessa Society of History and Antiquities. He also founded the newspapers *Odessa Herald* and the *New Russian Calendar*. In short, he was a worthy successor to the duke and his statue still stands in Cathedral Square. The Bolsheviks left it intact, although they tore down the cathedral and a monument to Catherine II.

That his memory is as solid as his statue was shown at the two-hundredth anniversary of the city when the Odessa composer Oleksandr Krastov premiered his opera *Mikhail Vorontsov*, as part of the celebrations of 1994. Vorontsov also left us his memoirs, a valuable historical source. Vorontsov was followed as head of Odessa and New Russia by Count Alexander G. Stroganov, a wealthy, wise, and tolerant leader. He also worked hard to improve municipal services such as gaslights, street paving, waterworks, and bridge building. He was one of the founders of the New Russian University, to which he bequeathed his library of 14,000 books that are still available to the reader with some of his notations in the margins. He pressed for the emancipation of the serfs, the building of railroads in the vicinity (here he was unsuccessful), and the founding of the Russian Steam Navigation and Trading Company for commerce on the Black Sea. Under his successor, Adjutant General Pavel E. Kotsebu, Odessa finally had a railroad connection and city improvements speeded up. Kotsebu founded an eye hospital and an asylum for orphans, later named "Pavlov'" for him. The American consul in Odessa reported that he was a very popular governor-general who was able to extract favors for the city from the tsar. After the transfer of Kotsebu in 1874 to Warsaw, Odessa was never to enjoy the personal favors of the tsars again. The early noble governors-general had been close friends of the monarchs they served and, since they took an intense interest and pride in developing the city, they had won concessions such as free-port status and money from the royal purse for the city's infrastructure and cultural institutions. With the advent of municipal government in 1863, there were some sincere and hardworking heads of the city, but they did not have close ties with the throne. Many members of the city council suffered not only from apathy, but often from a reluctance to tax themselves for the benefit of the city. Progress was much slower, and sometimes absent altogether. Odessa grew in the third quarter of the nineteenth century, but it was no longer the darling of the tsars.

Nonetheless, the city's population growth was phenomenal. Beginning with little over 2,000 persons in 1795, to 35,000 in 1815, the number of residents reached 116,000 in 1861. According to the 1897 census, the population was over 400,000, growing at rates on a par with some western cities in America. The growth came from the continual stream of immigrants from within the empire and from abroad, which made Odessa a boomtown, where as late as 1892 only 45 percent of the population had been born there.

By 1892, many of the early foreign immigrants: Greeks, Italians, Jews, Ukrainians, Poles, Tatars, Armenians, Belarusians, Mordvinians, and Georgians had become Russian subjects and were no longer counted among the foreign population. Russification of the city came slowly, however. As one traveler observed, Odessa possessed "Italian houses, Russian officials, French ships, and German artisans." Even the Duc de Richelieu, noting that so little Russian was spoken in the city, ordered the high school he founded to teach the Russian language. By 1892, the number of foreign nonsubjects was 7 percent of the population, a much larger percentage than in Moscow (0.75 percent) or even St. Petersburg, the much vaunted "Window to the West," whose foreigners constituted only 2.35 percent of its population. Odessa's colorful mix of population stamped the character of the city at least until the 1917 revolution. A native of the city, born in 1880, made this observation:

> Even if it was a city in Russia and in my time, very russified in language, Odessa was not a Russian city. Nor was it a Jewish city, though Jews were probably the largest ethnic community, particularly when one considers that half of the so-called Russians were actually Ukrainians, a people just as different from the Russians as Americans from Britons, or Englishmen from Irishmen. At least four great peoples—three ancient ones, and the fourth a young one—united to build the city: first the Greeks and Italians, a little later came the Jews, and only in the 1840s did the actual Russian influence begin to grow. The city was also full of Poles, Armenians, Caucasians, Tatars, Moldavians and a half dozen other peoples. In Odessa, everybody was an Odessan and everyone who was literate read the same newspapers and thought about the same Russian problems.[13]

A census tells us where these foreign residents of the city were from as of 1892. About 24 percent came from Turkey, 20 percent from Greece, 18 percent from Austria-Hungary and 13 percent from Germany, and, in descending order, from Romania, Italy, France, Great Britain, Slavic countries, Switzerland, Persia, Belgium, Sweden and Norway, Spain, Denmark, the United States and the Low Countries. People from all these countries lived in Odessa and were not tourists whose numbers go unrecorded. No other city in the Russian Empire hosted such a variety of people. Although economic opportunities undoubtedly brought them to the commercial seaport, the climate, cultural amenities, ambiance, and aesthetic enjoyment of the site help to explain why they remained in Odessa. No doubt each of these various ethnic groups contributed to the exotic flavor

Advertisement for Artistic and Industrial Exhibition 1910.

of the city, but since it bore a foreign imprint from the start, they often found congenial surroundings when they arrived.

Vladimir Jabotinsky, born in Odessa in 1880, a Zionist after the 1903 pogroms in Kishinev, provided his own distinct history of the various people who came to Odessa:

> From the hundreds of cities of Italy, from Genoa to Brindisi, a long procession of dark-eyed adventurers made their way towards Odessa: merchants, shipbuilders, architects, and smugglers of the choicest variety. They populated the young capital and gave it their language, their light-hearted music, their style of building and laid claim to the basis of its future wealth.

Car advertisement.

At approximately the same time the Greeks started pouring into Odessa, shopkeepers, boatmen and also, of course, masters of illicit trades. These connected the young port of Odessa with every nook and cranny of the Anatolian coast, with the Aegean Isles, with Smyrna and other ports. Then came Jews, who cut into the steppes a cobweb of invisible canals down which harvests from the rich Ukraine poured into Odessa. Thus, Odessa was built by the descendants of the three tribes, which once created humanity: the Greeks, the Romans and the Jews. Later came Russians and Ukrainians. The Russians ruled.[14]

As for the Ukrainians, Jabotinsky wrote, "they gave Odessa her superb sailors and masons and—most important—the salt of the earth, those pillars of the fatherland, those real creators of Odessa and of the whole of south Russia—those real, full-blooded human beings: I mean, of course, the tramps." Again, in his chronology, afterward came Turks and French and Armenians. In 1892, 58 percent of Odessa's population was ethnically non-Russian. It was the people of all of these nations and their cultures, richly interwoven, who together built Jabotinsky's birthplace "under the laughing sun, among the smells of the sea, of acacia and garlic, my town, the genuine and legitimate child though born before its mother—of a League of Nations."

These immigrants saw beautiful public and even private buildings designed by some of the empire's leading architects. While Odessa's buildings were stately and substantial, they were not monumental except for the Opera House. They were built to a human scale, and the center presented a harmonious ensemble to the eye. As early as 1809, the neoclassical court architect Thomas de Thomon of St. Petersburg completed two beautiful edifices in the city, the theater and the hospital. Two local architects of Italian origin, Francesco Frappoli and Francesco Boffo, also worked on the theater, so that Europeans would find familiar facades when coming to Odessa, where, in fact, were some of the finest in Russia.

Other artists came from St. Petersburg as well: the architects A. I. Mel'nikov and Auguste Montferrand, and the sculptor I. Martos. In 1829, the city had an exchange built by a local architect, G. Toricelli, following the plans, according to some and disputed by others, of the famous St. Petersburg architect Giacomo Quarenghi. At the time of its completion in 1834, it was a showy neoclassical building located at the southern end of the Prymors'kyi Boulevard on the top of the cliff looking over the Black Sea.

Engraving of the founding of Odessa, 1794.

At the entrance of the building were two rows of Corinthian columns, which led out from a covered courtyard that served as a place for trading operations. The composition and the style were reminiscent of the Alexandrovsky Palace in Tsarskoe Selo near St. Petersburg—not surprisingly, since the latter was also designed by Quarenghi. It cost the city 65,000 rubles to build, but private funds were used as well as public. In 1871, the architect F. O. Morandi rebuilt the edifice, the city's first exchange or *birzha*, converting the covered courtyard into a hall; he also tore down a second row of columns. Nonetheless, the building did not lose its architectural importance nor its beautifully proportioned first row of columns. In the second half of the nineteenth century when the New Exchange was built, the earlier *birzha* became the home of the city duma.

At the northern end of the Prymors'kyi Boulevard was another and even larger classical building, the palace of Count Vorontsov, constructed in 1828, according to the plans of Francesco K. Boffo. Vorontsov chose to erect it at the spot where the Duc de Richelieu had occupied a modest little house in the early days of the city. The most striking part of the palace is a detached portico of twenty semicircular Doric columns facing the sea that makes it the most easily observed landmark even at a distance for those coming to the city by water. It is prominent enough to serve as a landmark from various vantage points in the city as well. After the Revolution of 1905, it became the home of an engineering school. In Soviet times Vorontsov's home became the Palace of Pioneers, and during the Romanian occupation (1941 to 1944), it was the home of the governor.

Thomas de Thomon's first construction in Odessa was a massive classical building at the start of Pastera Street erected in 1806–7, a two-story building which was the first city hospital.

Cathedral Square. Postcard, early 1910s.

Two adjoining curved wings were added in 1821, surrounded by a six-columned portico. Almost at the same time, he designed the first Odessa Opera House, which burned in 1873. He also built stately granaries at the port, which appeared to be palaces that were perhaps unique to Odessa since they elicited so many comments from visitors to the city.

No discussion of the architecture of Odessa would be complete without at least reference to the gigantic stairway leading from Prymors'kyi Boulevard down to the port, the source of most of the city's wealth. It was designed by Francesco Boffo, the architect of the commune of Odessa from 1822 to 1844. Construction began in 1837 and was completed in 1842. Contemporaries called it the grand staircase but now it is better known as the Potemkin Steps, so named for the famous scene in Eisenstein's film *The Battleship Potemkin*. The staircase is still one of the most dramatic sights of the city, whether looking up from the port or down on the staircase from Prymors'kyi Boulevard. Before the Soviet period, there was a funicular alongside the staircase, which the Soviets tore down and later built a garish escalator in its place. (Happily, a funicular will occupy its old place in the near future.)

At the top of the staircase stands the statue of the Duc de Richelieu sculpted by Ivan Petrovich Martos in 1827. Behind the statue and built about the same time in the center of Prymors'kyi Boulevard are two semicircular buildings whose architect was Francesco Boffo, but whose final elaboration belongs to the well-known architect A. I. Mel'nikov from St. Petersburg. Among the most handsome edifices in the city, they frame the top of the staircase and the opening of Katerynyns'ka Street like parentheses, leading to the center of town. One of the curved buildings served as a hotel; the other was an office for city administrators. Katerynyns'ka was one of the main streets of Odessa that flowed into town from the grand staircase.

In 1830, Boffo also designed a handsome neoclassical building on Prymors'kyi Boulevard for M. N. Shidlovsky, who later was governor-general of the city (1865 to 1868). In 1835, Countess M. A. Naryshkina became the owner of the building. Rebuilt after the Second World War, it became the home of the Seaman's Club. Boffo created the "marine façade" of the city, that is, the buildings along Prymors'kyi Boulevard, the Potemkin Steps, and the concept of the statue of Richelieu. Governor-General Vorontsov nominated him in 1828 for the prize of the Order of St. Vladimir, Fourth Class, for which Boffo became a member of the Russian hereditary nobility. Even during the reign of Nicholas I (1825–55), Odessa's architecture continued to reflect a classical style. That is, until Nicholas began to favor pseudo-gothic architecture in St. Petersburg, so that in Odessa, too, private individuals built large houses in the pseudo-gothic style along the seashore. Although suburbs developed, the growth of population on the whole created a denser center city rather than urban sprawl. In 1849, the architect F. O. Morandi drew up a new master plan for the city in which all buildings had to conform to prescribed imperial plans for facades, which were essentially neoclassical in style. Not until the latter half of the century was more eclecticism displayed in the designing of buildings.

The new City Theater (Opera House), begun in 1883 and completed in 1887 at the cost of 1.3 million rubles, was designed in the Italian Renaissance and baroque style by two Viennese architects, Ferdinand Fellner and Hermann Helmer, who designed over seventy theaters during the last quarter of the nineteenth century and the twentieth up until World War I, principally in Eastern Europe. It is, after the Potemkin Steps, the most famous edifice

Church at the House of Industriousness. Lithograph, early 1900s.

in the city and certainly exceedingly grand. In the exterior niches of the Opera House are busts of Pushkin, Gogol, Griboyedov, and Glinka. The large hall, in the style of Louis XVI, was richly decorated with gilded stucco design and figures. Frescos on the ceiling depicted various Shakespearean scenes. In addition to the wide parterre, there were four tiers of loges, a dress circle, a balcony, and a gallery. The theater is located near the Prymors'kyi Boulevard. On October 13, 1887, at the opening of the new theater, the music-mad Odessa public was treated to a performance of excerpts from *Boris Godunov* by Mussorgsky and the third act of Griboyedov's play, *Woe from Wit*. The theater was illuminated by electricity, making it the first building in Odessa to employ the Edison Company. Unfortunately, there was a fire in 1925, but the building was restored and then later remodeled in the 1960s. Disastrously, the huge edifice sits atop shifting ground and is in danger of collapsing. A former opera singer in the theater, who happened to be trained as a geologist, is helping to advise on how the building can be saved, a costly enterprise.

That the imposing theater, often used as an opera house, occupied considerable space and resources is indicative of how much Odessites loved music, and still do. Apparently, the large Italian merchant community in the city provided the first impetus to produce Italian opera. But soon the entire city became enamored of the productions. It was said even Ukrainian grain carters were heard whistling Italian arias in the streets of Odessa. And a Russian declared that Jews were fanatics of the Italian opera, and indeed their attendance confirms their enthusiasm. Pinkhas Minkovskii, a cantor in Odessa, claimed that the reason that Odessa became such a strong center for cantorial music was because Jews were immersed in music.[15]

Beggars were supposedly happier in Odessa than elsewhere because they were surrounded by music. In Odessa, the fictional vagrant Fiske exclaimed:

> Well, you might even say that barrel organs has gone over mighty big in Odessa as a general thing. I mean you can't turn a corner anywheres, indoors or out, without you got a barrel organ or some such wheezebox grinding away at you there. Barrel organs in the street, barrel organs at home, barrel organs in taverns, barrel organs at the circus... they even got the shameless gumption to be playing them things at shul![16]

Alexander Kuprin uses music as a mirror to reflect changing times and political moods of the city in his famous short story "Gambrinus," in which Sasha the Jewish musician plays military marches, revolutionary tunes, and merry dance tunes. After the police brutally mutilate his arm so that he can no longer play the fiddle, he triumphantly plays a flute.[17]

A newspaper, *Troubadour d'Odessa*, founded in 1822, was devoted to news of the theater, the opera and other musical events. It included scores and lyrics for operas and musical scores for piano, harp, and guitar. During the early years of the theater, operas, ballets and vaudeville shows were staged in Italian, French, and Russian. But during the 1820s and 1830s, Italian opera predominated. As a music historian noted, "the earliest continuous Italian opera enterprise in nineteenth century Russia was based in neither capital, but in the Black Sea port city of Odessa, where a state theater for opera and ballet was opened in 1809."[18] When the great Russian poet Alexander Pushkin was sent in exile to Odessa in the early 1820s, he was delighted to engage in the cultural life of the growing city. In his masterful poem *Eugene Onegin*, he speaks of the dusty streets of Odessa and of its colorful polyglot population. He was an enthusiastic fan of the impresario Luigi Buonavoglia and his company. Pushkin, writing to a friend, noted "in the evenings I don't go anywhere except to the theater." Pushkin mentioned Rossini's operas, of which eight were performed before the poet was evicted from the city. Pushkin might have remained longer had he not flirted with Governor Vorontsov's wife.

In 1824, the impresario Cesare Negri signed a three-year contract for 38,000 rubles in addition to a 12,000-ruble subvention for his passage from Italy to put on eighty-six performances per year in Odessa. The poet and Polish patriot Adam Mickiewicz was a patron, and the Russian poet Konstantin Batiushkov pronounced Odessa's theater to be superior to that of Moscow. A German visitor to the Opera House in the 1840s was impressed that performances were given in five different languages.[19] Even while Vorontsov was city chief, he and his wife, as well as other aristocrats, invited chamber music groups to perform at their salons. By 1842, the Philharmonic Society of Odessa was founded. In February 1860, A. A. Tedesco formed Odessa's first symphony orchestra, and in the following year the first important program featured music by Russian composers. In 1864, the Society of Music Lovers was established in the city.

In 1834, Italians established the first music school. Violin classes at the school began in 1848. The pianist Demian von Ressel, supported by the composer-pianist Anton Rubinstein, opened a branch of the Imperial Russian Musical Society in Odessa in 1866. The first concert, conducted by W. Kaulbars, featured music by Felix Mendelssohn and Robert Schumann. In 1889,

View of the city from Katerynyns'kyi Yacht Club. Postcard, early 1910s.

Rubinstein himself played to celebrate the twenty-fifth anniversary of the society. This sparkling event was held in the New Bourse, or Exchange, which to this day is the home of the Odessa Philharmonic Orchestra. During the first quarter-century of the music society, they gave eighty-two symphony concerts. A German choir of local colonists regularly sang before the group. The Odessa Conservatory was established in 1913. Odessa was filled with music. Even the Reformed and Lutheran churches put on beautiful concerts of religious music. Music-loving Odessa Jews shocked conservatives by insisting that an organ be placed in their synagogue.

As Steven J. Zipperstein has noted, "The manifestation of a widespread interest in, and even a gift for, music on the part of Odessa Jews in the first half of the nineteenth century is intriguing, particularly in view of the large number of famous Jewish violinists, such as Mischa Elman and David Oistrakh, to emerge from Odessa several decades later."[20] The great violinist David Oistrakh was born in Odessa in 1908, studied at the Odessa Conservatory, and eventually went on world tours demonstrating his genius. According to one of his Odessa friends, Mark Zinger, when Oistrakh returned to Odessa in 1968 to give a concert, he insisted on going out for three hours to photograph his native city in colored film. In addition to taking the usual pictures of notable streets and monuments, he took pictures of P. S. Stolyarsky's home and then even his dacha, a loving tribute of a famous pupil to his first teacher.

Mischa Elman, another violin prodigy, known to Bel Kaufman and her family, was a local genius. In his autobiographical story, "The Awakening," Babel' wrote:

> All the people of our circle—middlemen, storekeepers, clerks in banks and steamship offices—sent their children to music lessons. Our fathers, seeing they had no prospects

of their own, set up a lottery for themselves. They built this lottery on the bones of their little children. Odessa was in the grip of this craze more than any other town. And sure enough, over the last few decades our town had sent a number of child prodigies onto the stages of the world. Mischa Elman, Zimbalist, Gawrilowitsch all came from Odessa—Jascha Heifetz started out with us. When a boy turned four or five, his mother took the tiny, frail creature to Mr. Zagursky [Stolyarsky]. Zagursky ran a factory that churned out child prodigies, a factory of Jewish dwarfs in lace collars and patent leather shoes. He went hunting for them in the Moldavanka slums and the reeking courtyards of the old bazaar. Zagursky gave them the first push, then the children were sent off to Professor Auer in St. Petersburg.[21]

Babel' continued by saying that his father decided when Isaac was fourteen that he too should become a prodigy and sent him to Stolyarsky for violin lessons. But "the sounds scraped out of my violin like iron filings. These sounds cut even into my own heart, but my father would not give up. All anyone talked about at home was Mischa Elman."[22] Young Babel' decided to skip the lessons to play at the beach. When finally the music teacher informed the family of Isaac's truancy, the boy had to lock himself in the lavatory against his father's rage in losing "the lottery." His aunt set him free during the night to take him to the safety of his grandmother's house.

Petro (Peisakh) Stoliars'kyi, born near Kyiv, was one of the founders of the violin school. He devised a method to teach young children how to play and by 1923 was a professor of the Odessa Conservatory. As the world now knows, Babel's music was in his prose. And while he never became a musician, he delighted in attending the theater, which was very popular in Odessa in the early twentieth century. Babel' described how, as a young man, he loved seeing the Sicilian tragic actor Di Grasso in *King Lear* and *Othello*, noting that scalpers obtained five times the regular price of tickets.[23]

Over the years, great names appeared on the Odessa stage, such as composer-conductors Tchaikovsky, Rubinstein, Rimsky-Korsakov, Napravnik, Arensky, and Glazunov. In 1847, Franz Liszt played six triumphant piano concerts in the theater. The Odessa pianist Svyatoslav Richter was self-taught. At the age of eighteen he was the accompanist and assistant conductor of the Odessa Opera, making his first solo concert debut in Odessa in 1935. Opera directors included the Italians Montovani and Zamboni. Famous singers also performed: Fedor Chaliapin, Enrico Caruso, Mattia Battistini, Giuseppe Anselmi, and Titta Ruffo. The Italian singer Moriconi came directly to Odessa when she finished the conservatory in Turin. She sang not only popular Italian operas but also became interested in Russian folk songs, learned Russian, and sang in Russian while appearing in Russian costumes. So, while Russians were becoming Italian opera fans, Italian opera singers became fascinated with Russian music.

Other Italian divas appeared as well, such as Caterina Amati and Adelanda Rinaldi, who earned as much as 500 rubles per month, a sizable sum compared with the 300 rubles earned by conductor and first violinist Sankte-Campioni. So engrossed in opera were music lovers that entire factions would form around particular divas; fans would sometimes come to blows with those supporting rival Italian singing stars. In fact, by 1911, the Opera House was staging more and more opera and less theater. In the 1920s and 1930s, productions became experimental, borrowing much from avant-garde cinema.

Why was Odessa so amply endowed with talented musical performers and appreciative audiences? Some have noted that one factor was geography. That relatively southern spot attracted from southern climates ethnic groups already famous for playing musical instruments and singing: Ukrainians, Jews, Gypsies, Armenians, Italians and southern Russians. As early as the 1820s, musicians from various nationalities organized musical unions or guilds (*tsekh muzykantov*) to perform at weddings, funerals, gala birthday parties, and other functions. If one studies a 1894 photo collage, dignitaries at the top, Catherine the Great and famous governors of the region and city, stand proudly with their medals, epaulets, and ribbons around Mother Russia with Infant Odessa on her lap (almost like the Madonna with Child). The common people at the bottom, mostly children, carry folk musical instruments: an Italian girl with a violin, a German girl with a guitar, a Polish girl with a lute, an Albanian girl with a triangle, a Ukrainian girl with a *domra*, and a Russian boy with a flute. It is significant that the picture assembled to represent the accomplishments of the city over a hundred years should feature so predominately musical instruments.

On the other hand, the most democratic and widely used instrument was the violin. Self-taught violin virtuosi were mostly Jews, Gypsies, and Ukrainians. The typical Ukrainian ensemble (*troisti muzyky*) was, and is, a trio: two fiddles and a flute. They never sang, only accompanied Ukrainian folk dancers. And of course, no Jewish celebration would be complete without a fiddler for dancers. Gypsy violinists often accompanied their own soloist singer. Thus, child prodigy musicians and virtuosi were relatively rare, even in Odessa, compared with the large numbers of people who produced and enjoyed music in that city with its soft inviting summers and autumns that encouraged people to dance, sing, and play music outdoors, a tradition that continues today with its outdoor cafes, bands, and even karaoke concerts.

The popular Soviet Odessa singer and bandleader of the 1920s, Leonid Utesov (L. I. Vaisbein), wrote in his memoirs about a piece he performed called "How Bands Play at Weddings in Odessa." He claimed that in Odessa, groups of musicians, *klezmorim* (probably following the old tradition of musical unions or guilds), who could not read music, showed up at ordinary weddings and functioned as a collection of soloists, producing music "in an original, freely improvised style." He went on to claim that "this curious manner of playing was then widely used in America some ten or fifteen years later by small amateur Negro bands in New Orleans. Like the poor Odessa musicians, the New Orleans amateurs did not use scores. They varied the themes of well-known melodies freely, and at times, with inspiration."[24] He concluded, in effect, that jazz was invented in Odessa, not New Orleans. This claim was made as part of a comic routine and thus in jest, but foreigners took it seriously.[25] This was, after all, the man who proudly said that Odessa should not be compared to Paris, for Paris should shine Odessa's shoes. His own chosen name Utesov comes from *utes*, meaning cliff, after the city's site. And the first lines of his memoirs are, "I was born in Odessa. You think I am bragging? But it's really true. Many people would like to have been born in Odessa, but not everyone

Cafe at Oleksandrivs'kyi Park. Postcard, early 1910s.

manages to."[26] Or as the cinematographer Kozak recently observed, whenever one informs others that he or she was born in Odessa, a smile comes to their lips and they mention, "Odessa humor, Odessa songs, Odessa jokes and the characteristic Odessa speech. An Odessite is without fail, merry, witty, sharp; he is never despondent, petty; he has a superior and fascinating personality."[27]

However valid Utesov's claim to Odessa's inventing jazz might be, the city has always patronized jazz players, including Peter Rozenkern's band of the 1930s that based much of its jazz music on lusty ballads from the Moldavanka Jewish district. Sooner or later, there was a blend of Yiddish music and jazz in Odessa. As Richard Stites noted, "The strains of an Odessa Jewish wedding were never far away [from jazz]."[28] Utesov's film, *Happy-Go-Lucky Guys*, also known as *Jolly Fellows*, of the 1930s was extremely popular. It reflected his European style as a typical Estrada entertainer, quick-witted, versatile, and funny. In 2001, Odessa placed a seated statue of Utesov on a bench, leaving room for someone to sit beside him. Nearby a machine plays songs sung by Utesov.

In 1916, Babel' conceded that Odessa chanteuses "might not have much in the way of a voice, but they have a joy, an expressive joy, mixed with passion, lightness and a touching charming, sad feeling for life. A life that is good, terrible, and *quand même et malgré tout*, exceedingly interesting."[29] Some of the better-known songs from Odessa, mostly sung in Yiddish, reveal the special characteristics of the city, like "Odessa Mama," in which some of the lyrics run, "What is Vienna or Paris to me. They're nothing, a travesty, no comparison, but Odessa—there you have a paradise, I tell you."[30] Another Yiddish song, "Akh, Odessa," proclaims: "there is only one of you, Odessa, in the whole world. Anyone who has not yet been in the beautiful city of Odessa hasn't seen the world at all, and he has no idea of progress."[31] Even Odessa folk songs sung in Russian include Jewish figures such as in "A Beer Hall Opened on Deribasovskaia," "The School of Ballroom Dancing," "The Story of the Kakhovka Rabbi," and "It's Terribly Noisy at Shneerson's House," in which the lyrics describe Abe the milkman and three of his brothers taking up instruments and constituting themselves into an impromptu jazz band.[32] The great modern balladeer, Vladimir Vysotsky, although he was not from the city, is said to have adopted the Odessa style of singing as well as Odessa songs.

Writing about the importance of music and comedy for the city, Stites noted that "Odessa exported its comedy and song patterns to Moscow. Odessa became renowned as a breeding ground for satirists, among whom Jews were especially prominent. But they dealt far more often with infidelity, high fashion and in-laws than they did with tsarist repression."[33]

Odessites are renowned for their sense of humor, and for their stand-up comics, some of whom have become popular in the United States. People recognize that these performers come from Odessa because of their Jewish intonations and gestures. Humor and music abounded in Odessa, but the inhabitants could be tough as well. Noted writer Konstantin Paustovskii described the role Odessites played in the First World War, "During the war the frivolous, garrulous Odessans, amateurs of comic songs and known as 'babbling brooks,' fought with grim courage—though they still cracked Odessan jokes—and showed such daring and selflessness that even the enemy were astonished."[34]

He continued by saying, "New songs came after the war, celebrating their feats and their unwavering love of their city." Music also marked the Civil War and NEP periods in Odessa, where the most popular unofficial song of the twenties "Bublichki" ("Pretzels" or "Bagels") was written by Yakov Yadov for an Odessa cabaret. Its lyrics about a drunken father and a whoring mother were later adapted to an indecent underground parody song on the Bolshevik Civil War hero, V. I. Chapayev.[35] All through the 1920s musicians such as Leonid Utesov, who were later canonized as Soviet culture heroes, cranked out songs about Odessa thieves and jailbirds.[36] An eyewitness of the 1917 Revolution and the Civil War, Paustovskii also remarked that "there was an orchestra here, in Odessa. They called it the Romanian orchestra but really it was made up of people of every sort—some from the Caucasus, some from Kishinev and some from our Moldavanka."[37]

Entertainment was always prized in Odessa, whether it was opera, drama, comedy, or the circus. There was a long tradition of the circus in the city. In the early twentieth century Olesha was fascinated by it and as a boy often went without lunch and solicited extra copecks from his grandmother to come up with the student fee of fifty copecks. He described his joy:

> The circus was always seen through a curtain of falling snow. Well, why not, since it was always winter when the circus came! I walked through the falling snow, marveling at the snowflakes. On the circus building hung wall posters with a picture of yellow lions and a lion tamer in red, a picture that moved, I thought, for it contained rings and a cracking whip and lions whose hind legs were thrust into the air... The lit-up wall, the poster. I read the words that would, in ten minutes, as soon as the lights in the arena were turned on,

be converted into clowns and mandolins and little dogs, into tambourines and horses and slender bodies, hurtling through the air between trapezes . . . As a boy, and for many years afterward as an adult, of all entertainments, I was fondest of the circus.[38]

Odessites also loved going to movies. With twenty-five theaters in 1913, Odessa was third after St. Petersburg and Kyiv in its number of movie houses. Because of the relatively mild weather in the area and the beautiful light, it was a good place for making movies as well, even after the 1917 Revolution, although during the Civil War the Odessa Studio was evacuated to the Crimea, the Caucasus, and Central Asia. Nikita Mikhalkov's popular 1970 movie, *Slave of Love*, was about moviemaking in the Odessa area before the revolution. It captured the lush scenery and beautiful light of the South. It happened that the great screen star Vira Kholodna died in Odessa in 1919 of the Spanish flu at the age of twenty-six. At the peak of her career, she was said to light up the screen with her luminosity in such movies as *The Last Tango* (1918), *Life for Life* (1916), *Children of the Age* (1915), and many more melodramas. There remain fragments of a newsreel of her funeral, which made her even more of a cult figure. The French comic Max Linder was also all the rage in Odessa. Sergei Eisenstein's famous 1925 silent film, *The Battleship Potemkin*, has become a classic, and through this movie millions have formed their visual images of the seaport.

As a seaport, Odessa was a melting pot. Not only did Odessa music blend Yiddish and Russian words, folk themes, and characters, but also each language absorbed a bit of the other and affected the other's syntax, lexicon, and phraseology. According to Babel', his grandmother mixed Polish and Hebrew words in with her Russian.[39] Perhaps that fact led him to state: "Odessa is a horrible town. It's common knowledge. Instead of saying 'a great difference,' people here say 'two great differences,' and 'tuda i syuda,' they pronounce 'tudoyu i syudoyu'! And yet I feel that there are quite a few good things one can say about this important town, the most charming city of the Russian Empire."[40]

According to the noted linguistics scholar Robert A. Rothstein, the Ukrainian language has also altered the Russian use of some prepositions to accord with Ukrainian usage. For a long time Odessites used the French forms of address *monsieur* and *madame*, and in 1895, a journalist proclaimed that the language of Odessa was "not even a language, but a language salad."[41] It is only natural that this city where so many languages were spoken would produce a kind of dialect of its own, or at least a nonstandard Russian that deviated from classical Russian in both pronunciation and vocabulary. Babel' called it simply "Odessa's hot, homegrown lingo."[42] So distinct is the language of Odessa that there is a website devoted to it on the Internet, called "Odessa Language Dictionary" (*www.odessit.com*).

One of Odessa's chief cultural legacies is the rich Jewish and Yiddish literature generated in Odessa, read by all Odessan society and now the world. Isaac Babel' and Sholem Aleichem are among the most famous of the writers. Although Babel's *The Red Cavalry* is his masterpiece, his *Odessa Stories* provide an indelible picture of Odessa and its Jewish Moldavanka district. Thoroughly trained in biblical studies and in French, Babel' wrote his early pieces in French and retained the storytelling style of Flaubert and Maupassant. Although he was influenced by Odessa's Yiddish writers, such as Mendele Moykher Sforim, he wrote his stories in Russian (including Odessa slang, ungrammatical Russian, and Yiddishisms) about very distinctive Jewish characters, most of whom are gangsters.

The leading bandit in these stories, Benya Krik, is modeled after a real-life gangster, Mishka Yaponchik (Mykhailo Vinnyts'kyi), who is said to have been a veteran of the Russo-Japanese War (1904–5), and married to a Japanese woman (hence his sobriquet). After serving time in prison, Yaponchik joined various groups—Bolsheviks, anarchists, and the anti-pogrom Jewish defense league. A writer living in Odessa during the Civil War wrote, "Three thousand bandits from the slums of Moldavanka with Misha the Jap at their head, looted half-heartedly. They were sated with fabulous loot from their previous raids. All they wanted was to relax from this strenuous occupation."[43] The situations described, mostly raids that took place when extortion money was not forthcoming, were all too real during the chaotic period of World War I and its aftermath, a time that witnessed brazen robberies in the city.

But even raids had a history in Odessa when political groups and individuals stole gold and other valuables from the state during the 1905 Revolution. Gangsters, thieves and criminal types are celebrated in Odessan underworld songs such as "Music Is Playing in Moldavanka" or "Kal'ka the Pickpocket," "From the Odessa Jail," and "Murka," in which a bandit speaks of justice when he murders a fellow bandit because she might endanger their safety. A special code of honor and sense of legality pervades these songs and tales. Such underground songs (*blatnye pesni*) and Babel's stories derive from common Odessa legends in which violence takes a form of revelry. Babel's Jewish gangsters, therefore, followed a long tradition and heralded a continuation of that tradition celebrating those who defied the law in Odessa.

During the 1920s and 1930s, Il'f and Petrov, writers from Odessa, created Ostap Bender, if not an outright criminal, at least a crafty and cool rogue who outwits his adversaries. His exploits are also stinging critiques of the New Economic Program and the first Five-Year Plan. The 1989 Odessa movie *Déjà vu* is also a spoof of the NEP era in Odessa with its jazz, bootlegging, and sex.[44]

Always a kind of free city with free spirits, Odessa, as a free port between 1817 and 1859, presented a temptation to smugglers, who would risk carrying duty-free goods to the interior. Since Odessa was built on quarried limestone used to construct the city, the honeycombed underground tunnels were ideal hiding places for contrabandists throughout the first half of the nineteenth century. Smuggling continued even after the abolition of the free port in 1859. Paustovskii wrote that in Odessa just before the First World War one could obtain tobacco from Constantinople that seemed to be pure shredded gold as well as "French cocaine, Greek vodka, Messina oranges of exceptional flavor and aroma."[45] Babel's list of contraband was similar: "cigars, delicate silks, cocaine, and metal jiggers, uncut tobacco from the state of Virginia and black wine bought on the Island of Chios."[46]

As a rough seaport, Odessa was famed for its criminals. One visitor noted that there were "adventurers and swindlers of the most ruthless kind, people who had learned their lessons in scoundrelism at Constantinople, Romania and the Levant, and had grown grey in vices and crimes of every description."[47] According to another, "Odessa turned out the most talented thieves in the world, certainly more ingenious, dexterous, and brazen than the Warsaw ones." And according to Roshanna P. Sylvester, Moldavanka criminals included many specialists: "gentlemen" pickpockets who operated in fancy stores, theaters, restaurants, lecture and meeting halls, banks, post offices, the stock exchange and in expensive hotels; "Saturday and Sunday men" who cruised the weekend crowds on the main streets; "cleaners" who offered to dust off gentlemen's coats while lifting wallets; and "sinners" who specialized in stealing purses in churches. Other specialists were shoplifters, counterfeiters, falsifiers of gold watches, con artists of every description, as well as second-story burglars.[48]

In the 1870s, a Russian visitor to Odessa declared, "this town has degenerated into a focus of crime and dissolute excess, such as none of the governors-general, town prefects or heads of police sent from St. Petersburg had even been able to master. Frauds and thefts of unprecedented extent, and murder and acts of violence committed in broad daylight, were daily occurrences."[49] So strong was Odessa's unsavory reputation that when Fedor Chaliapin, the famous basso, learned that Isaac Babel' was from Odessa, he refused to entrust a valuable vase to him, even though Maxim Gorky had sent him a letter to convey the object to the author of *The Odessa Stories*.[50]

Another Jewish writer, Sholem Aleichem, created a character who visited Odessa. Menahem-Mendl is perhaps the mirror image of the rogues Benya Krik and Ostap Bender. He is an exuberant, naive businessman, who in a letter to his wife raves, "I want you to know it is simply not in my power to describe the city of Odessa—how big and how beautiful it is— the people here, so wonderful and good hearted, and the terrific business one can do here."[51] These lines would not be so humorous if everyone, including the author, did not know how

Sanatorium on Andriivs'kyi Liman. Postcard.

shady business could be in Odessa. Menahem-Mendl thus was exceptionally optimistic at first about his business prospects in Odessa. But even he lost his money there. For most of its history Odessa has earned a reputation of defiance of Russian imperial and later Soviet law. As Paustovskii noted about the Civil War (1917–20), "even in those grim days racketeering flourished in Odessa. Even the most spineless caught the infection... In time the rackets infiltrated even our literary and journalistic milieu."[52]

Tongue in cheek, Babel' praises Romanians who came to Odessa after World War I:

> Nobody who loves Odessa can say a word against these Rumanians. They have brought life back to Odessa. They remind us of the days when the streets were full of trade, when we had Greeks trading in coffee and spices, German sausage makers, French book peddlers and Englishmen in steamship offices. The Rumanians have opened restaurants, play music with cymbals and fill taverns with their fast, foreign speech. They have sent us handsome officers with yellow boots and tall, elegant women with red lips. These people fit the style of our own.[53]

On the other hand, after World War II, during the Romanian occupation and administration of Odessa as part of Transnistria, crime and hooliganism reached new heights, matched perhaps only after 1991, when the nouveaux riches and mafiosi made their gaudy presence known.

Mention has been made of some of the famous writers of Odessa. Not only the physical beauty of the Southern Palmyra but also its lively population inspired a notable array of writers

Fountain and front of telegraph building on Andriivs'kyi Liman. Postcard, early 1910s.

to record their memories, as we have seen, but at the same time to create works of imagination. While Alexander Kuprin was not a native, he visited the city often because he had many friends there. He incorporated scenes from the city in his stories such as "The Ballroom Piano Player," "My Flight," and "The Miraculous Doctor." He wrote about the seamier side of the port city's life. His *Yama*, or *The Pit*, shows the degradation of one of Odessa's brothels, while "Gambrinus" depicts some of the nightlife in the city's many cheap taverns. He was fascinated by all of these people—"sailors of varied nationalities, fishermen, stokers, merry cabin boys, port thieves, mechanics, workmen, boatmen, loaders, divers, smugglers—all young, healthy, and impregnated with the strong smell of the sea and fish, knew well what it was to endure, enjoyed the delight and the terror of everyday danger, valued, above anything else, courage, daring, the ring of strong slashing words, and when on shore, would give themselves up with savage delight to debauchery, drunkenness and fighting."[54]

But Kuprin also noticed the brighter side of the city, "the dressed up, always holiday-like town, with its plate glass windows, its imposing monuments, its gleam of electric light, its asphalt pavements, its avenues of white acacias, its imposing policemen and all its surface of cleanliness and order."[55] Odessa was up to date in many aspects, first with its horse-drawn trolleys, then electric trolleys installed as early as 1910. Olesha described seeing and riding the first trolley:

> I remember standing in a crowd on Hrets'ka Street and waiting with everyone else for the appearance of the trolley that had that day just gone into service for the first time. Everyone was certain that the trolley would be exceptionally fast—like lightning—and that you wouldn't even have time to consider whether or not you could run across the street in front of it. Yellow and red with a glass-enclosed platform in front, the trolley finally appeared. It was moving quite fast, although nowhere near the speed we had imagined. Greeted by our shouts, it passed in front of us, its platform crowded with people, including even a high-ranking priest, who sprinkled water in front of himself and the mayor of Odessa, Tomachev, who wore glasses and had a rust-colored moustache. A gentleman in a derby was at the controls, and everyone spoke his name. "Legoder!" He was the director of the Belgian firm that had built that first trolley line in Odessa.[56]

The London Hotel was (and is) an elegant place on Prymors'kyi Boulevard. In 1904 it boasted electric lights, a salon, a reading room, baths, telephones, and a staff who could speak foreign languages. It was there that Kuprin first met the writer Anton Chekhov, whose roots were in nearby Taganrog on the Sea of Azov.

Yuri K. Olesha moved to Odessa as a child. His father, a Polish Catholic, was an excise officer in a vodka distillery. During the Civil War, Yuri's parents fled to Poland, but the young author remained in the city until his career as a journalist took him away eventually to Moscow, where he was friendly with other writers from Odessa—Kataev, Babel', Bagritskii, as well as Il'f and Petrov. Fascinated by painters, he saw the world with a painter's eye.[57] Olesha's most famous novel is *Envy* (1927), one that exhibited ambivalence toward the new Soviet values. He fell into disfavor with the regime; he returned to Odessa and during the Second World War went with the Odessa Film Studio to Turkmenistan. Olesha's memoirs reflect his fascination with film. His frequent references to Odessa, even when he lived in Moscow, confirm his statement that all that was lyrical and patriotic in his writing derived from his adopted city, Odessa, which he declared "was more closely tied to Europe than to Russia."[58]

Another translator confirmed the importance of Odessa in his writing, "nearly all of Olesha's writings are colored by the sudden discovery, when he was four years old, of the bright radiance of Odessa high on its cliffs with the dark-blue sea beyond."[59] Olesha himself wrote, "It was a sky-blue Odessa day with something golden in it."[60] Konstantin Paustovskii, another Odessa writer and critic and Olesha's friend ever since the Civil War, wrote after Olesha's death, "There was something of Beethoven in Yuri Olesha, a great power even in his voice. He saw with a wealth of magnificent details and he described them simply, accurately, and well."[61] More recently, a scholar wrote of Olesha's "comic genius, his skill as a storyteller, his slyly ironical and gamin slant on life (the birthright, apparently, of Odessa's writers)."[62]

Like Olesha, who saw the world through a special carnivalesque lens, Mikhail Bakhtin "was born with a gift of laughter and a sense of the world as slightly mad."[63] Already fifteen years old when his family moved to Odessa, like many other writers he was affected by that multilingual and multinational city where he attended secondary school and began his university studies: "Odessa was an appropriate setting for a chapter in the life of a man who was to become the philosopher of heteroglossia and carnival. The same sense of fun and irreverence that gave birth to Babel's Rabelaisian gangster or to the tricks and deceptions of Ostap Bender, the picaro created by Il'f and Petrov, left its mark on Bakhtin."[64]

One of Olesha's friends was the poet Eduard Bagritsky, born Eduard Dziubin to a middle-class Jewish family in Odessa in 1895. Olesha said in his memoirs, "As is well known, Bagritsky started out in Odessa. I was younger than he, yet not so much in years as they say, in the fact that he had already been published many times, while I had only been published once or twice. However, he liked me, and we were friends."[65] Bagritsky in turn had been powerfully influenced by the poet Vladimir Mayakovsky when Mayakovsky read his poems in Odessa at the Russian theater. In addition to Olesha, Bagritsky had as friends the writers Vera Inber and Valentin Kataev.[66]

Il'ya Il'f (Il'ya A. Fainzilberg) and Evgenii Petrov (Evgenii P. Kataev), both satirists from Odessa, drew on their youth in Odessa. When living in Moscow they wrote two popular comic novels with Odessa settings thinly disguised: *Twelve Chairs* (1928) and *The Golden Calf* (1931), both of them mocking the vice of acquisitiveness, a trait perceived to be common to many Odessites. Il'f wrote a humorous piece in the magazine *Chudak* in 1929, entitled "Trip to Odessa." In it he noted that before the revolution in Odessa there were only four monuments: to Richelieu, Vorontsov, Pushkin, and Catherine II. Then the number dwindled because the bronze autocrat was "overthrown." Tongue in cheek, he related that in the cellar of the Museum of History and Antiquities were scattered her extremities: her head, her skirt, and her bust, thus displaying her splendor to the occasional visitor. He went on to say (and the criticism only implicit of the Bolshevik penchant for erecting monuments) that now there were no fewer than three hundred sculptures adorning the gardens, piazzas, boulevards, and streets: marble maidens, copper lions, nymphs, shepherds playing pipes, urns, and granite piglets. There were some piazzas, he claimed, where all of a sudden twenty or thirty such monuments could be seen.

Among those marble groves sprang up two lonely acacia trees. Graffiti decorated both the tree trunk and the waist of a marble maiden; he hinted that the statues were becoming eyesores. Without making an editorial comment, Il'f made it plain to the discerning reader that he did not think that Soviet architecture had improved the city. One wonders what tart remarks he might have made had he lived long enough to see the Soviet realist monument erected in 1977 to the mutinous Potemkin sailors, which took the place of the elaborate bronze statue of Catherine, the founder of Odessa.

Another writer of distinction who had ties to Odessa was Ivan Bunin, born in Moscow in 1870, a first-rate writer, and recipient of the Nobel Prize for Literature in 1933. Bunin was attracted to Odessa and lived there between 1918 and 1920—that is, before the Bolshevik takeover of the city. Thereafter, he left his beloved Russia forever. A friend of Anton Chekhov, he is said by the writer Leonid Andreyev to have been influenced by his experience of Odessa so that had he not lived there, his writing would have been of another character altogether. Valentin Kataev, a native Odessite and a novelist loyal to the Soviet regime, wrote that Bunin, who had inspired Kataev, was compromised by his antirevolutionary views, but that he never tried to hide them during the Civil War. Kataev took the young Olesha to meet Bunin, of whom Olesha said, "he is a pessimist, a spiteful, gloomy writer."[67]

Women writers also flourished in Odessa. Lesya Ukrainka (Larysa Petrivna Kosach), a Ukrainian writer, visited Odessa frequently between 1880 and 1909, even taking a cure at a local spa. She published her first volume of poetry, *On the Wings of Song*, in 1893. Another

Derybasivs'ka Street. Postcard, 1900s.

poet, Vera Inber, born in 1890, became well known in her time. Her father owned a publishing company in Odessa, where she went to a girls' high school. While in her twenties she studied in Paris during the First World War and came under the influence of French and Russian Symbolism. She spent the Civil War years in Odessa. According to Paustovskii, Inber, who lived in a shady little street not far from him, was "a slight, frail woman." She spent many years in Western Europe, but returned to Leningrad before the Nazi invasion. She received a Stalin Prize for her account of the siege, *Almost Three Years*, a moving testimony to those awful times.

Perhaps the most famous poet born in Odessa was Anna Gorenko, who became a leading Acmeist. Indeed, she is probably the most famous of all Russian women poets. She took the name Akhmatova from her maternal Tatar great-grandmother. Her father was a maritime engineer and her aristocratic mother was a member of the revolutionary group The People's Will. Although she spent some time in Paris before the First World War, her name is associated with Leningrad. She also spent time in the Black Sea area, in Eupatoriia and Lustdorf. When she was fifteen years old, she visited the cabin where she was born in Velykyi Fontan, a suburb of Odessa. She said that someday there would be a plaque there, and indeed there now is one, put up by the city of Odessa. The city also changed the name of Ukrains'ka Street to Akhmatova Street in 1987. Her fellow Odessa poet and prose writer Olesha said of her, "I consider her one of the most talented poets of the Russian constellation of the twentieth century."[68] Her beautiful lyrical cycle *Requiem* (1935–40), expressing her emotions at the time of the arrest of her son Lev, has universal appeal. She is also of cosmic importance since a crater on the love planet Venus bears her name. Called daughter of Odessa by virtue of her birth, she is claimed by all as their muse.

In the nineteenth century before railroads linked the area to the capital, Odessa seemed remote from the watchful eye of imperial surveillance. Somewhat peripheral to the solid Russian core of the empire, ethnic minorities who were on the fringe, both geographically and politically, found the liberal city suitable for launching secret liberation movements. There was also the possibility that if the authorities were in pursuit, one could make a hasty exit by sea. Thus, Odessa was the site of the secret Greek society Filiki Eteria, which plotted the war for Greek independence from the Turkish Empire in 1821. Polish dissidents at the time of the 1861 uprising against Russian rule, together with their Ukrainian sympathizers, used the city as headquarters linking Kyiv, Warsaw, London, Paris, and Geneva.

A Russian newspaper complained that Odessa was "the chief operational base of Polish activity and the international center for communications with all the revolutionary centers of Europe." Some Poles left Odessa to go to the barricades of Warsaw in the uprising of 1861; others came back to Odessa in exile, with their property given over to Russians.

Ukrainians formed their own nationalist societies; the most prominent were the Hromadas in midcentury, and there was one in Odessa. Initially, they were loose associations of students and intellectuals interested in Ukrainian affairs, but then they took on a political slant, seeking reforms. Despite periods of repression, the Hromada in Odessa lasted until the Revolution of 1917. Another Ukrainian group, Prosvita, promoted the Ukrainian language by publishing literary and popular books and papers. It lasted for about a decade, but then it was suppressed so that only a cultural club for Ukrainians was allowed. The Bulgarian patriot Vasil Aprilov made Odessa a conspiratorial center for the raising of Bulgarian national consciousness through the Bulgarian Diocese. French Communards, defeated in Paris in 1871, also sought asylum in Odessa. Italian patriots manifested their enthusiasm for Garibaldi and his Red Shirts by putting in their shop windows signs with "Evviva Garibaldi." Even the great Garibaldi himself was a fisherman in the Black Sea area in his youth.

Like other ethnic groups, some Russians found the city to be a refuge, while others used it as a subterfuge for revolutionary activities. Before the emancipation of the serfs in 1861, many runaway serfs escaped to the port city. Odessa was considered by some to be a refuge, as were Kentucky and Massachusetts for American slaves. At the same time liberal Russians in Odessa part of or sympathetic to the Decembrist revolt, a rebellion of officers in December 1825, who attempted to unseat Nicholas I. Some wanted his more liberal brother Konstantin to rule; others were fighting for a republic. With some justification, therefore, Tsar Nicholas I called Odessa a "nest of conspirators."

Students formed a secret Society of Good Goals, fourteen years to the day after the Decembrist revolt. More reformist than revolutionary, it inspired students at Moscow University to form an Odessa Circle that was concerned with social issues. A couple of decades later, workers in Odessa created the first politically active labor union, the South Union of Workers. Much celebrated by the Soviets, this group was soon disbanded by the police. Radicals showed more enthusiasm for the populist terrorist group The People's Will. Not until 1900 was there a branch of the Social Democratic Workers' Party. This group

City Theater, side view. Postcard.

included a large number of Jews, some of whom left the Jewish Bund that had formerly represented Jewish workers.

As a result of a downturn in the economy at the turn of the century, the number of socialists of all kinds grew in Odessa by 1900. To head them off the police allowed a charismatic Zionist, K. Shaevich, to form a police union. The workers did not realize that the police sponsored the union with the goal of limiting workers' demands to economic ones and to make sure political issues were not raised. The union enlisted thousands of workers who frequently went on strike, making economic demands. The police did not interfere with their efforts until 1903, at a time when strikes became more and more frequent; then in a sudden turnabout, Cossacks and soldiers brutally suppressed workers' meetings and put an end to strikes. The government deemed the experiment too dangerous. But such oppression only made the Social Democratic Party look more attractive.

Along with Poles, Ukrainians, Bulgarians, Greeks, and Italians, Jews also expressed nationalist sentiment, making Odessa one of the most important centers for Zionism in Russia. At first Jews left the traditional Pale of Settlement or the Galician city Brody for Odessa in order to make a better life for themselves. Because of their exposure to commerce, foreigners, foreign languages, and nontraditional schools, many Jews became assimilated into Odessa's society, departing from their traditional roots. That does not mean that Jews and gentiles mixed socially. The Zionist leader Vladimir Jabotinsky wrote in his diary that as a young boy growing up in the 1880s and 1890s in Odessa, he did not have a single close gentile friend, although his family was secular. Yet Jabotinsky would reminisce poetically about the joys of his boyhood spent in the light-hearted city by the sea where the inhabitants "babbled in a dozen languages."

For most Jews, business and living in the same neighborhoods brought them into frequent contact with gentiles. Haskalah, or the Jewish Enlightenment, found great support in Odessa more for practical than intellectual reasons. As Zipperstein noted, "Many Odessa Jews studied foreign languages, because knowledge of Italian, French or German was deemed essential for participation in local economic life. Encouraged by the commercial opportunities open to Jews, many otherwise self-conscious traditionalists, unlike Orthodox Jews elsewhere in Russia, had their children study secular subjects to prepare for potentially lucrative commercial careers."[69]

In short, most of the Jews in Odessa were not rooted deeply in Orthodoxy. As Jabotinsky said of his youth, "Of the books we read, I do not recall one of Jewish content. The whole subject of Jews and Judaism just did not exist for us." He compared Jews in Odessa to those in Poland and Galicia: "In Odessa, I had not seen either the side-curls or the kapota, nor such wretched poverty. Nor had I seen grey bearded, old and respected Jews, taking off their hats when they spoke to the gentile 'squire' in the street."[70]

Michael Stanislawski described the city as "a unique port city located geographically in Ukraine but populated by a mix of inhabitants: Russian bureaucrats, Greek and Italian merchants, and tens of thousands of Jews fleeing both the economic constraints and the religious and cultural conservatism of the Pale of Settlement. Odessa in Jabotinsky's youth was still a frontier town, a place noted for its irreverence and heterodoxy, its strange mixture of cosmopolitanism and seediness, Russianness and Europeanism."[71]

By the 1870s, however, economic opportunities shrank for Jews as well as for many others in the city. The grain trade that had sustained Odessa was slipping away to other Black Sea ports and worse yet, to the United States, India, and South America, giving less employment to stevedores, middlemen, exporters, importers, and factory workers. The result was not only pogroms but also the radicalization of poor Jews along with poor Ukrainians and Russians. This radicalization of Jews manifested itself in their forming the Jewish Labor Bund and entering the ranks of the Social Democrats or the populists' terrorist groups.

Others decided it was useless to fight from within to better their condition; it was time to leave. The Odessa physician Lev Pinsker is typical of one who was much integrated into Odessa's cultural and intellectual life before the 1870s. But he had completely changed his mind about the future for Jews in Russia by 1882 (significantly, a year after a violent pogrom in Odessa), when he published a pamphlet, *Autoemancipation*, proposing that Jews leave the Russian Empire. Moshe Lilienblum, once a firm supporter of Haskalah, eventually also became an ardent Zionist in Odessa, although earlier he had proposed that Jews should become agricultural colonists within the Russian Empire. Part of his disillusionment with the possibility of Jews finding happiness in Russia was based on his negative views of the city itself. He found life there too frivolous, and he resented *la jeunesse dorée*, the obsession with commerce, money, and ease. In short, the materialism and superficiality of the city struck him as offensive. Only emigration to Palestine could solve the existential problems of life in Russia, especially in Odessa. For Lilienblum and for many other Jews, this commercial and luxury-loving city could be described as having the fires of hell burning around it, as a Jewish saying went.[72]

Other Jews loved the city for what it was. For example, Babel' observed that Odessa was "the most charming city of the Russian Empire. If you think about it, it is a town where you can live free and easy. To a large extent it is because of [Jews] that Odessa has this light and easy atmosphere."[73] While some Jews like Lilienblum sought a Jewish homeland with higher values, others decided to leave because of the pogroms that darkened the pages of Odessa's history. Diversity characterized the city from its inception. One Swiss visitor wrote, "a Russian jostles against a Turk, a German against a Greek, an Englishman against an Armenian, a Frenchman against an Arab, an Italian against a Persian or a Bucharestian."[74] As in many cities in which diverse ethnic groups vie for space and employment, Odessa was never free from tension. "Jostling" erupted into violence from time to time as early as 1821, and then again in 1849, 1859, and in 1871. For the most part these frictions occurred between two immigrant groups—Greeks and Jews who competed for positions as grain merchants—but admittedly religious prejudice was also a factor.

The pogrom of 1871 occurred just when Jewish merchants were displacing Greeks in the grain trade. The Greek Orthodox church in Odessa was located in the middle of a Jewish neighborhood. Easter was always an occasion for much feasting, drinking, and revelry, breaking a forty-day fast. On this particular Easter, random shootings, rock throwing, and three days of looting of Jewish shops and homes accompanied the celebration. The American consul in Odessa sent his report to Washington, DC, saying, "Between the Jews and Greeks, therefore, there are constant jealousies and animosities, originating, no doubt, mostly from differences of race and religion, but also, perhaps, excited and encouraged from the collision of business interests."[75] The city voted to give compensation to Jews deprived of property.

Ten years later a more general pogrom in South Russia took on political overtones. Odessa was not the first to be affected, but in May 1881, riots and destruction of Jewish property ravaged the city for three days. It is suspected that a reactionary group, such as the Holy Brotherhood, might have instigated the pogroms under the pretext that Jews were responsible for the assassination of Alexander II two months earlier. While the official explanation for the pogroms was that Jews were exploiting others in Odessa, most analysts spoke of economic rivalry for business in a city with declining opportunities and growing unemployment.

This pogrom resulted in the passing in 1882 of the May or Ignatiev Laws, which legalized discrimination against Jews in Russia. They could no longer reside in villages, not even in the Pale of Settlement. They could not own land outside of cities—that is, engage in agriculture. They could not work on Sundays or other Christian holidays so that they might not have a competitive advantage over Christians. In general, these laws did not afford Jews the full protection of state law. On the contrary, they formalized the status of Jews as second-class subjects of the tsar. When Jews reacted to the pogrom of 1881 by creating a self-defense league (that also included Christian university students), they were accused of threatening the public order. The defense league was still intact in 1905, the year of the next pogrom in the city. Jabotinsky belonged to it. The myth was solidified therefore that somehow Jews were less loyal than others.

And it was this issue of patriotism that lay at the bottom of the next and most violent pogrom against Jews in Odessa, or at least it was the excuse adduced for persecution. The

View from Rishel'ievs'ka Street. Postcard.

new wave of violence after twenty years of relative social peace came as the aftermath of the granting of a constitution by Nicholas II. This reluctant concession by the tsar was a result of massive strikes and revolutionary activity. Jews were accused of being in the forefront of those socialists, revolutionaries and radicals who "forced" the tsar to give up some of his autocratic power. Of course, many more gentiles than Jews were involved in revolutionary activity, but precisely because Jews were not the legal equals of others and were economic competitors, they provided a convenient target for blame.

Artisans were in general more radical than industrial workers and eagerly joined the Social Democratic Party, which had about a thousand adherents in Odessa by 1905. Since Odessa had a large number of artisans and most of them were Jews, there was the perception that revolutionaries in Odessa were Jews. By now economic tensions affected not only commercial enterprises but also every business affiliated with the proper functioning of the port. The closing of the port during the war dried up credit, closed down the business of middlemen and, most importantly, closed down factories and the work of those loading ships.

Thus, by 1905, the city was in turmoil, especially after the arrival of the mutinous battleship *Potemkin*. Most of the strike activity and violence, such as the burning down of the port, was directed against the autocracy and capitalists. But it took a certain nasty turn after the October Manifesto, when the tsar was forced to make political concessions. Public disorders could easily turn from revolutionary goals into attacks on Jews.[76]

There was a perception that Jews were either very rich, in which case they were called exploiters, or very poor, in which case they were called an economic drain on the city. Olesha recalled some names in the first decade of the twentieth century: "The Odessa rich, I never saw any of them. I only heard their names: Brodsky, Gepner, Khari, Ashkinazi, Ptashnikov, Anana. They were bankers, grain exporters—dark, sinister figures."[77] But the vast majority of Jews were very poor. Fierce competition among the poorest elements of the population, the longshoremen, inflamed hatred between Russians and Ukrainians against Jews. In 1905 Jewish casualties amounted to 302 known dead, including 55 from the self-defense force. Over 1,400 businesses were ruined. At this point many Jews decided that it was no longer possible "to live like God in Odessa." Thousands began their trek out of the city; between 1882 and 1908 a million Jews left Eastern Europe for the United States and elsewhere. Some of the Jews who remained did become socialists as a result of worsening economic conditions. For the most part they were Mensheviks, recruited from the economically and politically threatened artisans, merchants, and shopkeepers. Life went on in Odessa but under more unstable conditions.

Because of the relatively mild climate, as in many Mediterranean cities, so much of Odessa's vibrant life was led outdoors, either along its beaches, at the nearby dachas, in the parks, along Prymors'kyi Boulevard, at the outdoor cafes and wine shops, and in the many interior city courtyards where people conversed, were observed, overheard, and intensely discussed. Business deals were concluded, robberies planned, and family quarrels were aired out of doors. The courtyard (*dvor*) afforded social space for entire families and groups of families, semi-secluded from the street. In the Moldavanka they also served as inns for travelers. Statues, wells, tables, benches, and grapevines decorated the cozy space that also served as a kind of political forum and newsroom. In some courtyards, especially in the Moldavanka, the *dvorniki* (superintendents or janitors) served as police informants. The Odessa-born writer, photographer, and printer Arkady Lvov published his novel *Dvor* in 1982; it takes place in Odessa during the Stalinist era, an indication that the courtyard was still the informal gathering place for political discussions as well as for the exchange of neighborhood gossip.

Outdoor cafés in Odessa also served as places for conversation, business deals, and sheer enjoyment of the long Odessa summers. Sholem Aleichem's character Menahem-Mendl gushes to his wife that he was privileged to sit in Cafe Fankoni, "side by side with all the big speculators at the white marble tables, and order a portion of ice cream, because in our Odessa, it is a custom that as soon as you sit down, up comes a man dressed in a coat with a tail and orders you to order ice cream."[78] Odessans did enjoy their food and drink. Almost all Odessans remember or still enjoy the delicious candy made by the Krakhmalnikov Brothers. Founded as a bakery in 1820, by Abram Wolf Krakhmalnikov (1800–1883), the company was reorganized in 1893 by his sons Yakov (1860–?) and Lev (1864–1916) as a full confectionery. The chocolates, caramels, honey cakes, halva, and other treats were so fine that in the year 1904 alone, the company won international gold medals in Paris, London, Moscow, and Rostov. When the Bolsheviks took over the factory, it employed five hundred persons; they renamed the plant the Rosa Luxemburg factory, which after 1991 became simply the Odessa Candy Company. It was one of the first candy factories to use candy vending machines. Valentin Kataev, in his novel *White Sails Gleam*, has one character assure another that the gumdrop is a good one because it bore the Krakhmalnikov label.

The New Stock Exchange, built in 1894–99, designed by Aleksandr Bernardazzi. Postcard, 1900s.

Mentioning the Rosa Luxemburg candy label in his novel *Envy*, which he wrote while living in Moscow, Olesha showed nostalgia for that particular candy.

Odessa's mild weather and spectacular light encouraged not only outdoor socialization but also painting. One of Russia's most popular and prolific painters was Ivan K. Aivazovsky. Born in Feodosiia in 1817, the son of an Armenian merchant, he painted over six thousand pictures of sailors and Odessa seascapes, including *The Black Sea* (1881). Odessa's mists filtered the light, especially in autumn, so that both sea and sunlight inspired painters. In his stories, Kuprin verbally painted the fog and mist that often covered the northern Black Sea. Paustovskii also described the atmosphere: "Odessa wrapped herself in mist, like the old women in their shawls. Sea fog lasted all through the autumn. I have been fond of misty days ever since—especially in autumn when the watery light is lemon-yellow like turning leaves."[79] Babel' liked to describe the city in full light, "The sun hung from the sky like the pink tongue of a thirsty dog, the immense sea rolled far away to Peresyp, and the masts of distant ships swayed on the emerald water of Odessa Bay."[80]

While scenery inspired some, music seems to have been one of the sources of inspiration for Wassily Kandinsky. Born in Moscow in 1866, he was taken to Odessa when he was five years old and stayed there until he was twenty. He became first an amateur cellist and pianist, and then a painter of abstract art. It is said that his early art mimics the abstract language of music he learned while living in Odessa. Although Kandinsky did not spend much of his adult life in Odessa, he visited his mother there from time to time. Leonid Pasternak, father of Boris the famous writer and Nobel Prize winner, was also an Odessa artist. A famous Jewish graphic artist was born in Odessa in 1893, Mikhail Dlugach. Like many of Odessa's writers, Dlugach moved to Moscow when it became the capital of the new Bolshevik state.[81]

Odessa had a passion for change, novelty, and experimentation. The good weather and beaches also encouraged sporting activities. As Babel' noted of Odessa, "In the summer, the bronze, muscular bodies of youths who play sports glisten on beaches."[82] The writer Alexander Kuprin, "had he not become a writer, could certainly have been a champion boxer or wrestler ... Not satisfied with his prowess in these spheres, he threw himself into a host of others—fencing, skating, bicycling, horse riding and even ballooning and aviation."[83]

Perhaps the personification of an athlete daredevil was Serhii Utochkin. Born in 1876 to a merchant family in Odessa, he was orphaned at an early age. His guardian gave him a bicycle, on which as a boy he loved riding around town. He soon became a champion bicyclist in Russia, winning an international prize in Lisbon before moving to faster vehicles—first the motorcycle, and then the automobile.

Isaac Babel' celebrated Odessa's love affair with cars and Italian opera by depicting his most memorable character, the Odessan Jewish gangster Benya Krik, appearing at a funeral, "the red automobile came flying around the corner. It was honking *I Pagliacci*."[84] And who can forget the con man Ostap Bender of the twenties portrayed in *The Little Golden Calf*, in his car bumping along the dusty roads of Odessa and environs?[85]

But Utochkin moved beyond automobile racing. He was also a runner, boxer, fencer, skater, yachtsman, and swimmer. Attracted to ballooning, he went to Egypt and flew over the pyramids and the Sahara Desert. He made his reputation, however, as one of Russia's earliest aviators. By 1908, only five years after the Wright Brothers flew their first plane, he was a member of a select group belonging to the Emperor's All-Russian Air Club, Odessa branch, the only branch outside St. Petersburg. By April 1911, he was flying a French Farman IV biplane for the Odessa Naval Battalion. Earlier in 1910, he created a sensation in Baku, where he flew at an air show although he had never had flying lessons. So great was the interest in this spectacle that tickets cost over sixty rubles, the monthly wage of an oil worker. The audience gasped because it appeared that Utochkin would perish when his little plane went into a tailspin, but he managed to right it and land safely on the field. He had several other near misses in Katerynoslav and Rostov. Boasting that he would fly to Moscow in order to drink tea, he had a series of mishaps again en route with his plane. Lucky perhaps in flight but not in love, his beloved wife left him for a rich factory owner.

Not lucky for long, however, he injured himself severely during a difficult landing. At the hospital he was administered morphine; when he left, he became addicted to cocaine. He later was admitted to a psychiatric hospital in the capital, but was released in 1913, and went back to Odessa. When war broke out, he attempted to enlist in the air force but was refused. Even more humiliating, he was not allowed to work in an airplane construction factory. Returning to Petrograd, he was soon put back into the psychiatric hospital, where he died in 1916.

Babel' wrote an epitaph of sorts: "I saw Utochkin, *pur sang* Odessan, lighthearted and profound, reckless and thoughtful, elegant and gangly, brilliant and stuttering. He has been ruined by cocaine or morphine—ruined, word has it, since the day he fell out of an airplane somewhere in the marshes of Novgorod. Poor Utochkin, he has lost his mind. But of one thing I am certain: any day now the province of Novgorod will come crawling down to Odessa."[86] In his story "The Bicycle Chain," Olesha comments on Utochkin, "People regard him as a miracle. He was among the first to ride a bicycle, a motorcycle and an automobile, and one of the first to fly. He crashed on the Moscow-Petersburg flight and was gravely injured. They still laughed at him. He was the champion, and in Odessa he was regarded as a lunatic."[87]

In May 2001, Ukraine issued a special stamp in his honor. According to Kuprin, who first met the sportsman at Velykyi Fontan on the seashore in the summer of 1904: "From that time on, I never could imagine Utochkin without Odessa, or Odessa without Utochkin." In September 2001, Odessa commemorated its athlete-pilot by placing on the steps of the Utochkin Cinema a statue of him with a paper plane in his hand as though he were about to launch it—a whimsical but perhaps fitting tribute to the daring pioneer aviator.

Writers were impressed by other sportsmen as well as Utochkin. Olesha played soccer in school, and was a great admirer of the game and of its stars as shown in his story, *Envy*.[88] Over the years, Odessa produced outstanding athletes, including an Olympic champion in boating, Yuliia Riabchyns'ka, an Olympic champion in gymnastics, Margarita Nikolaeva, the gymnast Olena Vitrychenko, and the figure skaters Viacheslav Zahorodniuk, Viktor Petrenko, and the "Swan of Odessa," Oksana Baiul. Lenny Krayzelburg, born in Odessa, won gold medals in swimming for the United States during the 2000 Olympics. As Jabotinsky wrote in his journal, "Odessa reared healthier types than most traditionally Jewish cities. Odessa did not have any tradition, but it was therefore not afraid of new forms of living and activity. It developed in us

Одесса. Старый базаръ. Odessa. Le vieux bazar.

Old Bazaar.

more temperament and less passion, more cynicism, but less bitterness. Were I asked, I would not choose to be born in any other city."[89]

Odessa seemed to foster characters of originality and a unique culture. As Rothstein so aptly explained: "Thanks in large measure to the interaction of its populations of Russians, Jews, Ukrainians, Poles, Greeks and others, Odessa produced its own dialect, its own music, its own humor, its own literature—and even its own version of gefilte fish."[90]

There have been many elegies written concerning the decline of Odessa at various stages of its history. During World War I, Babel' wrote: "In Odessa there is a port, and in the port there are ships that have come from Newcastle, Cardiff, Marseille and Port Said; Negroes, Englishmen, Frenchmen and Americans. Odessa had its moment in the sun, but now it is fading—a poetic, slow, lighthearted, helpless fading."[91] Jabotinsky, a native Odessite and Zionist, mused nostalgically, "No trace of that Odessa [of his youth at the turn of the century] has existed for a long time, and there's no use hoping that I can ever return to it." And again he murmurs: "Most likely, I shall never see Odessa again. Too bad, I love her."[92] Oleh Hubar, Odessa's contemporary historian, lamented the passing of old Odessa when "the sun shone brighter and the sky was bluer."[93] Others might even declare, "Odessa doesn't live here anymore," but Odessa lives in these pages of history and, more important, in the memories of present and past Odessites.

Notes

Special thanks to Galya Diment, professor of Slavic Languages and Literatures, University of Washington, for help with this book.

1. Robert A. Rothstein, "How It Was Sung in Odessa: At the Intersection of Russia and Jewish Culture," *Slavic Review* 60, no. 4 (Winter 2001): 790.
2. Vladimir Jabotinsky, "Memoirs by My Typewriter," in *The Golden Tradition: Jewish Life and Thought in Eastern Europe*, ed. Lucy S. Dawidowicz (Syracuse, NY: Syracuse University Press, 1996), 397.
3. Patricia Herlihy, *Odessa: A History, 1794–1914* (Cambridge: Harvard University Press, 1986), 7.
4. François De Wollant, *Ocherk moei sluzhby v Rossii, 1787–1811* (Odessa: Optimum, 1999).
5. Konstantin Paustovsky, *Story of a Life*, vol. 2, trans. Manya Harari and Michael Duncan (London: Harvill Press; New York: Pantheon, 1965), 217.
6. Isaac Babel, *The Complete Works of Isaac Babel*, ed. Nathalie Babel and trans. Peter Constantine (New York: Norton, 2002), 79.
7. Herlihy, *Odessa*, 232.
8. Michele de Ribas, *Saggio sulla Città di Odessa*, ed. Giovanna Moracci (Genoa: Cassa di Risparmio di Genova e di Imperia, 1988).
9. Alexander de Ribas, *Staraia Odessa: Istoricheskie ocherki, vospominaniia* (Odessa: Knizhnyi magazin Georgiia Russo, 1913).
10. Yuri Olesha, *No Day Without a Line* (Ann Arbor, MI: Ardis, 1979), 142.
11. Patricia Herlihy, "Commerce in Russian Urban Culture, 1861–1914," ed. William Craft Brumfield, Boris Anan'ich, and Yuri A. Petrov (Washington, DC, and Baltimore, MD: Johns Hopkins University Press, 2001), 180–94.
12. Herlihy, *Odessa*, 115.
13. Jabotinsky, "Memoirs by My Typewriter," 398.
14. Shmuel Katz, *Lone Wolf: A Biography of Vladimir (Ze'ev) Jabotinsky*, vol. 1 (New York: Barricade Books, 1996), 14.
15. Steven J. Zipperstein, *The Jews of Odessa: A Cultural History, 1794–1881* (Stanford, CA: Stanford University Press, 1985), 66.

16 S. Y. Abramovitch, *Tales of Mendele the Book Peddler*, ed. Dan Miron and Ken Frieden (New York: Schocken Books, 1996), 257.
17 Nicholas Luker, *Alexander Kuprin* (Boston: Twayne, 1987), 199.
18 Richard Taruskin, *Defining Russia Musically: Historical and Hermeneutical Essays* (Princeton: Princeton University Press, 1997), 188.
19 Zipperstein, *Jews in Odessa*, 30.
20 Ibid., 66.
21 Babel, *Complete Works*, 628.
22 Ibid., 629.
23 Ibid., 701.
24 Rothstein, "How It Was Sung," 800.
25 S. Frederick Starr, *Red and Hot: The Fate of Jazz in the Soviet Union, 1917–1980* (New York: Oxford University Press, 1983), 144.
26 Rothstein, "How It Was Sung," 788.
27 Anatolii F. Kozak, *Odessa zdes' bol'she ne zhivet* (Samara: Gazeta *Tarbut*, 1997), 139.
28 Richard Stites, *Russian Popular Culture: Entertainment and Society since 1900* (Cambridge: Cambridge University Press, 1992), 75.
29 Babel, *Complete Works*, 76.
30 Rothstein, "How It Was Sung," 789.
31 Ibid.
32 Ibid., 800.
33 Stites, *Russian Popular Culture*, 21–22.
34 Paustovsky, *Story of a Life*, 4:90.
35 Rothstein, "How It Was Sung," 800.
36 Stites, *Russian Popular Culture*, 48.
37 Paustovsky, *Story of a Life*, 2:93.
38 Olesha, *No Day Without a Line*, 116–18.
39 Babel, *Complete Works*, 49.
40 Ibid., 75.
41 Rothstein, "How It Was Sung," 783, 785.
42 Babel, *Complete Works*, 81.
43 Paustovsky, *Story of a Life*, 3:205. Boris Briker, "The Underworld of Benya Krik and I. Babel's Odessa Stories," *Canadian Slavonic Papers/Revue Canadienne des Slavistes* 36 (1994): 115–34.
44 Stites, *Russian Popular Culture*, 188.
45 Paustovsky, *Story of a Life*, 2:90.
46 Babel, *Complete Works*, 158.
47 Herlihy, *Odessa*, 282.
48 Roshanna P. Sylvester, "Crime, Masquerade, and Anxiety: The Public Creation of Middle Class Identity in Pre-Revolutionary Odessa, 1912–1916" (PhD diss., Yale University, 1998), 237–40.
49 Herlihy, *Odessa*, 282.
50 Rothstein, "How It Was Sung," 791.
51 Sholom Aleichem, *The Adventures of Menahem-Mendl*, trans. Tamara Kahana (New York: Putnam, 1969), 17.
52 Paustovsky, *Story of a Life*, 4:10–11.
53 Babel, *Complete Works*, 82.
54 A. Kuprin, *Sasha*, trans. Douglas Ashby (London: S. Paul & Co., 1920), 11–12.
55 Ibid., 9.
56 Olesha, *No Day Without a Line*, 88.

57 Rimgaila Salys, "Sausage Rococo: The Art of Tiepolo in Olesha's *Envy*," in *Olesha's Envy: A Critical Companion* (Evanston, IL: Northwestern University Press, 1990), 103.
58 Victor Peppard, *The Poetics of Yury Olesha* (Gainesville: University of Florida Press, 1989), 15.
59 Yuri Olyesha, *Love and Other Stories*, trans. with an introduction by Robert Payne (New York: Washington Square Press, 1967), xi.
60 Olesha, *No Day Without a Line*, 137.
61 Olyesha, *Love and Other Stories*, xxiii.
62 *The Portable Twentieth-Century Russian Reader*, ed. Clarence Brown (New York: Penguin, 1985), 250.
63 Katerina Clark and Michael Holmquist, *Mikhail Bakhtin* (Cambridge, MA: Harvard University Press, 1984), 296.
64 Ibid., 27.
65 Olesha, *No Day Without a Line*, 146.
66 Maxim Shrayer, *Russian Poet/Soviet Jew: The Legacy of Eduard Bagritskii* (Lanham, MD: Rowman and Littlefield, 2000), 97.
67 Olesha, *No Day Without a Line*, 251.
68 Ibid., 170.
69 Zipperstein, *Jews of Odessa*, 21.
70 Katz, *Lone Wolf*, vol.1, 26.
71 Michael Stanislawski, *Zionism and the Fin de Siècle: Cosmopolitanism and Nationalism from Nordau to Jabotinsky* (Berkeley: University of California Press, 2001) 126.
72 Zipperstein, *Jews of Odessa*, 48.
73 Babel, *Complete Works*, 14–15.
74 Herlihy, *Odessa*, 123.
75 Ibid., 302.
76 Robert Weinberg, *The Revolution of 1905 in Odessa: Blood on the Steps* (Bloomington: Indiana University Press, 1993).
77 Olesha, *No Day Without a Line*, 110.
78 Sholom Aleichem, *The Adventures of Menahem-Mendl*, 32.
79 Paustovsky, *Story of a Life*, vol. 3, 200.
80 Babel, *Complete Works*, 157.
81 Robert Weinberg, *Stalin's Forgotten Zion: Birobidzhan and the Making of a Soviet Jewish Homeland* (Berkeley: University of California Press, 1998), 33.
82 Babel, *Complete Works*, 76.
83 Luker, *Alexander Kuprin*, 15.
84 Babel, *Complete Works*, 153.
85 Il'f and Petrov, *The Golden Calf*, trans. John H. C. Richardson (New York, 1965).
86 Babel, *Complete Works*, 76.
87 Olyesha, *Love and Other Stories*, 210–11.
88 Olesha, *Envy*, 5.
89 Jabotinsky, "Memoirs by My Typewriter," 399.
90 Rothstein, "How It Was Sung," 800–801. Babel' proclaimed that Odessa-style gefilte fish with horseradish was "a dish worth embracing Judaism for," *Complete Works*, 48.
91 Babel, *Complete Works*, 7.
92 Stanislawski, *Zionism*, 235, 237.
93 Oleg Gubar', *100 voprosov za Odessu* (Odessa: Polinom, 1994), 2. He wittily described his book as a "short course" on Odessa's history for "all-class reading."

Souvenir postcard (detail), early 1910s.

Oleksandrivs'kyi Park, early 1910s.

Monument to Alexander II.

City Theater. Postcards, early twentieth century.

Odessa Memories • CHAPTER 2 | 69

Odessa postcards, 1900–1910s

Odessa Public Library, built in 1907.

Odessa Memories • CHAPTER 2 | 71

City view from the Mykolaiv-Kherson dock.

The lighthouse at the Velykyi Fontan

The Quarantine Harbor.

The "Otrada" beach.

Malyi Fontan.

The Langeron beach.

The Vorontsov Lighthouse.

CHAPTER 3

How Ukrainian Is Odesa? From Odessa to Odesa

THERE'S SOMETHING ABOUT CATHERINE

In 1900, the city authorities of Odessa (in Ukrainian, Odesa) erected an impressive monument to Catherine II, who was surrounded on the base by her four principal administrators. When the Bolsheviks took over the city, they pulled down the monument with the help of a tractor and in 1920 put in its place a monument to Karl Marx. In 1977, Marx gave way to a Soviet realist rendition of the 1905 *Battleship Potemkin* mutineers. In the summer of 2007, the Potemkin monument was removed to another site in the city. On August 29, 2007, a new thirty-five-foot monument to Catherine II and her servitors was placed on the spot where the original statue had stood more than a hundred years earlier.[1]

This latest occasion of substitution stirred up quite a bit of fuss. In July 2007, a month before the installation, protestors knocked down a fence at the site and erected an Orthodox cross. Authorities removed the cross, but hundreds of Cossacks from various parts of Ukraine gathered days later, only to clash with the police.

When the new statue of Catherine was erected, the terrible heat wave reportedly kept people off the streets, although one Cossack vowed that a half-million Cossacks would see to it that the empress came down. The city vowed in turn that it would post a twenty-four-hour guard at the site while the statue awaited unveiling.[2] Those inclined to favor their connection to the Russian, but not Soviet, past claim that they wish to honor Catherine, the founder of their city.[3] They also argue that they are attempting to restore the historic center of Odesa in order to get support from UNESCO.

Some Ukrainian patriots find it reprehensible to celebrate the empress, who was, as one Ukrainian wrote, "Russia's ruling bloodthirsty she-wolf (in the words of Taras Shevchenko) who ordered the destruction of the Zaporozhian Sich and turned the Ukrainian peasants into serfs."[4] Professor Yurii Shapoval deplored "the unveiling of a monument to a German woman in Odesa, who hated Ukraine, regarding it as a source of freethinking and a threat to her cherished *alles ist in Ordnung* system in the Russian Empire."[5] Some Ukrainian groups petitioned the Security Services of Ukraine not to unveil the monument, which, in their opinion, "is planned

---

Originally published as Patricia Herlihy, "How Ukrainian Is Odesa? From Odessa to Odesa," *Place, Identity, and Urban Culture: Odessa and New Orleans*, Occasional Papers, Kennan Institute (2008): 19–27.

to be a permanent trigger of interethnic hostility to provoke chaos and anarchy in the country and first of all in Odesa."[6]

The Russian point of view on Catherine was expressed by Vladimir Yelenin, who asked, "Why did ridiculous yet malevolent Cossacks who descended on the seaport of Odesa in the fall of 2007 protest against the restoration of a monument to Catherine II? If it were not for the empress of Russia, they would have come not to Odesa but the Turkish town of Khadzhibei. There is a strong doubt that the Turks would have allowed them to enter."[7] This remark not too subtly asserts that Cossacks did not conquer the area from the Turks, but Russian generals did.

After two months of postponements, the unveiling, on October 27, revealed a statue no longer named for Catherine II but titled "The Monument to the Founders of the City." Fashioned in Kyiv, it again depicts Catherine standing in the midst of the same foursome of conquerors/administrators. Shouting and scuffles ensued after the unveiling.[8] While the Odesa Cossacks approved of the statue, Ukrainian Cossacks and members of the nationalist organizations Svoboda, the Ukrainian People's Party, and Our Ukraine shouted "Shame!" One Ukrainian Cossack likened the erecting of this statue in Odesa to placing one of Hitler in Babyi Yar.[9]

This tug of war is an example of the sensitivity engendered when claims are made on the symbols and meanings of Odesa's past, all of which are intended to shape the memory of Odes(s)ites.

THE RESONANT VOICE OF THE POLITICS OF LANGUAGE

Even more contested, in some respects, are the demands made on Odesites to shape the city's future identity, which involve not only memory but also language. Mute metal and stone can speak volumes, to be sure, but the politics of language, it can be argued, have an even louder resonance.

Only two years ago, the region of Odesa and others in eastern and southern Ukraine talked of secession out of fear of dominance by Ukrainian-speakers from western Ukraine. The debate over language was one of the most heated during the 2004 Orange Revolution. Official Russian reaction to a Ukrainian state resolution in 2000 titled "On Additional Measures to Expand the Use of Ukrainian as the State Language" was to protest. Russia's foreign minister denounced the "de-Russification of Ukraine" and predicted that such policies "directed against the preservation and development of the Russian language and culture" went against the Ukrainian Constitution's guarantee of the "free development, use, and protection of the Russian language."[10]

Ukrainian language policies and those of other states in the Near Abroad contributed to then-President Vladimir Putin's declaration of 2007 as "The Year of the Russian Language." Russia organized a conference on that topic in Moscow in May 2007, and others were held in the Commonwealth of Independent States and the Baltic states. That Sergei Lavrov, Russian foreign minister, gave the keynote speech and Vice Premier Dmitry Medvedev was chairman of the organizing committee, indicate the weight Putin gave the issue.[11]

Putin called for the creation of a "National Russian Language Institute," explaining in his 2007 State of the Nation address that "looking after the Russian language and expanding the influence of Russian culture are crucial social and political issues."[12] At the Moscow conference, it was reported that more than 30 percent of Ukraine is Russian-speaking. On the other hand, a reporter proclaimed that the "Russian language is in retreat in Ukraine," continuing that "16 years after shrugging off Moscow's rule, Ukraine is reclaiming a language that—like scores of other local languages across the former USSR—the Soviet leadership once disdained as inferior to Russian. Today Ukrainian has emerged from second-class status, slipping quietly into the chambers of governmental and popular culture. This marks more than a cultural change: it could doom any hopes Russia may have of restoring its traditional political influence over this country of 47 million."[13] Another reporter noted, "Little by little, the Ukrainian language is being used by the majority of the population as a first language. This is particularly true of the young generation, for whom it has become fashionable to use Ukrainian."[14]

Pop culture, especially music (including hip-hop and rap) with Ukrainian lyrics, has given the language a hip reputation. One indication of the appeal of Ukrainian to the young is the fact that the latest Harry Potter book was published in Ukrainian before it came out in Russian. A survey of 808 Ukrainians aged fourteen to forty-nine in the Ukrainian regions of L'viv, Kyiv, Odesa, and Kharkiv showed that only 11 percent were opposed to dubbing more movies in Ukrainian. It is significant that the people polled were relatively young and that Sony and Disney produced the movies under discussion, which included *Pirates of the Caribbean III* and *Ratatouille*.[15] On the other hand, Ukrainian legislation has prohibited the distribution of films dubbed into Russian, even if they have Ukrainian-language subtitles. Only films made originally in a foreign language that have received subtitles in Ukrainian will be accepted. Film exhibitors claim that such legislation will reduce the number of foreign films shown in Ukrainian theaters from 200, the number imported in 2007, to only 30 in 2008.[16]

Fashionable or not, it is practical to speak Ukrainian. More than 80 percent of the schools in Ukraine have changed the language of instruction from Russian to Ukrainian.[17] Because more universities are now also using Ukrainian as the language of instruction, parents are eager to have their children study it in school.[18]

In 2005, Hennadii Udovenko, a member of the Ukrainian parliament who chaired its Committee on Human Rights, National Minorities, and International Relations made a speech at the fourteenth "Ukrainian Yesterday, Today, and Tomorrow in Ukraine and in the World" conference assessing the state of the Ukrainian language and the need for its adoption by the citizens of Ukraine. Udovenko observed, "For 300 years the Ukrainian language was methodically and cruelly debased by imperial and communist dictates and regulations... Having gained an independent Ukraine, we have acquired the historical right to have a rebirth of a native language, and bestow it to an equal, deserving nation, one which gave to the world such geniuses as Taras Shevchenko, Lesia Ukrainka and Ivan Franko." Indeed, Udovenko argued that the state would not survive without the establishment of the Ukrainian language, "Without language there is no nation, and without a nation there is no state or government. These are the ABCs. Language has a central unifying role in the process of the formation of an ethnicity, nation and state."[19]

Udovenko is not historically correct in his depiction of Soviet language policy. Both Lenin and Stalin favored minorities being taught in their native language in school, with Russian to be taught as a second language.[20] Between 1936 and 1937 in Ukraine, 83 percent of pupils in general schools were studying in the Ukrainian language, a proportion that was similar to the proportion of Ukrainians in the population. In the 1950s and '60s, however, one-sided bilingualism was introduced: Ukrainians had to learn Russian, but Russians in Ukraine did not have to learn Ukrainian.[21] Ultimately, however, it is true that the Soviets expected Ukrainian (considered to be an inferior language) to fade away.

According to Anna Fournier, Russians in Ukraine (including Odesa) are resisting Ukrainian language laws, despite the fact that, as ethnic Russians, they are guaranteed the right to be educated in Russian (but in private schools). They are resisting because they have been put into an ethnic category, Fournier argues, in a country with common intermarriage between Ukrainians and Russians. Russians prefer to be classified with Ukrainian Russophones. In that way, they will not be considered an ethnic minority. According to a Russian source, Russians are only the second-largest cohort of the population in Odesa. Meanwhile, the number of Ukrainians is increasing. In 1989 they constituted 49 percent of the city's population, but by 2001, a decade after independence, the figure had risen to 62 percent. Russians, who were 39 percent of the population in 1989, have been reduced to 29 percent.[22] To Russians in Odesa, it seems anomalous to be considered a protected "ethnic minority," a designation that has the effect of increasing their discontent with the language laws.

THE CONFOUNDING EFFECT OF "LANGUAGE OF CONVENIENCE"

The increase in the number of Ukrainians is probably due to the fact that many Ukrainian Russophones declare Ukrainian to be their maternal tongue (*ridna mova*) "in the sense that it is the language of their indigenous cultural and ethnic heritage, which is essentially non-Russian."[23] In other words, they appear to be using the Soviet practice of allowing people to declare Ukrainian their "mother tongue" whether they are fluent in the language or not. Mother tongue was understood as the language of their nationality and not as the language of use. For example, "the last Soviet census, conducted in 1989, [showed that] Ukrainians comprised 72 percent of the population of the Ukrainian Soviet Republic, with 12 percent of those claiming Russian as a mother tongue. Had the Soviet Union used the category of 'language of use' instead . . . and presumed that language was a proxy of nationality . . . then the proportion of Ukrainians would have dropped to half of the population. Several surveys conducted in the 1990s have shown that Russian is used as the main home language by about half of Ukrainian citizens."[24]

Taras Kuzio agrees, "Based on 'language of convenience' [that is, everyday use] Ukrainianophones and Russophones were seen as roughly equal."[25] And Odesa would probably be counted among the cities where the use of Russian is more prevalent than the national average.[26] Two Odesa scholars, using four factors—economic, geographic, linguistic, and religious—to determine language use in three regions of Ukraine, concluded that historically these factors have resulted in Odesa's population's favoring the use of Russian.[27]

If ethnic Ukrainians who use Russian as their everyday language and ethnic Russians were lumped together into one Russophone group, and if all of them continued to retain Russian as their spoken language, then the Russian language would remain the dominant language and might, in time, cause the use of Ukrainian to die out, at least in Odesa. In short, in the thinking of some Ukrainian builders of national identity, either one must Ukrainianize ethnic Ukrainians or they will be Russified as they were under the tsarist and Soviet regimes. The question is, however, are ethnic Ukrainians resisting being singled out by ethnicity and forced to be educated in Ukrainian only, even though they speak Russian at home and perhaps even publicly?

In March 2007, a weeklong campaign for the use of Russian was mounted in Odesa. There were motor rallies, meetings, and the collection of 170,500 signatures in support of the Russian language.[28] As one indignant Russophone declared at the time, "I am against children studying Pushkin as a foreign writer and poet; I am against the Russian language being doled out on television; and I am against movies in the theaters being translated into Ukrainian."[29]

Odesa, however, did not go as far as other cities, such as Donets'k, Dinpropetrovs'k, Kryvyi Rih, Luhans'k, Mykolaiv, Sevastopol', Kharkiv, Kherson, and Yalta, which legalized Russian as a state language.[30] Odesa's municipal regulations merely state that the working languages of the city council are Ukrainian and Russian.[31]

A professor friend of nearly thirty years who teaches at Odesa State University wrote to me, "A country should have one state language. I am an ethnic Ukrainian; I had Ukrainian language and Ukrainian literature every single day of my school. I love the language. I am permanently reading contemporary Ukrainian authors; I don't resist its implementation. I simply believe that the language policy is desperately wrong, which is connected with an inferiority complex, the complex of the younger brother, that pesters our present elite. As to me, knowing the language, I, like all of the East, South and much of the Center, have never spoken it. And so naturally, I feel much more comfortable speaking, reporting at various meetings and conferences in Russian. I think that it would have been much wiser to give time for adjustment, not to push. You know that pushing always causes problems and this particular case in no exception." Another native Odesite, a journalist, observed to me, "The language problem is rather the subject of political manipulations than interpersonal relationships. One thing is clear, the more they force the so-called State language on us, the more it is going to be mocked and humiliated. I think it a nasty tendency, especially in the city that boasts its tolerance. Let the languages coexist, forget about revenge or getting even, and the attitude of Odesites toward Ukrainian will become less harsh. Let's not confuse the artificially cultivated enmity with the real neighborly relations."

Another friend, an ethnic Russian who is a translator living in Odesa, noted that various kiosks were distributing bumper stickers with the message "I Speak Russian," and that there were heated discussions on Internet forums.[32]

She continued, "I have always spoken Russian as my native tongue and never experienced any oppression concerning my way of self-expression. As for the Ukrainian language, there is definitely a historic injustice done to the language and the people. All of a sudden, people got divided by an issue, which in reality has little to do with their everyday life. I still claim that the Russian language dominates in everyday use in Odesa and nobody is trying to violently change this. Any efforts to promote Ukrainian are met as a personal insult by many and there seems to be a strong opposition and bitter feelings." She went on to say that her sympathies were with Ukrainian-speakers, but her democratic instincts allied her with Russian-speakers as a minority, even though in Odesa they are not a minority. She concluded, "I do not know how to feel—for Ukrainian-speakers or for us Russian-speakers. See what confusion? All of this is to say the situation is really a mess."

This dual self-identification or sympathy is expressed by Natasha Yermakova, a specialist in the history of the Ukrainian theater and a teacher who was born in Kyiv of Russian parents, who asserts, "I received Russian culture by blood, and I inevitably chose Ukrainian culture while growing up."[33] It seems that Ukrainians and non-Ukrainians are willing to speak or learn Ukrainian. But they feel that they should be able to make the choice and not have it legislated, an approach they consider divisive.

One direct method for spreading the use of Ukrainian is to expose Ukrainian citizens to the language via the media. In 2006, President Yushchenko signed a law stipulating that 75 percent of radio and television broadcasts had to be in Ukrainian. The Eastern Party of the Regions responded immediately by threatening to conduct a referendum on making Russian a second state language on a par with Ukrainian.[34]

Hennadii Udovenko expressed the Ukrainian viewpoint in 2005 on television programs. He lamented the "unending flow of Russian-language serials with the standard content, made with Ukrainian subtitles. But Ukrainians are not deaf! It is annoying and unpleasant how the Russian-speaking environment continues to plant itself."[35]

Other measures to foster the Ukrainian language in Ukraine's youth include Ukrainian-language versions of Windows Vista and Office System 2007 that Microsoft has introduced at the same price as the Russian versions.[36]

Teaching young children Ukrainian in school, along with popularizing the language through music, film, TV, and computer software, will help ensure that Ukrainians of the future know Ukrainian. These measures are less likely to arouse ire and irk elderly Russophones who find that it is too late to learn to speak Ukrainian fluently and correctly even though they can easily read and understand the language. As the scholar Yaroslav Hrytsak affirms, integration of eastern and western Ukraine is possible if leaders capitalize on similarities rather than on differences, and if they avoid hot topics such as the status of the Russian language.[37]

CONCLUSION

Most experts on language politics in Ukraine, such as Laada Bilaniuk, agree that more than 90 percent of the population understands both Ukrainian and Russian, but "speaking one or the other at any given time can attach social and political meanings to the act of speech."[38] Instead of choosing one of the languages to suit a given occasion or the other person, Bilaniuk suggests that "each speaker [use] whatever language she or he prefers (Ukrainian or Russian) regardless of the language the others are speaking, or if they wish, they can switch back and forth."[39] Certainly, this would be the ideal situation. It would show acceptance of ethnic and linguistic hybridity, thus defusing tensions.

Historically the most diverse, apolitical, and tolerant of Russian imperial cities, Odesa should be the first to embrace such a model.[40] My local Odesa respondents, whether Jewish, Ukrainian, or Russian, are willing to read both languages, and most of them speak both. Perhaps such flexibility might be possible as long as provocative gestures were avoided, at least nothing beyond the traditional teasing and joking that are so much part of the city's tradition, culminating each April 1 in the Iumorina festival.

Instead of classifying Odesites as ethnic Russians or Ukrainians, the state could facilitate—but not mandate—Russophones' and Ukrainophones' acquisition of each other's mother tongue, if only as a second language. It appears that Odesites do not base their friendships on language affinity. While geography and language use have a strong correlation with Ukrainian political positions, they are not exclusive markers of Ukrainian identity, any more than ethnicity. As one Odesite put it, "I am Ukrainian; I speak Russian, but I am Ukrainian."[41] Opinion surveys reveal that matters such as NATO membership and the strengthening or weakening of the status of the Russian language are not among the top twenty issues of importance to Ukrainians.[42]

On the matter of politics, Odesites should speak for themselves in whichever language they choose, and not have their language define how others perceive their views or gauge their loyalty as Ukrainian citizens. Odesa has always had a strong sense of its unique cosmopolitan history, priding itself on loose but real ties with the center. Rulers have often regarded it as an enfant terrible among cities, but nations, like families, should always have room for one slightly eccentric member.[43]

Notes

1. The four administrators, all associated with the establishment of Odesa, were Grigorii Potemkin, Prince Platon Zubov, José de Ribas, and François de Wollant (in Russian imperial adaptation, Frants de Volan). The original statue disappeared during World War II when parts of Catherine and the four gentlemen were found; they are now displayed in the sculpture garden outside Odesa's literary museum.
2. Ron Popeski, "Catherine the Great Sparks Cossack Ire," Reuters Press, August 29, 2007, http://www.reuters.com/article/inDepthNews/. Cossacks suggested a compromise: abandon the Catherine monument and complete a church in honor of Saint Catherine on the site. Oleh Hubar, a well-known Odesa journalist, said, "Cossacks swore allegiance to Catherine the Great, Polish kings and Turkish sultans. This was simply the nature of their work. Today these people are being manipulated. It is quite frankly, no more than a tragic, uncivilized joke."
3. The mayor of Odesa in 1994-1998 and 2005-2010, Eduard Hurvits, was in favor of the monument because it recalled the pre-Soviet past. He noted that he had removed 148 Soviet monuments, 104 of which were of Lenin, and had changed the Soviet names of 179 streets. Piotr Smolar, "Homo Ukrainus: An Emerging Species." *Le Monde*, September 28, 2007, http://iedg.blogspot.com/2007/09/lhomo-ukrainus-espce-en-voie.html.
4. *The Day Weekly Digest* (Kyiv, Ukraine), October 30, 2007, http://www.day.kyiv.ua/190492/.
5. Ibid. It was stated in the same article that 600 Cossacks were among the first 1,000 settlers of Odesa, so they too can be considered founders of the city.
6. *Ukrains'ka Pravda*, October 28, 2007. "Catherine II Sees Fights in Odessa," http://pda.pravda.com.us/emg/news/.
7. Vladimir Yelenin. "Catherine the Great Is More Valuable to Ukraine than Zaporizhian Cossacks," *The Ukrainian Times*, February 5, 2008.
8. A translator in Odesa sent me this report by email on November 5, 2007, "As for the opening the monument to Catherine II, I was there in that crowd and can tell how it was: jolly, noisy, quarrelsome, altogether quite normal for such an event. Some women managed to start a fight in a corner of the square, others laughed, the music was very loud and rhythmic, some danced, lots of pictures were taken, it was quite a show. After all that, there were fireworks and the Philharmonic orchestra played under the open sky for an hour. In terms of legal actions

there were no steps taken. The tension is still there and will be there for years to come as the experience of other countries tell us."

9   "Scuffles reported in South Ukraine over Controversial Monument," BBC Monitoring, report by Ukrainian channel UT1 on October 27, 2007, http://www.industrywatch.com/pages/iw2/print/; Unian, "Monument to Russian Empress Ekaterina II to Be Unveiled in Odesa," September 9, 2007, http://www.unian.net/news/print/.

10 Anna Fournier, "Mapping Identities: Russian Resistance to Linguistic Ukrainization in Central and Eastern Ukraine," *Europe-Asia Studies* 54, no. 3 (2002): 422.

11 ITAR-TASS, Moscow, May 28, 2007, "Russian Language Important for Enrichment of People World Over Says Foreign Ministry," http://ru-entraslator.livejournal.com/58823.html.

12 Mara D. Bellaby, "Russian Language in Retreat in Ukraine," Associated Press, May 1, 2007, http://www.washingtonpost.com/wp-dyn/content/article/2007/05/01/AR2007050101036.html.

13 Ibid.

14 Smolar, "Homo Ukrainus."

15 Unian, "Only 11 Percent of Ukrainians Opposed to More Films Dubbed in Ukrainian," February 5, 2008, http://www.unian.net.

16 Tom Birchenough, "Ukraine on Language Lockdown: Country Demands That Films Have Ukrainian Dub," *Variety*, February, February 22, 2008, http://www.variety.com/index.asp?layout+print_story&articleid+VR1117981323&-categoryid=2523.22. *Variety* reported that Anton Pugach, an exhibitor with Multiplex Holding, was trying to gather 100,000 signatures against the legislation to present to President Viktor Yushchenko. Exhibitors claimed, however, that such a stringent law would only encourage the sale of pirated Russian language DVDs.

17 During the 1935–36 academic year, 83 percent of students in Ukraine were studying Ukrainian. See Harold R. Weinstein, "Language and Education in Soviet Ukraine," *Slavonic Year-Book, American Series* 1 (1941): 142. But in 1933, as many as 88.5 percent of Ukrainian children were enrolled in Ukrainian schools. See Laada Bilaniuk, *Contested Tongues: Language, Politics, and Cultural Contestation in Ukraine* (Ithaca, NY: Cornell University Press, 2005), 82.

18 Belaby, "Russian Language."

19 Hennadii Udovenko, "Movna Polityka Ukrainy na Suchasnomu Etapi," *Ukraïnoznavsto* 4 (2005): 24–30.

20 See Weinstain, "Language and Education," 124–48. See also Yuri Slezkine, "The USSR as a Communal Apartment, or How a Socialist State Promoted Ethnic Particularism," *Slavonic Review* 53, no. 2 (1994): 414–52; Maxim Waldstein, "Russifying Estonia? Iurii Lotman and the Politics of Language and Culture in Soviet Estonia," *Kritika: Explorations in Russian and Eurasian History* 8, no. 3 (2007): 561–96; George Liber, *Soviet Nationality Policy, Urban Growth and Identity Change in the Ukrainian SSR, 1923–1934* (Cambridge: Cambridge University Press, 1992)'; and Bilaniuk, *Contested Tongues*, 80–81. *Contested Tongues* is the most useful book on the subject of language politics in contemporary Ukraine.

21 Waldstein, "Russifying Estonia?" 578.

22 ITAR-TASS, July 4, 2007. I do not know if the classifications are based on self-identification, but they must refer to ethnicity, since the majority of Odesites are Russophone. "Many Ukrainian citizens (as many as 56.1 percent of the adult population of Ukraine, according to Kyiv International Institute of Sociology) are thought to prefer interacting in Russian in the public sphere, regardless of their ethnicity and whether or not they are bilingual," Fournier, "Mapping Identities," 422.

23 Fournier, "Mapping Identities," 422.

24 Dominique Arel, "Language Categories in Censuses: Backward—or Forward-Looking," in *Census and Identity: The Politics of Race, Ethnicity, and Language in National Censuses*, ed. David I. Kertzer and Dominique Arel (Cambridge: Cambridge University Press, 2002), 104–5.

25 Taras Kuzio, "Census: Ukraine, More Ukrainian," *Russia and Eurasia Revue* 2, no. 3 (2003).

26 The 1989 Soviet census showed that 12 percent of the population of the Ukrainian Soviet Republic claimed to be Russian, whereas the same census showed 39 percent of the population of Odesa to be Russian.
27 Oleg Zorteev and Rostislav Zoteev, "Osobennosti funktsionirovaniia russkogo iazyka v polietnicheskikh regionakh Ukrainy," January 9, 2008, http://www.edrus.org/content/view/7121/69/.
28 "Odessa vsegda govorila po russki," April 4, 2007, http://forum.odessitka.net/index.php?showtopic=636.
29 Ibid.
30 ITAR-TASS, "Action to Protect Russian Language Launched in Ukraine's Odesa," March 3, 2007, http://www.itar-tass.com/eng/level2.html?NewsID.
31 "Reglament Odesskogo gorodskogo soveta v sozyva," *Rasdel I. Stat'ia* 2, no. 2 (June 27, 2006), http://www.odessa.ua/acts/council/5712/.
32 For examples of such discussions, see http://forum.pravda.com.ua/en. Purportedly, the "I Speak Russian" campaign is led by Valery Kaurov, head of the Odesa-based Union of the Orthodox Citizens of Ukraine. This organization pitched tents around Odesa where its members could collect signatures in support of giving Russian a protected status as a regional language. According to Kaurov, "With all the linguistic, religious, cultural differences, parts of the country can only coexist within a federally regulated polity." Paul Abelsky, "Building Its Own Destiny: Ukraine Seeks a Place between Russia and Europe," *Russia Profile*, May 30, 2007, http://www.russiaprofile.org.
33 Smolar, "Homo Ukrainus."
34 Ibid. Just before the September 2007 elections, the Party of Regions (PRU), led by Viktor Yanukovych, announced a campaign to organize a referendum asking Ukrainians whether Russian should be a second official language. But even some members of the PRU feel that the language issue is "too divisive." Pavel Korduban, "Party of Regions Challenges President with Referendum Plan," *Eurasia Daily Monitor*, September 12, 2007, http://eurasiandaily.org/article.
35 Udovenko, "Language Policy." "By 1937 when Stalin decided that some of Ukraine was over-Ukrainianized, he said more attention should be given to Russian popular literature, music, radio and cinema." Weinstein, "Language and Education," 145.
36 "Microsoft Puts on Sale Ukrainian-Language Windows Vista and Office System 2007," Ukrainian News. Agency, Kyiv, Ukraine, May 22, 2007, http://www.lucorg.com/luc/news.php?id=2478.
37 Abelsky, "Building Its Own Destiny." An article by Elena Yatsenko, "The Russian Language as the Geopolitical Potential of the Russian World," June 19, 2007, www.Eurasianhome.org, is an example of a provocative exhortation for Russophones in the Near Abroad to retain Russian so that they can leave their "diasporas," return to Russia and become more quickly reintegrated into Russia.
38 Laada Bilaniuk, "Language Politics in Ukrainian Popular Culture" [Event summary], Kennan Institute, April 16, 2007, www.wilsoncenter.org/index.cfm?.
39 Ibid.
40 Founded by a German empress of Russia, designed by a Netherlander and a Spanish-Irish Neapolitan, governed successively by two French administrators, suffused with Italian opera, Odesa was a city of foreign settlers, especially Greeks, in its early years, and eventually hosted a large population of Jews. The current conductor of its philharmonic orchestra is Hobart Earle, an American.
41 Abel Polese, "Where Marx Meets Ekaterina (the Great): The Dichotomy between National and Plural Identities in Odessa," paper presented at the convention of the Association for the Study of Nationalities, New York, April 2007.
42 Mykola Riabchuk, "Ukraine Torn between Russia, the West: A Commentary," *Edmonton Journal*, August 8, 2007.
43 As a Red Sox fan, I am tempted to say that in some respects Odesa is like Manny Ramirez, the talented but individualistic outfielder whose antics are explained by a shrug and the phrase, "Manny is just being Manny." Odesa is just being Odesa.

CHAPTER 4

Jewish Writers of Odessa
1800–1940

Although the efflorescence of Jewish literature in Odessa was compressed into less than a century (1860–1940), Odessa nourished an innovative and influential Jewish literary production in three languages: Hebrew, Yiddish, and Russian. To be sure, the "Odessa style" was sometimes criticized for its excessive rationalism, especially in the works written in Hebrew. Nonetheless, some Odessa Jewish writing has been admired as part of the Southwestern School. Nearly all the Jewish writers of note, natives and immigrants alike, felt a special affinity for Odessa. Even those who eventually left the city when the political, social, cultural, intellectual or economic milieu became less hospitable, often retained an affectionate nostalgia for the city of their inspiration.

For example, the Zionist Vladimir (Ze'ev) Jabotinsky (1880–1940) expresses through his alter ego, the narrator of *Piatero* (The Five, 1935), his aching sense of loss, "I'll probably never get to see Odessa again. It's a pity. I love the place. I was indifferent to Russia even in my youth ... but Odessa is a different matter ... [My love for it] has never passed and it won't."[1] Writing from Warsaw in 1896, another Zionist, Ahad Ha'am (Asher Zvi Ginzburg, 1856–1927), lamented, "My longing for Odessa and all that I love there is greater than I could ever have imagined."[2] Isaac Babel' (1894–1940), perhaps the foremost of Odessa's writers, admitted that Odessa was a "great city, which has more charm than any other in the Russian Empire. To a large extent it is because of [Jews] that Odessa has this light and easy atmosphere."[3] More recently the Jewish Odessan humorist Mikhail Mikhailovich Zhvanetsky (1934–) remarked, "You can leave Odessa, you can leave it forever, but you cannot not return."[4]

While many Jews such as Babel' were Russified, Babel' himself is identified especially with Odessan culture. According to the literary and cultural historian Joseph Klausner (1874–1958), all of the significant Jewish literature in Russia of lasting value was created in Odessa. Dan Miron (1934–), another literary historian, notes that Odessa was a crucible for the creation of a modern Jewish literary culture.

The roots of the Jewish community extended as far back as the founding of Odessa. A few Jews were already residing at Khadzhibei (the future site of Odessa) on the northwest coast of the Black Sea, when Russia captured the Ottoman fort of Yeni-Dünya in 1789. The Jewish population grew rapidly from 4,000 in 1815, to 7,000 in 1854, to 17,000 in 1861, to 75,000

Originally published as Patricia Herlihy, "Jewish Writers of Odessa," *Enzyklopaedie juedischer Geschichte und Kultur* vol. 4 (2014): 391–97.

in 1887, to 140,000 in 1897, and to 200,000 in 1912, comprising about one-third of the city's population. By 1926, the Jewish population had dropped to 153,000, but then rose to 180,000 in 1939, but by 1959 had declined once more—to 106,000—even as the population of the city had been continually increasing.

Odessa, founded in 1794, was a frontier boomtown lacking a historical tradition. Those who sought a haven there could take with them as much (or as little) of their heritage as they wished. Whether they were Italians, Greeks, French, Russians, Poles, Ukrainians, Moldavians, or Jews who moved to the port city from abroad or from within the Russian Empire, they had the possibility to construct a fresh identity with few constraints or expectations. The young city of Odessa therefore had a cosmopolitan, diverse, fluid, and enterprising population. The historian Simon Dubnow (1860–1941), who chose to live in Odessa during his productive years and who chronicled the history of Jews in Russia and Poland, called Odessa the least historical of cities, a cultural tabula rasa. Inhabitants could mold the city and themselves according to their own inclinations, restricted only by the prohibitions applied (rather loosely) by Russian law. Yet settlers could also bring with them their cultural, religious, and ethnic identities and form their own communities. The population of Odessa contained a mixture of both types: free uprooted spirits and community builders. As a microcosm of the population, Jews followed the same patterns. The only city within the Pale that freely admitted Jews throughout its history, Odessa attracted from the Pale of Settlement as well as from Galicia, Jews from all walks of life including intellectuals, merchants, artisans, and laborers.

Jewish religious attitudes represented a broad spectrum: from traditionalists (Orthodox including Hasidic), through secularists, agnostics (maskilim), and even including atheists who had rejected their traditional religious beliefs and practices but who nonetheless retained their cultural identity. Haskalah Jewish Enlightenment was especially strong in Odessa. The presence of so many secular, acculturated, and assimilated Jews, combined with Odessa's reputation for materialism and hedonism, prompted the Yiddish expressions, "to live like God in Odessa," and "seven miles around Odessa burn the fires of hell."

Politically (and reflecting the rest of the population) Jews ranged from conservative to liberal or to the extremes of socialism and Marxism. Zionists held varying visions of Jewish nationhood. Some like Moshe Leib Lilienbaum (1843–1910) believed that colonists should settle in Palestine as quickly as possible. Others such as Ahad Ha'am insisted that emigration should be gradual and should take place only after Jews had been educated and possessed an authentic, national Jewish consciousness. The historian Simon Dubnow believed that Jews should remain in the diaspora, but instead of assimilating, they should build a strong sense of their spiritual and cultural identity. Vladimir Jabotinsky, on a completely different tact, advocated a Revisionist Zionism, the building of a secular Jewish state in Palestine through violence if necessary.

Jews did not stand out as starkly in multiethnic Odessa, a port city, as they did in the *shtetlekh* and villages in the rural Pale of Settlement where the non-Jewish population was uniformly either Russian or Ukrainian. Even populations of Vilna and Warsaw were much less diverse than Odessa's. Therefore Jews had the option to adapt to a broader, hybrid Odessan lifestyle. Common commercial interests attenuated ethnic and religious differences, although at times sharp rivalry between Greek and Jewish merchants did erupt in violence, as in the 1871 pogrom. The many European settlers in Odessa provided westernized models for progressive Jews to emulate. Indeed, in Odessa the Jewish population itself sprang from a variety of historical and cultural backgrounds: Russian, Ukrainian, Galician, Lithuanian, Belorussian, Polish, and German.

Odessan Jews, especially those engaged in shipping grain and other commodities abroad, learned foreign languages and technical subjects in order to attain economic success. As early as 1826, wealthy Jews from Brody, undaunted by a weak traditional community, took the radical step of establishing a modern Jewish school in Odessa. Since the school was private, Jewish youth could learn such practical and secular subjects relating to the importance of Haskalah and conducting commerce in the city.

Like other Russian cities, Odessa contained no ghetto. Jews chose their place of residence according to their means; but in late imperial Russia, a rapidly increasing number of poor Jews inhabited the Odessa suburb of Moldavanka, which became known as the home of Isaac Babel's fictional Jewish gangsters. Laxer censorship and a higher degree of tolerance in Odessa than in most large Russian cities at the time also allowed for literary productivity.

In a city where most Jews were immersed in Russian/Odessan culture, it is only to be expected that those who tended to resist assimilation would choose to write their literature in Yiddish and Hebrew. However (and somewhat paradoxically), to reach a wider audience of assimilated Jews, these Jewish writers often reverted to Russian when writing articles, especially those in non-Jewish newspapers such as the city's leading newspaper *Odesskii vestnik* (Odessa Herald, 1828–62).

Jewish discussion groups of widely differing positions also helped to stimulate ideas that found their way to print. Estranged from their traditional *shtetlekh* or small town birthplaces, many intellectuals sought out Odessa, perceived as tolerant of diversity. Once there, they found themselves estranged from moneymaking, assimilated Jews, who had formed a visible component of the Jewish community. These *Khakhmey Odessa* (Sages of Odessa) formed tight circles of discussion groups, often meeting in one another's houses; one such circle consisted of Mendele Moykher Sforim (S. Y. Abramovitsh, 1835 O.S.–1917), Haim Nahman Bialik (1873–1934), Ahad Ha'am, Moshe Lilienblum, Elhanan Levinsky (1857–1911), Simon Dubnow, and others who became friends in their isolation, although they were often ideological foes. This wide variety of Jewish backgrounds and diversity of opinion contributed to the novelty and vibrancy of Jewish culture in Odessa. So far removed were these Jews from the mainstream of Odessa's Jewry, one contemporary observed, that a great generation of writers lived as if on their own, beautiful island.

Many of these writers, such as Ahad Ha'am, Ben-Ami (Mark Rabinovich 1853–1932), Y. H. Ravnitsky (1859–1944), and Haim Nahman Bialik belonged to charitable societies such as the Odessa branch of the Society for the Promotion of Enlightenment (OPE) founded in Odessa in 1867, and which by 1910, was supporting thirteen elementary and four schools of higher learning enrolling over two thousand students. Affiliating itself with OPE in 1897, the Historical-Literary Commission provided a forum for writers and intellectuals to discuss politics, culture, and philosophy. Once Zionism had largely displaced the Haskalah movement in Odessa, some of this group of writers, such as Elhanan Levinsky, Leon Pinsker, Ahad Ha'am, Haim N. Bialik, J. Klausner, Y. H. Ravnitsky, and Saul Tchernichovsky (1875–1943), joined *Hovevei Zion* (Lovers of Zion), a group which flourished until about 1900. S. Y. Abramovitsh served as principal of the Talmud Torah in Odessa from 1881 until 1916, excluding the two years that he spent in Geneva, Switzerland, following the 1905 pogrom in Odessa. The prevalence of literary and political circles, the expansion of reformed schools, and the early presence of a Jewish press contributed to a synergetic process of increasing literacy among the city's Jewish population and fed their appetite not only for news and political commentary, but also for imaginative literature.

JEWISH PRESS

Hebrew

Although Russian Jews read modern literature mostly in Russian in the late nineteenth century, Jewish intellectuals increasingly preferred Hebrew, a language favored especially by the early Zionists as a means to eliminate Yiddish. The first Hebrew journal published in Odessa was *Ha'melitz* (The Advocate, 1860–71), edited by Alexander Tsederbaum (1818–93). Intended for the general Hebrew-reading public, it reached 2,500 subscriptions. In 1871, a year of a pogrom in Odessa, the journal moved to St. Petersburg. Partially as a reaction to the pogroms in Odessa in the 1880s, the editor of Hebrew journals began to lose faith in Haskalah as a key to obtaining emancipation. Therefore Hebrew periodicals embraced a new movement, *Hovevei Zion* (Lovers of Zion).

In contrast to the more eclectic Hebrew press of Warsaw, Odessa's periodicals, chiefly under the influence of Ahad Ha'am, took on an elitist and conservative tone. The most notable journal of this type, the prestigious Hebrew monthly *Ha'Shiloach* (1896–1926), was edited in Odessa but until 1907, was published abroad; in 1919 it moved to Jerusalem, where it was published until 1926. Throughout his tenure as editor, Ahad Ha'am used this journal to promote the spirit of Jewish nationalism through education; he required that all of the journal's writers and its entire content were Jewish. Under the later editorship of Joseph Klausner in 1903 and Haim Nachman Bialik, literary editor from 1904–9, the paper became more inclusive, and published literary works of merit, no matter the author or content. Ahad Ha'am continued to promote his educational mission by editing *Kaveret* (Beehive, 1890), a literary compendium that contained works by Mendel Moykher Sforim and Ahad Ha'am, as well as literary criticism, articles on culture, politics, and education. Ahad Ha'am wrote for *Pardes* (1892–96), edited by Y. H. Ravnitsky, to which he contributed some of his finest articles. Haim Nahman Bialik's first published poem appeared in that distinguished journal. Elhanan Levinsky wrote the first science fiction novel in Hebrew, *A Trip to the Land of Israel in the 800th Year of the Sixth Millennium*, published in 1892 in the journal *Pardes*, describing Hebrew culture in a utopian Palestinian Jewish nation in the year 2040.

Founded in 1901 by Y. H. Ravnitsky, Haim N. Bialik, and S. Ben-Tsiyon (1870–1932), the Moriah publishing house was the major distributor of Hebrew textbooks to Europe. Between 1912 and 1914, the World Zionist Organization issued in Odessa a weekly *Ha'Olam* (This

World, 1912–14). Fourteen issues of the weekly *Barkai* (The Morning Star) were published in Odessa in 1919, until the Bolshevik regime put an end to it. All in all, through the course of forty years some thirteen Hebrew periodicals were published in Odessa and publication ceased only when the Soviets suppressed the Hebrew press entirely.

Yiddish

Some Jews in Odessa had the reputation of not being as pious or as learned as the Jews of Vilna. The former could read Yiddish more readily than Hebrew, the language of study, prayer, and law. To this day, the Russian spoken in Odessa contains many Yiddish (and some Hebrew) influences. Tsederbaum published *Kol mevasser* (The Herald, 1862–70), the only Yiddish newspaper in the Russian Empire at that time. For six years it was a popular independent weekly with the goal of enlightening Jews, promoting reforms, and providing articles both on literature and of general interest; notably, it was the first Jewish newspaper to publish articles written by women. Using his native Volhynian Yiddish dialect in his paper, Tsederbaum did much to modernize and standardize the language. In 1910 E. Levinsky founded in Odessa the first daily Yiddish newspaper, *Gut Morgn*. A second newspaper *Sholem Aleichem* was begun the following year.

Perhaps the paucity of Yiddish periodicals in Odessa, despite its precocity in producing the first Yiddish paper in the Russian Empire, reflects the fact that in Odessa, Russian-speaking Jews felt that Yiddish created a barrier between Jews and non-Jews. Many Jews, at least for the first three-quarters of the nineteenth century, wanted to demonstrate to non-Jews that they were a secular, modern, and progressive people—and thus worthy of emancipation—so they used Russian. Furthermore, periodic restrictions during the nineteenth century against publishing in Yiddish also discouraged Yiddish writers.

Russian

Osip Rabinovich (1817–69) and Joachim Tarnopol, merchant and author (1810–1900), published *Rassvet* (Dawn), the first Russian-language Jewish newspaper in Odessa (1860–61) and in the empire. Engaged in local politics, Rabinovich was a member of the commission to write a new charter for the city in 1861. Leon Pinsker (1821–91) was a physician and initially an assimilationist, but after experiencing pogroms, he wrote an early Zionist tract, *Selbstemanzipation*, in German (Auto-Emancipation, 1882), advocating the establishment of a Jewish state, whether it be in Palestine or elsewhere. It is not surprising that Leon Pinsker was made chair of the nationalist society *Hovevei Zion*. Pinsker and others published *Sion'* (Zion, 1861–62). Although written in Russian and meant to be a continuation of *Rassvet*, it was more nationalistic in tenor, promoting the use of Hebrew and cautioning its readers against assimilation with Russian culture. Since the paper attempted to appeal to both Jewish and Russian readers, it failed to interest a sufficient number in either community and lasted only nine months.

Seven years later, *Den'* (The Day, 1869–71), a Jewish-Russian newspaper, would succeed, partially because of financial support from the newly-founded Odessa branch of OPE, but mainly because Jews had become more attracted to Russian society as a result of the

Great Reforms of the 1860s. *Den'* boasted that Odessa was the nerve center of all of Russian Jewry. Unfortunately, subscriptions could not sustain the expense of publication and the publication could not evade the censors for long. In the last quarter of the nineteenth century, St. Petersburg became the center for Russian-language Jewish press.

In 1906–7, Zionists published in Odessa the weekly *Kadima* (Forward) in Russian.

LITERATURE

Hebrew

Odessa's Jewish periodical press published some works of fiction, poetry, and historical essays, but the city's Jewish authors are chiefly remembered for their books. Some wrote fiction and poetry for the same reason that Russians did: to disguise their political views from censors. Between 1881 and 1921, Odessa was perhaps the most enticing center of Hebrew literature in the Russian Empire. Young people flocked to be near the Sages, who formed a tight literary circle; or, as one young acolyte put it: they had homes that were like green oases of Hebrew culture in a desert of easy living.

One of the most versatile Jewish writers who settled in Odessa was S. Y. Abramovitsh, who moved to Odessa in 1881 and died there nearly forty years later. He began and ended his writing career using Hebrew; in the interim, however, he became known as the "Grandfather of Yiddish Literature," under the name of Mendele Moykher Sforim. His early Hebrew works concerned politics and natural history. His novel *Ha'avot vehabanim* (Fathers and Sons, 1868) was a reworking of an earlier novel *Limdu hetev* (Learn to Do Good, 1862). Like Ivan Turgenev's novel of the same title published also in 1862, Abramovitsh showed his talent for fiction and for delving into the psychological tension between traditional Jewish religious fathers and their progressive sons, but the book never became as popular as his Yiddish works. For the next twenty years he wrote his famous stories in Yiddish, but then returned to writing in Hebrew in 1886. In 1896, he began to translate into Hebrew his own famous Yiddish works. By incorporating Talmudic and biblical language along with a secular Hebrew vocabulary, he molded a modern literary Hebrew style, called *Nusah* (mode or style) or *Nusah Odesa*, which was clear, logical, erudite, eloquent, flexible, and compact. His realistic novels of Jewish contemporary life were published in three volumes, *Kol kitve Mendele Mokher Sefarim*, between 1909 and 1912. The famous Jewish libraries of the city were consolidated into a single library (named after Abramovitsh), but which was sacked and destroyed by the Romanian Nazi occupying forces in 1942.

Ahad Ha'am, from a younger generation than Abramovitsh, was the most prominent Hebraist in his time, who, like Abramovitsh, blended new and old vocabulary to enrich Hebrew as a literary language. He devoted much of his efforts to formulating his Zionist philosophy on the necessity of developing a national consciousness before a viable Jewish nation could be formed in Palestine. A charismatic individual, Ahad Ha'am commanded respect in his day, and his four volumes of collected essays, *Al parashat derakhim* (At the Crossroads, 1895–1914), influenced future notable writers such as Haim Bialik, Haim Weizmann (1874–1952) and Martin Buber (1878–1965). His great ambition was to create a modern, homogenous, coherent, national literary Jewish canon, a gathering (*kinus*) of material and selected Hebrew writing (but not religious classics) into anthologies in order to unify Jews in the diaspora and to prepare them for eventual emigration to Zion. However, he was never able to obtain sufficient funding for this project.

The poet Haim Nachman Bialik greatly admired Ahad Ha'am. Like most of the Jewish intellectuals who had moved to Odessa, Bialik received an Orthodox religious education but became attracted to Haskalah. Seeking to interact with writers such as Mendele Moykher Sforim and Ahad Ha'am, he went to Odessa at the age of eighteen. There he studied Russian and German languages and literatures. He became a pioneer in writing modern Hebrew poetry. His poem *El Hatzipor* (To the Bird) identifies him as a Zionist. A member of the literary circle *Hovevei Zion*, Bialik published his first book of poetry in Hebrew in Warsaw in 1901. This work earned him the title of "poet of the national renaissance." After writing a report, as requested by the Jewish Historical Commission of Odessa on the pogrom in Kishinev in 1903, he published his epic poem *Be'ir Hahareigah* (City of Slaughter).

He translated various European classical authors, such as Shakespeare, Schiller, Cervantes, and Heine into Hebrew; he also translated S. An-sky's *The Dybbuk* (Between Two Worlds) from Russian. When the Soviet authorities closed his publishing house Moriah, he moved to Berlin and finally, in 1924, to Tel Aviv. After his death he was acknowledged as Israel's national poet.

Saul Tchernic (1875–1943), a contemporary of Bialik and considered among the best of the renaissance poets, studied and lived in Odessa, where he published Jewish nationalist poems such as *Beleyl Hanukah* (On Hanukah Night) and *Seu nes tziyonah* (Carry the Banner to Zion). He studied German, French, English, Greek, and Latin, the knowledge of which allowed him to translate many authors and works into Hebrew including Sophocles, Horace, Shakespeare, Molière, Pushkin, Goethe, Heine, Byron, Shelley, the *Kalevala*, the Gilgamesh cycle, and the Icelandic *Edda*. He received his medical degree in Switzerland and practiced medicine in Odessa and later in Ukraine, Belarus, Russia, and finally in Tel Aviv. Associated with the sonnet and Greek themes in some of his poetry, he is sometimes called the Hellenic poet. Indeed he has been the subject of much Jewish criticism for his love (one not shared by Bialik) of foreign themes, pagan and erotic subjects, and nature. He was one of the first to write idyls in Hebrew, mostly about his childhood. He won the Bialik prize for poetry twice, and died in Jerusalem in 1943.

The summer of 1921 marked the closing of a chapter on Hebrew literature in Odessa. Forced out of the Soviet Union, twelve families of Hebrew writers, including the great poets Bialik and Tchernichovsky, left the city together and traveled to various Western European countries and to Palestine. Stalin so severely restricted any dissemination of the Hebrew language and culture that nearly all writing in Hebrew ceased, both in Odessa and in the rest of the Soviet Union.

Yiddish

The founder of modern Russian Yiddish literature as well as a writer of universal stature, S. Y. Abramovitsh was known popularly as Mendele Moykher Sforim, the name of one of his fictional characters, a book peddler. His *Fishke der Krumer* (Fiske the Lame) began as a short story in Yiddish in 1869 and expanded in 1888. His first novel, the satire *Dos Kleyne Mentshele* (The Little Man), appeared serially in the journal *Kol mevasser* between 1864 and 1865. His writings captured life in the shtetl with his conversational Yiddish prose that satirized the rich while sympathizing with the poor. His autobiographical novel *Funem yarid* (Back From the Fair) and other stories had a huge appeal, especially because most Jews, including nearly all women, could not read Hebrew.

Sholem Aleichem (Sholem Rabinovich, 1859–1915), a prolific writer of some twenty-eight volumes of novels, plays, and short stories, was a master of Yiddish humor, often using monologues and letters as his form of choice. Like Abramovitsh, he preserves in print the life of the shtetl that he and others so willingly left and yet could not forget. One of his best-known works is *Tevye der Milkhiker* (Tevye the Dairyman). Among his humorous works is *The Letters of Menakhem-Mendl and Sheyne-Sheyndl*, in which a dim itinerant seeking his fortune writes letters to his mystified, scolding wife, Motl. *The Cantor's Son* is a comic novel that recounts the observations of a sharp-eyed young boy who relates the breakdown of traditional Jewish culture after immigrating to New York.

Sholem Aleichem encouraged young writers of Yiddish in 1888 and 1889 by publishing two yearbooks, *Di Yidishe Folksbibliotek* (the Yiddish Popular Library), at his own expense. The next year he could no longer support the publication because he had lost his wife's entire fortune by playing the Odessan stock market. He wrote articles in Russian and in Hebrew for various Odessan newspapers, including *Ha'melitz* and an anthology edited by Y. H. Ravnitsky. The "Jewish Mark Twain" died of tuberculosis in New York City.

Russian

Because many of the Russian inhabitants of Odessa in the nineteenth century worked as administrators, bureaucrats, military officers, and other government functionaries, they produced little literature of note. It might be said that, until the twentieth century, Jewish literature comprised the bulk of Russian literature produced in Odessa.

Osip Rabinovich, known for using his journalism to teach Jews how to improve themselves and defend themselves against antisemitism, wrote novels as well. *Kaleidoscope* (1860) describes multiethnic Odessa in mid-nineteenth century, but it does not focus on Jewish characters, unlike his *Shtrafnoi* (Penal Recruit, 1859), which provided a realistic and unsentimental description of Nicholas I's policy of recruiting Jews into the tsarist army. This was perhaps the first major work of Jewish-Russian literature to flow into the Russian mainstream. His was the first of many recruitment stories. One of his last works, a novel, *Istoriia o tom, kak reb Khaim-Shulim Feiges puteshestvoval iz Kishineva v Odessu, i chto s nim sluchilos'* (The Story of How Reb Khaim-Shulim Feiges Traveled from Kishinev to Odessa and What Happened with Him, 1865), with its humorous depiction of an itinerant bumbler, anticipates Sholem Aleichem's fictional character Menakhem Mendl. Mixing Ukrainian, Hebrew, Yiddish, and Romanian words in his text, Rabinovich was the first to attempt to reproduce the unique Odessa speech that Babel' later called a "language salad," and which he famously perfected.

Semyon Yushkevich (1868–1927), the popular playwright and novelist, although he occasionally treated Jewish themes, wrote more often about the thoroughly Russified Jews of Odessa. Dwelling on the erotic in many of his works, he showed the seamier side of the city's Jewish life in his depiction of prostitution, poverty, and crime, prefiguring Babel's gangsters. For his frank exposure of the Jewish underside of Odessa, he was often criticized, but his works were popular in Russia. After he immigrated to New York in 1920, he continued to publish, but in the Yiddish press, and his Russian plays were translated for the Yiddish theater. He died in Paris in 1927.

Vladimir Jabotinsky, a native of Odessa, Russian writer, orator, solider, and Zionist activist, was also a gifted linguist who knew eleven languages. He translated Hebrew poetry, including Bialik's *City of Slaughter*, into Russian and Dante's *Inferno* into Hebrew. A great stylist and at times a humorist, he wrote newspaper articles, poems, plays, short stories, a partial autobiography, and two novels, *Samson Nazarei* (1926) and *Piatero* (The Five; 1935). His novel *Piatero*, narrated by a person presumably much like himself, recounts the story of a Russified Jewish bourgeois family in fin-de-siècle Odessa. Nearly all of the five children in the family come to a tragic or at least a sad end, a commentary on a decadent society for which there is no hope for the emancipation of Russian Jews. Evocative of the Odessa he loved, the lyrical novel nonetheless speaks of the disintegration of a family, but symbolically it is Russian Jewish society that is falling apart. Unspoken but implied in the narrative is the idea that only Zion can deliver Russia's Jews from the dead ended path of assimilation.

Thoroughly assimilated into Russian culture himself, Jabotinsky left Odessa for Rome at the age of eighteen to study law. He supported himself by writing articles for the *Odesskii listok*, a liberal daily paper, using the pen name Altalena. After his return to Odessa, the Kishinev Pogrom of 1903 prompted him to advocate Jewish self-defense leagues; soon he became fully engaged in the politics of Zionism, attending Zionist Congresses abroad and running for a seat in the post-1905 Revolution Duma, but lost twice. He began to learn Hebrew and took on the name Ze'ev (wolf). He was instrumental in forming a Jewish Legion within the British Army when they took over Palestine. Jailed by the British during Arab riots of 1920, he founded in 1925 the World Union of Zionist Revisionists that sought to mount a large-scale emigration to a Jewish state in Palestine on both sides of the Jordan. Highly controversial for his right-wing politics, he is honored in Israel, where his remains were transferred from New York in 1964.

Eduard G. Bagritsky (Eduard Godelevich Dziubin, 1895–1934) who was honored at his funeral by the officials of the Soviet Union as a great Romantic poet of the Revolution, earned this lofty status with the help of critics who had turned a blind eye to his Jewish themes and even to his fairly mild criticisms of the regime and who had portrayed him as a loyal, anti-tsarist and anti-fascist Soviet citizen. Born in Odessa, he wrote for literary journals there before the Revolution, served in the Red Army during the Civil War, and moved to Moscow at the age of thirty. His modernist poetry was a continuation of the tradition of pre-revolution avant-garde and the Silver Age. One of the great poets of the first generation of Soviets, Bagritsky was admired for his writing until the late 1940s and the 1950s when the anti-Cosmopolitan campaign began to attack his work posthumously. Soviet critics characterized his poetry as bourgeois-nationalist, and smacking of hoboism. His work was not reprinted nor was he recognized as a major Soviet poet until the Thaw (1953–64), when even some of his "Jewish" poems such as *Duma pro Opanasa* (Lay of Opanas, 1926) and *Proiskhozhdenie* (Origin, 1930) appeared, although there was no open discussion of their touchy themes. His last, and perhaps finest and most controversial poem, *Fevral'* (*February*, 1933–34; 1936), published posthumously, is set in Odessa during the first two decades of the twentieth century. In this poem Bagritsky passionately examines Jewish Russian identity in a period of violent change and ends with an expression of hope that Jews and Slavs might live in harmony.

A friend of Bagritsky, Isaak Emmanuilovich Babel', a master short-story writer and gifted playwright, received a secular education at the Nicholas I Commercial School in Odessa, where he learned French, among other subjects. As a teenager he composed his first stories in French in the style of Guy de Maupassant and Gustave Flaubert. In the home of his middle-class parents he received an Orthodox religious education. Influenced by Odessan writers in the Hebrew, Yiddish, and Russian languages, Babel', especially in his *Odesskie rasskazy* (Odessa Stories, 1921–23) incorporated Odessan slang and Yiddishisms, creating a unique style. His semiautobiographical *Odessa Stories* take place in the period between the Revolutions of 1905 and 1917 and purport to convey the carnivalesque and Rabelaisian goings-on of Jewish gangsters, prostitutes, and other colorful characters in the poor district of Moldavanka. These mock epics are filled with theatrical episodes, often permeated with humor. In 1927 he wrote his first play, *Zakat* (Sunset), set in Odessa and concerned with a generational conflict in which the dialogue is comic, but the mood melancholy. Odessan theatergoers loved the play and filled two theaters that simultaneously staged its own performance, one in Yiddish and the other in Russian. In the same year, the Soviet Union produced a silent movie, *Benya Krik*, depicting further adventures of Odessa's gangsters.

His most famous work, the cycle of stories *Konarmiia* (The Red Cavalry, 1926), based on his war diaries, consists of thirty-five pieces of supposed reportage on the Soviet-Polish War of 1920 by a Soviet war correspondent named Kirill Liutov. Since that is the name Babel' used when he was actually a war correspondent, the tightly-composed pieces recall, at least to some extent, scenes from the war as Babel' experienced them. By using striking metaphors and describing brutal scenes of unspeakable cruelty with both brevity and objectivity, Babel' shocks the reader but does not preach. Babel' became the first well-known Soviet writer at home and abroad. Silenced at the height of his creative power by the Stalinist reign of terror, he fell victim to one of its massacres.

Ilya Il'f (Ilya Arnoldovich Fainzilberg, 1897–1937), born into a poor Jewish family in Odessa, was a journalist and novelist. Together with a fellow, non-Jew Odessite, Evgenii Petrov (Evgenii Petrovich Kataev, 1903–42, younger brother of the novelist Valentin Kataev), they are known for two humorous novels set in the New Economic Policy (NEP) era 1921–29, when censorship was more lax just before Stalin came to power. Il'f and Petrov, as they came to be known (although they used several pseudonyms, including F. Tolstoevsky), met in Moscow in 1925, while working as journalists for *Gudok* (The Whistle), a newspaper for railroad workers. *Dvenadtsat' stul'ev* (The Twelve Chairs, 1929) is set during NEP, when limited capitalistic enterprises were allowed. The antihero Ostap Bender represents a greedy rogue who is attempting to recover diamonds hidden in a chair formerly owned by an aristocratic family. In a picaresque and Gogolesque fashion, Bender and a member of the aristocratic family roam all over the Soviet Union and become embroiled with various types of characters in their effort to recover the treasure. An Orthodox priest is likewise engaged in the pursuit of the diamonds. Not explicitly Jewish in theme, the adventure takes place during NEP, when, according to Stalin, Jews took advantage of a limited free market to exploit others. Although a different kind of rogue from Benya Krik, Bender might be considered something like a NEP-style con artist version of Benya Krik. Several movies were made in the Soviet Union and in the United States based on the novel, with the most recent one produced by Mel Brooks in 1970.

Il'f and Petrov's satiric novel *Zolotoi Telenok* (The Golden Calf, 1929–31) is a sequel to their first novel, with Ostap Bender brought back from the dead to continue his larcenous ways. The title, of course, refers to the golden calf in Exodus, which some Jews worshipped in the time of Moses. Bender pursues a covert multimillionaire in order to obtain some of his fortune, which the NEP entrepreneur dares not spend in a socialist society. Among the places visited is Chernomorsk, undoubtedly the authors' native Odessa. During the Great Depression, they toured the United States by motorcar and reported their travels in *Odnoetazhnaia Amerika* (One-Storied America, 1936). Il'f died of tuberculosis while Petrov was killed in a plane crash during the Second World War.

Arkady Lvov (Arkady Binshteyn, 1927–), born in Odessa to a working-class family, author of over two hundred stories and essays, taught history in Odessa. Perhaps his best-known novel, *Dvor* (The Courtyard, 1981), was smuggled out of the Soviet Union and published first in French in 1979. Set in a typical Odessa courtyard, it examines the lives of ten different families that include different character types, such as an ardent Communist who is Jewish. After the Odessa KGB accused him of being a representative of international Zionism in 1970, Lvov was stripped of his Union of Writers from Ukraine membership and his books were withdrawn from libraries. Lvov immigrated to the United States in 1979. Lvov continues the tradition of Rabinovich and Babel' by having his characters speak in the distinctive Odessa speech: Russian sprinkled with Yiddishisms and Ukrainianisms. His collected works were published in six volumes between 1998 and 2002 in his beloved Odessa.

As the example of Lvov shows, it was dangerous for Odessa Jews to publish anything that could arouse Soviet antisemitism, nonetheless, the entire world loves humor. If fiction in the tsarist regime could serve as a Trojan horse for political messages, humor during the Soviet era similarly masked Jewish commentary on life. The greatest example of ironic humor is that written and spoken by Mikhail Mikhailovich Zhvanetsky (1934–), born in Odessa. Trained as an engineer, he quickly found his métier by performing at low-profile comedy clubs and theaters in Odessa. The genius Jewish director and comic actor Arkady Raikin took note of Zhvanetsky's brilliance and hired him to become a scriptwriter for his humorous performances. In 1972 Zhvanetsky went on stage himself to deliver his famous monologues on Soviet life, but with only oblique references to Jewish topics. Still, his speech patterns were clearly that of an Odessan Jew. Even if he simply mentioned Odessa, the audience understood the reference was to a Jewish subtext. His self-irony is reminiscent of Sholem Aleichem. He published two anthologies before the fall of the Soviet Union in 1991, and since then, he has returned to Odessa from Moscow. Two of his more recent works are a revised version of *Moia Odessa* (My Odessa, 2007) and *Odesskie dachi* (Odessan Dachas, 2006). In 2009, on the occasion of his seventy-fifth birthday, President Dmitri Medvedev decorated this convert to Orthodox Christianity with the Order of Merit for the Fatherland, fourth class.

CONCLUSION

Odessa in the nineteenth century attracted Jews for many of the same reasons it served as a magnet to other groups: it was that rare city of opportunities, both commercial and cultural. Jewish literature took root for nearly a century because of the city's unique confluence of geography, history, and politics. This cluster of genius was unusual but hardly random. Enlightened Jews, witnessing the rapid secularization and assimilation of other Jews, especially the educated youth, attempted in their writing to show Russians that Jews—as a people— were modern, good citizens. Yet, fearing that more and more Jews would either completely assimilate or convert, these enlightened Jews began asking for emancipation as early as the 1840s. Like Abramovitsh's satirical mare (*Di Klyatshe*, 1873), Jews were asking for justice, not mercy. However, when it became increasingly clear that tsarist authorities would almost certainly never abolish the Pale of Settlement or give Jews full civil rights, many Jews turned to Zionism and added a new tone of urgency to their writings.

Antisemitism, especially the pogroms of 1871, 1881, and 1905, drove many Jews out of Odessa. Ironically, the February Revolution of 1917 ushered in a brief period of Jewish integration into Russian society. The Pale was abolished. Jews served once again in the local government; Jews could become army and naval officers, and Jewish societies, including Zionist ones, flourished. By the 1930s, however, Soviets had divided society by class and political loyalty, so that Jewish identity was submerged into the new ideological categories.

The first generation of Jewish writers went to Odessa to escape the shtetl; the second, such as Bagritsky, Babel', I'lf, and others, went to Moscow to escape Odessa, a city they now considered too confining, too provincial, perhaps even too Jewish. Nostalgia for Odessa replaced nostalgia for the shtetl. With few exceptions, Odessan Jewish writers from Mendele Moykher Sforim to Zhvanetsky deployed wry, ironical humor in their works, perhaps conscious of the anomaly of being a Jew immersed in Russian culture on Ukrainian territory, an existential marginality that would always exist, no matter how much at home they might have felt in Odessa.

Under the Soviet regime Jewish authors used the Russian language and Soviet subjects in their writing and in general drew little attention to their Jewish identity. Jewish culture as such was completely eradicated by the late 1930s. Odessan Jews themselves were soon to follow their literary culture into oblivion. The Romanian Nazis, who occupied Odessa in the early 1940s, found approximately 200,000 Jews in the city. They deported many of them, which merely postponed their deaths, while other Jews fled. When the Soviet Army recaptured the city in 1944, they found a scant forty-eight people who identified themselves as Jews. In the 1970s a number of Jews emigrated to Israel and the United States. After the fall of the Soviet

Union, there has been in Odessa a resurgence of Jewish religious and community life among the remaining and relatively sparse Jewish population. There are two Jewish periodicals published in Odessa in Russian: a monthly journal, *Dobroe Delo*, supported by the Orthodox Main Synagogue, and a paper issued twice weekly, *Shomrey Shabos*, sponsored by the Hasidic Synagogue.

Notes

1. *The Five*, 197.
2. *Igrot Ahad Ha'am* vol. 1, new ed. (May 1896), 95, as quoted by Zipperstein, *Elusive Prophet*, 67.
3. *Collected Works*, 14–15.
4. *Moia Odessa*, 1993, 30.

Bibliography

Primary Sources:

Abramovitsh, S. Y. (Mendele Moykher Sforim). *Tales of Mendele the Book Peddler: Fiske the Lame and Benjamin the Third*. Edited by Dan Miron and Ken Frieden. New York: Schocken Books, 1996.
Ahad Ha'am, *Igrot Ahad Ha'am*. 6 vols. Tel Aviv: Devir, 1956–60.
Babel, Isaac. *The Complete Works of Isaac Babel*. Edited by Nathalie Babel and translated with notes by Peter Constantine. New York: W. W. Norton and Co., 2002.
Bagritsky, Eduard. *Stikhotvoreniia i poemi*. Edited by G. A. Morov and afterword by Maxim D. Shrayer. St. Petersburg: Akademicheskii proekt, 2000.
Dubnow, Simon M. *Kniga Zhizni: Materaly dlia istorii moego vremeni: Vospominaniia i razmyshleniia*. Jerusalem: Mosty Kul'tury, Moscow: Gesharim, 2004.
———. *History of the Jews in Russia and Poland from the Earliest times until the Present Day*. 3 vols. New York: Ktav Publishing House, 1975.
———. *Ob izuchenii istorii russkikh evreev i ob uchrezhdenii russko-evreiskago istoricheskago obshchestva*. St. Petersburg: A. E. Landau, 1891.
Frieden, Ken, Ted Gorelick, and Michael Wex, eds. *Classic Yiddish Stories of S. Y. Abramovitsh, Sholem Aleichem, and I. L. Peretz*. Translated by Ken Frieden. Syracuse, NY: Syracuse University Press, 2004.
Jabotinsky, Vladimir. *Sochineniia v deviati tomakh*. Minsk: Met, 2007.
Jabotinsky, Vladimir. *The Five: A Novel of Jewish Life in Turn-of-the-Century Odessa*. Translated and annotated by Michael R. Katz. Ithaca, NY: Cornell University Press, 2005.
Lilienblum, Moshes L. *Kol kitve Mosheh Leib Lilyenblum*. Krakow, 1910–13.
Rabinovich, Osip. *Sochineniia O. A. Rabinovicha*. St. Petersburg: A. E. Landau, 1880.
Shrayer, Maxim D., ed. and trans. *An Anthology of Jewish-Russian Literature: Two Centuries of Dual Identity in Prose and Poetry*. 2 vols. Armonk, NY: M. E. Sharpe, 2007.
Zhvanetsky, Mikhail. *Odesskie dachi*. Odessa: Druk, 2004.
———. *Moia Odessa*. Moscow: Olimp, 1993.

Secondary Sources:

Abramson, Glenda, and Tudor Parfit, eds. *The Great Transition: The Recovery of the Lost Centers of Modern Hebrew Literature*. Totowa, NJ: Bowman and Allanheld, 1985.
Cammy, Justin, Dara Horn, Alyssa Quint, and Rachel Rubinstein, eds. *Arguing the Modern Jewish Canon: Essays on Literature and Culture in Honor of Ruth R. Wisse*. Cambridge, MA: Harvard University Press, 2008.
Hetényi, Zsuzsa. *In a Maelstrom: The History of Russian-Jewish Prose (1860–1940)*. Budapest: Central European University Press, 2008.
Herlihy, Patricia. *Odessa: A History, 1794–1914*. Cambridge, MA: Harvard University Press, 1986.
Horowitz, Brian. *Jewish Philanthropy and Enlightenment in Late-Tsarist Russia*. Seattle: University of Washington Press, 2009.
Iljine, Nicholas, ed. *Odessa Memories*. Seattle: University of Washington Press, 2003.
Litvak, Olga. *Conscription and the Search for Modern Russian Jewry*. Bloomington, IN: Indiana University Press, 2006.

Miron, Dan. *The Image of the Shtetl: And Other Studies of Modern Jewish Literary Imagination.* Syracuse, NY: Syracuse University Press, 2000.

Miron, Dan. *A Traveler Disguised: The Rise of Modern Yiddish Fiction in the Nineteenth Century.* Forward by Ken Frieden. Syracuse, NY: Syracuse University Press, 1996.

Nakhimovsky, Alice Stone. *Russian-Jewish Literature and Identity: Jabotinsky, Babel, Grossman, Galich, Roziner, Markish.* Baltimore: The Johns Hopkins University Press, 1992.

Nakhimovsky, Alice Stone. "Mikhail Zhvanetskii: The Last Russian-Jewish Joker." In *Forging Modern Jewish Identities: Public Faces and Private Struggles,* edited by Michael Berkowitz, Susan L. Tannenbaum, and Sam W. Bloom, 156–79. Portland, OR: Vallentine Mitchell, 2003.

Nakhimovsky, Alice Stone. "Vladimir Jabotinsky Russian Writer." *Modern Judaism* 7, no. 2 (May 1987): 151–73.

Orbach, Alexander. *New Voices of Russian Jewry: A Study of the Russian Jewish Press of Odessa in the Era of the Great Reforms, 1860–1871.* Leiden: E. J. Brill, 1980.

Shrayer, Maxim D. *Russian Poet/Soviet Jew: The Legacy of Eduard Bagritskii.* Lanham, MD: Rowman and Littlefield Publishers, 2000.

Stanislawski, Michael. *Zionism and the Fin de Siècle: Cosmopolitanism and Nationalism from Nordau to Jabotinsky.* Berkeley, CA: University of California Press, 2001.

Stanton, Rebecca J. "Odessa Selves: Identity and Mythopoesis in Works of the Odessa School." PhD dissertation, Columbia University, 2004.

Wisse, Ruth R. *The Modern Jewish Canon: A Journey Through Language and Culture.* New York: Free Press, 2000.

Yeykelis, Igor. "Odessa 1914–22: The Resurgence of Local Social and Cultural Values during the Times of Upheaval." PhD dissertation, The University of Melbourne, 1997.

Zipperstein, Steven J. *Imagining Russian Jewry: Memory, History, Identity.* Seattle: University of Washington Press, 1999.

———. *Elusive Prophet: Ahad Ha'am and the Origins of Zionism.* London: Peter Halban, 1993.

———. *The Jews of Odessa: A Cultural History, 1794–1881.* Stanford: Stanford University Press, 1985.

Part Two
Community

CHAPTER 5

Death in Odessa: A Study of Population Movements in a Nineteenth-Century City

Historians and demographers have long recognized that the cities of traditional Europe were demographically parasitic, that death rates within them consistently surpassed birth rates, and that even to maintain their numbers they were dependent on constant immigration.[1] Modernization in urban history consequently involved a type of "demographic transition," a reduction in death rates sufficiently substantial to allow the city to maintain and increase its size by natural reproduction. In this paper, we shall examine that transition in the city of Odessa in southern Ukraine, across the nineteenth century.

SITE AND SIZE

In 1794 Catherine II ordered the construction of a city on the west coast of the Black Sea; the following year it was given its historic name, Odessa.[2] Odessa's location by the sea conferred some advantages for the health of those who settled within it.[3] Its situation on a bluff about two hundred feet above sea level meant that the city was exposed to winds from all sides. According to one of the city's earliest health reports (1834), these winds freshened the atmosphere, presumably dispelling insects and, with them, "bad air" or malaria.[4] Odessa, the same report further observed, was not affected by some maladies, which frequently visited other large cities in warm climes. But if malaria was not a major menace to health at Odessa, it was not unknown. The medical report of 1834 noted the presence in the population of intermittent, surely malarial, fevers.[5] Nine years later, in 1843, another medical report stated that the number of cases of intermittent fevers was increasing.[6] Quinine and a small amount of rhubarb were recommended as antidotes and prophylactics. Since the *Anopheles* mosquito breeds in brackish waters along seacoasts, it is likely that the estuaries near the city harbored such insect vectors of malaria.[7]

Experts disagree as to how Odessa's climate affected health. To most Russians, it appeared mild. A volume published to celebrate Odessa's centenary claimed that the mean annual

---

Originally published as Patricia Herlihy, "Death in Odessa: A Study of Population Movements in a Nineteenth-Century City," *Journal of Urban History* IV (1978): 417–42.

temperature of the city, 48.5° F, compared favorably with that of Paris, Vienna, Strassburg, Cologne, Brussels, and Cambridge in England.[8] In fact, the contrast between the heat of July at Odessa (mean temperature, 72.8° F) and the cold of January (23.2° F) amounted to 49.6° F; the difference between the mean temperatures of July and January found at Moscow (52.5° F) and at St. Petersburg (49.0° F) were nearly the same.[9]

Visitors seldom mention climate as one of the attractions of the city. Travelers frequently complained of hot summer days, when the temperature soared to 104° F. In the judgment of one traveler, Odessa may have been on the latitude of Milan, but its climate was far from Italian. There were no hills, he explained, to protect the city from arctic blasts; he found there an extraordinary contrast between the heat and cold, while drought prevailed over most of the summer.[10] Climate and the seasonal changes in temperature and precipitation visibly affected patterns of mortality in Odessa, as they did in many traditional European cities. As we shall see in more detail later, the hot summer months carried off infants in large numbers, mainly through intestinal disturbances, diarrhea, and resulting dehydration.[11] Winter, on the other hand, took its heaviest tolls from among the elderly, although deaths in winter were much less clustered than those of summer (see Table 3).

Apart from extremes in climate, visitors in the early nineteenth century noted other dangers to health in the new and growing town. One element of the urban environment that attracted almost universal comment and complaint was dust and mud—the one pervasive in the city during the dry summer months, the other clogging the streets and all that moved on them in the rainy spring and autumn. To be sure, neither dust nor mud directly threatened human life, and they did not significantly raise the incidence of diseases.[12] But the dust certainly aggravated existing maladies, such as eye infections and respiratory ailments. Odessa's dust, raised by sea winds in the summer heat, was particularly fine, because it came from the porous debris of layered shellfish and cockleshells, which composed the limestone foundation of the city.

In some famous lines of poetry in *Eugene Onegin*, Alexander Pushkin complained of the city's air: "I lived then in dusty Odessa."[13] A traveler reported that the city "was invariably enveloped through the summer in whirling clouds of dust."[14]

A doctor noted in more detail:

> It is to be regretted that, notwithstanding the clear autumnal atmosphere, a grey mist spreads over the city in consequence of the quantity of dust, and never affords a clear prospect. The mist consists of the finest particles of the steppe limestone, and has a still more unpleasant effect, as it is extremely injurious to the eyes, especially to those of strangers, frequently producing serious inflammation.[15]

In the 1830s a noblewoman recorded in her memoirs, "At our arrival in Odessa, we were enveloped by clouds of dust which scattered a hail, the granules of which were the size of pigeons' eggs. Odessa is not yet paved nor sheltered neither by mountains nor by any forest.

The circulating air carries into the houses a fine and tiny sand which covers all the furniture, and against which one takes care to seal hermetically the doors and windows."[16] According to another English traveler, "The limestone dust two or three inches deep in the streets made its way into desks, drawers, and all corners of the house; every article of food [was] covered with it for the heat was too intense to allow of the windows being closed."[17] Echoing the English and American complaints was the lamentation of a French engineer: "Dust here is a real calamity, a fiendlike persecutor, that allows you not a moment's rest. It spreads out in seas and billows that rise with the least breath of wind and envelops you with increasing fury, until you are stifled, and blinded and incapable of a single movement."[18] "The argillaceous soil," he further explained, "the dryness of the air, force of winds, width of streets, the bad paving, the great extent of uncultivated ground and the prodigious number of carriages" all contributed to the noxious clouds.

The rains of spring and autumn turned the dust into mud, and this was equally annoying. Pushkin immortalized Odessa's mud along with its dust, saying that the streets and houses were flooded with the oozing mess five to six weeks of the year; to get around, it was necessary to wear stilts.[19]

All English travelers who have given any account of Odessa are unanimous in their complaints respecting the execrable state of its roads. This picture is confirmed by yet another visitor: "In winter they are said to be impassable for the mud ... When I first arrived at Odessa in March 1828, the streets were at least a foot deep in mud and water, which rendered a carriage necessary even to cross the way; and in many places there were deep holes which made them absolutely dangerous."[20]

Another witness called the main thoroughfare the very "slough of despond, where drunken men or old women suffocated at the crossing. Women servants had to wear Wellington boots in order to make their way about the city."[21] Nearly all the travelers repeated stories of horses, cattle, and Cossacks that reputedly sank into the mire and were never sighted again. One observer attributed the prevailing high death rates to the "miasmic vapour from the mud mixed with manure and churned up."[22]

Even more menacing to the health of Odessa's population was the meager available supply of fresh drinking water. When the town was founded, nearby streams and wells had at first met its needs. In 1792 the well water drawn in the vicinity of the city was described as "fresh and good."[23] However, as early as 1805 an Italian merchant trading in the new city affirmed that the water was bad and very scarce in summer.[24] Pushkin remarks, perhaps facetiously, that it was cheaper and surely more pleasant to drink wine in Odessa (a duty-free port) than the costly water.[25]

According to the French merchant Sicard, not only was there insufficient water for the population in 1818, but also the cattle needed to transport grain to the port could not be adequately watered.[26] The following year, a missionary described Odessa's well water as "hard and brackish."[27] In 1825 an English doctor wrote that one of the chief obstacles to the growth and commercial prosperity of the town was the want of a water supply adequate "for the purposes of life."[28] In contemporary opinion, the city's contaminated water was a principal factor in the outbreak of cholera epidemics, from 1831 on.[29]

Supplies of water grew even more expensive during the 1830s. Water carriers brought the precious liquid from springs about five miles distant, and sold pails for two copecks each. For water alone, the average urban family spent about five rubles per month—roughly equivalent to the wages earned by a skilled worker for five days of labor.[30] The costs rose if extra baths or washings were desired. Thirty years later, a German wrote that the cisterns were inadequate for the city's needs in normal times, and in drought years, such as 1859, they dried up entirely.[31] A popular travelers' guidebook from the same period warned the tourist that he would find little water in Odessa.[32]

The scarcity of water obstructed the disposal of sewage. Odessa's gutters and ditches were left without a natural flushing system, and they grew increasingly putrid across the hot and dry summer.

Table 1 The Population of the City of Odessa, 1795–1900

Year	Size	Annual Rate of Growth*	Year	Size	Annual Rate of Growth*
1795	2,345	13.74%	1856	101,320	2.07%
1808	12,500	12.25%	1867	127,000	7.27%
1814	25,000	9.36%	1873	193,513	2.37%
1817	32,700	6.95%	1883	244,609	3.65%
1820	40,000	2.21%	1897	403,815	3.68%
1842	76,862	1.99%	1900	450,000	2.20%

*Compounded

Sources: Grigorii Moskvich, *Illiustrirovannyi prakticheskii putevoditel' po Odesse* (Odessa, 1904). *Odessa: Ocherk istorii goroda-geroia* (Odessa, 1957). Henry S. Dearborn, *A Memoir on the Commerce and Navigation of the Black Sea and the Trade and Maritime Geography of Turkey and Egypt* (2 vols; Boston, 1819). Mary Holderness, *New Russia* (London, 1823). Thomas S. Fedor, *Patterns of Urban Growth in the Russian Empire during the Nineteenth Century* (Chicago, 1975). V. A. Zolotov, *Vneshniaia torgovlia Iuzhnoi Rossii v pervoi polovine 60–90 gody XIX v.* (Rostov-on-the-Don, 1966). *Statisticheskii vremennik Rossiiskoi imperii. Sbornik svedenii po Rossii za 1883 god.* (St. Petersburg, 1886).

In spite of these formidable difficulties, the population of the new town grew at an astounding rate (Table 1). As Table 1 illustrates, the growth of Odessa's population was dramatic. When the Duc de Richelieu was appointed governor of the city in 1803, there were only about 7,000 inhabitants in Odessa.[33] By 1814, when he returned to France, there were more than 25,000.[34] A major attraction for immigrants was the quickening trade between Odessa and Western Europe, to which the Napoleonic wars gave a powerful stimulus. Merchants, brokers, shippers, consular agents, innkeepers, stevedores, smugglers, and entertainers settled in the attractive port city. The city assumed many of the characteristics of a boomtown: a motley ethnic composition, much wealth and much poverty, and a public order frequently disturbed by vice, violence, and lawlessness.[35]

Colorful and prosperous, Odessa by 1860 had surpassed 100,000 in population—a feat which made it the third largest city in the Russian Empire. The United States then contained only nine cities with a population of 100,000 or more.[36] The late 1860s and early 1870s seem to have been a period of particularly rapid expansion. The emancipation of the serfs (1861) and the liberal reforms of Tsar Alexander II favored commercial and industrial expansion. Odessa's first railroad was completed in 1865, and by 1872, it was possible to travel all the way to Moscow by train.[37] At the same time, an enormous market for Russian wheat, much of which flowed through Odessa, developed in Western Europe. In 1860 wheat exports were about seven million quintal; they soared to more than twenty-eight million in 1878.[38] By then the city had a radius of about seven miles and contained more than 200,000 people.

Many new houses were constructed, predominantly of stone; wood was scarce and expensive on the treeless steppe. This may have conferred some small advantage—vermin could not readily infest stone walls. But rents remained high and crowding intense. Speculators, it was reported, purchased dwellings with the confident expectation that their value would soon double.[39]

Rapid growth aggravated the problems of dust, mud, water, and sewage. Moreover, the concentration of numerous humans in a small space raised the threat of communicable disease. "It seems to be a universal law," a Boston physician remarked in 1873, "that condensation of population lessens the chance of life."[40] Contaminated supplies of water and milk and crowded housing favored the spread of typhus (proverbially, the "poor man's disease"), typhoid, and tuberculosis. Moreover, some diseases, such as measles, smallpox, and mumps, require a large population in order to maintain their existence.[41] The penalties of size seem in the past to have placed limits on the expansion of cities, but they did not do so in the nineteenth century. How was this ancient ceiling on urban growth broken at Odessa?

IMPROVEMENTS IN PUBLIC HEALTH

The historian of public health at Odessa is fortunate in possessing not only much anecdotal information (contained in the abundant and vivid travel literature, consular reports, and contemporary newspapers), but also four lengthy papers on mortality in the city and its causes, dated 1834, 1843, 1865, and 1895.[42] The diseases mentioned in these reports can be conveniently classified according to the manner by which they were conveyed from person to person: through the air, through water and food, and through lice, fleas, mosquitoes, and other "vectors."[43]

Among the principal airborne diseases can be listed tuberculosis of the lungs, bronchitis, pneumonia, influenza, smallpox, whooping cough, measles, scarlet fever, and diphtheria. The reports of 1834 and 1843 also mention chicken pox, German measles, measles, inflammations of the eye, "catarrhal fevers," rheumatic fevers, and so forth. The author of the report of 1843, a professor of forensic medicine at the Richelieu Lyceum named A. Rafalovich, is the first to give extensive attention to tuberculosis, which seems to have been increasing in the population, as it was also in Western Europe. He correctly observed that Odessa's irritating dust could not be the sole cause of tuberculosis; cities such as Vienna, Prague, and London, where dust levels are lower, suffered even greater losses to the disease than did "dusty Odessa." He had as yet no perception of the relation of tuberculosis to cramped quarters and low living standards. These associations were only gradually impressing themselves on the consciousness of European doctors.[44]

Tuberculosis remained one of Odessa's principal endemic diseases and one of the most difficult to suppress. In 1895 tuberculosis was responsible for 10 percent of all the deaths in the city (still a moderate toll by the standards of many Western European cities). It chiefly claimed its victims from among adults between the ages of fifteen and sixty. Men were even more susceptible to the disease than women.[45] Still, these numerous deaths may exaggerate the virulence of tuberculosis among the urban population. This southern seaport seems to have attracted many persons already infected, who came in hopes of a cure in the favorable climate. The deaths of many of these sick visitors probably inflate our figures.

Among the chief waterborne diseases can be listed cholera, diarrhea, dysentery, tuberculosis (non-respiratory), and typhoid. Outbreaks of cholera occurred sporadically after its initial appearance in Russia in 1830.[46] Major epidemics occurred in 1848, 1855, 1865, 1872 (when the death rate climbed to 58.2 per 1,000), and 1892. The terrifying novelty of the disease, its tendency to strike all social classes indiscriminately and the ghastly torments it inflicted on its victims, probably inspired the composition of the valuable medical report of 1834. While the disease diminished in virulence over time, it still pays Odessa an occasional, unwelcome visit.[47]

Less violent but more persistent were other intestinal disturbances—diarrhea, dysentery, and the like. In his report of 1843, Rafalovich observed that the inhabitants of Odessa seldom escaped intestinal disorders from mid-June to mid-September and newcomers to the city were almost always stricken. He rejected the popular, but probably accurate, belief that the tainted well water was chiefly at fault. Rather, in his estimation, the chief cause of the malady was the consumption of raw fruits and vegetables, especially the local apricots. To counteract the attacks of diarrhea, vomiting, griping pains, and headaches, Rafalovich could only prescribe the application of mustard plaster or the taking of effervescent soda powders and weak mint tea. Only occasionally should leeches be applied, or almond oils taken with opium. In Rafalovich's eyes, the only sure relief for this epidemic intestinal malady was the cooler weather of late September and October, when, as experience showed, the disease gradually abated.[48]

The chief vector-borne diseases were malaria, plague, and typhus. Steady progress against malaria came almost as a welcome by-product of the city's own expansion. The draining of nearby marshes continuously reduced the breeding areas of the anopheles mosquito. Intermittent fevers gain no mention in the medical report of 1895.

Quarantine and fumigation were the traditional measures taken to repress plague. As a port, Odessa was constantly exposed to infection from abroad. Grain stored near the docks supported a sizable population of rats, hosts to the disease-bearing fleas. Only three years after the founding of the city, a ship arrived at port with plague on board. Thanks to the quarantine system already in effect, the disease did not spread into the city.[49] In 1812, on the other hand, despite the quarantine and heroic measures taken personally by the Duc de Richelieu, the plague raged for six months.[50] Remembering this epidemic, Pushkin asked in his poem, *Eugene Onegin*: "Have the casks of expected wines arrived? And how's the plague, and where the conflagrations?"[51] People tarred their clothes, bathed in the sea, soaked their possessions in water and their money in vinegar. Convicts, still in chains and attired in black leather suits soaked in oil, were used to cleanse houses twenty days after the dead had been removed. And the dead were many. Of a total population of some 20,000, the plague infected 4,038 persons and 2,632 of these succumbed.

The next major outbreak of plague in 1829 carried off 2,458 victims. In 1837–38, the then governor-general of Odessa, M. S. Vorontsov, gained distinction by the vigorous measures he took to contain a threatened epidemic.[52] He directed a door-to-door search to identify and isolate the stricken. A German doctor then visiting the city has left us the following description:

> During my first visit to Odessa, in January 1838, I [had] an opportunity of witnessing the plague ... At that time I more than once accompanied Prince Woronzoff [Vorontsov] on his visits of inspection, and beheld many of the unfortunate wretches who had been seized by that frightful disease, few of whom recovered their former health. I then saw with my own eye how the bodies of those who had died of the plague were thrown into pits with quicklime.[53]

Port officials at Odessa were strict in enforcing quarantine regulations on ships entering the harbor—excessively so, in the opinion of many captains, passengers, and consuls.[54] The advent of the telegraph, which carried almost instantly news of plague appearances, seemed to render superfluous the long quarantine of ships coming from plague-free ports. At all events, the plague declined at Odessa from the early nineteenth century, although it never disappeared entirely, as it did in Western Europe. Here the city's proximity to eastern centers of the disease probably explains the recurrences.

Typhus was another vector-borne disease, but not until the last quarter of the century was it distinguished from typhoid fever. With better knowledge came heightened awareness that the disease was closely related to dirt, lice, and poverty. In the last decades of the century, the authorities organized campaigns against the flophouses of the city; doctors were commissioned to visit flophouses and inspect their sanitary conditions.[55] These and other measures seemed to gain no small degree of success. The death rate from typhus was 16 per 10,000 in 1875; by 1895 it had been reduced to 1.5 per 10,000.

Specific measures taken against particular diseases would probably have had little significant impact on death rates in the absence of broad improvements in public sanitation. One major undertaking was the paving of urban surfaces, essential for cleansing the air of dust and the streets of mud. The saga of how the city streets came to be paved is a long one and can only be sketched here. As early as 1827, newspapers were advertising for stones suitable for pavement.[56] Captains, it was hoped, would willingly carry such stones as ballast when they sailed their ships to Odessa in search of grain. The stones of Trieste and its region were particularly desired. Through manifests, the city government kept captains and shippers continuously informed of the price it was willing to pay for suitable paving material. The appeal to shippers seemed to promise a cheap solution to the problem, but unfortunately it did not prove successful. The prices offered apparently did not persuade a sufficient number of captains to alter their usual routines and fill their ships with paving stones. It was the grain shipped out of, not the stones carried into, Odessa which caught and held the captains' interest.

Early attempts to macadamize the streets of Odessa had no happier results. The pavement was basically limestone. The city's many horses, armed with frost nails on their hoofs, quickly returned the pavement to the vile dust from whence it sprung. With rain, the streets were again mud flats.

In the 1840s, a French engineer convinced the authorities that wooden paving would save the situation.[57] Wooden blocks were laid down on some principal streets. The French consul declared the experiment a success. But the costs proved far too high to allow for the remaking of Odessa's streets in wood. The annoyed travelers hardly paused in their complaints. In 1861, joining a now strident chorus, the French consul declared, "This magnificent city might fall into ruin if something is not done about its streets."[58]

The aroused government now solicited bids to pave the streets and in 1862, French, German, and English firms entered into a spirited competition to win the award. The commission to pave the streets with granite was conferred on George Furness and Company of London. Two years later the American consul described the considerable progress of the enterprise:

> The paving of the streets with granite blocks progresses well and a curious feature of the work is that much of the granite is brought from Scotland as ballast although great quarries are worked on the borders of the Boug [Bug River] not far from Nicholaieff [Nikolaev] and only about one hundred miles from Odessa by sea, but a still more curious feature is that all the blocks as well as the sewers are laid with American cement.[59]

In 1868, the work was taken away from the English firm and entrusted to a Russian engineer. Eleven years later the French consul announced that all the streets of Odessa would be paved "in magnificent granite" within a year.[60] Of course, as it often does, progress came more slowly than anticipated. But by 1895, all the central area was paved and part of the outlying districts as well. It might appear that streets were slow to acquire a hard surface at Odessa, but we must remind ourselves that in New Orleans as late as the 1880s fewer than 100 of the 566 miles of streets were paved.

Even more essential to the good health of the city was a plentiful supply of pure water. Odessa's elevated site made the drilling of artesian wells all but impossible. The water carted into the city from outside wells was expensive and often of dubious quality. Early in the city's history, projects had been proposed to bring water from the Dnister River (a distance of twenty-seven miles) or even the Buh (seventy-five miles), but the Duc de Richelieu, governor of the city during its early years of rapid growth, accomplished nothing. Later visitors, who were usually full of praise for the governor, here took him to task for his failures to arrange for the transport of sufficient pure water into the city or to build a reservoir within it.[61] And the succeeding governors for long proved themselves unequal to this pressing task. Finally, on September 19, 1861, the French consul reported good news: the tsar had just approved the formation, by British investors, of the Company of the Aqueduct of the Dnister to Odessa (later to become the Odessa Waterworks Company).[62]

By 1873, water from the Dnister was flowing through pipes into the city. By the same year, 71 percent of the houses in Odessa had running water, although only 45 percent were connected to the city's sewer network.[63] The inhabitants of Odessa drew inestimable benefits from the new waterworks, but apparently not the English investors who provided the necessary capital to build the system. According to an English traveler writing in 1889, the British Odessa Waterworks Company, Limited spent over a million pounds sterling to bring water into the city. However, "the suffering shareholders are still wailing over the unprofitable (to them) investment of so much hard cash. The water is brought in from the Dnister, thirty miles distant, through thirty-inch pipes, after being carefully filtered."[64]

Once the city had piped water and steam pumps powerful enough to move it freely, it could also adopt improved methods of sewage disposal. In 1878, the major sewer system of Odessa was completed.[65] The very newness of the city facilitated rapid construction; no older and outmoded system obstructed the labors. In technical language, this was a "full floating system," which carried away both liquid and material wastes and storm waters.[66] It not only disposed of sewage but also drained the city streets. Odessa was the first large Russian city to possess an efficient sewerage system. Kyiv followed in 1894, Moscow in 1898, and Rostov-on-the-Don only in 1906.[67] In America, Boston did not complete its metropolitan sewerage system until 1897.[68] New Orleans began to lay its sewer pipes in 1903 and finished the undertaking in 1908.[69]

In 1895, Odessa's administrators attributed the encouraging decline in the official death rate (from 37.9 per 1,000 in 1874 to 31.3 per 1,000 in 1880) directly to the new waterworks and sewer systems.[70] Figure 1 illustrates the close association of these improvements and the declining death rate. As further illustration of the beneficent effects of good plumbing, these officials assembled statistics on various districts of the city, as Table 2 shows.

The coefficient of correlation between the two columns in Table 2 is -0.893; in other words, as the percentage of homes with indoor flush toilets rises, the death rate shows a strong tendency to drop. The relationship is, to be sure, in some measure not causal but "ecological." Many houses with flush toilets were doubtlessly also spacious, comfortable, and clean; their inhabitants probably ate better than the average residents of the city, kept servants, and enjoyed other advantages, which promoted longevity. While we cannot measure it exactly, the contribution of plumbing to the health of Odessa's people was nonetheless substantial.

By the end of the nineteenth century Odessa's death rate was lower than that of either Moscow or St. Petersburg. It was also lower than the contemporary death rates of Liverpool, Manchester, Le Havre, Königsberg, Danzig, Budapest, and Bucharest.[71] Of all the sanitary improvements made in Odessa during the nineteenth century, the new waterworks and sewer system had the most dramatic impact on mortality rates.

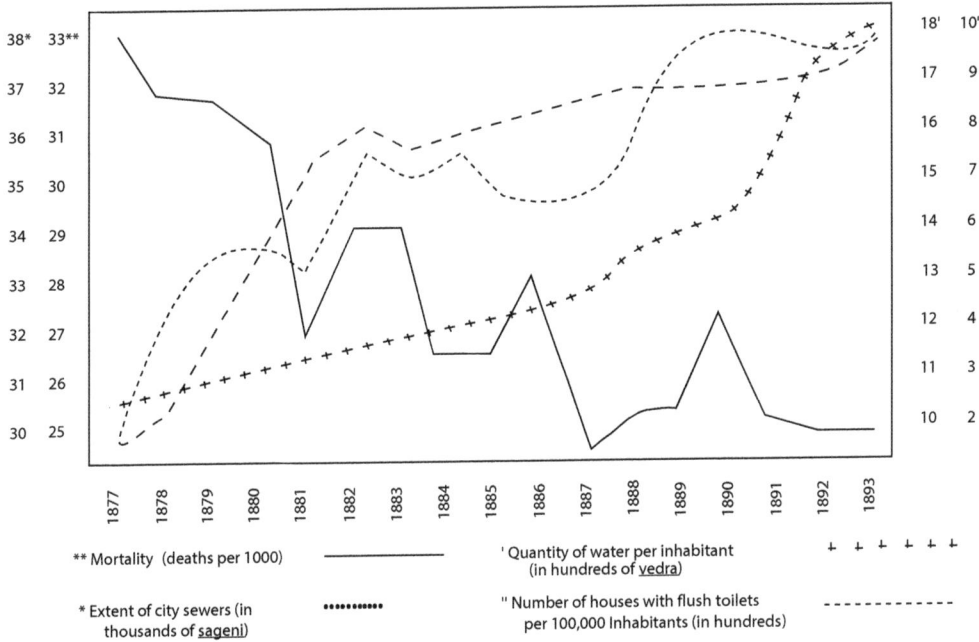

Figure 1 Mortality and sanitation in Odessa, 1877–93. (Source: *Odessa 1794–1894* [Odessa, 1895], 444.) Copyright 2003 ProQuest Information and Learning Company and Sage Publications, Inc.

Table 2 Plumbing and Death Rates in Districts of the City of Odessa, 1893

District	Percentage of Homes with Indoor Flush Toilets	Deaths/1,000
Bul'varnyi	87.0	17.19
Oleksandrivs'kyi	78.4	19.11
Petropavlovs'kyi	52.8	27.96
Khersons'kyi	78.6	20.82
Mykhailivs'kyi	16.2	28.20
Peresyps'kyi	3.2	29.07
Slobidka-Romanivka	11.5	35.39

Source: *Odessa 1794–1894* (Odessa, 1895), 455.

INFANT MORTALITY

Within Odessa's population, the last group or cohort to benefit from the improved standards of public health were babies. Over the period 1824 to 1827, the deaths of infants under one year of age constituted 44 percent of all the city's deaths.[72] By 1851–60, the rate had fallen to 28 percent but thereafter infant mortality began noticeably to increase. Between 1867 and 1884, deaths in the first year of life had come to average 35 percent of all deaths.[73]

The tendency for infant mortality to remain high or even to worsen over the middle and late decades of the nineteenth century is observable in many American and European cities as well. In the city of Rotterdam in the Netherlands, according to a recent study, infant death rates rose from early in the century until the 1870s.[74] In England and Wales the infant mortality rate was 148 per 1,000 births in 1841–45; 156 in 1851–55; 158 in 1875, and not until 1901–5 did it drop to 138.[75] In Boston rates of infant mortality decreased until the 1820s, but then began gradually to rise.[76] In 1853, observers noted that in New York City, "there was an alarming increase in infant deaths over the previous ten years."[77] It may be that an undercount of infant deaths in the early nineteenth century and improving registrations thereafter have distorted the record. Still it is odd that the same documentary fault should have been almost universally present. And it is incontrovertible that infant mortalities remained for long at high levels even in Western societies. In Germany, for example, death rates among those 10–14 years of age began to fall from about 1845, for those 55–64 years old from 1890, and for those less than one year of age from 1905.[78]

What explains this high and unresponsive death rate among infants? Early improvements in public health benefited most members of society, but did not immediately and decisively help the very young. Contemporaries, doubtlessly with reason, laid the principal blame on inadequate maternal care. Migrants, including many women, were flocking into the cities in search of employment. Mothers who left the hearth for outside employment frequently had neither time nor energy to devote to the careful nurture of their babies. Nearly all commentators ascribed premature deaths of babies to improper feeding—the refusal or inability of mothers to nurse their babies, the indiscriminate use of solid food in infant feeding, and even, on occasion, recourse to drugs.[79] One New York doctor described this frightening menu presented to infants, "Not merely molasses, or sugar and water, catnip tea, olive or castor oil, goose-grease, spoon victuals, and the like, but salt and water, soot tea, gin sling, and even urine, are incontinently forced into the infant's throat before it has known an hour of life."[80] According to several doctors, wars or strikes, which forced mothers to remain at home, benefited babies even when food was in short supply.[81]

At Odessa, too, experts in childcare stressed the importance of mother's milk for babies. To send babies to wet nurses in the countryside—evidently a common practice at Odessa—was tantamount to condemning them to death.[82] The heat of Odessa's summer gravely reduced the infants' chances of survival. The earliest medical report, dated 1834, gave much attention to the summertime ailment of infants:

> In summertime and especially in June and July children from a few months to four years are subject to a great disorder in the functioning of the gastro-intestinal tract, accompanied by diarrhea and vomiting, a rise in body temperature and accelerated pulse, and, along with this, convulsions and spasms appear. This is an illness without a clear cause, which affects children and consists evidently in great irritation of the nervous system and [produces] a flow of blood in the head (*congestio*) and, if it increases in severity, it then affects the organs (*gastro-entero-encephalitis*).[83]

In 1841, a former English soldier who had spent many years in India commented on hot summers and disease at Odessa, "Dysentery and nervous fevers prevail here [in Odessa] during the great heats; the former attacks children, who seldom recover; but those who can do so, generally remove them into the country in the summer. The greater number of deaths takes place in this season, and are on the whole population, about one in thirty. There is no rain until late in the autumn."[84]

Table 3 Percentages of Annual Deaths by Age and Season at Odessa, 1851–61

Deaths at Ages	Winter	Spring	Summer	Autumn	
0–5	21.1	18.4	36.7	23.8	percent
6–10	23.1	22.4	30.2	24.3	"
11–20	23.0	25.0	26.4	25.6	"
21–40	24.2	26.1	27.6	22.1	"
41–80	27.0	24.9	25.8	22.3	"
81–100	29.4	25.9	22.35	22.35	"

Source: Mark I. Finkel', "Issledovanie," 175–76.

Rafalovich in his oft-cited 1843 report also noted that children suffered irritation of the intestinal tract in the hot summer months from June to September.[85] In his words, "there is a close connection with the temperature of the air, so that the higher the mercury in the thermometer, the more numerous the children who will suffer from diarrhea." In his observation, the number of infant deaths correlated strongly with unusually hot summers. In his reckoning, during the average year at Odessa, of those children three years or younger in age, one out of 4.06 died. One out of 3.02 infants who died had yet to see their first birthday.

The third medical report, prepared in 1865, shows clearly that summer was for babies the cruelest season. Table 3 reproduces its data, giving for the period 1851–61 deaths by season at Odessa.

M. I. Finkel', who prepared the report of 1865, reported:

> By its character, by its phenomenon, by its sad result and killing impact on children [this disease] fully corresponds to the character and nature of that disease which rages in the United States of North America, which there the doctors call infantile cholera (*cholera infantilis*), but which we, the doctors of Odessa, call the epidemic irritation of the stomach and intestines (*gastro-enseritis epidemica infantum*). For us this disease has the same significance as in North America and together with the North Americans, we can call it the infantile pestilence. In this regard Odessa can share its sad reputation with New York, Philadelphia and Washington. For several years almost half of all children dying from the age of 0–3 years are taken away by this disease. Let us note, too, that this disease rages in Odessa especially fiercely in those years in which the temperature of summer undergoes rapid changes.[86]

If, as Dr. Finkel' maintains, it is permissible to draw comparisons between Odessa and American cities, we may note that a contemporary New York doctor also observed that a special kind of disease affected children in the summer. He called it "summer complaints" and claimed that it was exclusively an American, and not European, debility.[87] One-half of the mortality in the summer in certain American cities consisted of children under two years of age. Another doctor noted at the same time, "This is a disease peculiar to cities."[88] According to C. E. Winslow, a modern expert on public health, this summer diarrhea, "so prevalent in earlier days [within cities]," was the product of two factors: the lower resistance of the infant due to summer heat and the toxic effect of decomposed or infected milk.[89]

The tardy reduction of infant mortality at Odessa prompts this observation. By 1895, the city had made great strides in improving the life expectancies of its inhabitants. But the better survival of infants depended as much on social and cultural as on physical changes. Poverty, illiteracy, ignorance of the proper care of babies, and perhaps indifference took a heavy toll of infants. The quality of the environment, supporting or threatening human life at Odessa, had cultural as well as physical dimensions.[90]

THE SELF-SUSTAINING CITY

In spite of the continuing great loss of babies, the urban population of Odessa passed a milestone at about 1880. As late as 1877, one expert at an international demographic congress included Odessa among the world's cities that were not maintaining their own numbers through natural reproduction.[91] As Table 4 shows, this was no longer true in the early years of the following decade.

Table 4 The Demographic Transition at Odessa

Years	Births	Deaths	Excess
1867 and 1868	10,790	10,409	381
1870, 1872, 1873	19,489	18,646	843
1881, 1882, 1884	26,490	23,103	3,387

Sources: *Statisticheskii vremennik Rossiiskoi imperii* (St. Petersburg, for 1867 published in 1872; for 1868 published in 1877; for 1870 published in 1879; for 1872 published in 1882; for 1873 published in 1882; for 1881 published in 1887; for 1882 published in 1887; for 1884 published in 1889).

The city of Odessa in the nineteenth century grew at rates equaled only by contemporary American cities, but this rapid expansion posed formidable risks for the health of its inhabitants. As late as 1870, death rates lingered in the high 30s—occasionally, as in the cholera year of 1872, surpassing 50 deaths per 1,000. These dreadful tolls threatened the future growth and present prosperity of the city. In its struggle for improved assurance of life the city undertook the paving of its streets, which gave it purer air and cleaner surfaces. But the critical achievement seems to have been the construction of aqueducts, bringing pure water in abundant supply in the city and the citywide sewerage system finished in 1878. In what seems a clear correlation with these improvements, the urban death rate plummeted, declining to 25.4 deaths per 1,000—the mean for the years 1891–93. (The comparable rate at Moscow in 1891–95 was 29.2). Infant deaths remained high, but not high enough to offset this substantial improvement in the life chances of older children and adults. By 1900 social reform and education had become the new frontiers in the continuing struggle to protect and prolong human life at Odessa.

Notes

1. Adna F. Weber, *The Growth of Cities in the Nineteenth Century: A Study in Statistics* (New York and London: Studies in History, Economics and Law, Columbia University), 283: See also William H. McNeill, *Plagues and Peoples* (Garden City, NY: Anchor Press, 1976), 275.
2. For the early history of Odessa, see A. Orlov, *Istoricheskii ocherk Odessy s 1794 po 1803 god. Sostavil po dokumentam, khraniashchimsia v Moskovskom Arkhive Ministerstva Iustitsii* (Odessa: A. Shul'tse, 1885); A. A. Skal'kovskii, *Pervoe tridtsatiletie istorii goroda Odessy, 1793–1823* (Odessa: V gorodskoi tipografii, 1837); *Odessa 1794–1894* (Odessa: Izdanie gorodskago obshchestvennago upravleniia k stoletiiu goroda, 1895).
3. Robert E. Jones, "Urban Planning and the Development of Provincial Towns in Russia, 1762–1796," in *The Eighteenth Century in Russia*, ed. J. G. Garrard (Oxford: Clarendon Press, 1973), 337, 342. Jones concludes that Odessa was the most successful of Catherine's many new towns.
4. "Mediko-topograficheskiia svedeniia o g. Odesse" (henceforth, "Svedeniia") in *Zhurnal Ministerstva vnutrennikh del*, vol. 3 (1834), 408–9. In the 1820s, a visitor to Odessa wrote, "The air is pure and remarkably wholesome" (Joseph Conder, *The Modern Traveller* [London: J. Duncan, 1825], 233). On the other hand, another traveler said that the hot winds of summer forced all who could afford it to retire to the countryside (Charles Koch, *The Crimea and Odessa: Journal of a Tour* [London: John Murray, 1885], 265).
5. "Svedeniia," 409.
6. A. Rafalovich, "Meditsinskaia statistika Odessy za 1842 god" (henceforth, "statistika"), in *Zhurnal Ministerstva vnutrennikh del*, vol. 4 (1843), 173.
7. C. E. A. Winslow, *Man and Epidemics* (Princeton, NJ: Princeton University Press, 1952), 176.
8. *Odessa 1794–1894*, 16. The statement is repeated in Grigorii Moskvich, *Illiustrirovannyi prakticheskii putevoditel' po Odesse* (Odessa: Tekhnik, 1904), 68.
9. *The Encyclopaedia Britannica*, 11th ed. (New York: The Encyclopaedia Britannica Company, 1911), 20, 3 (for Odessa); 18, 891 (for Moscow); 24, 38 (for St. Petersburg).
10. William Jesse, *Notes of a Half-Pay in Search of Health: Russia. Circassia, and the Crimea in 1839–40* (London: J. Madden and Co. 1841), 1:239.
11. At an urban parish at Lyons in France in 1780–89, more than half the deaths of children in the first year of life occurred in summer (51.5 percent), and nearly half the deaths of children age 1–5 (48.7 percent), Maurice Garden, *Lyon et les Lyonnais au XVIIIe siècle* (Paris: Les Belles Lettres, 1970), 112.
12. On dust as a vector of disease, see Abram S. Benenson, *Control of Communicable Disease in Man*, 12th ed. (Washington, DC: The American Public Health Association, 1975), throughout (s.v. index under "Dust, transmission by"). Spore-laden dust is the chief menace to health.
13. *Eugene Onegin*, translated by V. Nabokov (New York: Bollingen Foundation, 1964), 1:340.
14. Anatole Demidov, *Voyage dans la Russie méridionale et la Crimée* (4 vols.; Paris: Ernest Bourdin, 1842), 1:290.
15. Koch, *The Crimea*, 259–60.
16. *Mémoires de la Comtesse Rosalie Rzewuska* (1788–1865), ed. Giovanella C. Grenier (Rome: Cuggiani, 1939), 2:320.
17. Jesse, *Notes*, 1:178–79.
18. Xavier Hommaire de Hell, *Travels in the Steppes of the Caspian Sea, the Crimea, the Caucasus, etc.* (London: Chapman and Hall, 1847), 8.

19 Eugene Onegin, 1:341.
20 Morton, *Travels*, 207–8.
21 Jesse, *Notes*, 1:178.
22 George Hume, *Thirty-Five Years in Russia* (London: Simpkin, Marshall, Hamilton, Kent & Co, 1914). For a brief discussion of medical theories of miasma and contagion in the spread of disease during the nineteenth century, see McNeill, *Plagues*, 265–68; and George Rosen, "Disease, Debility and Death," in *The Victorian City: Images and Realities*, ed. H. J. Dyos and Michael Wolff (London and Boston: Routledge & Kegan Paul, 1973), 633–34.
23 Frederick W. Skinner, "City Planning in Russia: The Development of Odessa, 1789–1892" (PhD diss., Princeton University, 1973), 36, citing a letter from V. K. Kakhovskii to Empress Catherine, May 5, 1792.
24 Notizie di Odessa scritte dal Sig. L. C. (Florence, no pub. 1817), 36.
25 Cited in Frederick W. Skinner, "Trends in Planning Practices: The Building of Odessa, 1794–1917," in *The City in Russian History*, ed. Michael F. Hamm (Lexington: University Press of Kentucky, 1976), 147.
26 Cited in V. A. Zolotov, *Vneshniaia torgovlia Iuzhnoi Rossii v pervoi polovine XIX v.* (Rostov: Izdatel'stvo Rostovskogo universitet, 1966), 28.
27 Robert Pinkerton, *Russia, or Miscellaneous Observations on Past and Present State of That Country and Its Inhabitants* (London: R. Watts, 1833), 136.
28 Robert Lyall, *Travels in Russia, the Krimea, the Caucasus and Georgia*, 2 vols. (London: T. Cadell, 1825), 1:169.
29 Archives du Ministère des Affaires Étrangères, Paris (henceforth, AMAE), Odessa, vol. 4, June 24, 1831. In the city of New York, the poor who could not afford to buy pure water were also the first afflicted with cholera in 1832, Charles E. Rosenberg, *The Cholera Years—The United States in 1832, 1849 and 1862* (Chicago: University of Chicago Press, 1962), 56.
30 The prices are given in Jesse, *Notes*, 1:196.
31 Wilhelm Hamm, *Sudöstliche Steppen und Städte nach eigener Anschauung geschildert* (Frankfurt am Main: Sauerländer, 1862), 105.
32 *Murray's Hand-Book for Northern Europe, Finland and Russia* (London: John Murray, 1849), 611.
33 Duc de Richelieu, "Mémoires sur Odessa, 1813," Sbornik imperatorskogo russkogo istoricheskogo obshchestva, vol. 54 (St. Petersburg: Tipografiia I. N. Skorokhodova, 1886), 369–70.
34 Charles Sicard, "Notice sur onze années de la vie du Duc de Richelieu," Sbornik irnperatorskogo russkogo istoricheskogo obshchestva, 54:71, 75.
35 For Odessa's early trade, see Patricia Herlihy, "Odessa: Staple Trade and Urbanization in New Russia," *Jahrbücher für Geschichte Osteuropas* 21 (1973): 184n3, for bibliographical references. For a description of the various ethnic communities living in Odessa, Patricia Herlihy, "The Ethnic Composition of the City of Odessa in the Nineteenth Century," *Harvard Ukrainian Studies* 1 (1977): 53–78. Odessa long retained its reputation for lawlessness, as the stories of its noted authors, Isaac Babel' and Il'f and Petrov, amply illustrate.
36 For the population of American cities, see Blake McKelvey, *American Urbanization: A Comparative History* (Glenview, IL: Scott, Foresman, 1973), 36–37.
37 The first railroad was a line of 180 versts between Odessa and Balta. On these and other changes, see S. Ia. Borovoi, "Odessa v period promyshlennogo kapitalizma," in *Odessa: Ocherk istorii goroda-geroia* (Odessa: Odesskoe oblastnoe izdatel'stvo, 1957), 53–78.
38 For the growth in cereal exports, see M. V. Kasperoff, "Commerce des céréales," in *La Russie à la fin du 19e siècle*, ed. M. W. De Kovalevsky (Paris: Paul Dupont, 1900), 724–43.
39 Public Records Office, London (henceforth, PRO), FO 65, vol. 860, February 18, 1873.
40 Edward Jarvis, "Infant Mortality," Fourth Annual Report of the State Board of Health of Massachusetts (Boston: n.p., 1873), 224.

41 For measles, M. S. Bartlett, "Measles Periodicity and Community Size," *Journal of the Royal Statistical Society* cl. 120 (1957): 48–70.
42 They are: "Svedeniia"; Statistika"; Mark I. Finkel', "Issledovanie o smertnosti v Odesse v desiatiletnii period, s 1851 po 1861 god vkliuchitel'no," in *Trudy odesskago statisticheskago komiteta, vypusk vtoroi* (Odessa, 1865), 1:153–99 (henceforth, "Issledovanie") and the chapter entitled "Narodnoe zdravie," *Odessa 1794–1894*, 433–569.
43 *Odessa 1794–1894*, 443. In 1895, by virtue of measures taken against these diseases, the city fathers claimed that Odessa "occupied in sanitary conditions the first place among the large Russian cities and far from the last among Europe."
44 "Statistika," 377. George Rosen, "Disease, Debility and Death," *Victorian City*, 2:643.
45 *Odessa 1794–1894*, 452.
46 For cholera and its impact on Russian society, especially the medical profession, see Roderick E. McGrew, *Russia and the Cholera, 1823–1832* (Madison: University of Wisconsin Press, 1965), and Nancy M. Frieden, "The Russian Cholera Epidemic, 1892–93, and Medical Professionalization," *Journal of Social History* 10, no. 4 (June 1977): 538–59.
47 During the author's visit to the USSR in August 1970, Odessa was quarantined as a result of an outbreak of cholera. Again, during a visit to Odessa in September 1974, the author was told that one of the bathing beaches was closed because cholera had been traced to that area.
48 "Statistika," 370–71.
49 *Odessa 1794–1894*, 435.
50 Ibid.
51 *Eugene Onegin*, 1:342.
52 AMAE, *Odessa*, vol. 6, fol. 382, November 6, 1837.
53 Koch, *The Crimea*, 261.
54 AMAE, *Odessa*, vol. 7, fol. 457, August 15, 1856.
55 *Odessa 1794–1894*, 463.
56 *Journal d'Odessa*, March 26/April 7, 1827.
57 On the episode, see AMAE, *Odessa*, vol. 7, fols. 291–96, March 23, 1843, and fols. 334–36, October 20, 1843.
58 AMAE, *Odessa*, vol. 8, fol. 240, May 6, 1861.
59 National Archives, Washington, DC (henceforth, NA), Odessa, Consular Report, July 1, 1864.
60 AMAE, *Odessa*, vol. 11, fol. 191, June 20, 1879.
61 Morton, *Travels*, 217.
62 AMAE, *Odessa*, vol. 8, fol. 290, September 19, 1861.
63 *Odessa 1794–1894*, 444.
64 Thomas Michell, *Russian Pictures* (London, Religious Tract Society, 1889), 139.
65 *Odessa 1794–1894*, 441.
66 The Russian term is "obshchesplavnii." See N. I. Fal'kovskii, *Istoriia vodosnabzheniia v Rossii* (Moscow and Leningrad: Izdatel'stvo Ministerstva Kommunal'nogo Khoziaistva RSFSR, 1947), 272.
67 Ibid.
68 Oscar Handlin, *Boston's Immigrants 1790–1865* (Cambridge, MA: Harvard University Press, 1941), 20.
69 Joy J. Jackson, *New Orleans in the Gilded Age: Politics and Urban Progress, 1889–1896* (Baton Rouge, LA: Louisiana State University Press, 1969), 156.
70 *Odessa 1794–1894*, 442–43. By 1893, the death rate for Odessa had fallen still further, to 25.4 per 1,000.
71 Ibid., 445.
72 *Journal d'Odessa*, October 6/18, 1828.
73 *Odessa 1794–1894*, 447.

74 H. Van Dijk, "Urbanisation and Social Change in the Netherlands During the Nineteenth Century," paper distributed at the Seventh Congress of the International Association of Economic History, Edinburgh, Scotland, 1978.
75 Rosen, "Disease, Debility and Death," 2, 649.
76 Barbara G. Rosenkrantz, *Public Health and the States: Changing Views in Massachusetts, 1842–1946* (Cambridge, MA: Harvard University Press, 1972), 18.
77 *Mr. Ely's Report on the Sanitary Condition of the City of New York* (New York: New York State Senate, n.d.), 92–93.
78 Wolfgang Köllmann, *Bevölkerung in der industriellen Revolution. Studen zur Bevölkerungsgeschichte Deutschlands* (Göttingen: Vandenhoeck & Ruprecht, 1974), 28.
79 Edward Willoughby, *Handbook of Public Health and Demography* (London, New York: Macmilan, 1893). Edward Jarvis, MD, "Infant Mortality," 206–9.
80 *Mr. Ely's Report*, 96.
81 Jarvis, "Infant Mortality," 207.
82 *Odessa 1794–1894*, 448.
83 "Svedeniia," 410.
84 Jesse, *Notes*, 1, 241.
85 "Statistika," 380.
86 "Issledovanie," 176–77.
87 *Mr. Ely's Report*, 101.
88 Jarvis, "Infant Mortality," 207.
89 Winslow, *Man and Epidemics*, 122.
90 That poverty was not the exclusive agent of these high infant mortalities seems indicated by the fact that Jewish babies, many of them found in impoverished households still survived distinctly better than their gentile counterparts. For the better survival of Jewish infants, which contemporaries attributed to superior maternal care, see "Statistika," 380. Even today, literacy is regarded as essential in lowering mortality among nonwhite infants in the United States. See Julius B. Richmond, "The Needs of Children," *Daedalus* (Winter, 1977): 247–59.
91 Weber, *Growth of Cities*, 239n2.

CHAPTER 6

The Ethnic Composition of the City of Odessa in the Nineteenth Century

The tongue of golden Italy resounds along the gay street where walks the proud Slav, Frenchman, Spaniard, Armenian, and Greek, and the heavy Moldavian, and the son of Egyptian soil, the retired Corsair, Morali.

—**Alexander Pushkin** (1820s)

In the streets [of Odessa] one hears Russian, English, Italian, German, Tatar, Polish, Turkish, Greek, Armenian, Moldavian, Bulgarian, Hungarian, Dalmatian, French, Swedish and Spanish, and these are not spoken merely by passing strangers, but by the regular inhabitants.

—**J. G. Kohl** (1830s)

There [in Odessa] the Russian jostles a Turk, a Frenchman an Arab, an Englishman an Armenian, an Italian a Bulgarian or Wallachian, a Pole a Circassian, a Hungarian a Persian or Bokharan.

—**Daniel Wegelin** (1840s)

Among the cities of the Russian Empire in the nineteenth century, Odessa was distinctive for several reasons.[1] Until the incorporation of Warsaw into the empire in 1863, it was the third-largest city in Russia, a position it held from midcentury. For most of the nineteenth century it was the fastest growing major city in the Russian Empire, rivaling in its rate of expansion such American cities as Chicago. And the ethnic composition of its population was the most complex of all large imperial cities.

This chapter will be concerned with this last aspect of Odessa's development in the nineteenth century. In examining the ethnic composition of Odessa, we shall make particular

---

Originally published as Patricia Herlihy, "The Ethnic Composition of Odessa in the Nineteenth Century." *Harvard Ukrainian Studies* I (1977): 53–78.

use of the rich data contained in the first All-Russian Imperial Census of 1897.[2] This census, although late, allows reliable comparisons between Odessa and other cities of the empire; it also contains a comprehensive listing of inhabitants by native language and by citizenship. All persons in all linguistic groups are classified by occupation, social class, religion, age, marital status, and literacy. This detailed survey affords numerous insights into the composition and contributions of non-Russians to the social and economic life of Odessa. The 1897 census, in sum, presents a solid, if static, picture of Odessa at the end of the century. Earlier, fragmentary data permit us to construct a more dynamic picture of Odessa's social development over the preceding decades. Consular reports, newspapers, travel journals, and imaginative literature, as well as subsequent official and nonofficial histories of Odessa, permit us to see well, if not always to measure, the growing city and the groups that formed it.

THE AGGREGATE POPULATION

At the time of the census the population of Odessa, including its suburbs, was 403,815 persons (the city alone numbered 380,541 inhabitants). In 1897, Odessa was still a growing community. Since 1856, its population had increased at an extraordinary rate—3.42 percent annually, compounded and calculated on an average yearly basis.[3] The comparable average annual rates of growth, over exactly the same period, are 2.34 percent for St. Petersburg and 2.56 percent for Moscow. From 1897, Odessa's headlong expansion shows signs of slowing; between that year and 1904, the average annual growth rate had dropped to 3.09 percent. But not until after 1905 does the city experience a really precipitous decline in its rate of expansion.[4]

Of the 403,815 persons living in Odessa in 1897, foreign subjects numbered 19,422. Many more were immigrants from within the Russian Empire. In 1897, only 43.6 percent of the population had been born in the city. Another 9.6 percent had been born in the Kherson gubernia, which included Odessa, while 44.3 percent of the population had birthplaces in other parts of the Russian Empire. Within this category are to be found numerous Russian subjects whose native language was not Russian: Jews, Poles, Ukrainians, Belarusians, Lithuanians, and so forth. Surprisingly, only 2.5 percent of the population had been born in foreign countries, despite the fact that nearly twice that percentage were foreign subjects. Presumably, many babies had been born in Odessa to foreign parents. The basic ethnic mixture of Odessa consisted of these foreign subjects, of Russians, and also of Russian subjects who spoke languages other than Russian as their native tongue.

In Odessa in 1897, 57.78 percent of the population (all ages included) could read, a literacy rate somewhat lower than that for St. Petersburg (62.6 percent) and slightly higher than the rate for Moscow (56.3 percent). In Odessa, however, literacy shows a distinctive association with age. In St. Petersburg the literacy rate peaks among school-age children and diminishes at the older levels of the population. This certainly reflects the lack of educational opportunities in the past and probably also the continuing immigration of illiterate peasants into the city. In Odessa the peaks of literacy are not found among the young school children. Rather, the highest rates are recorded in the groups between the ages fifteen and nineteen, and between thirty and thirty-nine. The delayed bulge in the literacy rate coincides at least in part with the age groups of the heaviest immigration into the city. The administrative, educational, mercantile, and cultural positions available in the city required literate persons to fill them. Perhaps even more than St. Petersburg, Odessa attracted those who could read.

According to the census there were fifty languages other than Russian spoken in Odessa by 166,345 individuals (41.20 percent of the population). Most of these people probably acquired Russian during their lifetime, but their literacy was calculated on the basis of their mother tongue. Fully 28.4 percent of Odessa's inhabitants reported Yiddish as their first language. But language alone does not reveal the true extent of the Jewish population. According to the 1897 tables, 138,935 persons, or 34.41 percent of the population, professed the Jewish religion. Presumably, most Jews who did not speak Yiddish as a first language were Russian speakers by upbringing.[5] The next largest communities of foreign speakers were the Poles (4.3 percent), Germans (2.5 percent), and Greeks (1.5 percent). Russian, Ukrainian, and Belorussian were spoken as mother tongues by 237,525 persons—58.8 percent of the city's population. In Moscow about 95 percent of the inhabitants spoke these languages, and in St. Petersburg, 87 percent. In Odessa only 56 percent of the people belonged to the Orthodox faith (or a schismatic sect thereof); in St. Petersburg 85 percent of the population were Orthodox, as were 93 percent of the inhabitants of Moscow. If we take either language or religion as an index, it could be affirmed that as late as 1897, Odessa was little more than half-Slavic in its ethnic composition.

The structure of the population in Odessa shows several distinctive characteristics. There were relatively more women in the Black Sea port than in the two northern capitals. The sex ratio for Odessa was 116 males for every 100 females, which compares with 120 males per 100 females in St. Petersburg and 133 in Moscow. It may be that these last two cities were more advanced industrially than was Odessa, and were therefore attracting young males in proportionately greater numbers to work in their factories. Still, a principal reason for the relatively large numbers of women was cultural rather than economic.[6] The Jewish population contained more women than men (sex ratio was ninety-eight). If the Jews are subtracted from the population of the city, then the sex ratio among gentiles in Odessa is 130, almost as high as Moscow's (133). The size of the Jewish community in Odessa, and the large numbers of women within it, thus helped tip the ratio for the city as a whole. Among the Russians men outnumbered women by 120 to 100; among the Ukrainians, males held an even greater preponderance—159 to 100. The predominance of males among Odessa's gentiles reflects the fact that many non-Jews were students, soldiers, convicts, and seasonal workers who were bachelors or had families elsewhere. The Jews, in contrast, when they immigrated, seem to have done so as entire families.[7] Their households, as we shall see, contained large numbers of children and were not lacking in females.

In Odessa, as elsewhere, girls entered the labor force, especially domestic service, at a very young age. Out of every 100 male workers in Odessa, only two were age fourteen and under. But nearly six girls of every 100 female workers were fourteen and under. The demand for domestics and seamstresses drew girls into the city when they were still quite young. Women began to work earlier and they worked longer than men, all the while for inferior pay. It is, however, interesting to note that among the Russian women, 33.33 percent were independently employed, as opposed to only 19 percent of the Jewish women. This seems to reflect the peculiar strength of the Jewish household in Odessa, which tended to retain its females and did not send them forth in large numbers to household service or to outside employment.

Sex ratios can also tell us something about the cultural life of the city. Although the number of French in Odessa was small (0.3 percent of the population), French women outnumbered males by nearly 164 to every 100 males. Those among them who were employed were nearly all governesses or teachers. The high literacy rates for Italian, American, English and German women, compared with males of the same nationalities, indicate that Odessa attracted many trained and plucky foreign women, who took up positions in the wealthy households and schools of the city. Finally, Odessa, like all large cities in the Russian Empire, attracted elderly women, many of them widows, some of them with means. For age sixty and older, the number of men per 100 women falls to only eighty-six. Females nearly equal males in number during childhood, fall well behind them during young adulthood, and dominate the ranks of the elderly. The relatively large numbers of women in Odessa and its attractiveness to the elderly testified to the elegance, amenities and cultural appeal of this southern seaport and summer resort, and served to stimulate the demand for theater, music, fashionable clothes, and luxury commodities.

The patterns of marriage observable in Odessa are also distinctive. Although women were present in somewhat larger numbers than in other towns, males showed no particular zeal to marry. Among the total population of males, only 45.36 percent were married in Odessa, below the 49.5 percent in St. Petersburg and substantially lower than the 57 percent found in Moscow. The most obvious explanation for this large proportion of bachelors in Odessa is the presence of a sizeable military garrison: 16 percent of the working male population were in the armed forces. Only 9 percent were so employed in St. Petersburg, and less than 5 percent in Moscow. Odessa was founded with a view to defending the imperial frontiers, and it remained an armed outpost in 1897.

Odessa also attracted many young men who were interested in pursuing careers in commerce or in the liberal professions. Intellectuals and dissidents also gathered there. Just as Novorossiia (New Russia) had traditionally been a haven for runaway serfs, prisoners, and the lawless, Odessa, its capital, drew émigrés from many societies. Unattached, impetuous males, living in crowded quarters, sought the many inns, pubs, and clubs for the exchange of stimulating ideas (as well as for the consumption of stimulating beverages). The University of Novorossiia, located in Odessa, and several scientific and learned societies also provided focal points for the exchange of ideas among both Slavs and Western Europeans. The active port and easy communications abroad added further to the intellectual vitality of the city.

With a social composition that included numerous, young, unattached males, and with a cosmopolitan cultural atmosphere and good contacts with the outside world, Odessa understandably became one of Russia's major centers of political activism. As early as 1821, the Greek secret society, the Hetaireia, was established in the city; it went on to plan the Greek national uprising against the Turks.[8] Bulgarian patriots (notably Vasil Aprilov) made the city a center in their efforts to raise Bulgarian national consciousness.[9] In 1861, a joint Polish and Ukrainian revolutionary committee set up its illegal headquarters in Odessa. From there it spun a conspiratorial network stretching to Kyiv, Warsaw, London, Paris and Genoa.[10] Jewish liberals, reformers and Zionists found Odessa hospitable to their movements.[11] Russian radicals also favored Odessa; the Independent Society functioned there, and several Decembrists were from the city.[12] The first labor union in Russia was formed in Odessa, although the city was not as industrialized as St. Petersburg or Moscow.[13] The Black Sea port was the major distribution point for Herzen's illegal paper, *Kolokol*, as well as the home of the most radical, legally printed paper, *Odesskii vestnik*. The rapid movement of men and goods through the port made censorship difficult—and the censors of Odessa had long enjoyed a reputation for corruption. Even the land frontier was difficult to patrol; contraband, whether in goods or ideas, slipped easily over the border. With reason, therefore, three-quarters of a century before the 1905 Revolution and the *Potemkin* mutiny, Nicholas I marked Odessa as "a nest of conspirators."[14]

In spite of the considerable numbers of single males, the average size of households was comparatively large at Odessa. The census does not give exact figures, so we must estimate average household size on the basis of aggregate information.[15] Although this limits the precision of the estimates, still the figures retain a comparative value. In Odessa, if we exclude convents, barracks, prisons, and other groups not based in the natural family, the average household size was 4.18 persons; the same figures, calculated by the same methods, are 4.01 for Moscow and only 3.78 for St. Petersburg.

Why were households larger in Odessa? We can only speculate about the answers. Single young men from distant areas were likely to lodge in the homes of relatives living there. The Jewish population in particular seems to have lived in large households, with members well balanced between the sexes and with relatively numerous children.[16] Perhaps, too, in this commercial city young men remained long in their households of origin, as they acquired the training and awaited the success, which allowed them to marry. Finally, the large average size of households may perhaps be an early sign of Odessa's slowing growth; perhaps its economy in 1897 was not buoyant enough to allow young people to marry at an early age and set up their own families. Large households tend to be the mark of a stagnating, rather than a growing economy.

The social divisions or *sosloviia* of the population further differentiated Odessa from the two northern capitals; in the latter, peasants formed the largest single class.[17] Since there was no category for industrial laborers, these workers appear in the census as "peasants" because they were recent emigrants from rural areas. The fact that Odessa had comparatively fewer "peasants" among its inhabitants does not imply, as one might think, a greater degree of industrialization, but the contrary. The inflated numbers of those classified as *meshchanin*—petty bourgeois—in Odessa, in comparison with the other two cities, indicate the vitality of trade and small crafts in the southern port and the large Jewish population.

ETHNIC COMPONENTS OF THE POPULATION

In surveying the various ethnic groups in Odessa, we shall begin with the largest—the Slavic-speaking peoples. Among the Slavs, the Russians predominated; they formed almost exactly one-half of the population (50.78 percent). The figure may, however, be inflated by a tendency on the part of many non-Russians to report Russian as their native language, and thus claim for themselves membership in the politically dominant group. In 1880, according to one observer, one-third of the family names in the city were Ukrainian, but in 1897, less than one out of ten inhabitants reported Ukrainian as their mother tongue.[18] Although the exact size of the Russian component in Odessa's population is questionable, still there can be no doubt that this was the largest single ethnic group in the urban population.

In terms of employment, more Russians living in Odessa in 1897 are found in "private work and service" than in any other occupation. This category, while it included some managers and employers, was largely made up of unskilled labor: servants, day laborers, and the like. The Russians so employed numbered 15,743 out of 75,983 males. The second largest occupational group of Russians (11,734) comprised those in the armed forces. In third place came the construction workers (5,824). Smaller, but still important groups of 2,000–3,000 Russians were engaged in the carrier trade (postmen, carters, and the like); the processing of food; carpentry and wood products; and the clothing industries. All these last occupations conferred relatively low status in the social hierarchy. But Russians were also well represented among those in government service (2,224); men who lived from stocks and savings (2,616); and those supported by land rents (1,954). These occupations conferred relatively high prestige. In sum, the Russians fill the lowest and the highest ranks of Odessa's society, but are singularly absent on the middle levels of the social pyramid, where most shopkeepers and small manufacturers are found.

This distinctive distribution of Russians in Odessa's society partially reflects the pattern of Russian immigration into Novorossiia. The opening of this new territory had attracted land speculators, developers, and some nobles who were anxious to duplicate on the southern steppes the manner of life they had known in the central regions. In Gogol's *Dead Souls*, P. I. Chichikov purchased his "souls" ostensibly to settle them on land in Novorossiia; the government, he explained, granted free land to those who brought the labor to work it.[19] In real life, Mikhail Vorontsov, governor-general of the region in the 1820s, transferred some of his peasants—live ones—from his less productive estates in central Russia to the new land. His palace in Odessa, although damaged by fire, is still one of the great monuments of the city. Besides opportunities in agriculture, the growth of governmental bureaucracy also attracted Russians. On the other end of the social scale, the work available in the booming port and the nascent industries drew large numbers of unskilled, often illiterate workers.

The social position of Russians in Odessa was a microcosm of their status in the empire as a whole. They dominated the landholding aristocracy and the government service, and they also helped fill the lowest social orders; but they contributed relatively few members to Odessa's middle class.

The census of 1897 allows us to investigate, although indirectly, the fertility and the natural increase of the various components of Odessa's population. We can calculate ratios between the numbers of young children in the population and women of childbearing age. These child–woman ratios indirectly reflect both the fertility of women and the survival of their offspring, and give us a rough but usable way of measuring the comparative success of the various ethnic groups in rearing children. The age categories utilized in the census require that we consider women between twenty and thirty-nine as representative of all women able to bear children. In Table 2 in the appendix, we have calculated ratios between women in that age category with babies less than one year of age, and then with children from one year to nine years inclusively.

Russian women were considerably more prolific than Ukrainian, Polish, and German females. For every 100 babies born to the Russian women and surviving up to age one, there were eighty-seven Ukrainian, seventy-three Polish, and sixty-four German babies born and surviving.[20] One factor here was the large number of unmarried, employed women among these last groups. German women, for example, frequently served as teachers and governesses, and many doubtlessly returned home to marry. Then, too, with the exception of the Germans, these last groups were generally on a lower socioeconomic level than the Russians, and this apparently affected the size of their families. On the other hand, Russian women were distinctly less fertile than Jewish wives; for every 100 babies born and surviving in Russian families, there were 127 Jewish babies. We shall presently examine some of the reasons for this remarkable contrast.

Ukrainians formed another large group of Slavic speakers in Odessa. Although Odessa is located in Ukraine, only 9.39 percent of its population was registered as Ukrainians in the city and suburbs. In the city alone, only 5.66 percent reported Ukrainian as their mother tongue. These percentages, as we have seen, may well be too low, but the Ukrainian component at Odessa is still surprisingly small. In founding Odessa, the Russian government deliberately encouraged Russians to move to the area with their serfs, and it invited foreign settlers; but it did not actively recruit Ukrainians. The Ukrainians who immigrated to Odessa were predominantly poor, male, and unmarried. Very few were rentiers of any sort. Of the 11,172 Ukrainian men living in Odessa, only 224 were supported from interest on savings or stocks, and only 100 from land rents. In the first quarter of the nineteenth century, we know of at least two extremely wealthy Ukrainian capitalists—Lakhnenko and Symyrenko—but they were exceptions.[21]

More Ukrainians were in the military than in any other occupational category. About 14 percent of the males were to be found in the local quarries and mines. (Only 1.5 percent of Russian males were miners). Among Ukrainians, 12 percent were in manufacturing on a small scale and about 8 percent were in transport. The Ukrainian carter, the *chumak,* had long been a familiar sight on the roads to Odessa, carting grain from the hinterland to the port. By 1897, the railroad had largely supplanted the ox-drawn wagon, but Ukrainians continued to work on the still important river barges.

Few Ukrainian women came to Odessa (the sex ratio among Ukrainians was 159), and they appear with comparatively few babies in the census. Moreover, rates of child mortality must have been high among them.[22] All these characteristics seem to be linked with their low socioeconomic status.

Among the Slavic groups in Odessa, there were some 1,100 Belarusians in the city, exclusive of its suburbs, and a few Serbs, Slovenes, Bulgarians, and Czechs. The other sizable Slavic group was the Poles, who numbered about 17,000 in the city itself. In their socioeconomic position and their demographic characteristics, they resemble both the Russians and the Ukrainians. They included relatively more rentiers than the Ukrainians (259 Poles supported themselves from land rents and another 335 from interest and dividends), and some Poles appear in the relatively skilled occupations of tailor, metalworker, and even medical doctor. But many Poles were also employed in low-level occupations. A large proportion (4,144) were soldiers. The second largest group (1,490) were day laborers and servants. The high sex ratio (191) and low child–woman ratios among the Poles would indicate a population predominantly composed of the poor.

After the Slavs, the second major component of Odessa's population were the Jews. Most of Odessa's Jews were Russian subjects, although there was a group of foreign Jews as well, chiefly from Austria. Subject to various civil disabilities, the Jews were frequently regarded as foreigners, but they were in fact among the earliest settlers of the region. Jews were probably already in the area when the Russian state acquired the small Turkish fort that became the site of Odessa.[23] The city possessed a Jewish cemetery soon after its founding in 1794.[24] Catherine II, while hardly partial toward the Jews, encouraged their settlement in Novorossiia.[25] Alexander I, in the first quarter of the nineteenth century, tried to establish colonies of Jewish cultivators on the virgin lands of the region.[26]

The hardships of rural life on this new frontier led many colonists to give up farming in order to settle in the growing city of Odessa. Other Jews streamed to the city from the formerly Polish provinces and from Galicia. By 1828, according to the city's newspaper, the population of Odessa, which then numbered 32,995, contained 4,226 Jews—12.81 percent of the total.[27] According to the same newspaper, a new Jewish school had been founded in 1827; within it, some 200 pupils were learning Hebrew, Russian, and German.[28] By 1844, Jews made up some 33 percent of the guild membership of the city, although still comprising a much smaller proportion of the population.[29] In 1856, when they formed 10.3 percent of the urban population, Jews made up 46 percent of the guild membership. The American consul reported in 1856 that Odessa contained three synagogues (one of which served Karaite Jews) and 36 Jewish houses of prayer.[30]

In 1843, in one of its sporadic antisemitic campaigns, the Russian government sought to restrict the activities of foreign Jews in the empire. The then governor-general of Novorossiia, Prince Vorontsov, petitioned the authorities in St. Petersburg to exempt his region from the new regulations. He argued that many of the bankers in Odessa were Austrian Jews whose departure would disrupt the business of the city.[31]

The size and economic importance of Odessa's Jewish community continued to grow after the Crimean War and during the period of the Great Reforms. Several Greek firms departed the city, and Jewish merchants took their place as shippers and bankers. Although the cereals of southern Ukraine faced increasing competition on world markets, still the export retained importance, and the Jews were coming to play an ever-larger role in it.[32] Conversant with the ways of the Russian peasant and landlord, well-informed in foreign commercial practices, the Jews provided a vital link between native suppliers and foreign consumers of Russian wheat. Some observers ascribed the success of Jewish merchants to their alert use of the telegraph to ascertain European grain prices, and others, more simply, to their invaluable "universal connections."[33]

The '60s and '70s of the nineteenth century represented almost a golden age for Odessa's Jews. As one visitor remarked: "Judaism held up its head as it never dared to do in Moscow or

St. Petersburg." The same commentator further noted the handsome synagogues, the participation of Jews in municipal management, and their contribution toward the social life and the culture of the city. So satisfied were the Jews with their condition, he affirmed, that few ever converted to Christianity.[34]

In 1863, the French consul reported that Jews were free to follow professions and some became bourgeois notables. They could hold office, and, in his words, were liberated from the "moral ghetto" in which they were confined elsewhere in the empire.[35] To be sure, in the same year, the British consul related the incident of a Jewish banker who aspired to election to the Club of Notables but was rebuffed in his efforts. It is significant, however, that he tried, and significant, too, that the British consul noted "general public indignation" in the city over his humiliation.[36]

From the late 1870s, the status of Jews in Odessa entered a period of slow deterioration. The Ignatiev or May Laws of 1882 and the crop failures of the early 1890s injured both the social position and the economic status of Odessa's Jews.[37] Mounting discrimination and poor economic times prompted many Jews to emigrate to Germany and the United States. The hostile attitude of Alexander III and his antisemitic ministers, and the pogroms which darkened the epoch further promoted emigration. On the other hand, the Russian government never officially encouraged the exodus of Jews. In fact, Russian law did not even recognize a right of emigration.[38]

Odessa was not spared the social disorders of the period. In 1884, Prince Demidoff (or Demidov) San Donato sought to explain the deepening hostility toward the Jews and the acts of destruction against their property perpetrated in Odessa, Kyiv and Rostov-on-the-Don; he affirmed that "a considerable portion of the population of these towns consists of trading and industrial classes inimically disposed toward the Jews, for there is very dangerous rivalry in almost every branch of trade and industry."[39] The frugality, sobriety, energy, and, above all, the success of the Jews aroused animosity among their competitors. The discriminatory laws of the empire further imparted the belief that the Jews were somehow foreign and disloyal, and this in turn invited further persecution. Odessa in particular was "distinguished for its turbulent instincts and for its readiness to manifest them in some form or other." The restless, rootless, mateless men of Odessa were not only potential revolutionaries, but could also turn into hoodlums when moved by fear, frustration, or greed.

According to the census of 1897, Jews remained chiefly traders and shopkeepers. Of the ten occupations in which most of their numbers were enrolled, four categories involved some kind of trade (in agricultural products, grain, clothes, and general trade), and a fifth included middlemen or brokers. Jews were not, on the other hand, numerous in industry. Only in the manufacture of metal and wood products are there any significant numbers. Over 5,000 males (out of 37,000) were engaged in the making of clothes. Clearly, these were tailors rather than industrial workers. Another 3,000 men were employed as servants and day laborers, and slightly more than 1,500 served in the armed forces. Unlike any of the ethnic groups we have so far considered, the Jews belonged preeminently to the middle classes of society.

In many respects the Jews seem to have been the most stable component of Odessa's population. The sex ratio among them is nearly normal (ninety-eight men per 100 women), and the Jewish household appears to have been large and cohesive. Jews were also the fastest growing major group in the city. In 1873, members of the Jewish faith constituted 26.55 percent of Odessa's population. By 1892, the portion had grown to 32.96 percent; by 1897, it rose further to 34.41 percent. Concurrently, the Orthodox population at Odessa declined from 64.79 percent in 1873 to 57.46 percent in 1892. It reached a new low of 55.93 percent in 1897. Despite all the efforts of Alexander III to promote Russification and Orthodoxy, Odessa was rapidly becoming a predominantly Jewish city. While this indicates that conditions were still favorable for Jews in Odessa, it doubtlessly also contributed to the antagonism of many gentiles toward them.

The growth of Odessa's Jewish community was partially due to continuing immigration, but also to high fertility among Jewish women and comparatively low death rates among their children. Table 2 in the appendix shows that Jewish women of childbearing age appear in the census with considerably more babies under age one than do the women of any other of the groups surveyed. If we compare the Jewish women with the number of older children, age one to nine, in the census, then the number of Jewish children increases in relation to two groups, the Ukrainians and the Poles, while remaining stable in relation to the Russians. This suggests that child mortality was particularly high among the Poles and Ukrainians, who included, as we have stated, many disadvantaged members of urban society.

Not all the Jews of Odessa were wealthy, and this high rate of survival was not entirely a reflection of affluence. Stable family life and the traditional care of Jewish mothers for their children doubtlessly also contributed. The Jewish family and child benefited from both material and cultural resources.

Mortality rates for the Jews had been lower than those for the general population well before 1897. In a survey conducted in the 1860s, the redactors noted that the mortality rate among Jews was distinctly low.[40] A book commemorating the centennial of the city specified the advantage in 1895: from the ages of six to fifteen, only five Jewish children died per 1,000, whereas nine non-Jewish children perished. The authors concluded that the Jewish population in Odessa was growing at the rate of 36.4 per 1,000, while the gentile population was increasing at the rate of only 21.4 per 1,000.[41] Well before the census of 1897, contemporaries were aware of the remarkable increase of the Jewish communities. A study of the census itself revealed that in the southern Ukraine, the population grew between 1881 and 1897 by 37.8 percent, but the Jews had increased their numbers by 60.9 percent.[42] This enormous growth was the combined result of immigration, high fertility, and low mortality.

In the years immediately preceding the First World War, many Jews emigrated from Odessa and its hinterland. According to the Jewish Statistical Society, by 1904, the percentage of Jews in Odessa had dropped from 35 to 30.5 percent of the total urban population.[43] But many remained. An American reporter who visited Odessa in the first decade of the twentieth century wrote, "all the wealthy classes are Jews." He gives us this remarkable description of their status:

> There are more than 200,000 Jews in Odessa—exceeding one-third of the entire population—and, as everywhere else, they control the banking, the manufacturing, the export

trade, the milling, the wholesale and retail mercantile and commercial enterprises. And, naturally, they are hated by the Russians and envied for their success and prosperity. The prejudice against the Jewish population elsewhere as well as here is due to economic rather than religious reasons—simply because they are getting richer and more prosperous, while the Russians are losing ground in all the occupations and professions. They have wasted their capital in bad investments and dissipations and extravagance, and are forced to mortgage their property to the Jews to keep up appearances. In the meantime the Jews have been securing control of all the profitable enterprises and lines of business in Odessa. Their sons show the same earnestness and zeal in the university that they show in the counting-room. Therefore, they make the best doctors and lawyers and engineers, and their services are in demand, while the Russian members of the profession are all idly waiting for business.[44]

Jews fared well, but also suffered in Odessa. Shortly after World War I, Isaac Babel', one of the city's most accomplished writers, expressed these ambivalent feelings about Odessa, which both nurtured Jews and rejected them: "Odessa is an awful place. Everyone knows how they murder the Russian language there. All the same, I think there's a lot to be said for this great city, which has more charm than any other in the Russian Empire."[45]

Much fewer than the Jews, but no less intimately connected with Odessa's commercial development, were the Greeks. For centuries—or millennia—Greeks had sailed the waters of the Black Sea. Well before the time of Christ, they had traded for grain from the Pontine steppes.[46] After the Russian conquest of the area, many Greek firms established agencies on the shores of the Sea of Azov and on the western littoral of the Black Sea. Only three years after the founding of Odessa, twenty-five Greek merchants arrived with their families.[47] Many came from the island of Chios. In 1798, at least twenty-one more Greek merchants settled in the city, some of them with substantial capital. Famous mercantile names, such as the Mavrokordato, appear in Odessa's records. In 1824, an English traveler wrote that among the many foreigners in Odessa, the Greeks were the most numerous.[48]

Among the most prominent commercial firms were the Ralli brothers and the Rodokanaki Company. In 1846, Theodore Rodokanaki was the leading merchant of Odessa. The monetary worth of his transactions totaled three or four million rubles—at least one million more than his closest competitor handled. His commercial operations alone constituted about 10 percent of the total trade of Odessa for that year.[49]

Members of the Rodokanaki family were already well established in the principal Mediterranean ports before coming to the Russian Empire. By the end of the eighteenth century, Michael Rodokanaki was a prosperous merchant in Livorno, which seems to have served as the center of the family's commercial network.[50] This network of family support enabled the individual branches to survive even in the face of local disasters. The embargo on Russian grain exports during the Crimean War severely taxed the operations of Theodore Rodokanaki in Odessa, but simultaneously his brother George, from his base in Livorno, was importing grain from the Danubian ports of Galați and Braila. One man's woe was another man's profit, but both men were members of the same family enterprise.

The Ralli Brothers Company similarly maintained partners or agents in many ports, not only across the Mediterranean Sea but also over the world. They traded in Livorno, New York, London, Calcutta, and Odessa, as well as other cities.[51] Their London headquarters operated until 1961. John Ralli, the company's founder in Odessa, was also the first American consul there, serving until his death in 1860.[52] By the end of the century, Odessa's Ralli family had intermarried with Russians, so that they no longer appear in the 1897 census among the foreign population.

Indeed, by 1897, native-speaking Greeks represented only 1.3 percent of Odessa's population, and even this represented a decline from the 1.6 percent registered only five years earlier.[53] Although few in number, the Greeks in Odessa were found in almost all occupations. The majority of them, however, were connected with trade. The next largest group worked in the processing of food and animal products and in the manufacture of clothes. Some of the Greek residents of Odessa in 1897 were wealthy: more than 100 of their small group lived from interest and dividends. But many Greeks were in Odessa only temporarily—a fact that seems reflected in the small number of Greek women. Only 58.6 Greek women could be found in Odessa for every 100 males. Clearly, when the young Greek merchant achieved success, he returned home to marry.

Among the more exotic residents of Odessa were the Tatars, who numbered 1,835 in 1897. More than 300 were serving in the military, and about 100 worked in making foods of various types—macaroni, coffee, oil, baked goods, flour, and the like. A substantial number of Tatars appear in the ranks of unskilled laborers and domestics, and some were traders on a small scale. Among the Tatars, men outnumbered women by more than 2.5 to 1; males came to the city to work primarily in unskilled trades, and those who wished to marry usually returned home.

Many nationalities of Western Europe are represented in Odessa in the census of 1897, but none of them in great numbers. The French early recognized the commercial importance of the new port and of the cereal export, which soon flowed through it. Even before the foundation of Odessa, French merchants were trading in Kherson, and they were among the first participants in Odessa's early growth. Antoine de Saint-Joseph Anthoine and Charles Sicard, both merchants, have given us two of the oldest and best depictions of the city.[54]

Newspapers in the French language—the short-lived *Troubadour d'Odessa* and the *Messager*—were the first to be published in Odessa; the long-surviving *Journal d'Odessa*, which first appeared in 1824, had a Russian counterpart only from 1827.[55] The Duc de Richelieu, an émigré who served as the first governor-general of Novorossiia from 1803 until 1814, laid out the large boulevards, regular streets, trees, parks, and public buildings which made Odessa so attractive.[56] His successor, another Frenchman, Count Langeron, who served from 1814 to 1822, did not acquire the same brilliant reputation, but added further to the French influence on the city. French immigrants came to Odessa in small but not insignificant numbers. They occupied themselves in viticulture, small manufactures such as soapmaking, and in the wool industry (the duke introduced Merino sheep to the steppe). In 1858, at least thirty French families belonged to the second and third guilds of Odessa.[57] French influence on the city's culture was manifest. The theater was called the Palais Royal, and the plays performed there were often in French. The language was commonly spoken in the elegant clubs and salons of the city. By 1869, the balls given by the French Benevolent Society were among the social highlights of the season.[58]

French technical assistance was also of considerable importance in the growth and design of the city. The dirt streets of Odessa seemed always covered with mud or dust, depending on the season, and French engineers designed projects for paving them.[59] The building of the railroad in southern Ukraine brought a wave of engineers and construction workers. Substantial French and Belgian investments in the 1890s in the economy of southern Ukraine led to a renewed influx of Gallic visitors.[60]

Still, the French population of Odessa remained largely transient. In 1897, there were only 319 employed Frenchmen in the city. Most of them worked in the metal-processing industry. The high esteem accorded French culture is, however, evident in the numerous governesses—some 208 among the 383 working Frenchwomen in the city. Frenchmen came and departed, but their influence abided.

The same judgment would apply to the Italians in Odessa. In 1897, there were only 286 working Italian males in the city. Most were merchants dealing primarily in luxury commodities, or skilled artisans such as, for example, ceramists. Italians were also prominent as proprietors of hotels and restaurants. Like the Greeks, the Italians had first come to the city as merchants trading in grain and in other agricultural commodities, but they had abandoned such interests by the end of the century. While Italy itself remained a principal consumer of Russian wheat, the large commercial firms in Odessa were no longer Italian.[61]

Italian culture exerted a continuing influence on the city. The Italian language was the commercial lingua franca of the region. Street signs were given originally in both Italian and Russian, and notarial documents were redacted in Italian, as were passports, lists of current grain prices, and even theater notices.[62] The first publication by a local press was a sonnet in Italian. The architectural style of the growing city showed many Italian influences. Most operatic productions were of Italian works. On hearing Rossini's *Barber of Seville* and other works by Italian masters, Pushkin proclaimed them to be "representatives of heavenly paradise."[63] Even the great hero of the Italian *Risorgimento*, Giuseppe Garibaldi, lived briefly in Odessa.[64] And Odessa was involved, although in a minimal degree, in the growing hostility that Italians felt against Austria. Tuscan merchants vociferously complained that the Austrian consul, who supposedly represented their interests in Odessa, was more concerned with developing the rival Austrian port of Trieste than their own Livorno.[65]

The style of the city, its distinctive combination of climate, culture, and cuisine, prompted one visitor to remark in 1835, "I was almost tempted to believe that, by some hocus-pocus, we had tumbled on an Italian town.... There was little or nothing Russian about it. Its inhabitants were chiefly Italian or Greek, with a sprinkling of French, German and English."[66]

If Odessa impressed some visitors by its old-world charm, it appeared to Samuel Clemens (Mark Twain) as almost an American city:

> I have not felt so much at home for a long time as I did when I "raised the hill" and stood in Odessa for the first time. It looked just like an American city; fine, broad streets, and straight as well; low houses (two or three stories), wide, neat, and free from any quaintness

of architectural ornamentation; locust trees bordering the sidewalks (they call them acacias); a stirring business-look among the streets and stores; fast walkers, a familiar *new* look about the houses and everything; Look up the street or down the street, this way or that way, we saw only America. There was not one thing to remind us that we were in Russia. We walked for some little distance, reveling in this home vision, and then we came upon a church and a hack-driver, and presto: the illusion vanished![67]

If Odessa looked like an American city to Mark Twain, it never contained many Americans—or Englishmen either. The American government had an early interest in the city, and appointed a permanent consul as early as 1832. But the two countries sold to the world many of the same products, and a vigorous trade never developed between them. An American traveling to Odessa in the 1830s was amazed to find an émigré from Philadelphia, General Sontag, who had lived in Odessa twenty years. He married a Russian noblewoman, raised grain on a vast estate outside the city, and had adapted well to his new environment. His daughter played "Hail, Columbia!" and "Yankee Doodle" on the piano for the visitor.[68] But the 1897 census tells us that there were only thirty-six American citizens living in Odessa. We cannot determine what they were doing there, as they are treated with Englishmen in a single category in regard to occupations.

The English themselves maintained close diplomatic and commercial ties with Odessa, but sent few immigrants. The British consuls at Odessa regularly filed informative reports at the Foreign Office, and English firms were among the principal purchasers of Russian grain.[69] More numerous and more diverse were the German speakers of Odessa.[70] Many retained their foreign citizenship; in 1897, some 3,435 were citizens of Austria and 2,790 of the German Empire. But German-speaking subjects of the tsar were also numerous. From the time of Catherine II German colonists had come to Novorossiia, chiefly as farmers, although some drifted to the city. Among the German speakers in 1897, there were substantial numbers of rentiers—perhaps retired peasants—and many skilled workers in metal products, food processing, carpentry and in the making of clothes. But the German contribution to the development of the region seems to have been more in agriculture than in the urban trades.

We shall not examine the still smaller ethnic groups—Armenians, Turks, Georgians and so forth—even though their presence added further to the cosmopolitan flavor of the city. And we must recognize that our analysis is incomplete for other reasons. While we have said something about the composition and characteristics of the separate ethnic groups, we have not considered, and cannot here consider, how these groups interacted, clashed, and cooperated, and how they formed a living city. We hope to do this in the future. Odessa, remarkable for its nineteenth-century expansion, remarkable, too, for the many cultural communities that contributed to it, eminently deserves much further study

APPENDIX

The following tables are based on data from the city alone, exclusive of its suburbs.

Table 1 The Ten Largest Groups by Native Language in the City of Odessa, 1897

Language	Males	Females	Total	Percentage Total Pop.
1. Russian	104,172	89,081	193,253	50.78
2. Yiddish	61,156	62,530	123,686	32.50
3. Ukrainian	13,224	8,302	21,526	5.66
4. Polish	11,174	5,864	17,038	4.48
5. German	5,253	4,680	9,933	2.61
6. Greek	3,166	1,847	5,013	1.32
7. Tatar	970	459	1,429	0.38
8. Armenian	929	470	1,399	0.37
9. French	423	701	1,124	0.30
10. Belorussian	799	296	1,095	0.29

Source: *Pervaia vseobshchaia perepis'... 1897 g.*, vol. 47.

Table 2 Women and Children in the City of Odessa, 1897

	Russians	Ukrainians	Poles	Jews	Germans
Infants, to One Year	4,246	364	245	3,466	142
Children, Age 1–9	30,715	2,376	1,382	25,398	1,160
Women, Age 20–39	31,811	3,146	2,514	20,548	1,868
Ratios:	Russians	Ukrainians	Poles	Jews	Germans
Infants/100 Women	13.35	11.57	9.75	16.87	7.60
Index (Jews = 100)	79	69	58	100	45
Children/100 Women	96.56	75.52	54.97	124.33	62.10
Index (Jews = 100)	78	61	44	100	50

Source: *Pervaia vseobshchaia perepis'... 1897 g.*, vol. 47.

Notes

1 For a bibliography on the history and growth of Odessa in the nineteenth century, see Patricia Herlihy, "Odessa: Staple Trade and Urbanization in New Russia," *Jahrbücher für Geschichte Osteuropas* 21 (1973): 184n3. I would like to thank Dr. Barbara A. Anderson for the opportunity of reading her PhD dissertation, "Internal Migration in a Modernizing Society: The Case of Late Nineteenth-Century European Russia" (Princeton University, 1973).

2 *Pervaia vseobshchaia perepis' naseleniia Rossiiskoi imperii, 1897 g*, 80 vols. in 24 (St. Petersburg: Tsentral'nyi statisticheskii komitet Ministerstva vnutrennikh del 1899–1905). The data for Odessa appear in vol. 47; for St. Petersburg, in vol. 37; for Moscow, in vol. 24. For a brief history of the census and a critical evaluation of the results, see P. I. Pustokhod and V. K. Voblyi, *Perepisi naseleniia* (Moscow and Leningrad: Gos. Sots.-ekon. izd-vo, 1940), 97–98 and B. Ts. Urlanis, *Rost naseleniia v SSSR* (Moscow: Nauka, 1966), 17. For additional and more lengthy criticisms of "the first and last census of Tsarist Russia," with a bibliography and résumés in French and English, see A. I. Gozulov, *Perepisi naseleniia SSSR i kapitalisticheskikh stran* (Moscow: Redaktsionno-izdatel'skogo upr. TsUNKhU, 1936), 185–221.

3 For the populations in 1856 of Odessa (101,302 persons), St. Petersburg (490,808), and Moscow (368,765), *Statistische Tabelle des russischen Reiches für das Jahr 1856 in ihren allgemeinen Resultaten zusammengestellt und heraus gegeben auf Anordnung des kaiserlich-russischen Ministeriums des Innern durch das statistische Central-Comité*, ed. E. Olberg (Berlin: E. S. Miller und Sohn, 1859), 113.

4 An American reporter wrote in 1910 that Odessa's population was 520,000, "but there has been a steady decrease during the last five years, which is due to the rivalry of other ports which are attracting trade because of better harbours, better railway connections and better facilities for doing business. The strong and violent socialist element in Odessa has also injured the city by frightening away capital and preventing the establishment of manufacturing industries because of the fear of labour strikes." He also suggested that the tsar was deliberately fostering Mykolaiv to favor his friends and harm the Jewish capitalists in Odessa. See William E. Curtis, *Around the Black Sea* (New York: Hodder and Stoughton, 1911), 327–28, 336–38.

5 We are cautioned by the Jewish Statistical Society in Russia to count Jews on the basis of religion rather than language: *Evreiskoe naselenie Rossii po dannym perepisi 1897 g. i po noveishim istochnikam* (Petrograd: Kadima, 1917), iii. The same group, using the figures for religion and for the city with suburbs, concluded that the Jewish population for Odessa in 1897 was 35 percent of the total: Ibid., 72.

6 The sex ratios of persons in the population age twenty to twenty-nine were 177 men per 100 women in Odessa, 156 in St. Petersburg, and 167 in Moscow. This indicates that Odessa was attracting young male adults as much as these last two cities.

7 Although Jewish immigration into Odessa was substantial, the population does not show the bulge of males in the young adult years characteristic of other ethnic groups. Among Jews, the sex ratio of those aged twenty to twenty-nine was ninety-nine men per 100 women. Clearly, Jewish men did not immigrate unaccompanied by women. The cohesiveness of the Jewish family is also shown in the illegitimacy rates (0.1 percent of all births among the Jews, and 11.9 percent, more than ten times greater, among the Orthodox). See *The Jewish Encyclopedia* (New York and London: Funk and Wagnalls Company, 1905), s.v. "Odessa," citing rates for 1902.

8 G. L. Arsh, *Eteristskoe dvizhenie v Rossii: Osvoboditel'naia bor'ba grecheskogo naroda v nachale XIX v. i russko-grecheskie sviazi* (Moscow: Nauka, 1970).

9 On the life and activities of Aprilov and other Bulgarian patriots at Odessa, see Nikolai Genchev, "Odeskoto Bulgarsko nastoiatel'stvo," *Godishnik na Sofiiskiia universitet, Filosofsko-istoricheski fakultet*, vol. 64, bk. 3 (Sofia: Nauka i izkustvo, 1972); G. A. Kashirin and V. S. Alekseev-Popov, "K voprosu o roli Odessy v istorii sviazei russkogo i bolgarskogo narodov: Obzor pechatnykh istochnikov, khraniashchikhsia v fondakh Odesskoi

gosudarstvennoi nauchnoi biblioteki imeni A. M. Gor'kogo," *Izvestiia na narodnata biblioteka i bibliotekata na Sofiiskiia derzhaven universitet*, vol. 3 (9) (Sofia, 1963); M. Arnaudov, *Vasil El'statiel' Aprilol': Zhifotu, deinost', suvremennitsi 1789–1847* (Sofia: Durzhavna pechatnitsa, 1971).

10   B. S. Itenberg, *Iuzhnorossiiskii soiuz rabochikh* (Moscow: Gos. izd-vo polit. lit-ry, 1974), 40–41.

11   For Jews in Odessa, see especially I. I. Lerner, *Evrei v Novorossiiskom krae* (Odessa: I. M. Levenson, 1901). The article, "Odessa," in *Encyclopaedia Judaica* (New York: Keter Publishing House, 1971) reviews social and intellectual movements among Odessa's Jews.

12   S. la. Borovoi, "*Kolokol* i obshchestvenno-politicheskaia zhizn' Odessy v gody pervoi revoliutsionnoi situatsii," in *Revoliutsionnaia situatsiia v Rossii v 1859–1861 gg.* (Moscow: Nauka, 1974), 195.

13   Itenberg, *Soiuz rabochikh*, 31ff.

14   Quoted by Borovoi, "*Kolokol*," 195. Borovoi also attributes a "revolutionary tradition" to Odessa. A visiting Englishman observed in the 1820s that Odessa was the seat of Polish agitation: "Odessa was one of the chief seats of the conspiracy against Russia, and is viewed with proportionate suspicion by the government" (James Webster, *Travels through the Crimea, Turkey and Egypt*, 2 vols. [London: H. Colburn and R. Bentley, 1830], 1:42). Webster claimed that despite governmental suspicion, "There is, perhaps, more political freedom enjoyed in this town [Odessa] than in any other of the empire. This probably arises from the high and liberal character of Count Woronzow [Vorontsov], the present Governor-General of New Russia," *Travels* 2:342. A quarter of a century later, another Englishman repeated the assertion: "There is a great deal more liberty enjoyed by the inhabitants than by those of any other town in the empire," Laurence Oliphant, *The Russian Shores of the Black Sea in the Autumn of 1852* (New York: Redfield, 1854), 234.

15   Households *(khoziaistva)* are grouped in the census according to the following number of persons: two, three, four, five, six to ten, and more than ten. It should be noted that these household figures include only the head of household and his relatives, not lodgers or servants. Without the complete, ungrouped distribution, it is impossible to calculate precisely the average household size. I estimated the average by adding to the distribution the number of one-person units (not regarded as households by the census takers) and by assuming an average size of eight for all households in the category six through ten, and an average size of eleven for those in the category of more than ten.

16   The census gives no direct information on family size for the various ethnic groups. It does, however, list according to ethnic groups those employed in some occupation, whom it calls "independent," and those "members of the family" who were economically dependent on them. The ratio of dependents to employed workers would thus reflect family size (of course, a single family could well have more than one member employed). For the city of Odessa as a whole, there are 146,064 independent men and 51,546 independent women, or a total of 197,610 persons. Again for the city proper, the male "members of the family" number 58,713, and the female 124,218, for a total of 182,931. The ratio of dependents to employed is therefore 0.93. Among the Jews, considered separately, there are 37,054 independent men and 11,970 independent women; and 24,102 and 50,560 male and female family members, respectively. Among the Jews, the ratio of dependents to employed is 1.52—more than a third greater than that found in the entire urban population. Although we cannot convert these ratios into exact estimates of family size, it is manifest that the Jews were supporting numerous dependents in their households. For further comment, see below, 65ff.

17   In the census of 1897, the population was classified by class according to the following categories: (1) hereditary nobles and their families; (2) personal nobles, officials, and their families; (3) clergy and their families; (4) personal and honorary citizens and their families; (5) merchants and their families; (6) petty bourgeois; (7) peasants; (8) military Cossacks; (9) aliens; (10) native Finns without class; (11) persons not belonging to the above classes; (12) persons of unspecified class.

18. V. Zagoruiko, *Po stranitsam istorii Odessy i Odesshchiny*, 2 vols. (Odessa: Odesskoe oblastnoe izdatel'stvo, 1957–60), 2:42. Zagoruiko cites a book by a Dr. Pantiukhov, published in 1885, in which the author noted that one-third of Odessa's population bore Ukrainian names; one-third, Russian, Polish, Armenian, and Greek names; and one-third, Jewish and other names. Zagoruiko believed that the Ukrainians made up a large portion of the population, but he did not venture to say that they formed the major part.
19. Nikolai Gogol, *Dead Souls* (London: J. M. Dent and Sons, 1931), 132, 199.
20. These figures are comparative indexes of the child–woman ratios, which result when the figure for the Russian babies and women is set equal to 100. The data on which this calculation is based are given in Table 2.
21. Zagoruiko, *Po stranitsam*, 2:36. Zagoruiko notes that there were many large landlords in the southern Ukraine, but few made their homes in Odessa. See also Ibid., 1:73. There were sufficient Ukrainians in the city, however, to patronize plays given in Ukrainian; see Ibid., 2: 123.
22. See below, 20, and Table 2 in the Appendix.
23. For the early arrival of Jews in Odessa, s.v. "Odessa," in *Jewish Encyclopedia*.
24. *The Jewish Encyclopedia*, s.v. "Odessa."
25. N. D. Polons'ka-Vasylenko, *The Settlement of the Southern Ukraine (1750–1775)*, vols. 4–5 (New York: Ukrainian Academy of Arts and Sciences in the US, 1955), 263.
26. S. Ia. Borovoi, *Evreiskaia zemledel'cheskaia kolonizatsiia v staroi Rossii* (Moscow: Izd. M. i S. Sabashnikovykh, 1928), 43ff.
27. *Journal d'Odessa*, October 6/18, 1828.
28. *Journal d'Odessa*, July 20/August 1, 1827.
29. A. A. Skal'kovskii, *Population commerciale d'Odessa* (Odessa: Gorodskaia tipografiia, 1845), 4.
30. National Archives, Washington, DC (hereafter NA), Dispatches from US Consuls in Odessa, April 12, 1856.
31. Archives du Ministère des Affaires Étrangères, Paris (hereafter AMAE), Odessa, vol. 6, fol. 344, December 14, 1843.
32. Public Record Office, London (hereafter PRO), FO 65, vol. 647, February 23, 1863. See also *Encyclopedia Hebraica* (Jerusalem and Tel Aviv: Encyclopaedia Publishing Co., 1949), s.v. "Odessa," in Hebrew, translated for the author by Professor Richard A. Webster of the University of California.
33. PRO, FO 65, vol. 647, February 4, 1863.
34. Harold Frederic, *The New Exodus: A Study of Israel in Russia* (New York: W. Heinemann, 1892), 255.
35. AMAE, Odessa, vol. 9, January 4, 1863.
36. PRO, FO 65, vol. 647, February 23, 1863.
37. The May Laws were designed to evict Jews from rural areas where they had gone from overcrowded cities and towns. See I. M. Rubinow, *Economic Condition of the Jews in Russia* (Washington, DC: Bulletin of the Bureau of Labor, US Department of Commerce and Labor, September 1908), 492.
38. Hans Rogger, "Tsarist Policy on Jewish Emigration," *Soviet Jewish Affairs* 3, no. 1 (1973): 26. For an example of this policy in practice, see NA, Odessa, December 8, 1880. A Jewish boy of fourteen who had left Odessa as a baby, became an American citizen, and could no longer remember Russian, was seized and put into the army in Odessa on his return there, on the basis that he had no right to emigrate.
39. For this and the following quotation, see Prince Demidoff San Donato, *The Jewish Question in Russia* (London: Darling and Son, 1884), 98.
40. Mark I. Finkel', "Issledovanie," 181–82.
41. *Odessa 1794–1894* (Odessa: Izdaniia gorodskogo obshchestvennogo upravleniia k stoletiiu goroda, 1895), 450. There is evidence that mortality rates for Jews in Europe and in the United States were also lower than for the general population, especially among the young. For example, Jakob Lestschinsky, *Probleme der Bevölkerungs Bewegung bei den Juden* (Padua: Metron, 1926); and H. Seidman, L. Garfinkel, and L. Craig, "Death Rates in New York City by Socio-Economic Class and Religious Groups, 1949–51," *The Jewish Journal*

of *Sociology* 4, no. 2 (1962): 254–73. I am grateful to Professor Bernard D. Weinryb for the last two citations and for other useful information concerning Jewish mortality rates. For attempted explanations for the low mortality rates among Jews in nineteenth-century Manchester, England, see Hugh T. Ashby, *Infant Mortality* (Cambridge: Cambridge University Press, 1915), 25–26.

42 Rubinow, *Jews in Russia*, 496.
43 *Evreiskoe naselenie*, 72.
44 Curtin, *Black Sea*, 4.
45 Isaac Babel, "Odessa," in *You Must Know Everything*, ed. Nathalie Babel (New York: Farrar, Straus and Giroux, 1969), 26.
46 M. Vol'skii, *Ocherk istorii khlebnoi torgovli Novorossiiskogo kraia s drevneishikh vremen do 1852 g.* (Odessa: V tip. Frantsova i Nitche, 1854), 11–62. I am indebted to E. I. Berkovich for obtaining this rare book for me. See also A. Jardé, *Les céréales dans l'antiquité grecque* (Paris: E. de Boccard, 1929).
47 A. Orlov, *Istoricheskii ocherk Odessy s 1794 po 1803 god* (Odessa: A. Shul'tse, 1885), 104–22.
48 John Moore, *A Journey from London to Odessa with Notices of New Russia, etc.* (Paris: Printed for the author, 1833), 149.
49 *Journal d'Odessa*, January 28, 1847.
50 M. Baruchello, *Livorno e il suo porto: Origini, caratteristiche e vicende dei traffic livornesi* (Livorno: Livorno soc. an. editrice riviste techniche, 1932), 380–81, 563. Much material on the Rodokanaki family in Tuscany may be found in the Archivio di Stato, Firenze (hereafter ASF), Affari Esteri.
51 Chr. Moulakes, *Oikos Adelphon Ralli* (Athens: n.p., 1964).
52 For information on John Ralli and his son Stephen, see NA, Consular Reports, May 20, 1845; October 14, 1849; January 1, 1854; October 29, 1854; December 5, 1856; June 25, 1860; and July 19, 1861. I am grateful to Marfa Viktorovna Tsomakion, great-niece of Stephen Ralli and niece of Paul Ralli, for granting me an interview in Odessa in September 1974. The interview provided me with valuable information on the later history of the Ralli family in Odessa.
53 *Pervaia vseobshchaia perepis'... 1897 g.*, vol. 47: *Gorod Odessa*, vi–vii, in which the redactor notes that Greeks, Germans, and Rumanians were fewer in Odessa in 1897 than in 1892.
54 Antoine Ignace Anthoine, Baron de Saint Joseph, *Essai historique sur le commerce et la navigation de la Mer-Noire ou voyages et entreprises pour établir des rapports commerciaux et maritimes entre les ports de la Mer-Noire et ceux de la Méditerranée* (Paris: Agasse, 1805). For Anthoine's career, see Hans Halm, in his edition of J. Weber, *Die Russen oder Versuch einer Reisebeschreibung nach Russland und durch das Russische Reich in Europa* (Innsbruck: Das Sprachwissenschaftliche Institut der Leopold-Franzens-Universität, 1960), 164–68. For Charles Sicard, see *Lettres sur Odessa par Sicard ainé, négociant* établi *dans cette ville* (St. Petersburg: Imprimerie de Pluchard, 1812); and his *Lettres sur la Crimée, Odessa et la Mer d'Azov* (Moscow, n.p., 1810).
55 Zagoruiko, *Po stranitsam*, 1:86. For the history of the *Journal d'Odessa* in the 1870s, see Alexander de-Ribas, *Staraia Odessa: istoricheskie ocherki i vospominaniia* (Odessa, 1913), 314. For an excellent survey of printing, books, and periodicals in early Odessa, see S. Ia. Borovoi, "Kniga v Odesse v pervoi polovine XIX v.," in *Kniga: Issledovaniia i materialy* 14 (Moscow: Nauka, 1967): 145–59.
56 His memoirs are published in vol. 54 of the *Sbornik Imperatorskogo russkogo istoricheskogo obshchestva* (St. Petersburg, 1864–1916). See also Léon de Crousaz-Crétet, *Le Duc de Richelieu en Russie et en France, 1766–1822* (Paris: Firmin-Didot et cie., 1897). For a favorable appraisal of his career, see E. I. Druzhinina, *Iuzhnaia Ukraina, 1800–1825 gg.* (Moscow: Nauka, 1970), 187–202.
57 AMAE, Odessa, vol. 8, January 20, 1858.
58 AMAE, Odessa, vol. 10, February 12, 1870. In 1843 the French consul claimed "Odessa has borrowed from France more than from any other country; of all the foreign languages ours is the most widespread. It is spoken

not only in salons, but also in all the stores, in most of the shops and workshops. Our customs, our habits, our tastes have become those of the area and everything which comes from France, from Paris especially, is well received." AMAE, Odessa, vol. 6, fol. 293, March 4, 1843.

59 AMAE, Odessa, vol. 6, fol. 293, March 23, 1843.
60 Some sixty to eighty French families accompanied the 120 to 150 railroad engineers and workers who came to Odessa in the 1850s. See AMAE, Odessa, vol. 8, fol. 177, August 20, 1859. For French and Belgian investments and participation in industry in the southern Ukraine, see John McKay, *Pioneers for Profit: Foreign Entrepreneurship and Russian Industrialization, 1885–1913* (Chicago: University of Chicago Press, 1970).
61 For grain purchases by Italy, see Vincenzo Cacciapuoti, *Relazioni commerciali tra l'Italia e la Russia* (Naples: N. Jovene, 1928); and Jean Gorrini, *La Russie moderne et les rapports italo-russes* (Turin: Schioppo, 1918). Vincenzo Giura, *Russia, Stati Uniti d'America e Regno di Napoli nell'età del Risorgimento* (Naples: Edizioni Scientifiche Italiane, 1967) gives much material on the earlier period.
62 *Odessa, 1794–1894*, 585. There is a theater notice published in Italian in the Historical Museum in Odessa. For passports, see PRO, FO 65, vol. 257, September 4, 1821. For the street signs, see Edward Morton, *Travels in Russia and a Residence at St. Petersburg and Odessa in the Years 1827–1829* (London: Longman, Rees, Orme, Brown and Green, 1830), 198.
63 J. Thomas Shaw, ed. and trans., *The Letters of Alexander Pushkin*, 3 vols. (Bloomington: Indiana University Press and Philadelphia: University of Pennsylvania Press, 1963), 1:143.
64 Ribas, *Staraia Odessa*, 322.
65 ASF, Affari Esteri, protocol 207, no. 7, December 24, 1830, in which the Tuscan Council of State wrote to the Grand Duke of Tuscany: "Se è evidentemente preso a promuovere i vantaggi di Trieste contrariando Livorno."
66 Henry Wikoff, *The Reminiscences of an Idler* (New York: Fords, Howard, & Hulbert, 1880), 231.
67 *Innocents Abroad, or the New Pilgrim's Progress, Being Some Account of the Steamship* Quaker City's *Pleasure Excursion to Europe and the Holy Land*, 2 vols. (New York: Grosset, 1911), 2:116.
68 John Stephens, *Incidents of Travel in Greece, Turkey, Russia and Poland*, 2 vols. (New York: Harper and Brothers, 1838), 1:264. Wikoff, *Reminiscences*, 233 also recalls a meeting with General Sontag in Odessa.
69 James Yeames was a merchant and consul at Odessa as early as 1819. At the same time, William Yeames was vice-consul at Taganrog. See PRO, FO 65, vol. 257, June 7, 1819; and vol. 258, no. 3, September 22, 1823.
70 See Herlihy, "Odessa," 189n27, for a bibliography on the German colonists.

CHAPTER 7

Greek Merchants in Odessa in the Nineteenth Century

With the conclusion of the Treaty of Kuchuk-Kainardji in 1774, the Russian Empire under Catherine II succeeded for the first time in obtaining and holding a portion of the Black Sea coast.[1] Peter the Great had founded Taganrog on the Sea of Azov in 1706 and had built a port there, only to lose the city to the Turks in 1711. In 1783, the Crimea was annexed; the empire thereby broadened its access to the Black Sea and obtained dominion over the coastline of the Sea of Azov. Finally, through the Treaty of Jassy concluded in 1791 after a victorious war against the Turks, the Russian Empire acquired the Ochakov region, a glittering prize, for it included the site of what was to become the greatest emporium of the Black Sea—Odessa.

Russia was, however, ill prepared to exploit the commercial opportunities, which the acquisition of these southern outlets offered. With virtually no merchant marine, few trained sailors, and even fewer mercantile houses, Russia established a policy of inviting merchants of various nationalities, religious beliefs, and skills to populate the newly founded ports. Almost at once, foreign merchants arrived to explore and exploit the commercial possibilities offered by the new lands and the new waterways. Greek colonists, for example, settled in large numbers in Mariupol' (in Soviet times, Zhdanov); by 1816, there were 11,500 Greeks in or near the city.[2] Coming chiefly from the Crimea, they in dress and language more closely resembled the Tatars than did their compatriots on the Aegean. A French merchant, Antoine de Saint-Joseph, was one of the first to open a firm at Kherson, near the mouth of the Dnipro River.[3] His firm, which included four of his brothers, dealt in wool, hemp, iron, leather, and ship stores. The German merchant Johannes Weber similarly organized commercial ventures out of Kherson.[4] Mykolaiv, which had been founded ten years after Kherson, in 1788, at the mouth of the Buh River, likewise attracted foreign merchants. However, like many other Euxine ports, it did not achieve major commercial importance until the late nineteenth century. As early as 1802, there were 850 Greek males settled in Taganrog, the most important port on the Sea of Azov.[5]

In the nineteenth century Odessa was the most flourishing of all these ports. Founded in 1794, happily endowed with a deep, sheltered harbor and ably administered by the Duc de Richelieu (1803–14), the city grew in close correspondence with the increasing demand for grain from the Russian Empire.[6] This favorable conjuncture—the convenience of the

---

Originally published as Patricia Herlihy, "Greek Merchants in Odessa in the Nineteenth Century," *Eucharisterion: Essays Presented to Omeljan Pritsak on His Sixtieth Birthday by his Colleagues and Students. Harvard Ukrainian Studies* vol. III/IV, part 1 (1979–80): 399–420.

Ukrainian plain to Odessa and the rising demand from foreign markets—attracted strangers in great numbers to the southern city. Greeks, with their valued maritime skills, were among the first to settle in the area. At the end of 1795, the government brought sixty-two families into Odessa from the Archipelago and other Greek sites.[7] In addition, twenty-seven Greek merchants and fourteen others of various trades came into Odessa with state support.[8] Within a year after the founding of the city, Greeks comprised nearly 10 percent of the population (224 out of 2,340).[9] Twenty-five more Greek merchants with their families arrived in the city in 1797.[10] An additional twenty-one joined them the following year.

By 1795, the Greek community of Odessa was so large that it was possible to organize a special battalion made up of Greeks and Albanians residing in or near the city.[11] Paul I disbanded the unit, but it was recommissioned by Alexander I in 1803. The battalion fought bravely in the war against the Turks from 1806 to 1812. In 1814, when it was again disbanded, the tsar rewarded the Greek soldiers with land in the village of Aleksandrovka near Odessa. Many of these Greeks, however, preferred to rent out their lands while they themselves resided in the city, where some made considerable sums in commerce. Odessa's Greek community soon organized various cultural institutions. As early as 1800, a school founded by the collegiate assessor Vreto was teaching the Greek language as well as the Italian and Russian. Two private Greek schools were accepting pupils by 1811.

We know the names of the ten richest Greek merchants of Odessa in 1817: Theodore Serafino, Alexander Mavros, Dimitrios Inglesi, Alexander Kumbaris, Vasilii Iannopulo, Grigorii Marazli, Kyriakos Papahajis, Il'ia Manesis, Iohannis Ambrosiu, and Dimitrios Paleologos.[12] A contemporary estimated the value of their combined fortunes at 10 million rubles. Interestingly enough, a report written less than a decade later which named the richest merchants in the entire Russian Empire listed four of the same surnames: Serafino, Iannopulo, Marazli, and Paleologos.[13] Although they were not among the empire's wealthiest houses, the Inglesi family was hardly less prominent. Its members appear frequently in the documents between 1803 and 1814. Dimitrios Inglesi was mayor of Odessa from 1818 to 1821.[14] By 1847, the firm was described as representing one of the leading mercantile houses of the empire.[15] In 1820, in connection with the visit to Odessa of the famous Greek patriot Alexander Ypsilanti the rich Greek merchant Alexander Kumbaris also named the wealthiest families among his compatriots.[16] These were the Inglesi, Marazli, Mavros, and Christodoulou. All these houses were active in the city six years later, and several of them remained prominent for many more decades. At a time when fortunes were made and lost quickly—for much depended on crop failures in Western Europe—this continuity indicates a high degree of stability among the resident Greek merchants of Odessa in the first half of the nineteenth century.

The wealthy Greeks were not without a sense of loyalty to their adopted city. During the Napoleonic Wars, the Duc de Richelieu appealed to the Greeks of Odessa to support the Russian war effort. In 1812, out of a total of 280,000 rubles contributed (the governor himself gave 40,000), the Greeks provided 100,000 to the defense of their new home.[17]

The governmental policy, initially highly favorable to foreign merchants at Odessa, gradually changed over the early decades of the nineteenth century. The authorities acknowledged the fact that skilled foreigners served as channels through which golden grain could be turned into golden specie. But they no longer felt compelled to extend unlimited privileges to the foreigners. In 1812, for example, the Duc de Richelieu exempted the Greeks of Kerch and Enikale from military service, but the imperial government repudiated the act.[18] Moreover, the authorities wished to encourage the participation of Russian citizens in this lucrative trade. To that end, an ukase of January 1, 1807, forbade foreign firms from buying grain wholesale for shipment abroad.[19] The law effectively required the foreigners to use citizens of the empire as brokers and agents. Many of these middlemen were local Jews, who knew the current prices, the Russian language, and the local laws and customs. According to an Italian merchant living in the city, the services of an official broker were obligatory in some transactions as early as 1804, "Contracts made in this square to consign merchandise at certain times must be registered by the *makler*, who is a middleman appointed by the government to the job."[20]

Doubtlessly, the government hoped that this measure would persuade many foreigners to adopt Russian citizenship. In December 1845, however, the requirement that Russian subjects serve as middlemen was abrogated, perhaps because the law was too easily evaded.[21] By then, too, cereal exports were mounting rapidly and the government sought to facilitate this profitable enterprise.

In spite of these shifting policies, Greeks continued to immigrate to Odessa in considerable numbers. In 1817 a correspondent for a Greek newspaper published in Vienna waxed eloquent over the town, "How is it possible to leave Odessa, a land where milk and honey flow, where trade flourishes, where the government is mild, where tranquility and freedom are complete and where the plague does not bother us?"[22]

Many Greeks must have been in agreement with this glowing assessment. In 1822 an Italian merchant wrote that Italian was the language of commerce in Odessa, but Greek was the tongue one heard most often, "because of the great number of Greeks who live there."[23] As early as 1817, three Greek insurance companies were established in the city. These companies, which also served as benevolent aid societies, supported a Greek commercial school. The school, which opened in November 1817, with great fanfare—Governor-General Langeron, the metropolitan and all the Greek notables were in attendance—instructed Greek youth not only in commercial subjects, but also in Russian, ancient and modern Greek, religion, natural sciences, humanities, and Italian.[24] It soon enjoyed the reputation of being the second-best school in Odessa, after the Richelieu Lyceum. Supported entirely by the local Greek community, it attracted students from other Greek colonies and from the homeland itself. Greek theater made its debut in Odessa in 1814 and flourished, especially after 1817.[25] All these cultural resources drew more Greek immigrants to the city. In 1824 an English visitor to Odessa remarked that among the city's many foreigners, the Greeks were the most numerous.[26] Even in 1832, the French consul described the national composition of Odessa's merchants as follows:

> There are 40 foreign firms, established by Greeks, Italians, Slavonians, Triestians, Genoese, French, German, English, Swiss and Spanish. These enterprises are all regular and permanent.... The Greeks are the most numerous and the richest. The greatest fortunes are from 800,000 to one million rubles. Of these there are only three. There are some others

from 300,000 to 400,000 rubles, most of them are from 50,000 to 100,000 rubles and the majority [are] with even less capital.²⁷

The consul, François Sauron, noted that in addition to the forty permanent firms, there were about 100 foreign firms with representatives in Odessa. The parent companies that maintained these agents were located in Constantinople, Malta, Trieste, Livorno, Genoa, Marseille, Barcelona, and so forth. Of all the companies trading in cereals, only two were in a strict sense "Russian." These were the houses of Steiglitz from St. Petersburg and of Demidov. These two companies were, however, "powerful," according to Sauron. About two-thirds of the commercial firms were Greek. The remaining houses were for the most part Italian, with headquarters in Genoa, Livorno, or Trieste. French companies numbered only four or five, and English, German, Swiss, and Spanish enterprises were still fewer.

In 1834, at the government's behest, a German expert wrote a report on the commerce of the province of Novorossiia, which confirmed Sauron's observations:

> Foreign trade is almost exclusively in the hands of persons of foreign origin, the greater part of whom are Greeks and Italians. The merchants of Russian origin are comparatively few in number, and are chiefly employed in the sale of the different manufactures of the country, such as cordage, glass and iron and copper articles. The purchases of the produce of the country in the interior are commonly made by the indigenous Jews, who are very numerous in Odessa. It is to the foreigners, as we have observed before, that the town owes its present flourishing condition. By their industry and capital they have laid open the resources of the country...²⁸

The presence of the foreign traders obviously stimulated—or rather, sustained—Odessa's commerce. But the government still pressured them to become Russian citizens. In 1858, for example, the government determined that foreign merchants could belong only to the first of Odessa's three guilds.²⁹ Annual membership dues were 1,000 rubles, then the equivalent of $827.06 or 400 francs. Few could afford, or were willing to pay, that exorbitant amount. Many foreign merchants assumed Russian citizenship, which allowed them to enroll either in the second guild, at an annual fee of 401 rubles, ninety-seven copecks or the third, which required an annual payment of only 116 rubles. French merchants, in particular, were vociferous in objecting to the stipulation that only Russian citizens could remain enrolled in the second or third guilds. Some forty-seven French merchants signed a cranky protest. They were allowed to retain their former status for one year without changing nationality, but no new Frenchmen would be allowed to join the second or third guilds without assuming Russian citizenship.

How was one to become a Russian subject? Nothing could be simpler, according to the English consul at Odessa, James Yeames.³⁰ A formal declaration of intent, made before the appropriate authorities, could make anyone a citizen; the procedures were accomplished in the course of a few hours. Yeames cited the example of the Ralli and Scaramanga families of Taganrog and Odessa, who were obviously Greeks but, "who are inscribed in the guild as Russian subjects." Clearly, the government was ambivalent in its attitudes and policies toward the foreigners. It recognized that they brought valued capital, entrepreneurial spirit, and commercial expertise to Odessa. Yet it feared that these strangers would skim the cream, as it were, off the booming export trade and carry off the profits to distant lands. The government therefore wanted a commitment from the foreigners to the city and the empire, but it did not intend to kill the goose that laid the golden eggs. The merchants of the first guild, who were willing to pay for the privilege, were largely left undisturbed.

The policy of encouraging the foreign merchants to become Russian nationals enjoyed a partial, if superficial, success. In 1844 a prominent historian and scholar, Apollon Skal'kovs'kyi published a pamphlet entitled *The Commercial Population of Odessa*.[31] In it he sought to refute the common charge of "so-called patriots" that foreigners dominated Odessa's trade. In a strict sense, he argued, only about one-sixth of the commercial houses in Odessa belonged to foreign nationals. The rest were "Russian," in that their owners had assumed Russian citizenship. Table 1 reproduces the statistics he assembled.

Table 1 Russian Citizens and Foreigners (Gosti) in Odessa's Guilds

Year	Firms	Russian	Foreign
1837	765	598	167
1838	765	602	163
1839	738	589	139
1840	693	578	115
1841	719	582	127
1842	702	584	118
1843	704	589	115
1844	700	588	112

Source: A. O. Skal'kovs'kyi *Population commerciale d'Odessa* (Odessa, 1845).

Skal'kovs'kyi rejoiced to see the diminishing number of foreign firms, and he clearly believed that the foreigners who had adopted Russian nationality were sincere in the gesture.

The exact role of foreign merchants in Odessa's commercial development during the nineteenth century has been a vexed question among both contemporaries and later historians. In 1858, the French consul observed that the natives greatly feared that foreigners were carrying off the national wealth. The concern, he believed, was totally unfounded, for, "foreigners alone have made Odessa what it is."[32] Soviet historians have interpreted the role of foreign capital at Odessa variously. Zolotov, for example, condemned the foreigners of Odessa for spending tens of millions of rubles abroad.[33] E. I. Druzhinina, on the other hand, gives them a somewhat more positive assessment, "The diverse national composition of the merchants guaranteed the success of trade relations of Russia with various countries. All of this contributed to the primitive accumulation of capital in Russia."[34]

How well did the foreign merchants integrate into the society of the region, and how much did they contribute to its growth? The Greek community holds our special attention here, and many families within it would merit close study. Among them would be the Avierino, the first family from Chios to establish a firm in Taganrog (1803); the Marazli, who were among the earliest arrivals in Odessa and remained actively involved in its affairs even while vigorously supporting the movement for Greek independence; the Mavrokordato, present in Odessa from at least as early as 1798; the Negroponte of Taganrog; the Petrocochino, prominent not only in Odessa and Taganrog but also in Rostov-on-the-Don; and the Scaramanga, great merchants in grain whose reputation as fair dealers lingered on in the region, even among peasants, even after their departure.[35] But the two leading Greek families whom we shall examine here are the Ralli and the Rodokanaki. To be sure, their private records are not extant, as far as I know. Still, through newspapers, almanacs, government reports, consular letters, travel accounts, university records, genealogical tables and city directories, it is possible to reconstruct the remarkable activities and achievements of these two great Hellenic houses.

THE RALLI FAMILY

In 1847, according to the list of Odessa's commercial houses prepared that year, the fifth largest in the city belonged to the Greek merchant John Ralli. (Another Ralli, John Christopher, appears on the same list, but his relationship to John is obscure, as is his subsequent career.[36]) John Ralli was indubitably a substantial trader. The value of the goods he imported into Odessa in 1846 amounted to 506,717 rubles; the value of all imports into the city during the same year was 7,745,567 rubles. He exported commodities worth 1,089,176 rubles, out of a total of 22,787,589 rubles for the entire city. The turnover in his affairs exceeded 1.5 million rubles—about 5.2 percent of the entire overseas trade of the city in 1846.

Who was John Ralli? We know a fair amount about him, partly because he served as consul for the United States in Odessa from 1832 until his death in 1859.[37] He was not, however, a United States citizen, although he was familiar enough with American overseas trade. In 1854, when the United States Department of State inquired into the background of its consul, Ralli explained that he was "a Russian subject, born on the Island of Scio [Chios] in the Archipelago, and was by birth of Greek origin."[38] According to other, more detailed sources, John (or Zannis, his Greek name) Ralli was born in Chios on November 3, 1785. His father, Stephen, had been born in Chios in 1755; doubtless he, too, had been a merchant, for he died in Marseille in 1827. John married an Italian girl, Lucia, who had been born in Pisa in 1797. They were married in Odessa, but we do not know the year. Their only child, Stephen, was born in London in 1821. As a young man John was clearly accustomed to moving frequently!

He was also the oldest surviving son within a large family, and he had close relatives all along the Mediterranean and beyond. His sister Ploumos died in Marseille, as did his brother August. Another brother, Pandia, was a Greek consul in London, where he and two other brothers eventually died. An American traveler noted that John had several brothers—in England, Trieste, and the Greek Islands.[39] All were merchants. In his reports to Washington, John frequently asked for permission to take leave in order to go abroad on business. Together with four younger brothers, he founded in London in 1818 a firm called Ralli and Petrocochino; after a subsequent reorganization, it was renamed simply Ralli Brothers. This company existed continuously until 1961.[40] At various times it maintained branches in the Danubian Provinces, Persia, the East Indies, and America, besides the Russian Empire. The vast network recently elicited this comment from S. H. Chapman:

In their migration westward, the more successful Greek houses spawned new branches and tracing these reveals the pattern of extension of their interests. Ralli Brothers, the Chian family in the vanguard of the migration, opened branches at Odessa, Marseille, London and Manchester (1828), and were soon exporting cotton twist to Germany as well as the Levant. In 1865, at the summit of their mercantile achievement, the Rallis were operating through interlocked partnerships in fifteen centres, spread across Europe and the Middle East.[41]

The English branch of the family achieved numerous distinctions. John's nephew Pandely became a member of the British Parliament.[42] In 1912, the British government conferred the hereditary title of baronet on the then head of the firm, Lucas Eustratius Ralli, who died in 1931. His son and his nephew served in the British army during the Boer War—one died of typhoid fever, the other survived to fight in World War I and was decorated with the Military Cross.

Other members of the family earned honors from other governments. John's first cousin, Ambrose Ralli of Trieste, received the hereditary title of baron from the Austrian emperor. His father, Stephen, was a great merchant and banker active in Smyrna and Constantinople. Another member of the family, Panajoti, was engaged in the thriving grain import business at Livorno during the French revolutionary wars. There in 1847, the Ralli firm was still listed as "Greek."[43] It was reckoned among the *fidate*, or those enterprises not required to pay their taxes in advance, in recognition of their faith and substance.

In 1838, an American visitor to Odessa wrote that Ralli had left his native island as a boy and had visited every European port as a merchant before settling permanently in Odessa in about 1830.[44] In fact, John left London in 1827.[45] It is very likely that the death of his father at Marseille in the same year called him, as the eldest son, back to the Mediterranean, the center of the family's far-flung commercial interests. While his younger brothers and close relatives were receiving hereditary titles in London and Trieste, John built up business in the booming city of Odessa. Already in 1826, before his own permanent settlement there, the Ralli Company in Odessa was importing and exporting goods valued at 290,524 rubles. In 1827, exports declined to 149,342 rubles. However, as we have seen, under John's immediate supervision the company was trading more than 1.5 million rubles' worth of commodities, chiefly cereals, by 1846.

From 1832, John Ralli represented the United States government at Odessa. He was appointed on the recommendation of an American diplomat, Charles Rhind, who had negotiated a treaty between his country and the Porte and who had employed Ralli as an agent, apparently without ever having made his personal acquaintance. Rhind described the candidate to the Department of State as being talented and "rich and respectable."[46] An American traveler who met Ralli in 1835 praised the courtesy with which the consul treated him and his partners.[47] They were allegedly the first Americans the American consul had ever met. In spite of the time he spent in England, Ralli still spoke English with difficulty. Shortly afterwards, John Stephens, an American world traveler and adventurer who later became president of the Panama Railroad Company, also met Ralli. He described the consul as follows: "Mr. Ralli is rich and respected, being vice-president of the commercial board, and very proud of the honour of the American consulate, as it gives him a position among the dignitaries of the place, enables him to wear a uniform and sword on public occasion, and yields him other privileges which are gratifying, at least, if not intrinsically valuable."[48]

Ralli fulfilled the duties of consul with a high degree of competence, as his long tenure suggests. His dispatches to Washington were always well informed and written in correct English. He alerted the government to commercial opportunities for American ships in the Black Sea, and he stressed the profits to be made by shipping colonial products directly to the empire. In making his assessments Ralli had the advantage of information coming in from his offices in Rostov, Taganrog, and other Azov cities, as well as from his numerous connections in the West. One example of his good commercial sense was his advice to the United States to increase its grain shipments to Europe during the Crimean War, so as to take advantage of the prohibition against cereal export, which the Russian government had recently imposed, "The present circumstances may be advantageously profited by the United States, from whence great quantity of bread stuffs may be exported to Europe."[49]

In 1857, the American government tried to prohibit its consuls abroad from engaging in private commercial ventures. Ralli appealed the decision to President Buchanan and described his own career: "I have been a merchant for a great number of years. . . . I have not only a commercial house at Odessa, and branch houses in other parts of Russia, but likewise houses in England, France, Turkey, Persia and also the East Indies."[50] To retain his consular post, Ralli was willing to renounce his stipend, but he would not end his commercial career. His son Stephen was likewise willing to serve as consul for the honor alone, he wrote. Ralli also reminded the president of his father's friendship for him when they had been together at the court of St. James. His petition was favorably received, but John died soon after, in 1859, while abroad in Paris. His widow went to Paris to live, but died in Livorno in 1873, in the country of her birth. John's only son, Stephen, remained in Odessa and served as vice-consul from 1854 until his father's death.[51] He then became deputy consul until the arrival of Timothy Smith of Vermont, the first native American to occupy the post of American consul in Odessa.

Stephen continued the family's traditional involvement in the cereal trade, and also built up a substantial landed endowment. Like his father, he was a Russian citizen and took active part in civic affairs. In 1863, he was appointed a member of a commission to study proposed reforms of the city government, and he was also named to the city council.[52] After the Crimean War, when he was regarded as one of the richest landowners in the Russian Empire, Stephen's wealth and services won him new titles, including honorary justice of the peace and actual counselor of state. The story spread that he kept large sums of gold and silver in his house and was constantly preoccupied with matters of security.[53]

In 1850, Stephen married a woman born in Odessa to a Greek family.[54] The twin sons born to them the following year were given the names Peter and Paul. Daughters followed in rapid succession—one in 1852, and four more before 1872. All the children were born in Odessa. The youngest daughter, Elizabeth, eventually married Prince Alexander Lobanov-Rostovskii. The alliance indicates how closely the family had become connected with the Russian social establishment. Peter Ralli became a captain in the Imperial Guards, while Paul retained close ties with his native city.

Much gossip circulated about the family. According to a newspaper report dated May 7, 1885, the Rallis had recently erected a large, expensive, and ornate building. With ill-concealed cynicism, the reporter demanded to know whether the millionaires had built it for the unfortunate, the sick, or the elderly. In truth, it was designed to house dogs—a "dogs' kingdom (*sabach'e tsarstvo*)," he called it. According to the Soviet historian who uncovered this bit of scandal, the Ralli dogs were so ferocious that they chewed to death some of the family's own servants; allegedly, their bodies were found floating on the Black Sea.[55] Whether or not these tales deserve credence, the Rallis had clearly become rich enough to excite jealousy and resentment on the part of their fellow townsmen. Since Paul appears in the city directory of 1910 as the president of the Odessa Society for the Protection of Animals, it is more than likely that the Rallis were simply devoted to raising pedigree dogs.[56]

The twin sons were educated in Odessa. At age twenty-six they received law degrees from the imperial university, which had been established in Novorossiia. They are listed as Orthodox hereditary honorary citizens of the city.[57] Peter then left Odessa to take up his career in the Imperial Guards. He married in St. Petersburg in 1889; there are no recorded offspring. Death overtook him in Pau, France, in 1896. His father, Stephen, survived him until 1901. His widow, Peter's mother, left Odessa and died in Cannes, France, in 1903.[58]

The surviving twin, Paul, assumed the leadership of the clan in Odessa. In addition to his work for the protection of animals, he served as president of the Odessa Discount Bank.[59] In 1974 the niece of Paul Ralli, Marfa Viktorovna Tsomakion, graciously granted me an interview in Odessa. In her recollections, Paul was not as dedicated to the pursuit of commerce as his forefathers had been. Rather, he invested his money in land, notably in a huge estate south of Kyiv. He was also the owner of a sugar refinery. His wife, Catherine Tymchenko, who was born in Odessa in 1861, encouraged him to undertake various philanthropies. He maintained a well-staffed hospital on his estate and sent ailing servants off for seaside cures. Once, he discovered that a young peasant was endowed with a fine voice and paid for his musical training; the protégé eventually became a leading singer on the Moscow stage. His sugar refinery was said to have been the first in the vicinity to initiate an eight-hour working day.

Paul Ralli undertook many trips to Western Europe, often in the company of his niece Marfa. His own daughter, Madeleine, born in 1896 at his estate, Suprumiv, in Podillia, died in Bavaria in 1921 at the age of only twenty-five. As he had no sons, Paul Ralli was the last male of his line in Odessa; he died in St. Petersburg in 1911. Of his five sisters, Helen, born in 1852, lived the longest; she died in Odessa in 1923.[60]

THE RODOKANAKI FAMILY

Hardly less extended in their commercial interests was the Rodokanaki family, who also came from the island of Chios. One of the first bases for their commercial operations was Livorno. One Michael Rodokanaki was a prominent trader in that Italian port in the last decades of the eighteenth century.[61] He may be identified with a Michael who was born at Chios in 1775, and married at Livorno in 1835, at the age of sixty. This was his only known marriage, but probably not his first, for his bride was herself forty-seven years of age. In any event, the fortunes of the house prospered at Livorno. The wars of the French revolution and the Napoleonic era opened significant trading opportunities. Many Italian firms entered on bad days during the French occupation of Tuscany, but the Greeks, politically uninvolved, reaped substantial profits.

In 1815, the Rodokanakis were listed among the privileged foreign firms of Livorno, who did not have to pay taxes in advance.[62] Michael had no known children, but his death in 1843 did not leave the house leaderless. Direction of the family firm in Livorno fell to George, son of Paul Rodokanaki, who had been born at Chios in 1795. He was one of nine children and the oldest surviving son (an elder brother, Peter, had been hanged by the Turks at Chios in 1822). His younger brothers and close relatives established themselves at the principal Mediterranean ports. Theodore settled in Odessa and a nephew, Paul, at Marseille. This tight family network linked the large trading marts of the Mediterranean. All the Rodokanaki enjoyed nearly spectacular success. Paul, for example, at one time served as head of the Chamber of Commerce of Marseille. In 1851, he petitioned the Grand Duchy of Tuscany for appointment as its consul-general in the French port, although it is unclear whether he was a Tuscan citizen. At any event, we have this contemporary Tuscan assessment of his talents, "M. Paul Rodokanaki is very much esteemed here. His firm holds the first position among the Greek houses of Marseille. His political opinions are those of the conservative party, his intelligence and aptitude for commercial affairs lead us to declare that he would be a good choice."[63] In Odessa, Paul's uncle Theodore had likewise proved himself to be a shrewd and sensible merchant. He arrived in Odessa at age fifteen (in 1812), when the city itself was only eighteen years old. By the time he was twenty-one, he was directing a firm under his own name. He was among the first to recognize the opportunities in carrying grain from southern Ukraine to Western Europe. With brothers and nephews at the chief Mediterranean ports, he had informed sources of commercial intelligence and reliable agents. As S. D. Chapman recently noted,

> The supra-nationalist outlook of religious and ethnic minorities gave them distinct advantages. Intimate local knowledge was the best defence against commercial and political threats, and the family network transmitted intelligence most readily and was quickest to respond to it. And while each family maintained a rivalry with others in the "tribe," there was sufficient understanding between them for members to insulate each other against crises and to act collectively to improve or maintain their national image.[64]

By 1826, Theodore Rodokanaki was one of the leading merchants of Odessa, doing transactions totaling 465,082 rubles. In the following year, his turnover jumped dramatically to 1,144,296 rubles.[65] By 1847, his firm was the largest in the entire city. He imported goods to the value of 659,402 rubles and exported commodities valued at 2,771,548 rubles. The total value of goods traded, nearly 3.5 million rubles, was larger by a million than that of his closest competitor.[66] This one firm accounted for some 10 percent of Odessa's overseas commerce. Not surprisingly, Theodore's name appears among the members of the first guild in 1861.[67] According to the local newspapers, Theodore was the proprietor of several ships. One purchased in 1849 was loyally called the *Niccolo Primo*, and another, which made frequent calls at the port of Odessa, was suitably named the *Rodocannachi*.[68] In 1832, Theodore applied for the post of Tuscan consular agent in Odessa. At that time he wrote that he had become a citizen of the Russian Empire.[69] Another Theodore (a second cousin) settled in St. Petersburg, and he, too, petitioned to become the Tuscan consul in the imperial capital. On August 11, 1851, Grand Duke Leopold II of Tuscany confirmed his appointment. Theodore's petition stated that he was born in Livorno (we know that the year was 1825).[70] He was still a Tuscan subject as late as 1849, but at some point in his career, he also acquired British citizenship. This was a source of embarrassment to him during the Crimean War, since he was now a resident of the Russian Empire. Clearly, national allegiances weighed lightly on the Rodokanakis. This Theodore Rodokanaki of St. Petersburg became a very rich man. His palace, one of the most beautiful in the capital, was a gathering place for the elite of the city. Theodore died in Baden in Germany in 1889 without heirs. His wife, Catherine Mavrokordato, born and married in Odessa, died in Paris in 1923; her will left to the land of her Greek ancestors all the splendid objets d'art she and her husband had avidly collected.[71] One of the sons of Theodore Rodokanaki of Odessa, named Pericles, also gained recognition in the highest social circles of St. Petersburg. Philip Argenti claimed that he was the first person of Greek ancestry to be made a member of the hereditary Russian nobility. The emperor elevated him to this singular honor in recognition "of the great and rapid development of his house of commerce."[72] While the distinction was unquestionable, Pericles Rodokanaki may not have been the first Greek to achieve it. According to Gregory Arsh, Ioannis Varvakis had been made a hereditary noble by Alexander I.[73] Gossip surrounded the rich Rodokanaki, as it did the Rallis. A contemporary account said that Pericles had a reputation as a ladies' man. At the Opera House, he was prone to circulate, with a monocle in his eye, from loge to loge, peering at one lady after another. Because of his extreme myopia, he so closely scrutinized the faces of the women that he reputedly aroused the anger of more than one husband.[74] However, doubtless in recognition of his exalted status, none of the offended spouses dared challenge him openly. Pericles, born in Odessa in 1841, died in Paris in 1899 without heirs; his noble title expired with him. He had been Theodore's only son. Of Theodore's two daughters, we know only the issue of the youngest, Ariane, born in Odessa in 1842. She married Nicolas Mavrokordato, member of another prominent Greek mercantile family. Ariane died in Vienna in 1900; Nicolas had died in Odessa in 1893. Their three children, two sons and a daughter—all born in Odessa—bore, of course, the name of their father, Mavrokordato. The Rodokanaki commercial house continued to do business in Odessa as late as 1894. However, no member of the family is mentioned in the directory of the city for the year 1910.

A citation in the *Journal de St. Pétersbourg* for April 24, 1844, salutes the importance of the Rallis and the Rodokanakis in the commerce of Odessa during the mid-nineteenth century. "The house of Ralli," it reads, "holds the first place, both in exports and in imports taken together, and in exports taken separately; for imports alone, the Rodokanakis [are the leaders]."[75]

CONSIDERATIONS

The success of the Greek firms and families at Odessa had several roots. As early arrivals in a new city, they were able to establish their businesses before rivals could. They took advantage of the capital and connections that brothers, relatives, and compatriots extended to them in the major ports of the Mediterranean and beyond. The Greek firms were competitive with one another, but they also frequently shared commercial intelligence and resources. They formed, as an English traveler to Odessa observed in 1824, a moral family, "The Greeks are very intelligent and artful; they have agents of their own country in all parts to which they trade; they form, as it were, one large family and manage to lay their neighbors under contribution."[76] This moral solidarity became especially apparent and powerful in periods of crisis. In 1848, for example, a year of financial panic, the English consul at Odessa remarked that the Greeks, who dominated the import trade, disposed of abundant cash and hence were not severely affected by the commercial downturn, "The Greek houses, whose branch establishments have of late been remarkable in most of the great towns of Europe, and whose character and solidity had become a matter of inquiry and of jealous attention, have in particular borne the late trial in a way much to add their credit and power."[77] During a subsequent financial crisis in 1857, the French consul explained why Odessa suffered so little: "To begin with, the largest companies in Odessa are Greek firms, and it is known to what degree of prudence and skill Greek traders conduct their operations. Linked with each other at all points of the globe, they help each other, supporting each other so that it is rare to see them in difficulties."[78] Clearly, in diversity and geographic dispersal there was strength.

The commercial disruption caused by the Crimean War offers a good example of the benefits which dispersion could provide. The wartime embargo against the export of grain out of Odessa hurt the business of Theodore Rodokanaki. But the embargo proved a windfall to his brother George in Livorno. George developed an alternate source of grain in the Danubian ports of Galați and Braila, and he sold it in Western Europe at the inflated prices that the Russian embargo had engendered.[79] One man's woe was another man's profit, but both men were members of the same family enterprise. The Greeks across the diaspora assiduously cultivated family solidarity and cohesiveness. They shared information on prices, established a network of credit and debt clearances, and trained and tested younger members of the clans as suitable business partners. Finally, they contracted marriages, which added ties of sentiment to ties of cash.

Social cohesion was advanced by the fact that the Greeks in foreign cities very often lived together in compact neighborhoods. In Odessa they settled on the side streets jutting off from the main artery, the Derybasivs'ka. Even the affluent who could have afforded more spacious quarters preferred to reside among their poorer compatriots. Some scholars have seen in this sense of ethnic solidarity, first noticeable among the Greeks of the diaspora, a source of the national fervor that ignited and sustained the movement for Greek independence.[80] In Odessa, as elsewhere, Greeks faced a difficult dilemma. Should they assimilate into the larger society, at the cost of losing their valuable connections with their conationals abroad? Or should they retain their Greek identity, and thus visit on themselves the resentments and disabilities which are the usual deserts of outsiders? Some Greeks chose assimilation, partial or total. Dmitri Inglesi rose to become mayor of Odessa from 1818 to 1821, as we have seen. Many members of the prominent families—Ralli, Sevastopulo, Mavrokordato, and others—became honorary citizens of their cities; conferral of the dignity indicated long years of community service in some productive profession. Some few, such as Paul Ralli, became full members of the Russian aristocracy. On the other hand, many others clung to their Greek identity and never looked on Odessa as their permanent home.

Indeed, the very presence of Greek merchants at Odessa begins to wane from the middle nineteenth century. For example, the number of Greeks attending the University of Novorossiia was surprisingly low. Of the 1835 students who graduated from the university between the years 1868 and 1890, only fourteen have evident Greek surnames.[81] And the old, familiar names are few among them. Vladimir and Egor Dimo, for example, members of the merchant class, received law degrees in 1871 and 1873, respectively. In 1826, Sotiri Dimo was a leading merchant of the city, doing commerce valued at 346,961 rubles.[82] The Ralli twins, Peter and Paul, were likewise the recipients of law degrees, as we have seen. Matthew Sevastopulo, who became a high state official, was also a graduate of the University of Novorossiia. A Dmitri Inglesi appears among the graduates; his ancestors had come to Odessa in the first decade of the nineteenth century, and one Dmitri Inglesi had been an early mayor. In 1847, an Inglesi was listed as a leading merchant of the city, with a trade turnover of 93,410 rubles. Several members of the family are mentioned in the city directory for 1910 as officials in banks and credit societies.[83] The paucity of Greeks at the university reflects their small numbers in the city as a whole. In 1897, according to the first All-Russian census, native speakers of Greek constituted only 1.3 percent of the population;[84] they had comprised 1.6 percent only five years earlier. The sex ratio among them was very unbalanced: 58.6 women for every 100 males. Most Greeks in Odessa were newly arrived males in search of jobs who were unmarried or who had left their families at home. The older wave of Greek immigrants had either assimilated and disappeared, or had left the city. The directory for the year 1910, which lists the notables of the city, offers further evidence of the declining Greek presence. The directory gives some 2,523 names, with indications of social class and offices held in government, military service, teaching, business, and so forth. Only sixty-nine residents are identified as merchants, whereas forty-eight are honorary citizens, a category which traditionally included successful businessmen of foreign origin. Of these 117 names (only 5 percent of the city's notables), we recognize only three: Marie Sevastopulo, the patroness of orphanages; Paul Ralli, the president of the Odessa Discount Bank and protector of dogs; and Petr Amvrosievich Mavrokordato, president of the Imperial Society for the Study of History and Antiquities. Evidently, very few Greeks remained among Odessa's elite.

Where had the Greeks gone? According to a contemporary observer who wrote in 1863, Greek merchants were leaving the city and Jews were taking their places in commerce.[85] Wilhelm Hamm, who visited Odessa in the early 1860s, noted that the Greeks once held the major share in the commerce of wheat, wool, tallow, skins, and linseed. Now, however, he observed, "the Greeks were in great decline."[86] University lists, consular reports, and city directories all indicate that Jews were entering large-scale commerce in unprecedented numbers. They had always been, to be sure, numerous among the small brokers and traders, but overseas commerce was now falling into their hands more and more. In 1913 an American from Toledo, Ohio, commented on their commercial prominence: "The business of Odessa is largely in the hands of the Jews, and prosperous Jews or their families may be seen at all times on the street. . . . The Russians all dislike them in Odessa, it seems, but no doubt this hatred is partly the result of envy."[87] The Jews were superbly suited to take up the slack left by the departure of the Greeks. They had much the same cohesiveness, family connections, and invaluable experience in intermediate business roles. They were, on the whole, content with slimmer margins of profit than the Greeks. The Greek mercantile houses, on the other hand, favored more risky and speculative ventures.[88]

While the grain trade increased in absolute volume during the latter half of the nineteenth century, the entry of the Americans on the international grain market whittled down the profits to be expected from the export of the empire's wheat. The Greeks were ready for more profitable, if riskier, enterprises. Textiles, not grain, attracted them in the late nineteenth century. Ralli Brothers established branches in Calcutta (1851), Bombay (1861), and New York (1871). Its trade in India and America was primarily in cotton. In 1866, in a major reorganization, the firm gave up its business in the Russian Empire altogether; it fell to a company known as Scaramanga and Associates.[89]

According to the firm's historian, success came to Ralli Brothers because the partners had always observed the dictum engraved on the family coat of arms, "Walk the straight path."[90] Perhaps more truly, the key to success for all the Greek merchants lay in taking a circuitous path around the Mediterranean and well beyond its shores, in perpetual search of remunerative ventures. In the early nineteenth century, the enterprise of Greek merchants gave a powerful boost to the export of Ukrainian wheat. Pioneers in the trade along the many ports of the Black Sea coast, they contributed in a special way to the cosmopolitan atmosphere of the area's largest port, Odessa. Odessa, in turn, offered a hospitable environment for the Greek community. Some of its members integrated themselves smoothly into the city's life. But others, as their easy shift of national allegiances would lead us to expect, left the site when commercial opportunities beckoned elsewhere.

Notes

1 E. I. Druzhinina, *Kiuchuk-Kainardzhiiskii mir 1774 goda* (Moscow: Akademii nauk SSSR, 1955); E. I. Druzhinina, *Severnoe prichernomor'e v 1775–1800 gg.* (Moscow: Akademii nauk SSSR, 1959).

2 G. L. Arsh, *Eteristskoe dvizhenie v Rossii* (Moscow: Nauka, 1970), 144.

3 Antoine Ignace Anthoine (Baron de Saint-Joseph), *Essai historique sur le commerce et la navigation de la Mer-Noire* (Paris: Agasse, 1805).

4 Johann P. B. Weber, *Die Russen oder Versuch einer Reisebeschreibung nach Russland und durch das Russische Reich in Europa*, ed. H. Halm (Innsbruck: Sprachwissenschaftliche Institut der Universität, 1960); Hans Halm, *Oesterreich und Neurussland*, vol. 1, *Donauschiffahrt und -handel nach dem Südosten 1718–1780* (Breslau: Thiel & Hintermeier, 1943).

5 Arsh, *Eteristskoe dvizhenie*, 141.

6 *Odessa, 1794-1894:* (Odessa, Izdaniia gorodskogo obshchestvennogo upravleniia k stoletiiu goroda, 1895).

7 Arsh, *Eteristskoe dvizhenie*, 136.

8 Ibid.

9 Ibid., 141.

10 A. Orlov, *Istoricheskii ocherk Odessy s 1794 po 1803 god* (Odessa: A. Shul'tse, 1885), 104–22.

11 Arsh, *Eteristskoe dvizhenie*, 136–38.
12 Ibid., 142.
13 *Gosudarstvennaia vneshniaia torgovlia 1826 goda v raznykh ee vidakh* (St. Petersburg: n.p., 1827).
14 *Odessa, 1794–1894*, 791.
15 *Journal d'Odessa*, January 28, 1847.
16 Arsh, *Eteristskoe dvizhenie*, 260.
17 G. L. Arsh, *Tainoe obshchestvo "Philiki Eteriia"* (Moscow: Nauka, 1965), 46–47.
18 Arsh, *Eteristskoe dvizhenie*, 147.
19 V. A. Zolotov, *Vneshniaia torgovlia iuzhnoi Rossii v pervoi polovine XIX v.* (Rostov-on-the-Don: Izdatel'stvo Rostovskogo universiteta, 1963), 170.
20 *Notizie di Odessa di Sig. L. C.* (Florence: n.p., 1817), 13.
21 Zolotov, *Vneshniaia torgovlia*, 172–73.
22 Quoted by Arsh, *Eteristskoe dvizhenie*, 211.
23 Renato Risaliti, *Studi sui rapporti italo-russi (coi "Ricordi di viaggi" inediti di Luigi Serristori)* (Pisa: Libreria Goliardica, 1972), 154.
24 Arsh, *Eteristskoe dvizhenie*, 212.
25 Arsh, *Eteristskoe dvizhenie*, 303.
26 John Moore, *A Journey from London to Odessa with Notices of New Russia*, etc. (Paris: Delaforest, 1833), 149.
27 Archives du Ministère des Affaires Étrangères, Paris (hereafter AMAE), Mémoires et Documents, Russie, vol. 44, fol. 24.
28 Julius de Hagemeister, *Report on the Commerce of the Ports of New Russia, Moldavia, and Wallachia Made to the Russian Government in 1835* (London: E. Wilson, 1836), 74.
29 For the various French consular reports discussing the regulations and the reactions of the French merchant community to them, see AMAE, Odessa, vol. 8, January 20, 1856, fols. 1–5; February 5, 1858, fols. 10–20; April 27, 1858, fol. 50; July 25, 1858, fols. 70–75.
30 Public Records Office, London (hereafter PRO), Foreign Office (hereafter FO) 257, March 13, 1850.
31 Only the French translation was available to me: *Population commerciale d'Odessa* (Odessa: Gorodskaia tipografiia, 1845).
32 AMAE, Odessa, vol. 8, July 25, 1858, fols. 87–89.
33 Zolotov, *Vneshniaia torgovlia*, 155.
34 E I. Druzhinina, *Iuzhnaia Ukraina 1800–1825 gg.* (Moscow: Nauka, 1970), 360–61.
35 The genealogies of most of these houses have been reconstructed in the remarkable work by Philip P. Argenti, *Libro d'Oro de la noblesse de Chio*, 2 vols. (London: Oxford University Press, 1955). On the abilities of the Greeks as merchants, see the incisive comments of David S. Landes, *Bankers and Pashas: International Finance and Economic Imperialism in Egypt* (New York: Harper and Row, 1969), 24–27.
36 *Journal d'Odessa*, January 28, 1847.
37 National Archives of the United States (hereafter NA), Dispatches from the United States Consuls in Odessa, May 31, 1831.
38 NA, Odessa, Consular Report, October 20, 1854.
39 John Stephens, *Incidents of Travel in Greece, Turkey, Russia, and Poland*, 2 vols. (New York: Harper and Brothers, 1838), 1:260.
40 Chr. Moulakes, *Oikos Adelphon Ralli* (Athens, no. pub. 1964), 9.
41 S. D. Chapman, "The International Houses: The Continental Contribution to British Commerce, 1800–1860," *Journal of European Economic History* 6 (1977): 38.
42 Argenti, *Libro d'Oro*, 2:103.

43. Archivio di Stato di Firenze (hereafter ASF), Ministero delle Finanze, Capi Rotti, no. 20. Report from G. Cantini to G. Baldasseroni, July 7, 1848.
44. Stephens, *Incidents*, 1:260.
45. Moulakes, *Oikos*, 10.
46. NA, Odessa, Consular Report, May 30, 1831.
47. H. Wikoff, *Reminiscences of an Idler* (New York: Fords, Howard, & Hulbert, 1880), 234.
48. Stephens, *Incidents*, 1:260.
49. NA, Odessa, Consular Report, March 1, 1854.
50. NA, Odessa, Consular Report, February 20, 1857.
51. NA, Odessa, Consular Report, December 5, 1856.
52. Odessa, 1794–1894, 88.
53. Personal interview with his great-niece, Marfa Viktorivna Tsomakion, Odessa, September 1974.
54. Argenti, *Libro d'Oro*, 2:147.
55. V. Zagoruiko, *Po stranitsam istorii Odessy i Odesshchiny*, 2 vols. (Odessa: Odesskoe oblastnoe izdatel'stvo, 1957–60), 2:104–5.
56. *Adres-kalendar' Odesskogo gradonachal'stva na 1910 god* (Odessa: Vedomosti Odesskogo gradonachal'stva, 1910), 336.
57. A. A. Markevich, *Dvadtsatipiatiletie Imperatorskogo Novorossiiskogo universiteta* (Odessa, Ekonomicheskaia tipografiia, 1890), xxxvii.
58. Argenti, *Libro d'Oro*, 2:147.
59. *Adres-kalendar'*, 196.
60. Argenti, *Libro d'Oro*, 2:151.
61. For information on the Rodokanaki family in Livorno, see M. Baruchello, *Livorno e il suo porto: Origini, caratteristiche e vicende dei traffici livornesi* (Livorno: Livorno soc. an. editrice riviste techniche 1932), 380–81, 563.
62. ASF, Ministero delle Finanze, Capi Rotti, no. 20, July 7, 1848.
63. ASF, Affari Esteri, Protocollo 435.34, January 12, 1851.
64. Chapman, "International Houses," 46.
65. *Gosudarstvennaia vneshniaia torgovlia* for the years 1826 and 1827.
66. *Journal d'Odessa*, January 28, 1847.
67. *Gosudarstvennaia vneshniaia torgovlia* for the year 1861.
68. *Giornale del Commercio, delle Arti e delle Manifatture con Varietà ed Avvisi Diversi*, May 20, 1838, and subsequent issues for ship arrivals and departures.
69. ASF, Affari Esteri, Protocollo 266, no. 22, May 24, 1832.
70. Argenti, *Libro d'Oro*, 2:180.
71. Ibid.,1:106.
72. Ibid.
73. *Eteristskoe dvizhenie*, 143n34.
74. A. de Ribas, *Staraia Odessa: Istoricheskie ocherki i vospominaniia* (Odessa: Knizhnyi magazin Georgiia Russo, 1913).
75. *Journal de St. Petersbourg*, April 24, 1844.
76. Moore, *A Journey from London*, 154–55.
77. PRO, FO 65 355, February 28, 1848.
78. AMAE, Odessa, vol. 7, December 15, 1857.
79. ASF, Affari Esteri, Protocollo 485.85, May 10, 1853; April 28, 1855.
80. Arsh, *Eteristskoe dvizhenie*, 148–49. Deno J. Geanakoplos, "The Diaspora Greeks: The Genesis of Modern Greek National Consciousness," in *Hellenism and the First Greek War of Liberation (1821–1830): Continuity and*

Change (Thessaloniki: Institute for Balkan Studies, 1976), 59–77. On the other hand, V. A. Iakovlev claims that the Greeks of Odessa did not keep apart from the Russian population of the city, "The Greeks were not greatly alienated (*otchuzhdalis'*) from the Russian population and always responded enthusiastically to the demands of their new fatherland." See his essay "Koe chto ob inoplemennikakh v istorii g. Odessy," in *Iz proshlogo Odessy: Sbornik statei*, ed. L. M. de-Ribas (Odessa: G. G. Marazli, 1894), 377–78.

81 Markevich, *Dvadtsatipiatiletie*, xiii–lxxix.
82 *Gosudarsvennaia vneshniaia torgovlia* for the year 1826.
83 *Journal d'Odessa*, January 28, 1847. *Adres-kalendar'*, 195, 199.
84 *Pervaia vseobshchaia perepis' naseleniia Rossiiskoi imperii 1897 g.*, 80 vols., in 24 (St. Petersburg: Tsentral'ni statisticheskii komitet, 1899–1905), vol. 47: *Gorod Odessa*, vi–vii.
85 PRO, FO 65 647, March 4, 1863. The British consul, Grenville-Murray, reported to London that the Jews were then "pushing the Greeks altogether aside, and they have become the first bankers and merchants of South Russia."
86 *Südöstliche Steppen und Städte* (Frankturt-am-Main: Sauerländer, 1862), 103. See also V. A. Iakovlev: "[In both export and import] they held first place up to the 50s, but at the present time in this business they have gone back to a second level, leaving their place to the Jews." *Iz proshlogo Odessy*, 376.
87 Nevin U. Winter, *The Russian Empire of To-Day and Yesterday* (London: Simpkin, Marshall, Hamilton, Kent & Co, 1914), 136. A few years previously, another American journalist noted that while Jews of Odessa represented one-third of the population, "they control the banking, the manufacturing, the export trade, the milling, the wholesale and retail mercantile and commercial enterprises." William E. Curtis, *Around the Black Sea* (New York: Hodder and Stoughton, 1911), 329–30.
88 Chapman, "International Houses," 39.
89 Moulake, *Oikos*, 13. According to Iakovlev, the peasants retained in his own day (the 1890s) happy memories of the fair treatment they received in doing business with this Greek firm. *Iz proshlogo Odessy*, 376.
90 Moulake, *Oikos*, 17.

CHAPTER 8

The Greek Community in Odessa, 1861–1917

THE GREEKS AND THE BLACK SEA

The Greeks have always been a seafaring people, interacting with lands in easy maritime access to their homes. The northern littoral of the Black Sea is one such accessible region. In ancient times Greeks often visited this coast, dotting it with numerous colonies and trading stations. In the late eighteenth century, Greeks again came in considerable numbers to the region, now part of the Russian Empire. Expanding commercial opportunities, especially the booming export of cereals from the southern steppes to Western Europe beckoned them.

This essay describes the Greek community in one city of the Russian Empire, Odessa, for a particular period in its history. For contrast, characteristics of the German and Jewish communities of the time are occasionally referred to. The principal sources for the study are two: census reports and material to supplement them. The censuses, valuable as they are, provide aggregate and rather static information. To gauge the direction and degree of change, I have also examined life histories and have conducted oral and written interviews with elderly people of Greek descent who either lived in South Russia or had close relatives who did so. Some of the questions addressed are: Who were the Greeks who came to the southern territories of the Russian Empire? How did their economic interests and activities change as the area's initial prosperity gradually waned in the late nineteenth century? What factors either hastened or obstructed assimilation with the native peoples among whom they settled? The present study offers only partial answers with respect to the situation in approximately the last half-century of tsarist rule in Russia.[1]

The Greeks living in the Russian Empire have not been closely studied. Much less is known about Greeks in the northern Euxine regions (now South Ukraine) in modern times than about their ancient predecessors. G. Arsh's research has done much to rectify this, but his studies are largely limited to the Greek settlement in the late eighteenth and early nineteenth centuries when the region first became part of the Russian Empire. He was chiefly interested in the contribution that Greeks of the northern diaspora made to the independence movement in their homeland and only secondarily in their experiences abroad.[2] No one, to my knowledge,

---

Originally published as Patricia Herlihy, "The Greek Community in Odessa, 1861–1917," *Journal of Modern Greek Studies* VII (1989): 235–52.

has paid attention to the history of the Greek populations in Russian territory over the late nineteenth century.

ODESSA

In order to reconstruct their history, special attention must be paid to Odessa, long the queen city among Black Sea ports and one that had early attracted a large and prosperous Greek community. In the history of Black Sea commerce, the Crimean War (1853–56) marked a watershed. Over the last half of the nineteenth century, the cereal exports of the Russian Empire continued to grow in absolute volumes, but also declined in relative share of the world market. The United States, Canada, Argentina, and other countries emerged as vigorous competitors. Odessa in particular now faced diminishing commercial opportunities. Several of its prominent Greek mercantile families abandoned South Russia altogether in order to pursue more promising commercial enterprises elsewhere. Still others among the wealthy early arrivals transferred their businesses to other ports along the Black Sea and the Sea of Azov. Odessa did, however, continue to attract immigrants from Greece and the Turkish Empire. Doubtless, it also lost emigrants back to the homeland, particularly among those older persons who wished to retire in the country of their birth and had earned the means to do so. I want to look closely at the residual community of Greeks who made Odessa at least their temporary home in the late nineteenth century in spite of the city's weakening economic fortunes.

NUMBERS

Two censuses give us glimpses into the size and general characteristics of Odessa's Greeks. They were redacted in 1892 and 1897 respectively, and both included the entire city.[3] The census of 1897 was part of a monumental survey of the Russian Empire, the only such general scrutiny undertaken in tsarist times. The 1892 census is interesting as its takers sought answers to a long set of questions regarding one of Odessa's most salient social features: its large colonies of foreign language speakers and foreign nationals. The information recorded includes the identification of foreign nationals, their languages, religions, sex ratios, literacy levels, birth rates, residence patterns, and occupations.

The census takers of 1892 used two criteria to identify foreigners within the city, neither one of which is entirely free of ambiguity. Some of the published tables classify the city residents by maternal tongue, without specifying their places of birth (apart from those born in Odessa). Other tables use nationality or foreign citizenship. For economy of expression, we shall refer to those of Greek maternal tongue as Greek-speakers, although most of them doubtlessly knew and used other languages.

In 1892, there were 5,283 Greek-speakers in Odessa—not an insignificant number, although constituting only 1.6 percent of the 340,526 residents of this big city. By 1897, the number had declined slightly to 5,013 persons. The city meanwhile had grown to over 400,000 people (403,815), and this reduced the proportion of Greek-speakers to 1.3 percent. In 1892, of the 5,283 Greek-speakers, 4,182, or 79.1 percent, retained their Greek citizenship. This is a much larger percentage than we find, for example, within the German-speaking community. There, only 2,755 persons out of 9,163, or 30 percent, remained foreign citizens. The large number of Greek citizens within the Greek-speaking community could mean that they were retaining continuing close ties with their homeland.

In 1892, the Greeks at Odessa were recorded in overwhelming numbers as members of the Orthodox faith. Only five Greek-speaking Jews were recorded, although the city had a huge Jewish population.

The distribution of the Greek community by sex is revealing. Men predominate among the Greek-speaking population; there are 165 males for every 100 females. Among the Greek nationals, the ratio is 128, somewhat lower but still high. For all Odessa's residents, the ratio is 110 males per 100 females. A high sex ratio was not characteristic of all Odessa's foreign colonies. Of the more than 21,000 (21,727) foreign nationals registered in the census, the sex ratio was 114, slightly higher than in the entire population. Among the German-speakers, women were actually more numerous than men, 4,627 to 4,536, for a sex ratio of 98.

The unusually high sex ratio among Odessa's Greeks suggests that the community included a large and presumably transient population of young males in search of jobs, not all of whom made the city their permanent home. The low sex ratio among the German nationals, on the other hand, points to a similar transient element in their midst, but this time made up of young women. Many German girls came to work as governesses, teachers, or translators. High literacy rates confirm the presence of educated German women. Of German women over age six, 62.8 percent knew how to read and write, the same percentage as with German males. In contrast, only 41.5 percent of adult Greek women were literate; this is lower than the level for all foreign women (43.4 percent). Adult Greek males, on the other hand, show a literacy rate of 50.8 percent, nearly the same as that registered by males in the entire foreign community (51.3 percent). The contrast between Greek and German women is further borne out by their comparative birth rates. For Greek women between the ages of 16 and 45, the ratio of children under age five is .53 child per woman. For German women, the comparable ratio is a low .36. These data strongly suggest that many German women were not married as were many Greek women.

Of 2,346 Greek males who retained their foreign citizenship, 1,013, or 43 percent, were born in Odessa. Of 1,836 Greek women in the same category, 1,153 or 63 percent were born in the city. Not surprisingly, males were visibly more mobile than females.

NEIGHBORHOODS

The census of 1892 also gives the distribution of the population and its many constituent groups by nine urban districts. Since it also provides information about water supply and sewage, it allows us to judge the quality of the physical environment and thus the relative affluence of these different neighbors. The "comfort index" I utilize here is the percentage of houses with toilets connected to sewers, as provided by the census itself. Table 1 shows where the persons of Greek maternal tongue are found in the city, in relation to the Russian-speaking population, the Jews and the Germans.

Table 1 Distribution of the Population by Neighborhoods, Odessa, 1892.

Figures represent percentages.					
Neighborhood	Buildings with Sewers	Russians	Greeks	Jews	Germans
Bul'varnyi	84	12.5	27.1	11.0	19.4
Oleksandrivs'kyi	72	14.0	19.7	32.8	15.0
Khersons'kyi Slobidka	70	17.0	17.8	6.0	23.0
Romanivka	12	4.6	2.4	0.8	1.0
Petropavlovs'kyi	45	20.7	10.1	23.7	15.6
Mykhailivs'kyi	18	14.7	9.0	22.0	16.2
Peresyps'kyi	2	5.9	9.9	3.0	5.7
Port	34	1.1	2.6	0.02	0.3
Dal'nyts'kyi	0	9.6	1.3	0.7	3.7
Total pop.		196,440	5,283	105,670	9,163

Source: Rezul'taty 1894.

The ethnic communities show a pronounced tendency to cluster. Nearly a third of the Jews are found in the relatively well-to-do neighborhood of Oleksandrivs'kyi and upwards of 45 percent in the somewhat poorer districts of Petropavlovs'kyi and Mykhailivs'kyi. Jews are very few or altogether absent in five of the nine neighborhoods. Over a quarter of the Greeks are found in the city's best neighborhood, that of Bul'varnyi; this would indicate the presence in the Greek community of a prosperous element, or "middle class." Not even the Germans show as large a concentration as the Greeks in Odessa's better neighborhoods. On the other hand, another quarter of the Greek population is found in five neighborhoods, which have the fewest houses with sewage connections. The Greek community clearly also included many poor members.

OCCUPATIONS

The census of 1897 classifies the population by occupation, and this allows us to seek confirmation for the conclusions concerning wealth and education proposed above. The census lists sixty-five occupational categories and further divides the population into "independent" and "dependent" persons. The data presented here are based on those individuals regarded by the census takers as "independents." I have grouped the original sixty-five occupations into ten categories. Table 2 shows the distribution for Greeks, Germans, and Russians.

Table 2 Distribution of the Population by Occupation, Odessa, 1897.

Category	Greeks			Germans			Russians		
	M	W	Per.	M	W	Per.	M	W	Per.
Govt. & Army	90	0	3.2	894	0	15.8	14304	1	13.2
Liberal professions	48	33	2.9	147	210	6.3	2,606	1,607	3.9
Domestic service	473	77	19.8	477	771	22.1	18,314	18,234	33.7
Rentiers & Pens.	138	170	11.1	307	353	11.7	4,624	5,450	9.3
Agricultural prdcts	65	3	2.4	162	5	3.0	1,714	160	1.7
Manufactures	588	53	23.0	1,218	163	24.4	13,871	3,362	15.9
Construction	56	1	2.0	261	3	4.7	7,901	65	7.4
Travel and Comm.	133	2	4.9	135	8	2.5	7,202	120	6.8
Commerce and Bank	812	10	29.5	438	51	8.6	5,969	1,157	6.6
Miscellaneous	19	11	1.1	28	27	1.0	903	715	1.5

Source: *Pervaia perepis'* 1899–1905, vol. 47.

The Greeks are well represented in what seems the wealthiest entry in the list of sixty-five occupations, those who live from dividends, rents, pensions and the like. In addition, we also have an indirect indication of the relative affluence of this group in the number of dependents that the census attributes to it. If we take the Russians (the largest group recorded in the census) as an example, then the 5,086 capitalists appear with 5,549 dependents, for a ratio of 1.1 to 1. In contrast, those obviously poor persons who were supported by the state, social organizations, parents, and relatives numbered 4,988 but appear with only 107 dependents for a ratio of 0.02. The capitalists and rentiers show a large number of dependents in spite of the fact that this category included many widows.

Among the Greeks, 105 men and 135 women, or 8 percent of all those independently employed, live from returns of stocks, bonds, and government securities. The same group among the Germans enlists 6.7 percent of both sexes, 4.7 percent among the Russians, and 3.1 percent among the Jews.

Both Greeks and Jews have a large number of their members employed in some sort of retail trade. Nearly 30 percent of those Greeks declaring an occupation were engaged in some form of trade; Jews similarly employed were 30.1 percent. The largest in the Greek community is that of merchant in agricultural produce apart from grain; 395 Greek men give this as their occupation. It is interesting to note that grain traders, which the census lists as a separate occupation, did not include a large number of Greek men, only sixty-four.

In contrast, 2,039 Jews were engaged in the cereal trade. We might note that the big Russian population shows only 446 male grain dealers. The Jews seem to have dominated the marketing of grain. Large numbers of Greeks were also found in the occupations of manufactures and household service. Many of these were doubtlessly governesses, and this would help explain the high literacy level shown by German women in 1892.

The Germans also appear in unexpected numbers in the army, for reasons I cannot at present explain.

CHARACTERISTICS

Here then are the prominent characteristics that the two censuses reveal about the Greek community at Odessa in the late nineteenth century. It was still attracting immigrants, and men in significantly larger numbers than women. Many Greek women were actually born in the city, married there, reared their children, but seem not to have pursued careers outside of the home, at least not in large numbers. The Greek males were in the majority recent immigrants, and many remained unmarried as they sought to find work and make a career. However, not all these males quickly left Odessa when opportunities beckoned elsewhere. Some married and seem even to have brought in brides from Greece, as hinted by the numbers of women who declare Greek nationality.

The Greek community appears also to have been socially much more variegated than, for example, the German nationals. To judge by their rather modest literacy levels and residency patterns, many poor Greeks were coming to Odessa, although the community also retained many prosperous members.

Perhaps we are observing here a shift in the character of Greek immigration between the early and late nineteenth century. At first Odessa attracted colonists of means, but late in the century it was drawing its share of less prosperous immigrants—poorer persons who were pouring out of the homeland in search of jobs and a better life. In this respect Odessa's Greek community probably resembles what we would find in a large American city in the same period.[4] The chief difference would be that Odessa's Greek community still included comparatively larger numbers of distinctively prosperous members.

The two censuses provide valuable aggregate information on Odessa's Greeks, but as I have already indicated, they necessarily present a somewhat static picture. When we turn to life history materials, understandably, almost all the available information on Odessa's Greek residents concerns the wealthiest and most prominent of the Greek families. Their experiences are not typical of all Greeks at Odessa, but given their status as the community's leaders, they hold an independent interest. We want to know what happened to the traditional Greek involvement in commerce, and what new economic interests occupied their energies and their capital as the old century moved into the new. And how well did Odessa's Greeks retain their Hellenic culture? These two aspects of their lives—economic and cultural—are, I shall argue, tightly intertwined. Certain types of economic activity favored contact with the homeland and knowledge of its language, while others rather promoted assimilation into Russian and Ukrainian society.

Of immeasurable help in this inquiry are the works of Philip Argenti and Mikhail Dimitri Sturdza.[5] They have compiled respectively two comprehensive genealogies of prominent Greek families, many of whose members spent part or all of their lives in Odessa. In addition, I have interviewed by mail several now elderly persons of Greek descent who either lived in South Ukraine or who had close relatives who did so.

THE RETREAT FROM OVERSEAS TRADE

After the Crimean War the changing and declining (in relative terms) export of cereals out of Odessa drove many of the major Greek export firms from the city. Among the prominent Greek mercantile firms who departed from Odessa but not from commerce was the house of Ralli.[6] One of several great mercantile families from Chios, the Ralli family had arrived early in Odessa; John Ralli even served for many years as American consul in the port. But by 1866, the Ralli Brothers' firm had left the empire in favor of engaging in the textile trade in India and banking in America. It sold its Russian interests to Scaramanga and Associates who continued to trade in Taganrog and other ports of the Black Sea and the Sea of Azov. John Skaramanga died at Taganrog in 1902. It is likely that his sons continued to manage the firm until the Bolshevik revolution.

Rostov, Mykolaiv, Mariupol', and Taganrog continued to be important centers of Greek mercantile activity. Mikhail Langada, the father of Helen Langada Sutsos, a woman I was able to interview, emigrated from the Greek island of Santorini and settled in Taganrog in the 1880s or 1890s. He remained in the grain-exporting business until the Bolsheviks took power in 1920. Together with the census data, his career suggests that the poorest Greeks continued to emigrate to Odessa in the late nineteenth century, but those with some means and with a mercantile career in mind had come to favor the more easterly ports.

The history of the Avierino family shows a similar pattern. Its founder, Theodore, was one of the several Greek merchants of Odessa active in the secret society for Greek Independence, the Filiki Eteria. While we have no reason to believe that the Avierino family continued to export cereal after the middle of the nineteenth century, other members of the family continued to function as merchants at Taganrog. Alexander (brother of Theodore) may have been the first Greek from Chios to open an exporting firm in Odessa. In 1803 he founded A. Avierino and Sons and, according to Argenti, the integrity of his character and the renown of his intelligence made him esteemed by Greeks and Russians alike until his death in 1843.[7] It is not clear from our data how long the company operated in Taganrog. As late as 1861, however, the firm was still listed among the merchants of the first and wealthiest guild. Helen Avierino Negroponte, the last Avierino we know of who resided there, died in 1909. Her long presence may indicate that the Avierino family continued to trade in cereals, but she was also the wife of a Negroponte. The Negroponte company was still active in Taganrog at least as late as the 1900s.[8]

Members of the Mavrokordato family also illustrate our point. The name, incidentally, is spelled in Russian with a "k," and thus in English, Mavrokordato; the branch in Western Europe spelled it with a "g," Mavrogordato. The name also acquired a special renown as it was attached to the most powerful bank of Eastern Europe, with headquarters at Constantinople and branches at Odessa, London, Paris, Marseille, and Trieste.[9] The Paris office remained open until the 1970s.

Laurenzi Mavrokordato arrived in Odessa as early as 1798 with investment capital of 10,000 rubles.[10] But the Odessa branch abandoned the grain trade after 1863. Among the family's distinguished members was Dmitri, who was born in Odessa in 1851 and died there in 1917. He became an admiral and a prince of the Russian Empire.

John Mavrokordato, born in Chios in 1845, was married in Nikolaev in 1872. He and his wife died in Nikolaev in 1922. Their last years must have been difficult. Their son George, chamberlain to the Tsar, a state councilor and a member of the Order of St. Vladimir, was killed by the Bolsheviks in 1918.

Other members of the family found their way to Mykolaiv, Taganrog, and Rostov-on-the-Don. They became involved, for example, in the shipment of wool from Rostov-on-the-Don, the major port for wool exports to England and the United States. An American consular dispatch, dated March 23, 1879, mentions that C. N. Mavrokordato was acting as agent in wool shipments for the firm of P. P. Rodokanaki in London.[11] Matthew Mavrokordato, born in 1860, served as consul general of Greece in Taganrog and Rostov-on-the-Don, where his daughter Helen was born in 1906. The imperial government decorated him with the orders of St. Anne and of St. Stanislaus. His son Constantine was born in Taganrog in 1901. The family apparently fled Russia in the face of the revolution: Constantine was married in Paris in 1926.

Many other examples could be offered of Greek families that came early to the south of Russia to participate in trade, only to leave commerce or the city altogether as its commercial fortunes declined. Smaller Jewish traders took up the slack, as the census of 1897 makes apparent.[12] The Greeks who remained in Odessa tended to shift their resources and energies in other directions: real estate holdings, industrial enterprises, banking, insurance, and government service.

DIVERSIFIED INTERESTS

Greeks, to be sure, had cultivated activities such as maritime insurance as early as the 1820s.[13] Insurance and banking enterprises attracted the interests of the prominent houses of Rodokanaki and Ralli. In 1910 Paul Ralli was director of the Odessa Discount Bank.[14]

The list of businesses in which Greeks can be shown to have invested after 1860 is dazzling for its variety: construction firms, cotton spinning and weaving factories, steam-powered flour mills, beet-sugar plants, distilleries, printing presses, food packaging plants (including jams and chocolate), champagne, cognac, and wine distributors and leather works.[15]

The Petrocochino family from Chios was among the first Greek families to arrive at Odessa (a branch also settled at Taganrog). They were former partners with the brothers in the cereal export business. In 1913, according to a commercial handbook of the empire, the Petrocochinos were the owners of one of Odessa's largest department stores.[16] Their great store was appropriately located at 28 Hrets'ka Street.[17] Another of the earliest Greek families to arrive in the new town of Odessa, the Raftopoulos, were engaged in the grocery and restaurant business on the eve of the First World War.[18]

Odessa's affluent Greeks were also moving heavily into real estate. Table 3 gives a list of some of the prominent Greek property owners within the city in 1873.

Table 3 Some Large Greek Property Owners in the City of Odessa, 1873.

Name	Street	Assessed Value (rubles)
Grigorii Marazli	Italiis'ka	80,000
Grigorii Marazli	Katerynyns'ka	24,000
Grigorii Marazli	Chervonyi provulok	6,000
Grigorii Marazli	Kolodiaz'na	11,000
Grigorii Marazli	Kolodiaz'na	4,000
Grigorii Marazli	Hrets'ka	50,000
Grigorii Marazli	Derybasivs'ka	60,000
Grigorii Marazli	Prymors'kyi	4,000
Grigorii Marazli	suburbs	29,783
Grigorii Marazli	suburbs	28,000
		296,783
Elena Ralli	Chervonyi provulok	39,000
Elena Ralli	Chervonyi provulok	5,000
Stephen Ralli	Preobrazhens'ka	27,000
Konstantin Ralli	Preobrazhens'ka	30,000
Stephen Ralli	Troitska	68,000
Stephen Ralli	Derybasivs'ka	150,000
Stephen Ralli	Teatral'na	54,000
Stephen Ralli	Teatral'na	254,000
Stephen Ralli	Teatral'na	130,000
		775,000
Fedor Rodokanaki	Teatral'na	5,000
Fedor Rodokanaki	Teatral'na	32,000
Fedor Rodokanaki	Kazarmovyi provulok	18,000
Fedor Rodokanaki	suburbs	27,500
		82,500
Papudov	suburbs	109,275
Greek School		96,000
Grand Total		1,262,558

Source: Odessa Oblast' Archives, Vedomosti, fond 274, opus 1: 64–85.

Among the Greek grain merchants who remained at Odessa was Marco Sevastopulo, the paternal grandfather of Elisabeth Stenbock-Fermor, one of my correspondents. In 1855 he married Erato Mavrokordato of the great commercial family. His two brothers, Charles and Constantine, were the company's representatives at Livorno. Constantine, a lover of Hellenic antiquities, accumulated a distinguished collection of ancient statuary, some pieces of which have found their way into museums at Athens and Stanford University.

Elisabeth's father was also named Charles, and typically was not a merchant. He entered government service as an agricultural expert, and spent considerable time studying silkworm culture in Italy and France. He also did pioneer work in photography. His career shift out of commerce into government service seems to illustrate a general trend. For a family of considerable means long settled in Odessa, the change from commerce to government service and other forms of civic activity was a natural evolution.

In 1896, Charles married at Odessa Maria Lignine, not of Greek extraction, whose father (Elisabeth's maternal grandfather) had been professor of mathematics at Odessa University and a former mayor of the city. He was a member of the horticultural society and active in many civic and charitable affairs. Elisabeth recalls that in the early 1900s her father's family still held wheat storage barns in Odessa's suburbs—relics of the once thriving trade. Elisabeth was related to another old and prominent Greek family, the Mavrokordatos previously mentioned. Their wealth then seems to have been primarily in vast landholdings.

In sum, those wealthy Greeks who remained in Odessa tended to shift their resources away from overseas commerce and also importantly into land. They came to resemble the Russian gentry, fraternized and intermarried with them, and often pursued careers similar to theirs. I. A. Tolli, for example, the descendant of Greek immigrants who had come to Odessa during the reign of Catherine the Great, was a millionaire who in 1884 served as mayor of Kyiv.

COMMUNITY

Odessa's Greeks maintained an organized community (koinonia) with a president and a council.[19] In 1901 the philanthropist Grigorii Marazli was its "president for life." The consul of Greece in Odessa, Fontana, hailed him as "first in all things good and all things Greek." The community sponsored a high school for girls, named for another philanthropist, Theodore Rodokanaki, and there was also a Greek high school for boys. The girls were regarded as the hope of the community as they were expected to be the parent who would pass on to their children language and traditions.[20]

In 1901, and in collaboration with the Greek consul, Fontana, the community sponsored a lavish celebration of the eightieth anniversary of the Greek revolution. Representatives of the imperial Russian government and of foreign powers participated in the thanksgiving services held in the Church of the Holy Trinity. The assembly then moved to the girls' school for speeches and music, and then to the Stock Exchange, whose great hall was appropriated for the day. Three hundred subscribers sat down to a special meal, enlivened by many toasts with Greek and Russian wine. The festivities continued far into the night and pictures and a description of the affair were published in Odessa in the Greek language. In his address, Consul Fontana congratulated Odessa's Greeks for their loyalty to the homeland and expressed the hope that a Greek club could be formed to enhance solidarity.

Greek philanthropic work in Odessa benefited both fellow Greeks and the larger society. Perhaps no one gave so much of himself or his property than Grigorii G. Marazli, mayor of Odessa from 1879 to about 1900. His gifts included a Christian cemetery, a bacteriology laboratory, a children's garden, a palace which is now the Museum of Art in Odessa, a mansion on Pushkins'ka Street, a dacha to house the Imperial Horticultural Society, a night lodging house, a public library, a reading room, and two schools. He also supported a poorhouse, a girls' orphanage, the Odessa theater and the publication of the *Novorossiiskii kalendar'*.[21] It may be that many Greek families were grateful to their adopted land for their fortunes and wished to repay Odessa and Russia.

SOCIAL RELATIONS

Those I interviewed report that the relations between Greeks and Russians were consistently cordial. Religious affinity was certainly an important factor in contributing to this. In addition, the Greeks were positively regarded as helping in the commercial and economic development of these new regions. Pericles Rodokanaki was ennobled in 1896 by Tsar Nicholas II expressly for the family's development of commerce in Odessa.[22]

Although we have no exact data on marriages between Greeks and Russians, the pattern seems to be the following. The great Greek families that arrived early in Odessa usually married among themselves. Indeed, the many from Chios tended to intermarry with families from the same island. Thus, the Sevastopulos were linked to the Mavrokordatos, Petrokokinos, Negropontes, Skaramangas, Rodokanakis, Rallis, and so forth.[23] But since religious affinity between the Greek and Russian churches placed no obstacle to intermarriages, it seems that they occurred with increasing frequency from the late nineteenth century. For example, Charles Sevastopulo (Elisabeth's father) married a Russian woman, Marie Lignine. Many such marriages are represented in Argenti's and Sturdza's genealogies. The Ralli twins, Peter and Paul, born in Odessa in 1851, were married in the 1880s and 1890s, the former to Maria Kurovski and the latter to Catherine Tymachenko, both Slavic surnames. At least four out of five of their sisters also married non-Greeks. My correspondent, Elisabeth Sevastapulo, married Count Ivan Stenbock-Fermor, a member of the Imperial Horse Guards in the First World War, in 1933. He later served with the White armies.

CULTURE AND LANGUAGE

The leaders of the Greek community warmly recalled the cultural achievements of the fatherland. In 1881, for example, Lysander Konsta, the director of the Odessa Greek commercial school, lauded the wealth of the ancient Greek language and stressed the need of giving instruction in it at the school. His own speech was appropriately written in the high style and was published at Odessa.[24] The school itself was an institution of major importance to the community. It enrolled 208 students, of whom 160 were Greeks, 33 were Russians, and others of assorted nationalities.

Two factors weakened the cohesion of the Greek community. Since both Greeks and Russians were communicants in the Orthodox Church, no religious barrier separated the two peoples. Social contacts, even intermarriages, as we have seen, were frequent. The community of Greeks at Odessa thus appears much more porous and open to the surrounding world than is the case among the Greeks settled at Alexandria in Egypt, a Muslim country.[25] Moreover, in the days when the export trade dominated Greek economic interests, it was essential that the Greek merchants speak their mother tongue (for purposes of internal communications) and also some western languages, such as French and Italian. But as their financial interests came to focus on local enterprises, the Greek language had diminishing economic value for them.

My correspondents disagree regarding the knowledge of Greek retained in the Black Sea diaspora. John Sevastopulo stated that "they all spoke Greek between them, also their second language was French; Russian came third. I met many Greeks from Odessa in Paris; they always spoke Greek…."[26] Still, the frequent intermarriages of a Greek male with a Russian woman must have made it difficult to maintain the language in the households where the children were reared. There appear to be fewer cases of Greek women married to Russian men. And the lack of Greek-speaking nurses, governesses and servants helped establish Russian as the chief domestic language.

The family histories suggest an ebbing knowledge of Greek. Marco Sevastopulo, for example, paternal grandfather to Elisabeth Stenbock-Fermor, spoke Greek as well as French and Italian. But his descendants did not retain this full panoply of linguistic equipment. His son Charles could communicate with his parents in Greek, and once surprised and disappointed the prime minister of Greece, Eleutherios Venizelos, with his poor command of the language. Charles's own library consisted of 2,000 volumes, all in Russian or French. The descendants of the great merchants commonly knew French (many were sent abroad to be educated and Italian). But they did not retain their Greek. Elisabeth Stenbock-Fermor reports that the language of her generation—the last before the First World War—was Russian.

In Elisabeth Stenbock-Fermor's household, her mother (who was not Greek) tried to learn Greek after her marriage in 1896 in order to please her father-in-law. However, she soon abandoned the effort. Her father spoke Greek with his mother only when he did not want the conversation understood by the four children. The children themselves were encouraged to speak French with their grandmother (who spoke it well). Their mother feared that if they spoke Russian with their grandmother, they would acquire the Odessa accent, "the worst in Russia." It is interesting to note that while modern Greek was apparently not taught in the boys' gymnasium, instruction in classical Greek was available to those students who wished it.

The only Greek cultural activities of which Elisabeth was aware as a young girl growing up in Odessa were religious. When still very young, the children were taken to the Greek cathedral several times by their grandmother. The archimandrite would send blessed bread (*artos*) and come to bless the house on the day of the Epiphany. But except for special occasions, the family worshipped in Russian churches and received religious instruction in that language. Clearly the common religious affiliation of Greeks and Russians favored assimilation.

On the other hand, Helen Langada Sutzos reported that at Taganrog, her family, relatively recent arrivals in the region, spoke Greek at home. They also attended the Greek church (there were two in Taganrog); but they also spoke Russian fluently and had many Russian friends. She reports that they had no sense of isolation within or separation from the larger community.

But in spite of their common use of the Russian language, the Greeks of the Black Sea diaspora still retained a sense of their ethnic identity. According to Helen Laganda Sutsos who lived in Taganrog until the 1917 Revolution, even the Bolsheviks treated the Greeks differently from the Russians. They did not, for example, immediately requisition their homes. They allowed them to leave the country without harassment. This favorable treatment was not, to be sure, the universal experience and not that of two of her relatives (cousins) in Odessa. These two brothers, young cadets, sons of a Russian father and Greek mother, were killed during the Bolshevik seizure of the city.

Many who had retained ties with kin in Greece or Turkey fled there after the 1917 Revolution. Others settled in Europe, but many more found a new home in the United States.

CONCLUSION

From its founding in 1794 through to the start of the First World War, Odessa and other Black Sea cities attracted many immigrants from Greece. Initially, they had been well-to-do merchants who had led in the development of grain export during the early part of the century. In the late 1800s, many poor Greeks were also arriving. As Odessa's commercial fortunes ebbed, many of the older families left the city, and those that remained tended to invest in land and in enterprises other than overseas export. They came to resemble the Russian gentry in their economic endeavors. As their international contacts weakened, they tended to lose their Greek language, and they largely adopted Russian as their common language. Intermarriage became common. Shared allegiance to the Orthodox faith can account for and may have facilitated a high measure of assimilation. But as late as World War I, the Greeks of the Black Sea diaspora had not entirely lost their ethnic and cultural identity. While their association with Russians and others in this corner of the world was close and, it is fair to say, productive for more than a century, it did not obliterate national and cultural differences.

ACKNOWLEDGMENTS

I would like to express my gratitude to the following people: Elisabeth Sevastapulo Stenbock-Fermor of Palo Alto, California; John Sevastopulo of Paris and Athens; and Helen Langada Sutsos of Sonoma, California.

Notes

1 I have elsewhere examined Greek settlement on the Black Sea shore in the late eighteenth and early nineteenth centuries. Patricia Herlihy, *Odessa: A History, 1794–1914* (Cambridge, MA: Harvard University Press, 1986), 125–27; Patricia Herlihy, "Greek Merchants in Odessa in the Nineteenth Century," *Harvard Ukrainian Studies*, 3–4, part 1 (1979–80): 399–420. For the history of the emigration of poor Greeks, mostly miners and farmers from Turkey in the eighteenth and nineteenth centuries to the region of the Caucuses, P. A. Akritas, "Greki Kavkaza," in *Narody Kavkaza*, ed. S. P. Tolstov, vol. 2 of *Narodny mira* (Moscow: Akademiia nauk SSSR, 1962), 421–32.

2 G. L. Arsh, *Eteristskoe dvizhenie v Rossii* (Moscow: Nauka, 1970).

3 *Rezul'taty odnodnevnoi perepisi g. Odessy 1 dekabria 1892 goda* (Odessa: Odesskoe gubernskoe zemstvo. Statisticheskoe biuro, 1894). *Pervaia vseobshchaia perepis' naseleniia Rossiiskoi imperii, 1897 g*, 80 vols. in 24 (St. Petersburg: Tsentral'nyi statisticheskii komitet Ministerstva vnutrennikh del, 1899–1905).

4 Theodore Saloutos, *The Greeks in the United States* (Cambridge, MA: Harvard University Press, 1964), 1–8.
5 Philip P. Argenti, *Libro d'Oro de la noblesse de Chio*, 2 vols. (London: Cambridge University Press, 1955). Mihail-Dimitri Sturdza, *Dictionnaire historique et généalogique des Grande Familles de Grèce, d'Albanie et de Constantinople* (Paris: M-D. Sturdza, 1955).
6 Moulakes, Chr. 1964, Oikos Adelphon Ralle (Athens: privately published, 1964).
7 Argenti, *Libro d'Oro*, vol. 1, 57–58.
8 Information supplied in a private communication from Helen Langada Sutsos.
9 Information provided in a private communication from John Sevastopulo.
10 A. Orlov, *Istoricheskii ocherk Odessy s 1794 po 1803 god. Sostavil po dokumentam, khraniashchimsia v Moskovskom Arkhive Ministerstva Iustitsii* (Odessa: Tip. A. Shul'tse, 1885), 123–27.
11 National Archives. United States Consular Despatches, Odessa, 1879, Washington, DC.
12 Herlihy, *Odessa*, 212–14.
13 I am indebted for information on the Marine Insurance Company founded by Konstantin Papudov to Professor Thomas Owen. On early insurance at Odessa, Herlihy, *Odessa*, 320.
14 *Adres-kalendar' Odesskogo gradonachal'stvo na 1910 god* (Odessa, Vedomosti Odesskogo gradonachal'stva, 1910), 196.
15 These are industries found in the list of Russian corporations supplied to me by Professor Thomas Owen.
16 *Vsia Rossiia*, spravochnaia kniga (Kiev: L. M. Fish, 1913), 947.
17 According to Elisabeth Sevatopulo Stenbeck-Fermor, the department store was eventually inherited by Nikolain Xida, nephew of Petrocochino.
18 *Odessa 1794–1894* (Odessa: Izdaniia gorodskogo obshchestvennogo upravleniia k stoletiiu goroda, Tip. A. Shul'tse, 1895), 158; *Vsia Rossiia*, 1913, 931.
19 I ogdohkontaeteris tis ethnikis palingenesias en Odessoi (Odessa: N. Chrusoqelos, 1901).
20 Palingenesis, 13.
21 *Odessa 1794–1894*, 726–54.
22 Ibid.
23 Argenti, *Libro d'Oro*, vol. 2, 249–52.
24 Lysander G. Konsta, *Logos anagnosteis en ti ellhniki emporiki scholi th 20h Ianouariou* (Odessa: P A. Zelenoi, 1881).
25 Athanase G. Politis, *L'Hellénisme et l'Egypte moderne*, 2 vols. (Paris: Félix Alcan, 1929–30), 1:250.
26 Information provided in a private communication from John Sevastopulo.

Part Three

Commerce

CHAPTER 9

Odessa: Staple Trade and Urbanization in New Russia

One of the more promising developments in Russia during the first half of the nineteenth century was the spectacular rise of the Black Sea port of Odessa.[1] Catherine II, through the successive partitions of Poland, had established Russian control over a vast expanse of the western and southern steppes. In 1774, through a victorious war against the Turks, she extended the Russian frontier to the western littoral of the Black Sea. Russian dominion over the littoral was gradually enlarged, eastward into the Crimea, and, in 1791, toward the west, into the area containing the site of the future city of Odessa. In 1794, to stabilize these conquests and promote trade, Catherine ordered a new city to be built where a small Turkish fortress, Khadzhibei, had once stood. In the classical spirit then fashionable, the new settlement was called Odessa, after an ancient city which had supposedly stood there, and which in turn recalled the name of the wandering Greek mariner, Ulysses or Odysseus.[2] Thirty-two years later, its population numbered 33,000; by the middle of the nineteenth century, it had grown to 100,000. Odessa was not among the ten largest Russian cities in 1811, but by 1863, it ranked third.

A review of trade statistics should convince historians, as it did contemporaries, that Odessa was a dynamic city.[3] In 1798, Odessa's exports were valued at 90,977 silver rubles, and its imports at 117,888 rubles.[4] By 1805, exports had grown in value to 3,399,291 rubles and imports to 2,156,844. In eight years, the worth of imports increased eighteen times while that of exports was growing forty-four times. In 1847 (although it should be noted that this was an exceptional year), Odessa's exports surpassed in value forty-four million rubles, which amounted to about a third of the worth of all exports from Russia. Between the two periods 1824–33 and 1844–53, the average annual export of wheat from Russia tripled, and in both periods, more than half of the wheat was sent through Odessa.[5]

Even before 1850, signs of prosperity excited the visitor to Odessa: the broad boulevards, elegant buildings, numerous schools, including the Richelieu Lyceum (later to become the University of New Russia) and a flourishing academy for young noble ladies.[6] In 1819, 700 houses were built and plans were laid out for 800 more the following year.[7] Between 1824 and 1827, 4,020,000 rubles (assignats) were spent on private construction in Odessa, 242,000 for shops and 620,000 for grain storehouses. The government expended 808,000 rubles on public buildings, bringing the total spent on construction of all sorts to 4,828,000 paper, or

---

Originally published as Patricia Herlihy, "Odessa: Staple Trade and Urbanization in New Russia," *Jahrbücher für Geschichte Osteuropas* XXI (1973): 184–96.

1,379,142 silver rubles.⁸ An English woman who visited Odessa in 1816–20 noted, "The town of Odessa is a very flourishing seaport, and a most astonishing place if it be remembered that about twenty years ago a few fishing huts comprised the whole of its inhabitants, and that in 1812, a third of its population was destroyed by the plague."⁹

According to the calculations of William L. Blackwell, the growth total for Odessa between 1797 and 1840 was 1200 percent.¹⁰ Between 1811 and 1863, only neighboring Mykolaiv among Russian cities grew at a faster rate than Odessa, but from smaller beginnings. Odessa's rate of growth averaged 10.8 percent annually, while St. Petersburg grew at an average annual rate of only 1.6 percent and Moscow by 1.7 percent during the same period. "One can boldly assert," the Soviet historian V. Zagoruiko justly concludes, "that there was no other city in Russia which in so short a period of about 50 or 60 years grew so remarkably as did Odessa."¹¹

One of the earliest great buildings was the city theater (replaced in 1887 by the present city theater constructed in Italian baroque style). Comfortable villas lined the tree-shaded streets. Even some grain storehouses were built in the architectural style of the adjacent mansions. Early city planning! Hotels, restaurants, clubs, gardens—all attested not only to the liveliness of the city but also to the cosmopolitan comforts which made Odessa a luxury sea resort as well as a bustling commercial depot. In 1823, the poet Pushkin complained that Odessa was so much a Western European city, no Russian books could be found there.¹² In *Eugene Onegin*, he alluded to Odessa's European character.¹³

> I lived then in dusty Odessa . . . There for a long time skies are clear. There, stirring, an abundant trade sets upon its sails.
> There all exhales, diffuses Europe, all glitters with the South, and brindles with variety.
> The tongue of golden Italy resounds along the gay street where walks the proud Slav, Frenchman, Spaniard, Armenian, and Greek, and the heavy Moldavian, and the son of Egyptian soil, the retired Corsair, Morali.

The street signs were in Italian as well as in Russian, and the Russians themselves supposedly called the city the Florence of their empire.¹⁴ Italian, in which most legal documents were redacted, served for many decades as the lingua franca of the city. Until 1827, the only newspaper of the town was a commercial journal printed in French.¹⁵ During Catherine's reign, Greek, Swiss, German and Bulgarian colonists were induced to settle in New Russia, of which Odessa was the administrative center.¹⁶ The colonists were to provide examples of good husbandry to Russian farmers.

Imperial policy also favored the city. In an ukase of April 16, 1817, Tsar Alexander I declared his intention of making Odessa a free port.¹⁷ Odessa opened as a free port in 1819 and retained this status until August 15, 1857. In sum, statistical, literary, and architectural evidence indicates that Odessa was a nineteenth-century *Wirtschaftswunder*. Favored by nature and imperial policy, the city and its exports flourished. Or so it seems.

Other measurements can be taken, however, which render the picture less glowing. If one examines the impact of Odessa's growth, the capital its merchants accumulated, and the repercussions this had on other economic sectors, a different assessment must be made. To gauge the nature of urbanization in New Russia, one must inquire into the relationship between Odessa and its hinterland. Did Odessa become a regional city or a portal city, in the sense used by J. C. Russell?[18] That is, did it spawn subsidiary towns and industries? Did the lure of foreign markets attract settlers to New Russia who were intent on exploiting the commercial possibilities of the area? To some extent, this was so. Some entrepreneurial landlords such as Mikhail Vorontsov, who became governor-general of New Russia in 1823, were quick to recognize the potential of black soil joined to Black Sea. With an eye to distant markets, Vorontsov bought up land, transferred northern serfs to the empty southern properties, and engaged in large-scale production of cereals.[19]

Melville H. Watkins has developed a "staple theory of economic growth," which seems quite applicable here. The prerequisites he identifies as essential for economic development in new territories are: "a new or empty land, a favorable man/land ratio, and an absence of inhibiting traditions."[20] By these criteria, New Russia would seem to have been magnificently endowed. The land was open and empty. The laws of serfdom still technically prevailed, but were moderated by frontier conditions. The settlers were not inhibited by the customs and rigidity of the communal system established in the older central regions. Profits made through the export trade should have, at least in theory, generated "backward linkages," working to stimulate economic activities in the hinterland: the domestic manufacture of agricultural machinery, farm services, improved transportation. "Forward linkages" should also have occurred, in such activities as the milling of flour; manufacture of candles, wool and linen cloth; processing of skins and leather. With new profits gained from agriculture, commerce and industry, further investment might have been predicted in a wide variety of industries, serving the growing community. This is a rough model, approximately describing how a staple economy promoted economic growth in Canada and to a certain extent in the United States. But here, as elsewhere in Russia's economic history, all factors did not effectively coalesce. Not much industry took root either in the city of Odessa or in New Russia in the first half of the nineteenth century. Not until Odessa and other Black Sea ports fell relatively behind in exporting grain abroad did the government deliberately attempt to foster industry.[21] By 1900, the population of Odessa had reached 450,000, but only 20,000 were employed in industry.[22]

What went wrong? One primary reason for the slow development of industry in Odessa was the scarcity of water and the high cost of fuel; until the exploitation of the Donetsk and Kryvyi Rih area late in the century, coal had usually to be imported from England.[23] Another chief reason, noted by many, was the high cost of labor. "One will no doubt be astonished to hear spoken of the dearness of labor," the *Journal d'Odessa* reported in 1827, "in a country where the daily wage of a strong man is from 60 to 80 kopecks when there are countries such as England where [wages] are two or three times this rate."[24] But food was so cheap at Odessa, the *Journal d'Odessa* explained, that the worker still could save one-half his salary. According to the British representative at Taganrog on the Sea of Azov in 1845, labor was so scarce that in years of abundance one-third the harvest was "not infrequently" left to perish in the field.[25] Thin population meant "each new article of production is cultivated only at the expense of some other of less profit to the landowner, e.g. linseed to the detriment of wheat, sheep to cattle." "This evil might in some measure be remedied," the British observer continued, "by permitting free egress to the redundant population of Great Russia, but the stringent system of Passports, retains in idleness at home thousands who might under a more liberal policy find beneficial employment abroad...." Twenty years later, in 1865, the British consul at Taganrog was still complaining that manual labor was dear in that port, the cost of conveyance burdensome, and capital scarce.[26]

Still, according to the staple theory of economic growth, high costs of labor are to be expected in new areas, and restrictions on labor mobility did not visibly slow the growth of Odessa itself. An equally critical obstacle was the manifest dearth of entrepreneurs, both in agriculture and in industry, whose activities might have generated strong backward and forward linkages. The model colonists from abroad were always to remain a minority, culturally isolated and of doubtful utility as examples to Russian producers. Some of the German colonists did not survive their first Russian winter; others drifted to an easier life in the crafts and trades.[27] Most colonies more nearly resembled the compact Russian servile villages than settlements of dispersed homesteads, characteristic of prosperous farming areas in the New World. The houses of the colonists, largely for administrative purposes, were grouped closely together. The inhabitants consequently shared the common lot of Russian serfs—their plagues, animal diseases and catastrophic fires.[28] Not all who raised grain for export prospered.

And what of the entrepreneurial Russian landlords, the men who, like Vorontsov, sought to develop commercialized farming in New Russia? Did they not create strong demand linkages? They invested in land, but, endowed with a supply of unpaid labor, that is, with serfs, they had little inducement to invest in innovative labor-saving devices. And their ultimate goal as entrepreneurs was not further investment and additional profits, but the maintenance of a certain seigneurial style of life. Here it seems that the aristocratic tastes of wealthy Russian *pomeshchiki* paralleled those of American southern planters; they dissipated their profits on luxuries (nearly always of foreign origin) or on travel abroad. They also had easy access to the tempting goods of foreign manufacture smuggled out of Odessa or across the Austrian border. By law, these goods were exempt from duty only within the city of Odessa itself. They were not to be taken into the interior without paying the full tariff.[29] Smuggling, however, developed into a lively form of commerce, and it no doubt whittled down the favorable balance of trade recorded in the official statistics. A recent Soviet historian claims that the chief reason for the lack of industry in Odessa and its environs was this smuggling of manufactured goods from the free port to the suburbs and the hinterland.[30] As for the serfs, there was little demand on their part of goods of domestic manufacture; the scant surpluses they commanded gave them little purchasing power.

With the commercial opportunities opened up through the Black Sea, one would expect a strong movement to build railroads, so that regions distant from the ports could supply foreign markets. The government took little official note of the need to thread the southern provinces with lines to the sea, and there was surprisingly little effort or agitation on the part of landlords in the '40s to bring railroads to New Russia.[31] "Why empty the state treasury to build a railroad to Odessa," asked E. F. Kankrin, minister of finance from 1822 to 1844, "when the winds of the Russian rivers and the Black Sea are free?"[32] Not until after the military debacle of the Crimean War was Odessa served by a line from the interior. Even that was not constructed until the late '60s.³³ As late as 1865, the British consul reported that the landed proprietors of New Russia looked on railroads "as matters of the future and not of the present."³⁴ Accordingly they supported the demands of peasant carters for the construction of bridges, the repair of roads, and other privileges. Again, we note a reluctance to invest in labor-saving machines, this time in transportation.

To government and landlords alike, the simple ox-drawn cart, the traditional means of transport on the steppe, sufficed. Relative to costs, the carts were indeed amazingly efficient. Thousands of them crossed hundreds of miles of prairie with little expense. The peasant carted as part of his labor rent, the oxen grazed their way to port across the grasslands and were at the end often slaughtered for tallow or meat, and the cart itself was frequently sold as firewood at the terminus.³⁵ As late as 1866, the British consul stated that each year over a million wagons arrived at Odessa.³⁶ The carts that returned usually were empty—a sign of the low intensity of exchange between Odessa and the hinterland. While the costs of carting were low, foreigners still wondered at the failure to build railroads in New Russia. "At present, the great want of Odessa, then," the American consul observed in 1862, "is the means of communication with the far interior, the country which really sustains and supports it, by means of railroads and canals."³⁷ Even earlier, in 1860, the then American consul, Stephen Ralli, stated quite flatly: "No country is more in want of railroads than Russia, and the tardiness of establishing them is really surprising, particularly after feeling their necessity during the Crimean War."³⁸

Although the prosperous Russian proprietor did little in the way of investing in or stimulating backward linkages, some did develop agricultural industries on their estates. This was especially true in the Polish provinces and in Ukraine, where labor was relatively plentiful. Sugar beets were raised and refined, flour was milled and grain distilled, but these enterprises, rather than encouraging regional industrialization, tended to obstruct the development of manufactures in the nearby towns. This pattern presents a striking parallel to contemporary conditions in the American South, as described by Julius Rubin:

> More important than the reduced scale of industry was its dispersion. Instead of centering in towns it became to a significant extent the activity of slaves on plantations. At the same time the commercial basis of local towns was weakened by the planter's proclivity for long-distance trading with the factors of the port cities and by his consequent ability to supply surrounding farmers and small planters from his own store. As in industry, commerce was not destroyed, but the basis for agglomeration was weakened. The farmers in plantation areas were thereby deprived of the northern type of variegated and enterprising industrial town and had to rely instead on a country store with a narrow range of goods operating in the economically passive environment of the county courthouse town.³⁹

The factories of the Russian *pomeshchiki* also seem to have undermined the development of small interior industrial towns, since the estates tended to become if not totally, then at least partially self-sufficient. The distant, largely self-sufficient estates delivered products to the ports and made their principal purchases there. This direct exchange bypassed the intermediate towns. There were consequently very few of what J. C. Russell calls "rank cities" or "satellite towns" in the region; neither the commercialized farming of New Russia nor the massive export through Odessa was able to launch a wave of urbanization in the hinterland.

This was a critical failure. Rubin has also described the beneficial effects of hinterland cities on economic growth in the northern United States in the nineteenth century, and again provides us with an instructive comparison.[40] Between the ports and the hinterland cities of the northern United States there occurred a distribution of economic functions, supplying the countryside with a variety of goods and services. The presence of interior towns stimulated the farmers to develop their own productive skills and to adopt more intensive methods of cultivation. Port towns also benefited from the growth of these hinterland cities, which offered enlarged markets for port goods and services, and supplied a better quality of raw materials and produce for manufacture or for export. Interaction between ports and interior towns produced a regional cultural homogeneity, which in turn prepared the way for an eventual "metropolitan dominance." This brought about a growing similarity of town and country inhabitants. No such smoothing out of differences between town and country took place in New Russia, or, for that matter, elsewhere in the empire. Still today, the eradication of differences between and the equalization of the rewards of living in the country and in cities—long an aspiration of Marxism–Leninism—challenge Soviet policy.[41] The moderating and blending influences, engendered by small towns and their attendant industries and attitudes, were absent in New Russia as they were absent too in the southern United States in the early nineteenth century.

Of course, the emancipation of the serfs in 1861 brought some fundamental changes.[42] Many marginal estates were sold by their timid owners to the more enterprising landlords and peasants. The loss of serf labor, as well as part of their lands, pressured some debt-ridden *pomeshchiki* into abandoning agriculture. Conveyances of land became frequent, and this indicates that some landlords and peasants were attempting to rationalize their holdings and engage in intensive cultivation for the export market.[43] Although these cultivators were soon aided by the construction of railroads, they had also to combat the growing competition from North and South America, Australia, and the Indies on the world grain market. Consular reports from Odessa overflow with fearful expressions concerning the mounting competition from the New World. As early as 1842, an Italian commercial journal published in Florence predicted that European grain imports from America would grow.[44] In 1850, the Russian scholar G. P. Nebolsin similarly foresaw the coming American competition.[45] An article in a commercial journal published in Vienna noted, in 1856, that the Crimean War had turned European purchasers to the lands across the Atlantic as suppliers of grain.[46] The French consul at Odessa summarized the situation in 1861, "Under the present circumstances, the quantity of cereals exported from the United States to England gives reason for concern [to the merchants of Odessa]. They already anticipate a menacing competition in the future, with which they must from now on reckon more than they had realized."[47]

Ironically, while some Russian proprietors were striving to improve the quality of their production, the entrance of peasant producers for the first time on a large scale into the export market brought about a general deterioration in the quality of exported wheat. The peasants had difficulty maintaining high standards of purity and cleanliness in the wheat they sold.[48] Russian wheat could seldom be sold more cheaply than competing varieties, nor could it match them in quality. A decline in sales to Russia's former, favored customers inevitably ensued. To some extent, Russia was able to compensate for this loss in wheat sales by concentrating on the production of cheaper cereals, such as rye, but her preeminence as the breadbasket of Europe was never to be regained. The ill-fated kulak of later years had to face the fierce competition of the cheap, good grains from other lands as well as to contend with the inefficiencies of Russian transport, the entanglements of the mir, and the perennial absence of capital. Thus, agricultural enterprise alone could not generate sufficient capital to make a major, spontaneous contribution to industrialization in the pre-Witte era, or indeed during the entire period to the Revolution of 1917.

If the wealthy wheat growers were unwilling and the serfs (later, the emancipated peasants) were unable to invest in industry, what happened to the mercantile fortunes amassed in opulent Odessa? Although there were some Russian export firms, almost all of the larger ones were foreign. Several of the greatest traders were Greeks, but Italians, French, English, and other foreigners were also represented in mercantile circles. In the 1850s, a French observer described the merchant firms in Odessa as follows, "The number of foreign houses is about forty, established by Greeks, Italians, Slavonians, Triestians, Genoese, French, German, English and Spanish . . . The Greeks are the most numerous and the most affluent."[49] Many of these foreign merchants found it to their advantage to acquire Russian citizenship.[50] Foreign nationals, for example, were required to join the "first guild," membership in which meant paying particularly onerous dues. But it was a simple procedure to become a Russian subject. Merchants slipped into different nationalities as easily as ships hoisted various national flags at various places and times to suit their convenience. Certainly, the wealthy merchants of Odessa stimulated the building trades and patronized the arts in Odessa, but there is no evidence and little likelihood that they ever transferred substantial sums into industry. Many of the foreign companies, especially those belonging to Greek owners, operated throughout the Mediterranean. Profits were widely distributed among distant family members, reinvested in other commercial enterprises in other ports, or kept liquid.[51] "Everyone knows," the French consul at Odessa remarked in 1857, "the prudence and skill which the Greek merchants usually bring to the conduct of their affairs. As they are bound together at all points of the globe and mutually aid and support one another, it is rare to see any of them fall into difficulty."[52] Not only at Odessa but also in other Mediterranean ports, officials repeatedly complained that foreigners were skimming off commercial profits and going elsewhere to spend their money. In 1841, for example, a Livornese complained about rich foreign merchants carrying off the fruits of their speculations to other lands. In the same vein, a Soviet historian denounced the foreign merchants of Odessa for spending tens of millions of rubles abroad.[53]

Jewish merchants, who were subjects of the tsar, formed a special class at Odessa. During the early growth of the grain export, Jews served primarily as agents, middlemen, brokers—members of the "third guild," engaged in small-scale trade. As the large foreign houses left Odessa in the face of ruinous overseas competition, Jewish firms took over the larger share of Odessa's export trade.[54] According to a British report in 1863, the Jews were then "pushing the Greeks altogether aside and they have become the first bankers and merchants in South Russia."[55] These Jews, native Russians like the *kulaki*, might have been inclined to invest in industry, but time ran out on them also. At all events, both tsarist policy and cultural attitudes toward the Jews hardly encouraged their willingness to risk their capital on new and hazardous enterprises.

Foreign merchants should not, however, be regarded only as persons who carried off their profits while contributing nothing to the city. As early as 1835, a German in the service of Nicholas I reported to the tsar that "it is to foreigners . . . that the town [Odessa] owes its present flourishing condition. By their industry and capital they have laid open the resources of the country. . . ."[56] In a recent study, John P. McKay comes to the same general conclusion concerning the role of foreign entrepreneurs in industry in southern Russia in the latter part of the nineteenth century.[57] The appropriate question is not how much profit was carried off, but how much of what was accomplished would not have been accomplished in the absence of foreign capital. Indigenous Russian shippers were too few, too poor, or too cautious to encourage capitalized farming on the steppes.

In sum, neither the commercial farmers of the late nineteenth and early twentieth centuries nor Odessa's merchants developed into industrial entrepreneurs on any significant scale. In the early twentieth century, foreigners were to play a principal role in establishing industrial enterprises in South Russia—Belgians in Odessa, for example, or in Kryvyi Rih. It is, however, worth noting that this generation of foreigners had no direct ties to the old foreign mercantile houses of Odessa, which had laboriously built up expertise in the laws, languages, customs, and idiosyncrasies of the Russian bureaucrat and businessman. All these matters had to be relearned, sometimes painfully. The second wave of foreign investment in southern Russia had little or no relationship with the first significant arrival of foreign capital in Russian commerce.

Here then is how we would summarize the economic experience of New Russia in the nineteenth century. The opening up of foreign markets acted as a powerful stimulus for the growth of the commercial city of Odessa. However, the traditional organization of Mediterranean trade did not allow an easy transfer of capital from commerce into industry. In the inland areas of southern Russia, cereal production grew enormously, but, surprisingly, in the first half of the century, the old system of serfdom was able to provide the increased output demanded, without revealing for a long time marked strains. Rigid as the system appeared, there was enough play in it to adapt to new circumstances. The cheap labor of the serfs encouraged, as mentioned, investment in the land of South Russia and the growth of a commercially oriented agriculture. Paradoxically, the appearance of new market possibilities lent vitality to a system increasingly condemned by the "enlightened" of Russia. Had serfdom been less adaptable and less viable, the results of the commercial expansion might have been more beneficial. For while allowing growth, serfdom also limited possible spinoffs, setting obstacles in the path of the linkages, which might have resulted from the wheat trade. The attachment of the Russian serfs to the soil of the South helps explain the reluctance to invest in industry and the effective limitation of urbanization to the city of Odessa. When emancipation finally came in 1861, intense competition on the world wheat market had developed, and the main chance for New Russia had already passed. The commercial success of Odessa and the paradoxical industrial failure of New Russia combine to furnish another example in Russian history prior to 1917 of a *révolution manquée*.

Notes

1 An earlier version of this paper was read at the annual meeting of the American Historical Association, New Orleans, Louisiana, in December 1972.

2 According to legend, the ancient city was called Odessos, but Catherine changed its gender. "Let Khadzhibei bear the old Hellenic name," she is reported to have commanded, "but in the feminine gender." On the naming of Odessa, A. Orlov, *Istoricheskii ocherk Odessy s 1794 po 1803 god. Sostavil po dokumentam, khraniashchimsia v moskovskom arkhive Ministerstva iustitsii* (Odessa: A. Shul'tse, 1885), xi–xii.

3 For accounts of the history of the founding, growth, and commercial development of Odessa, A. A. Skal'kovskii, *Opyt statisticheskogo opisaniia Novorossiiskogo kraia*, 2 vols. (Odessa: V tipografii L. Nitche, 1850–53). Other useful studies are the following: A. A. Skal'kovskii, *Pervoe tridtsatiletie istorii goroda Odessy, 1793–1823* (Odessa: Gorodskaia tipografiia, 1837); E. I. Druzhinina, *Severnoe Prichernomor'e v 1775–1800 gg* (Moscow: Akademii nauk SSSR, 1959); Hans Halm, *Österreich und Neurussland*. Vol. 1: *Donauschiffahrt und -handel nach dem Südosten 1718–1780* (Breslau: Thiel & Hintermeier, 1943); vol. 2: *Habsburgischer Osthandel im 18. Jahrhundert. Donauhandel und -schiffahrt 1781–1787* (Munich: Osteuropa Institut, 1954); M. Vol'skii, *Ocherk istorii khlebnoi torgovli*; Mose L. Harvey, "The Development of Russian Commerce on the Black Sea and Its Significance" (PhD diss., University of California at Berkeley, 1938); Patricia Herlihy, "Russian Grain and Mediterranean Markets, 1774–1861" (PhD diss., University of Pennsylvania, 1963); L. M. de Ribas, *Iz proshlago Odessy. Sbornik statei S. Borinevicha*, et al. (Odessa: G. G. Marazli, 1894); *Odessa 1794–1894* (Odessa: Odesskoe gorodskoe obshchestvennoe upravlenie, 1894); V. Zagoruiko, *Po stranitsam istorii Odessy i Odesshchiny*, 2 vols. (Odessa: Odesskoe oblastnoe izdatel'stvo, 1957–60). For a Soviet interpretation of the growth and importance of the cereal export, V. A. Zolotov, *Vneshniaia torgovlia Iuzhnoi Rossii v pervoi polovine XIX veka* (Rostov: Rostovskii gosudarstvennyi universitet, 1963); V. A. Zolotov, *Khlebnyi eksport Rossii cherez porty Chernogo i Azovskogo morei v 60–90-e gody XIX v.* (Rostov: Rostovskii gosudarstvennyi universitet, 1966); Erik Amburger, "Zur Entstehung und Entwicklung russischer Häfen," in *Beiträge zur Stadt- und Regionalgeschichte Ost- und Nordeuropas. H. Ludat zum 60. Geburtstag*, ed. K. Zernack (Wiesbaden: O. Harrassowitz, 1971), 173–207.

4 For yearly statements of exports of wheat, wool, tallow, and linseed from Odessa for the years 1814–61, Herlihy, "Russian Grain," Appendixes I and II; for the total trade figures, Appendix V.

5 M. L. de Tegoborski [Tengoborskii], *Commentaries on the Productive Forces of Russia*, vol. 2 (London: Longman, Brown, Green, and Longmans, 1855–56), 304. For aggregated statistics on Russian trade in the nineteenth century, F. W. von Reden, *Allgemeine vergleichende Handels- und Gewerbs-Geographie und Statistik. Ein Handbuch für Kaufleute, Fabrikanten und Staatsmänner* (Berlin: T. C. F. Enslin, 1844); J. M. Crawford, ed. and trans., *The Industries of Russia. Manufactures and Trade. With a general industrial map. By the Department of Trade and Manufactures, Ministry of Finance, for the World's Columbian Exposition at Chicago*, 2 vols. (St. Petersburg: Imperial Ministry of Finance, 1893); J. Kuczynski and G. Wittkowski, *Die deutsch-russischen Handelsbeziehungen in den letzten 150 Jahren.* (Berlin: Verl. Die Wirtschaft, 1948); V. Giura, *Russia, Stati Uniti d'America e Regno di Napoli nell'età del Risorgimento* (Napoli: Istituto universitario navale de Napoli, 1967); P. Köppen, *Statistische Reise in's Land der Donischen Kosaken durch die Gouvernements Tula, Orel und Woronesh im Jahre 1850* (St. Petersburg: Kaiserliche Akademie der Wissenschaften, 1852); P. Köppen, "Über den Kornbedarf Russlands," in *Mémoires de L'Académie de St. Petersbourg*, vol. 5 (St. Petersburg: Imprimerie de l'Académie, 1845), 490–579; O. Friebel, *Der Handelshafen Odessa* (Leipzig: Teubner, 1921); V. Cacciapuoti, *Relazioni commerciali tra l'Italia e la Russia* (Naples: N. Jovene, 1928); J. F. Crozat, *Rostoff-sur-le-Don et le commerce des céréales* (Paris: V. Giard & E. Brière, 1910); *Gosudarstvennaia vneshniaia torgovlia 1826 v raznykh ee vidakh* (St. Petersburg: Tipografia departamenta vneshnei torgovli, 1827); *Journal d'Odessa* and *Sanktpeterburgische Handelszeitung*.

6   The lyceum was named for the energetic Duc de Richelieu, a French émigré who was appointed governor of the city of Odessa in 1803 and governor-general of New Russia in 1805. He held the latter office until his return to France in 1814. For his memoirs, *Sbornik Imperatorskago russkago istoricheskago obshchestva*, vol. 54 (St. Petersburg, Izdatel'stvo tip. I. N. Skorokhodova, 1886). On his life, Léon de Crousat-Crétet (Paris: Firmin-Didot et cie., 1897).

7   Mary Holderness, *New Russia: Journey from Riga to the Crimea, by Way of Kiev; with some account of the colonization and the manners and customs of the colonists of New Russia . . .* (London: Sherwood, Gilbert, and Piper, 1823), 103.

8   *Journal d'Odessa*, November 23 / December 5, 1827.

9   Holderness, *New Russia*, 77. Anatole de Demidoff, *Travels in Southern Russia and the Crimea: Through Hungary, Wallachia and Moldavia, during the Year 1837*, vol. 1 (London: J. Mitchell, 1853), 295 similarly comments on the astonishment felt by Europeans at the rapid growth of Odessa.

10 W. L. Blackwell, *The Beginnings of Russian Industrialization, 1800–1860* (Princeton, NJ: Princeton University Press, 1968), 97, 428.

11 Zagoruiko, *Po stranitsam* 1:65.

12 J. Thomas Shaw, ed. and trans., *The Letters of Alexander Pushkin*. vol. 1 (Bloomington: Indiana University Press, 1963), 141. For Pushkin's stay in Odessa, Aleksandr Shik, *Odesskii Pushkin* (Paris: Dom knigi, 1938).

13 Alexander Pushkin, *Eugene Onegin, a novel in verse*, trans. V. Nabokov, vol. 1 (New York: Bollingen, 1964), 340.

14 Edward Morton, *Travels in Russia and a Residence at St. Petersburg and Odessa in the Years 1827–1829* (London: Longman, Rees, Orme, Brown, and Green, 1830), 198. See *Odessa 1794–1894* (Odessa: Izdanie gorodskogo obshchestvennogo upravleniia k stoletiiu goroda, 1875), 585 for further comment on the common use of Italian among the merchants. For Italian architecture in Odessa, *Odessa 1794–1894*, 383, 764. An Italian Philanthropic Society was flourishing at Odessa in 1863. Charles Koch, *The Crimea and Odessa: Journal of a Tour with an Account of the Climate and Vegetation* (London: John Murray, 1855), 256 notes the title "Florence of Russia" applied to Odessa. Dr. Koch then dryly comments that Odessa reminded him of Italian towns principally because the inns were so dirty. Much more enthusiastic in his comparisons with Italy was the American diplomat Henry Wikoff, *The Reminiscences of an Idler* (New York: Fords, Howard, & Hulbert, 1880), 231.

15 This was the *Journal d'Odessa* founded in 1824.

16 Druzhinina, *Severnoe Prichernomor'e*, 66ff.

17 Nearly all Western European consuls included translations of this ukase in their reports back home, for example, Archivio di Stato di Trieste, I. R. Governo per il Litorale (1814–50), Atti Generali, Busta 1242 (8/4), fasc. 50, which includes an Italian translation. For a detailed description of the regulations governing the port, National Archives, Washington, DC (henceforth, NA), Despatches from US Consuls in Odessa, July 1, 1854, November 2, 1857, and October 12, 1858. The dues imposed on goods entering Odessa were several times modified. Before 1849, the tariff imposed was one-fifth the normal duty, but in that year it was raised to two-fifths. Wine, sugar, and tea paid three-fifths the normal duties, while tobacco, liquors and eau de vie were given no reductions. Archives du Ministère des Affaires Étrangères, Paris (henceforth AMAE), vol. 7, Odessa, fol. 175, Huet to Minister of Foreign Affairs, August 3, 1849. According to the American consul in Odessa, even those goods paying full duty (tea, sugars, strong spirits, black and gray cloths, printed cottons, silks, and wools) were not to be taken outside the city of Odessa. NA, Ralli to Secretary of State, July 1, 1854. Still, the fact that Odessa remained to any degree a free port hurt the Russian treasury, according to Zolotov, *Vneshniaia torgovlia*, 149, "It can be said with certainty that as a result of the establishment of the free port of Odessa, millions of pounds sterling, tens of millions of francs and lire remained in the safes of London, Marseilles, Genoa and other centers of European trade."

18 J. C. Russell, *Medieval Regions and Their Cities* (Bloomington: Indiana University Press, Indiana, 1972), 23–30.

19 For an account of Vorontsov's career as an entrepreneurial *pomeshchik*, E. I. Indova, *Krepostnoe khoziaistvo v nachale XIX veka po materialam votchinnogo arkhiva Vorontsovykh* (Moscow: Akademii nauk SSSR, 1955), 41ff.

20 M. H. Watkins, "A Staple Theory of Economic Growth," *The Canadian Journal of Economics and Political Science* 29 (1963): 143.
21 *Illiustrirovannyi putevoditel'* (Odessa: D. I. Vainer, 1900), 7. One of the new enterprises promoted was that of health spas.
22 Ibid., 5–6.
23 *Odessa 1794–1894*, 150.
24 *Journal d'Odessa*, March 9 / March 21, 1827.
25 Public Record Office, London (henceforth PRO), FO 257, vol. 3, Memorandum from Taganrog, January 14, 1845.
26 PRO, FO 257, vol. 12, Monthly Commercial Report, February 12, 1865.
27 P. Conrad Keller, S. J., *The German Colonies in South Russia, 1804 to 1904*, trans. A. Becker (Saskatoon, SK: Western Producer, 1968), for some of the trials of the early German colonists in the region near Odessa. On German colonists in southern Russia, also Joseph S. Height, *Paradise on the Steppe* (Bismarck, ND: North Dakota Historical Society of Germans from Russia, 1972) and Karl Stumpp, *The German-Russians. Two Centuries of Pioneering* (New York: Edition Atlantic-Forum, 1978). For a bibliography of Russian works on colonists in southern Russia, S. A. Sekirinskii, "Nekotorye cherty razvitiia sel'skogo khoziaistva Kryma i prilegaiushchikh k nemu zemel' iuznoi Ukrainy v kontse XVIII–pervoi polovine XIX v.," *Ezhegodnik po agrarnoi istorii Vostochnoi Evropy 1960 g.* (Kiev: Izd-vo Akad. Nauk USSR, 1962): 407n33. For the attempts of Catherine II and Alexander I to induce Swiss colonists to settle in the same region, Walther Kirchner, "Emigration to Russia," *The American Historical Review* 60 (1950): 552–66.
28 Holderness, *New Russia*, 110–11.
29 Ibid., 7.
30 Zolotov, *Vneshniaia torgovlia*, 145.
31 Zolotov, *Khlebnyi eksport*, 31.
32 Quoted by Blackwell, *Beginnings of Russian Industrialization*, 273–74. Walter M. Pintner, *Russian Economic Policy under Nicholas I.* (Ithaca, NY: Cornell University Press, 1967), 133.
33 The Odessa-Balta line was finished on November 3, 1865. Zagoruiko, *Po stranitsam*, 2:26. This was only the beginning of the Ukrainian network.
34 PRO, FO 257, vol. 11, Miscellaneous Report, June 11/23, 1865.
35 Henry S. Dearborn, *A Memoir on the Commerce and Navigation of the Black Sea and the Trade and Maritime Geography of Turkey and Egypt*, vol. 1 (Boston: Wells and Lilly, 1819), 246; and G. P. Nebol'sin, *Statisticheskoe obozrenie vneshnei torgovli Rossii*. Two parts in one. (St. Petersburg: Tip. Departamenta vneshnei torgovli, 1850), 51. A description of the burning of the carts and the slaughter of oxen may be found in Archives Nationales, Paris, F 12, 2683.
36 PRO, FO 65, vol. 711, January 8, 1866.
37 NA, Consular Report, February 15, 1862.
38 Ibid., November 9, 1860.
39 Julius Rubin, "Urban Growth and Regional Development," ed. David T. Gilchrist, *The Growth of the Seaport Cities, 1790–1824* (Charlottesville, VA: University of Virginia Press, 1967), 15.
40 Gilchrist, "Growth of the Seaport," 3–21.
41 Basile Kerblay, "Le village russe va-t-il disparaître? Réflexions sur l'avenir de l'habitat rural," *Cahiers du Monde russe et soviétique* 10 (1969): 5–6, "La volonté d'égaliser les conditions de vie entre les travailleurs des villes et des campagnes a toujours été une des constantes de la doctrine marxiste."
42 P. A. Zaionchkovskii, *Otmena krepostnogo prava v Rossii* (Moscow: Gos. uchebno-pedagog. izd.-vo, 1960).

43 Fear and uncertainty concerning the future might have prompted some landlords to sell their land, but in the years immediately following emancipation, other factors influenced them as well: poor harvests, the rising cost of labor, devastation by steppe rats, fires on the steppes, animal diseases among the sheep and cattle, and other natural disasters. For contemporary comment, PRO, FO 257, vol. 11, Miscellaneous Report, June 11/23, 1865. In the empire as a whole, there was a trend in these years toward a reduction of lands held by nobles and an increase of those in the hands of peasants. Harry T. Willetts, "The Agrarian Problem," in *Russia Enters the Twentieth Century, 1894–1917*, ed. George Katkov et al. (London: Methuen, 1971), 119. Another immediate consequence of the emancipation was an increase in the leasing of lands by the lords to the peasants. PRO, FO 257, vol. 11, Monthly Trade Report, April 16/28, 1863.

44 PRO, FO 65, vol. 647, E. C. Grenville-Murray to the Rt. Hon. Earl Russell, February 4, 1863; AMAE, Odessa, vol. 11, Cochet to the Minister of Foreign Affairs, May 24, 1879; and *Giornale del Commercio, delle Artie delle Manifatture con Varietà ed Avvisi Diversi*, September 7, 1842.

45 Nebol'sin, *Statisticheskoe obozrenie*, 133.

46 *Il Corriere Italiano*, February 15, 1856.

47 AMAE, Odessa, vol. 8, Saint-Robert to the Minister of Foreign Affairs, October 28, 1861, fol. 297.

48 I. M. Rubinow, *Russia's Wheat Trade* (Washington, DC: National Government Publication, 1908), 18. By 1900, the reputation of Russian grain for uneven quality forced the merchants of Odessa to take measures to reduce the level of foreign matter found within it. The French consul at Odessa gives a detailed description of the sampling and testing procedures, by which the merchants hoped to attain levels of purity approaching American wheat. Archives Nationales, F 12, Commerce et Industrie, 7133, Odessa, letter from A. Sauvaire to Minister of Foreign Affairs, dated February 7, 1901.

49 AMAE, Russie, Mémoires et Documents, vol. 44, 1850–57, fol. 24. For additional comment Hagemeister, *Report*, 74; I. M. Kulisher, *Ocherk istorii russkoi torgovli* (Petrograd: Atenei, 1923), 271; A. A. Skal'kovskii, *Population commerciale d'Odessa* (Odessa: Gorodskaia tipgrafiia, 1845), 2. The last author states, "Les diverses nations qui composent la classe commerçante de notre ville, sont: les Grecs (sujets turcs ou grecs); ceux de la race slave, comme: Boulgares, Illyriens, Serbes, etc.; Les Italiens, surtout les Génois, anciens dominateurs de la Russie du sud; les Allemands, les Anglais et les Juifs autrichiens."

50 AMAE, Odessa, vol. 7, fol. 446, Voisins to Minister of Foreign Affairs, July 18, 1856, which describes the advantages of Russian citizenship for foreign merchants. On the same subject, AMAE, Odessa, vol. 8, fols. 1–10, Jaegerschmidt to Minister of Foreign Affairs, January 2, 1858.

51 The French consul noted that the merchants in Odessa were only moderately speculative and did not have large industrial stocks in their portfolios. AMAE, Odessa, vol. 7, Jaegerschmidt to Minister of Foreign Affairs, December 15, 1857.

52 Ibid.

53 Zolotov, *Vneshniaia torgovlia*, 155. For the Livornese complaint, Archivio di Stato di Firenze, R.R. Rendita, 1841, Entry 541.

54 *Encyclopedia Hebraica*, vol. 1, s.v. "Odessa" (Jerusalem, Tel Aviv: Encyclopedia Publishing Company, 1949), 705–14 (in Hebrew) describes this rise of Jewish merchants to dominance by the end of the century. Professor Richard A. Webster of the University of California kindly translated this article for me.

55 PRO, FO 65, vol. 647, Grenville-Murray to Earl Russell, March 4, 1863.

56 Hagemeister, *Report*, 74.

57 John P. McKay, *Pioneers for Profit. Foreign Entrepreneurship and Russian Industrialization, 1885–1913* (Chicago: University of Chicago Press, 1970), 37–39.

CHAPTER 10

Commerce and Architecture in Odessa in Late Imperial Russia

Odessa, one of the world's great cities and one of the Russian Empire's outstanding ports and cosmopolitan urban centers, was founded by Catherine II in 1794.[1] Only two years earlier, the Ottoman Turks had conceded the territory to Russia by the Treaty of Jassy. Its site on a bluff overlooking the Black Sea had made it a logical place for the Turks to build a fort, Yeni-Dünya (New World) in 1764, as part of a string of Turkish fortifications along the northwest coast of the Black Sea. But it was not to hold. In the course of a war waged between 1787 and 1791, Don Joseph de Ribas, a soldier of fortune born in Naples of Spanish and Irish stock and one of the many adventurers in Catherine's service, stormed the fortress and helped to secure it in September 1789.[2] Catherine II added this area to the new province of Novorossiia, which she had created in 1764, comprising other southwest territories wrested from the Ottoman Empire in earlier wars.[3]

The destruction of the fort combined with the absence of an urban center presented a tabula rasa to the empress so that she could create a city and port on the Black Sea, thus emulating Peter I who nearly a century earlier had also constructed a fiat city—the new capital St. Petersburg—on empty swamps near the Baltic Sea. Catherine wanted to build a city on the Black Sea worthy of the many battles against the Turks it had taken to seize the territory, solid enough to defend itself, and attractive enough to lure settlers to enrich it. Each of those two monarchs, bearing the epithet the Great to some, wanted to establish a window facing Europe, the first commanding the north and the second the south. Each wanted to establish a presence on territory taken from perennial enemies: the Swedes in the north, the Turks in the south; each in turn at the beginning and at the end of the eighteenth century built a dazzling city of defiance and defense. Of the newer city it has been said, "Born, like Aphrodite from the foam of the Black Sea, young and beautiful Odessa has a special character."[4]

From the beginning, Catherine's city received a foreign imprint; in the spring of 1794, she sent twenty-six thousand rubles to de Ribas and a close associate, Flemish engineer named François de Wollant, to build a harbor. She gave the site the Greek name Odessa (reportedly the feminine version of Odessos), and Greeks were the first major immigrants who came in significant numbers to the new port city of Novorossiia.[5] De Ribas was named

---

Originally published as Patricia Herlihy, "Commerce and Architecture in Odessa in Late Imperial Russia," in *Commerce in Russian Urban Culture 1861–1914*, ed. William Brumfield, Boris V. Anan'ich, and Yuri A. Petrov (Baltimore, MD: Johns Hopkins University Press, 2002), 243–63.

the first *gradonachal'nik* (city chief) in 1797, and the much beloved French émigré, the Duc de Richelieu, ruled benignly and efficiently over the city from 1803 until his return to France in 1814. After that, a military commandant served for two years until another Frenchman, Count Alexander F. Langeron, headed the city's administration until 1820.[6] The common commercial language, and very nearly the lingua franca of the city, was Italian. The street signs and many of the shop signs as well were written in both Russian and Italian.[7]

De Wollant's plan for Odessa was "in keeping with other western ideas of the time."[8] Because the city was divided by ravines, he laid out two gridirons intersecting at a forty-seven degree angle. To preserve uniform rectangularity in the city blocks, the principal gridiron had to be set at an angle to the shore.[9] De Wollant's plan envisioned spacious streets one hundred feet wide; an esplanade was to separate the old Turkish fort from the residential area. In 1827, K. I. Potier, an engineer, designed the beautiful Prymors'kyi Boulevard stretching along the bluff overlooking the gulf.

The regular design was popular in the new towns of the American West, as Mark Twain's impressions of the city in the 1860s confirm:

> I have not felt so much at home for a long time as I did when I "raised the hill" and stood in Odessa for the first time. It looked just like an American city: fine, broad streets, and straight as well; a stirring, business-look about the streets and the stores: fast walkers, a familiar new look about the houses and everything; yes, and a driving and smothering cloud of dust that was so like a message from our own dear native land that we could hardly refrain from shedding a few grateful tears and execrations in the old time-honored American way. Look up the street or down the street, this way or that way, we saw only America.[10]

While to some Odessa had an American appearance, to others it suggested a West European city. One native of Odessa, writing her memoirs in the twentieth century, claimed, "This city is light and clean, hopelessly, how hopelessly modern, on the style of the 20th century, solid, comfortable, well articulated and neutral. It is the most European city of Russia because of its architecture, its conception, its rhythm."[11]

The imperial government provided nearly 2 million rubles to be spent over a five-year period for the construction of the port, the admiralty, barracks, and warehouses. In 1796, the city received an additional 312,135 rubles to pay for the construction of a hospital, cathedral, and administrative offices as well as 405,000 rubles to construct docks.[12] Within the first year or two, de Ribas supervised the building of a new fortress, barracks, mole, military harbor, warehouses for provisions, a quarantine, a customs house, churches, and an arsenal—among other buildings.

The oldest private houses are on Chervonyi Provulok (Nos. 6–8, 18–24) with wooden loggias, diminutive in size but still reflecting the classical style. For the last four years of the century, building almost came to a halt as the government was preoccupied with revolutionary activities in Western Europe. But beginning with the reign of Alexander I in 1801, construction began energetically again under the guidance of the Duc de Richelieu. The neoclassical architect, Thomas de Thomon, court architect under Alexander I and the builder of the Petersburg

Stock Exchange, completed two beautiful monuments of architecture by 1804: the theater and the hospital.[13] A local architect, Francesco Frapolli, supervised the work.[14] In 1822, Francesco Boffo reconstructed the theater that has been described as "a lyrical theater relatively small (for eight hundred spectators), in the imperial style, and in the first half of the nineteenth century, it was considered one of the best in Russia from both the aesthetic and the functional point of view."[15]

The duke set up a building committee that was to oversee the designs of private construction. All facades of private houses, for example, had to be built according to prior approved models. M. M. Siniaver, a leading architectural historian of Odessa, claimed that the influence of St. Petersburg and the Building Committee of Odessa forced the city to maintain the regularity of the initial plan of de Wollant.[16] As one recent book notes, "Odessa is one of the rare Russian cities which did not develop in a chaotic manner."[17]

The founding of the city coincided with the height of Russian classicism, an adaptation of the neoclassical style, and some of the most famous classical architects of St. Petersburg also worked in Odessa, such as A. I. Mel'nikov in addition to Thomas de Thomon.[18] Initially, imperial funds flowed into the city in order to provide basic structures but, unlike the capital St. Petersburg, which continued to be ornamented by emperors and empresses after Alexander I's reign, which ended in 1825, Odessa was left to its own devices for embellishment. The thriving commerce of the city became both the motor and the source for the city's imposing structures. Merchants such as Val'b, Potapov, Androsov, Orlov, Tomasini, Latti, and K. Butyrskii all financed private and public buildings—Butyrskii, for example, helped build the Odessa (English) Club in 1842 designed by architect G. Toricelli. As early as 1829, the city built an exchange following the plans, according to some and disputed by others, of the famous St. Petersburg architect Giacomo Quarenghi that were executed by a local architect, Toricelli.[19] At the time of its completion in 1834, it was a showy neoclassical building located at the southern end of Prymors'kyi Boulevard on the top of the cliff overlooking the Black Sea. At the entrance of the building were two rows of Corinthian columns that led to a covered courtyard that served as a place for trading operations. The composition and the style were reminiscent of the Aleksandrovskii Palace in Detskoe Selo near St. Petersburg, not surprisingly, since the latter was also designed originally by Quarenghi. It cost the city sixty-five thousand rubles to build, but private funds were used as well as public funds.[20] In 1871, the architect F. O. Morandi rebuilt the edifice, converting the covered courtyard into a hall; he also tore down a second row of columns. Nonetheless, the building did not lose its architectural importance nor its beautifully proportioned first row of columns. In the second half of the nineteenth century when a new exchange was built, the earlier *birzha* became the home of the city duma.

At the northern end of Prymors'kyi Boulevard was another and even larger classical building, the palace of Count Mikhail Vorontsov, constructed in 1826, according to the plans of Francesco C. Boffo. The most striking part of the palace is a detached portico of twenty semicircular Doric columns facing the sea that makes it the most easily observed landmark even at a distance for those coming to the city by water. It is prominent enough to serve as a landmark from various vantage points in the city as well.

Thomas de Thomon's first construction in Odessa was a massive classical building at the start of Pastera Street erected in 1806–7, a two-story building that was the first city hospital. Two adjoining curved wings were added in 1821, and they are surrounded by a six-columned portico. Almost at the same time, de Thomon designed the first Odessa Opera House, which unfortunately burned down in 1873. He also built stately warehouses at the port that appeared to be palaces that were perhaps unique to Odessa since they elicited so many comments from visitors to the city.

No discussion of the architecture of Odessa would be complete without at least reference to the gigantic stairway leading from the Prymors'kyi Boulevard down to the port, the source of most of the city's wealth. It was designed by Boffo, the architect of the commune of Odessa from 1822 to 1844 and a member of the Odessa Building Committee mentioned above. Construction began in 1837 and was completed in 1842. Contemporaries called it the Great Staircase but now it is better known as the Potemkin Steps, so named for the famous scene in Eisenstein's film *Potemkin* in which Cossacks march down the steps shooting a mother who is holding on to a baby buggy that then goes out of control careening down the staircase. It is still one of the most dramatic sights of the city, whether looking up from the port or down on the staircase from Prymors'kyi Boulevard.[21] At the top of the staircase stands the statue of the Duc de Richelieu pointing to the sea; it was sculptured by Ivan Petrovich Martos in 1827, but the concept to place the statue at the top of the giant staircase appears to have been that of Boffo.[22] Behind the statue and built about the same time in the center of Prymors'kyi Boulevard are two semicircular buildings, both designed by Boffo but whose final elaborations belong to Mel'nikov. Among the most handsome edifices in the city, like parentheses they frame the top of the staircase and the opening of Katerynyns'ka Street leading to the center of town. One served as a hotel and the other as an office for city administrators.[23]

Boffo also designed in 1830 a handsome neoclassical building on Prymors'kyi Boulevard for M. N. Shidlovskii, who later became governor-general of the city from 1865 to 1868. In 1835, it was acquired by Countess M. A. Naryshkina.[24] Later it went into the hands of D. K. Volokhov, a well-known contractor who at one time headed the building committee. After several changes of hand, it went to the city, becoming the residence of the commander of the Military District, and finally, after being rebuilt after the Second World War, it became the home of the Seaman's Club.[25]

Boffo created the marine facade of the city, that is, the buildings along Prymors'kyi Boulevard, the Potemkin Steps, and the concept of the statue of Richelieu. Governor-General M. Vorontsov nominated him in 1828 for the prize of the Order of St. Vladimir, Fourth Class, for which Boffo became a member of the Russian hereditary nobility.[26] Even under the reign of Nicholas I (1825–55), Odessa's architecture continued to reflect a classical style. That is, until Nicholas began to favor pseudo-gothic architecture, so that in Odessa too, private individuals built large houses in the pseudo-gothic style along the seashore. As Siniaver noted, "With the development of the city, all administrators and propertied people of the time who were building their residences outside the city, strove to imitate the magnificent palaces surrounding Petersburg."[27]

Although suburbs developed, the growth of population on the whole created a denser center city rather than urban sprawl. In 1849, the architect F. O. Morandi drew up a new master plan for the city in which all buildings had to conform to prescribed imperial plans for facades that were essentially neoclassical in style. Not until the latter half of the century was eclecticism displayed in building design.[28]

The new Opera House begun in 1883 and completed in 1887 at the cost of 1.3 million rubles was designed in the Italian Renaissance and baroque style by two Viennese architects, Ferdinand Fellner and Hermann Helmer, who designed some seventy theaters during the last quarter of the nineteenth century and the twentieth up until World War I, principally in Eastern Europe.[29] It is, after the Potemkin Steps, the most famous edifice in the city and certainly exceedingly grand.

In the exterior niches are busts of Pushkin, Gogol, Griboyedov, and Glinka. The large hall, in the style of Louis XVI, was richly decorated with gilded stucco design and figures. Frescos on the ceiling depicted various Shakespearean scenes. In addition to the wide parterre, there were four tiers of loges, a dress circle, a balcony, and a gallery. The theater is located near Prymors'kyi Boulevard.[30]

A national competition was held for the design (announcements were placed in major newspapers of Russia, Western Europe, and the United States). The local architect Alexander Bernardazzi and the architectural company of Fellner and Helmer were asked to furnish designs. The Viennese architects were chosen. Two Austrian firms, first Frey & Co. (until it went bankrupt) and then Tsifer & Co., constructed the building. On October 13, 1887, at the opening of the new theater, the music-mad Odessa public was treated with a performance of excerpts from *Boris Godunov* by Mussorgskii and the third act of Griboyedov's *Woe from Wit*. The theater was illuminated by electricity, making it the first building in Odessa to employ the Edison Company. Nina Gourfinkel said of the theater, "The point of convergence, the indisputable center of the city, its heart marked by magnificence and munificence, was the large Municipal Theater, the passion and the pride of Odessans."[31]

Designed, built, and ruled mostly by foreigners in its early years, Odessa with a large immigrant population became a kind of commercial and cultural interface between the Russian Empire and the outside world, especially with Europe and the Middle East. The city grew at a phenomenal rate, tripling in size from 35,000 persons in 1815 to nearly 116,000 in 1861. By midcentury, some twenty languages were regularly spoken; ten religions were practiced. The marriage between the grain produced by the black soil (*chornozem*) of Ukraine and the exporters on the Black Sea coast produced Odessa's wealth as well as fortunes for many of the people involved with the growing, marketing, and shipping of wheat.

At first many of the exporters were Greeks and Italians who were members of family firms with branch offices around the Mediterranean Sea.[32] As these families of substance settled down in this attractive city, they built townhouses, and many summer villas (dachas) along the seashore. It was their generosity, civic consciousness, and perhaps love of ostentatious display of wealth that resulted in the construction of many handsome buildings, especially for public use, in the fast-growing city of Odessa.

The introduction of the railroad, the availability of easier credit with the formation of the Odessa Municipal Credit Society (1871), the rising wealth and confidence of the entrepreneurial classes and the new assertiveness of the municipal government all contributed to the building boom of the 1870s, 1880s, and 1890s. Next to commerce, building activity became the most important source of employment.... By the turn of the century, on average, 1000 buildings were being constructed annually.[33]

Greeks were among the first to make their fortunes in Odessa, and they left enduring monuments attesting to their success. As George Candelis wrote concerning his family and other Greeks of the diaspora, they sought to become members of the bourgeoisie and sought titles of distinction, such as "honorary citizen" in order to promote their economic interests. They also built substantial personal palaces and public theaters (as did the Scaramanga family in Taganrog, who built a theater there and invited French performers for the entertainment of the population).[34] Among those responsible for much building in Odessa was the civic-minded Marazli family, which made a fortune in the grain trade. By 1879, one of them, Grigorii Marazli, became mayor of the city. Before he became mayor he had been a member of the city council for five years; he was then to serve the city as mayor for nearly a quarter of a century. During that period, Marazli established forty social and educational institutions and made many municipal improvements. When his father died in 1851, Grigorii continued in the family export business, but because of the relative decline of the grain trade from Odessa after the Crimean War, he invested the family fortune into property and industry in Odessa.[35] The tax register of 1873 shows that he owned more than a dozen pieces of choice real estate worth then about 300,000 rubles, or about 0.7 percent of the value of all the private buildings in Odessa.[36] In 1899, he and several others, including Edmund G. Harris, an engineer, applied to set up a joint stock company in the construction business with offices in Odessa, Kherson, Bessarabia, Podillia, Katerynoslav, and Taurida.[37]

Thanks to the success of his many business ventures, Marazli was able to indulge his generous impulses such as subsidizing the publication of many books on Odessa's history.[38] As mayor, he attempted to introduce electric lights into the city. With his own money he built a chapel in the Christian cemetery. He gave the city a neoclassical palace built in 1805 by Count Stanisław-Felix Potocki on Sofiivs'ka Street according to the plans of an unknown architect. It became a museum, which it is to this day—the Museum of Art on what was in Soviet times known as Korolenko Street.[39] Another showplace, a French neoclassical mansion built in 1856 with some baroque elements on Pushkins'ka Street by the architect L. Otton for the rich merchant A. Abaza, was also the Marazli family's gift to the city. Since 1920, it has housed the Western and Eastern Arts Museum.[40] Otton also designed another neoclassical palace in the 1850s, which now houses the Odessa Literary Museum.[41]

In 1883, Grigorii Marazli engaged the architect F. Gąsiorowski to build a huge public library on Exchange Square to which nine years later he added another building that doubled the library in size to make room for its eighty thousand volumes. It was the first building constructed in Odessa specifically for public use.[42] This Palladian palace now houses the Archeological Museum.[43] In 1892, Marazli built another enormous public reading room in the Greek revival style with two public schools attached, designed by Iu. M. Dmytrenko and also a gift to the city. These libraries served until 1904, when the city built a neoclassical library (now Odessa National Scholarly Library) on Pastera Street according to the plans of the architect F. P. Nesturkh.

Marazli paid the local architect I. F. Iatsenko from his own means to make an addition to the almshouse. Like the Duc de Richelieu, he was particularly interested in gardens, so he gave one of his dachas, located about four kilometers from the city, to the Odessa branch of the Imperial Horticultural Society founded in 1884. In 1886 and 1889, he had the architects Roman Klein and M. Tołwiński redesign the dacha to make a school for studying botany, gardening, and farming. One building housed the students, teachers, and dining hall. Another served as a workshop and the third was a two-story church. Not only did this extensive area (five *desiatinas*, or thirteen and one-half acres) house a boarding school, but also the three hundred or more members of the Horticultural Society met there regularly to present scientific papers.

Marazli's interest in science was further reflected in his equipping from his own pocketbook the bacteriological laboratory in the city. This was the first of its kind in the empire; there the Nobel Prize winning scientist I. I. Mechnikov made his valuable experiments in microbiology. Today Odessa University is named for Mechnikov. Marazli also initiated the publication of the *Novorossiiskii kalendar'* (Novorussian calendar) in 1891, first edited by Ia. A. Iakovlev and then by A. S. Borinevich. He built a children's park in the duke's gardens for the poor children of Moldavanka and Slobidka-Romanivka districts. He paid for an addition to the Sturdza Almshouse for children. In 1870, in memory of his mother, Zoe Theodorovna, he contributed five thousand rubles to support girls living in the Maria Theodorovna Orphanage. In 1892, he financed a retirement home for veterans and gave as a donation to the city a large shelter for the homeless. Among his many charities, he gave large subventions to the City Theater, especially to support Italian opera.[44] Odessa had given the Marazlis an opportunity to gain a fortune in the grain trade and, fittingly, on the first anniversary of the founding of the city, a descendent of that family, a major patron of the city's architecture and philanthropies, Grigorii Marazli, presided as mayor.

Greeks were not unique in their architectural contributions to Odessa. Another heir to a family's fortune in the grain export trade from at least 1838 was the German Baron A. E. Mahs (Maas).[45] His house on Katerynyns'ka Square and Vorontsovs'kyi Lane was a sturdily built two-story building with a simple facade. His wealth was displayed primarily in the interior, which was done by the Italian artist A. Vanini, who put in an extremely luxurious parquet flooring of black, red, and lemon wood fashioned in such intricate patterns that they resembled the best Florentine mosaics, according to the authors of a history commemorating the centenary of the founding of the city.[46] In 1882, Mahs's heirs commemorated his memory by constructing on Staroportofrankivs'ka Street an enormous night shelter of two stories, which was built according to the plan of the architect A. D. Todorov and which cost 84,000 rubles and could house up to 725 homeless persons. His descendants continued to honor the baron by contributing 15,000 rubles to build an almshouse with one section for thirty-four persons called the Mahs Section. The family also provided a 15,000-ruble capital fund to maintain the poor there.

Avram Brodskii, a wealthy Jewish merchant and industrialist, was no less involved in Odessa's civic affairs. In 1873, he was one of the six men who formed the executive committee of the city's government. He supported the Jewish Hospital and in 1861, he bought a stone building on Oleksandrivs'kyi Prospekt for 20,000 rubles as a shelter for poor Jews. In 1872, the asylum was named Talmud-Torah and was expanded. In 1879, Brodskii built a gigantic Jewish orphanage, a solid classical edifice that occupied an entire block on Bazarna (Bazaar) Street that cost him 72,000 rubles. At the orphanage were a prayer house and a school. In 1891, he bought a large tract outside the city where he established yet another orphanage for Jewish children who could learn farming and the trades of blacksmith and wheelwright.[47]

The Polish grain merchant Count Isador Sabanski built a granary to resemble a palace of a rectangular shape, three stories high with three massive porticos with Ionic columns; this particular palace could contain 36,000 *chetvert's* of wheat (about 207,788 bushels). In 1830, Sabanski joined the Polish uprising, and the Russian government seized the building and converted it to army barracks. Located on Kanatna Street (No. 23), it is the only extant, disguised warehouse, although some 720 of them existed in 1857.[48]

Another Polish landlord, A. Brzezinski, paid for a remarkable house on Gogolia Street built in 1852 according to the plan of F. Gąsiorowski, who might have been influenced by Nicholas I's love of the pseudo-gothic style of architecture mentioned above. It looked like an English castle with towers, turrets, peepholes, and interior courtyards. On a hill, it commanded a view of the sea. In 1909, when a Persian revolution occurred, the shah fled to Odessa, renting the building; ever since then it has been known as the shah's palace. It became the House of Culture under the Soviet regime.[49]

Russian merchants also embellished the city. In 1874, a merchant by the name of M. R. Gladkov died and left a will requesting that his widow, Natalia Ivanovna, build an orphanage. In 1879, she built an orphanage that housed forty-eight boys of the Orthodox faith. Furthermore, she put 103,200 rubles into the State Bank as a capital fund for the continuing support of the orphanage. Apparently that sum was not sufficient, for she is reported to have covered the annual deficits during her lifetime. The boys studied to become cobblers, tailors, and artisans of various sorts.[50] Another Russian, the wealthy merchant A. Abaza, had constructed according to the design of L. Otton a building in Renaissance and baroque style on Pushkins'ka Street (No. 9). A sumptuous palace with broad stairs of white marble, adorned with molded ceilings and parquet floors, this private home was taken by the Soviet regime and became the Museum of Western and Eastern Art in 1920.

Mikhail Dmitrievich Tolstoi, another landlord made prosperous through the grain trade and later very active in civic affairs, built a two-story mansion in 1830 near Prymors'kyi Boulevard.[51] One of his descendants, M. M. Tolstoi, added in 1897 to the original palace another two-story house with an Italian baroque facade that was designed by Helmer and Fellner, under the supervision of a local architect G. Shevrembrandt.

Anonymous merchants also left an architectural stamp on the city of Odessa.[52] Typical of a wealthy merchant's home was one located on a precipice and appropriately enough on Torhova (Trade) Street with its face turned toward the sea. The courtyard into which jutted one wing of the house was protected by a translucent wooden fence of latticework on a stone base alternating with Doric columns. One of the characteristics of the city was large houses with interior courtyards that reflected the southern location of the city. These houses were usually set off from the street by open arched tunnels that led to the tiled courtyard, usually surrounding a cistern. Arched ceilings, pilasters, niches, and paintings were the usual elements of artistic adornment of the tunnels serving as entryways to the courtyards.[53]

The functions of commerce demanded suitable structures, as shown by the need for an exchange discussed above and the Palais-Royale, a row of forty-four shops built between 1842 and 1844 on Teatral'na Square by Toricelli. At the turn of the century, a larger Victorian shopping complex, the Passage, built by the architects L. L. Vlodek and T. L. Fishel', served the wealthy shoppers of the city.[54]

Testimony to the vibrant economy of the city was the new Exchange Building constructed according to the design of Alexander Iosifovich Bernardazzi, begun in 1894 and completed five years later. Bernardazzi was the descendant of a family of architects originally from Switzerland. Born in Piatigorsk, he came to Odessa in 1878 where he lived until his death in 1907. In those thirty years, he ornamented the city by creating dozens of prominent buildings.[55]

Of the twenty or so edifices Bernardazzi designed in Odessa, perhaps his most significant creation was the new Exchange Building, in the style of early Italian Renaissance that possessed a splendid loggia and outdoor stairs made of white Carrara marble, which also decorated the facade. An innovator, Bernardazzi used concrete instead of granite for its construction. The huge hall, paneled with cedars from Lebanon, covered 910 square meters. The height of the rooms was fifteen meters. Above the three entrances to the Trading Hall were panels representing allegories of Agriculture, Trade, and Industry painted by a Florentine artist. With the collapse of capitalism in 1917, the need for a stock exchange ended; the building under the Soviet regime and today houses the Odessa Philharmonic Orchestra.

Bernardazzi also built a large bank, also in the Italian Renaissance style, on Pushkins'ka Street, not far from the exchange. The windows are huge semicircles. From the lobby, a marble staircase led to the hall on the first floor.[56] He also designed the ornate five-story Bristol Hotel (or the Krasnaia, as it was known in Soviet times) that was constructed in 1898–99 in Italian Renaissance and baroque styles. Of Bernardazzi, Skinner wrote, "To a large extent, the Odessa that one sees today is the work of this prodigious and talented architect."[57]

At the same time that the Bristol Hotel was constructed, the London Hotel (such British names must have conveyed an air of business and luxury to guests) was built along Prymors'kyi Boulevard by a local architect, Iu. M. Dmytrenko, in Italian Renaissance style to blend in with the other edifices. By 1911, the Passage Hotel was the largest in the city. The English (and smaller American) business presence in the port city was marked by the construction in 1842 of the English Club by Toricelli. To suggest English Wedgewood ceramics, the building was white and blue, and looked out from its slope onto the Opera House.

In 1927, the State Museum of Art opened a special exhibition of paintings, lithographs, engravings, and photographs depicting interesting architectural structures of Odessa and environs.[58] The authors of the catalogue claimed there were five hundred architectural monuments in Odessa "worthy of attention and study," a statement supported by illustrations from the exhibit.[59] A more modest number—forty-three—buildings and monuments were listed in 1985 by the authors of a four-volume catalogue of architectural monuments in the entire Soviet Ukrainian Republic.[60]

The "monuments worthy of attention and study" were erected by private citizens, mostly merchants and businessmen, and by the city duma. Since nearly one-third of the city revenue was generated by real estate taxes (which were the largest single source of the city's revenue from 1864 to 1900), the wealthy citizens of Odessa indirectly subsidized public buildings such as the City Theater.[61] This kind of local support must be contrasted with the imperial largesse described by John Norman for St. Petersburg, "It is necessary to recognize the vital role state funds and imperially sponsored institutions played in the remarkable artistic flowering that occurred in the last decades of tsarist Russia. It was, after all, the tsars who provided both the institutional infrastructure and the massive patronage that were prerequisites for the thriving fine arts community that eventually resulted in an independent and distinctly Russian contributions to world artistic culture."[62]

Odessa, on the other hand, beyond its founding years, enjoyed very little imperial patronage. Architectural monuments, whether public buildings or private residences, stand as testimony to the industriousness, tastes, generosity, and, at times, vanity of Odessa's wealthy population. Most of Odessa's architecture of note had been built before 1900. Indeed, the most visible central edifices were erected during the first half of the nineteenth century when neoclassical architecture was at its height in Russia: Odessa's first theater and hospital (1804 and 1806), the first Exchange (1829), Vorontsov's Palace (1826), Mel'nikov's two semicircular buildings at the head of the Potemkin Steps (1827)—all of these were built along Prymors'kyi Boulevard, the city's marine facade, which gave the city an architectural unity, at least at first glance. Buildings erected later, such as the railway station (1884), New Exchange (1894), and the new theater (1883), were also neoclassical in style. Perhaps because of the absence of imperial patronage, or perhaps because around the turn of the century Odessa was no longer the prosperous seaport it once was and no longer attracted foreign merchants, the city did not undergo a revival of neoclassical building as did St. Petersburg in the first decade of the twentieth century.[63] To use the economic historian Alexander Gerschenkron's felicitous phrase, "the advantages of backwardness" spared Odessa the nouvelle vague of neoclassicism and thus conferred on it the opportunity to retain a harmonious complex of nineteenth-century neoclassical buildings, an advantage that lasted up until the Revolution of 1917, after which the city was not spared the excesses of so-called proletarian classical architecture.[64]

I am grateful to Professor Jürgen Schulz of Brown University for his helpful comments on this chapter.

Notes

1. For a general history, Patricia Herlihy, *Odessa: A History, 1794–1914* (Cambridge, MA: Harvard University Press, 1986). For a brief history, emphasizing the earlier period of the Tatar settlement dating back to the early fifteenth century, "Mizhnarodna Naukovo-Teoretychna Konferentsiia, Prysviachena 200-Richiu Mista, September 6–8, 1994," *Odessa-200* (Odessa: Odessa State University, 1994). For a broad yet penetrating study of the significance of the entire area, Neal Ascherson, *Black Sea* (New York: Hill and Wang, 1995).
2. The attack was led by Gen. I. V. Gudovich who reported to Gen. Alexander V. Suvorov. I. I. Kotkov, *Gorod-geroi: Odessa* (Moscow: Stroiizdat, 1977), 7.
3. Frederick W. Skinner, "City Planning in Russia: The Development of Odessa, 1789–1892" (PhD diss., Princeton University, 1973). For a history of the formation of Novorossiia, E. I. Druzhinina, *Kiuchuk Kainardzhiiskii mir 1774 goda* (Moscow: Akademii nauk SSSR, 1955).
4. Marie-Paule Vial, ed., *La Mémoire d'Odessa* (Paris: Hatier, 1989), 41.
5. A. Orlov, *Istoricheskii ocherk Odessy s 1794 po 1803 god* (Odessa: A. Shul'tse, 1885). See also Chapter 7 in this book.
6. For more information on these early foreign figures of importance in Odessa's history, Alexander de Ribas, *Staraia Odessa: Istoricheskie ocherki, vospominaniia* (Odessa: Knizhnyi magazin Georgiia Russo, 1913), 16–26.
7. For a discussion of the impact made on the city by the many foreigners in Odessa. See also Chapter 6 in this book.
8. David J. Fox, "Odessa," *Scottish Geographical Magazine*, 79, no. 1 (1963): 9.
9. The streets led from the top of the bluff inward toward the center of the city by the shortest routes, preserving the views of the Black Sea as much as possible. Ivan I. Kotkov, *Arkhitektura Odessy* (Odessa: Maiak, 1967), 58.
10. Mark Twain, *The Innocents Abroad, or the New Pilgrim's Progress, Being Some Account of the Steamship* Quaker City's *Pleasure Excursions to Europe and to the Holy Land* (New York: Grosset, 1911), 116.
11. Nina Gourfinkel, *Naissance d'un monde* (Paris: Édition du Sueil, 1953), 17.
12. *Odessa, 1794–1894* (Odessa: Odesskoe gorodskoe obshchestvennoe upravlenie, 1894), xiv.
13. Thomas de Thomom (1754–1813) was born and trained in France. *Macmillan Encyclopedia of Architects*, vol. 4 (New York: Free Press, 1982), 206.
14. M. M. Siniaver, *Arkhitektura staroi Odessy* (Leningrad: Leningradskii oblastnoi soiuz sovetskikh pisatelei, 1935), 10. Francesco Frappoli also began work on the cathedral and designed the City Hospital in Odessa. Ettore Lo Gatto, *Gli artisti italiani in Russia*, vol. 1 (Milano: Libri Scheiwiller, 1990), 132.
15. V. Bogoslavsky, "Boffo," in *Dizionario biografico degli italiani*, vol. 11 (Rome: Istituto della enciclopedia italiana, 1969), 170. For illustrations of the original theater and of Boffo's reconstruction of 1822, *Odessa, 1794–1894*, 404–5.
16. Siniaver, *Arkhitektura staroi Odessy*, 10.
17. Vial, *La Mémoire d'Odessa*, 42.
18. Kotkov, *Arkhitektura Odessy*, 58.
19. Ibid., 68, for details of the dispute. Some of the architects who came from St. Petersburg to work on Odessan projects were Mel'nikov, de Thomon, O. Montferrand, and the sculptor I. Martos. Some of the local architects of note were Boffo, Toricelli, E. Kozlov, N. Cherkunov, F. Gąsiorowski, M. Tołwiński, Morandi, Dall'Aqua, and A. Bernardazzi. G. A. Karev, *Odessa—gorod-geroi* (Moscow: Voenizdat, 1978), 14–16. Giorgio Toricelli, born in Switzerland in 1798, began his career in Lugano. Arriving in Odessa in 1818 at the invitation of Count Langeron,

he worked with Boffo until 1826, when he was named the city architect in charge of construction. His most important works were the houses of Khorvt on the Sabanievski bridge, Julien on Derybasivs'ka Street, and Camo on Tyraspil's'ka Square as well as the Mykhailivs'kyi Cathedral in 1835, the church of the Presentation of Christ, the Palais Royal (1840–43), and the English Club. He died in Odessa in 1843. Vial, *La Mémoire d'Odessa*, 76.

20 Odessa Oblast Archives, GAOO. f. 5, op. 1, d. 388, 11. 12–25.
21 For a description of the staircase, the city's "architectural emblem," size, number of steps, and composition, Kotkov, *Arkhitektura Odessy*, 67–68.
22 Martos is also the sculptor of the monument to Minin and Pozharsky in Moscow.
23 The slightly newer building on the right facing Katerynyns'ka Street was once the site of the Hotel St. Petersburg. Vissarion Belinsky, a noted literary critic, visited the hotel in 1846. Kotkov, *Arkhitektura Odessy*, 66.
24 Countess Naryshkina was the mistress of Alexander I. She settled by the sea for the health of her sickly daughter, Sofia. Ribas, *Staraia Odessa*, 46.
25 *Odessa, 1794–1894*, 408, and Bogoslavsky, "Boffo," in *Dizionario biografico degli italiani*, 171 and *Pamiatniki gradostroitel'stva i arkhitektury ukrainskoi SSR 3* (Kyiv: Budivel'nyk, 1983–86), 246–47.
26 Bogoslavsky, "Boffo," in *Dizionario biografico degli italiani*, 171. It was during the administration of Vorontsov that the city flourished. The funeral monument on his grave was made by the celebrated architect Eugène Viollet-le-Duc. Vial, ed., *La Mémoire d'Odessa*, 42.
27 Siniaver, *Arkhitektura staroi Odessy*, 1.
28 Skinner, "City Planning," 190.
29 About fifty opera houses were built, including those in Berlin, Odessa, Zurich, Wiesbaden, Sofia, and New York. George C. Izenour, *Theater Design* (New York: McGraw-Hill, 1977), 82. Izenour describes the style as "Italian horseshoe-shaped," and "eclectic neo-Renaissance."
30 In 1925, a fire destroyed the stage so that a fireproof curtain was installed. During World War II, the Germans tried to mine the building, but the bomb did not go off. In 1966, a large-scale renovation took place. Kotkov, *Arkhitektura Odessy*, 75–76.
31 Gourfinkel, *Naissance d'un monde*, 17. Typical of a native's impression was that of Abraham T'homi: "Of my hometown, Odessa, I remember only the straight streets lined with acacia trees and the Opera House. I was much impressed with our Opera House. I believed it was the most magnificent structure in the whole world." Abraham T'homi, *Between Darkness and Dawn: A Sage of the Hehalutz* (New York: Bloch, 1986), 19.
32 Herlihy, *Odessa*, 88–95.
33 Frederick W. Skinner, "Odessa and the Problem of Urban Modernization," in *The City in Late Imperial Russia*, ed. Michael F. Hamm (Bloomington: Indiana University Press, 1986), 221.
34 G. Candilis, *Treis Oikogeneies tes Diasporas. Chios-Pontos-Rosia, 1822–1924* (Athens: Hermes, 1994), 5.
35 N. A. Teren t'eva, "Sem'ia Marazli v Odesse," *Odesi-200 Materialy Mizhnarodnoi naukovo-teoretychnoi konferentsii*, 132–34. For the decline in the grain trade after the Crimean War and the reasons for it, see Herlihy, *Odessa*, 202–32.
36 The tax record is in the Odessa Oblast Archives, GAOO, f. 274 op. 1, d. 2, 11. 64–85.
37 Professor Thomas Owen, private communication.
38 In 1903, Marazli sent two Greek books to President Theodore Roosevelt as reported by the American consul at Odessa. National Archives, Washington, DC, NACRO, October 2, 1903. Unfortunately, the consul does not give the titles. The president wrote Marazli a grateful letter of acknowledgment, saying that he would donate the books to the Library of Congress.
39 The massive classical building has a portico and a courtyard. The interior is decorated with rich stucco molding, ornate friezes and magnificent parquet floors. This current museum of Ukrainian and Russian art from the

seventeenth century to modern times occupies nineteen halls. The old palace once had a secret passageway to the sea. Kotkov, *Arkhitektura Odessy*, 28–32.

40 Kotkov, *Arkhitektura Odessy*, 28–32.

41 It is on Lastochkina Street (No. 2). *Pamiatniki gradostroitel'stva*, 3:246.

42 *Pamiatniki gradostroitel'stva*, 3:244. Felix Gąsiorowski was born in Poland ca. 1815 and died in 1891 in Odessa. He began his architectural career in Warsaw. From 1849, he was in Odessa, first building homes for Poles and then he received commissions from Russian aristocrats as well as Russian, Italian, and German merchants. His most important buildings are the palaces for Brzezinski, Sabanski, Rzewuski, and Mochevski. He was one of the founders of the Society of Engineers and Architects and of the architectural section of the Technological Society of Odessa. Among his other outstanding works are the Imperial Hotel on Derybasivs'ka Street, the School of Commerce (1877), as well as the Archeological Museum. Vial, *La Mémoire d'Odessa*, 68.

43 A museum for antiquities was founded in Odessa as early as 1825, making it one of the oldest museums in Ukraine and even older than most in Russia.

44 Private communication from the late Professor M. M. Postan.

45 Guido Hausmann gives a full account of Baron A. Mahs and his family's role in the grain trade in Odessa in "Deutsche Kaufleute und Unternehmer im Wirtschaftsleben Odessas Ende des 19. und zu Beginn des 20. Jahrhunderts," unpublished paper, 7–11.

46 *Odessa, 1794–1894*, 412.

47 Ibid., 100, 738–39.

48 V. Zagoriuko, *Po stranitsam istorii Odessy i Odesshchiny*, vol. 1 (Odessa: Odesskoe oblastnoe izdatel'stvo 1957–60), 77.

49 V. I. Timofeenko, *Odessa: arkhitekturno-istoricheskii ocherk* (Kyiv: Budivel'nyk, 1983), 19.

50 *Odessa, 1794–1894*, 740.

51 For his numerous offices on city committees including that of building a water system, *Odessa, 1794–1894*, 88, 90–92, 100, 248, 285; for his gift to the city of a large tract of land on which was built a children's clinic, 560.

52 Ethnic and religious groups of wealthy merchants, grain growers, and industrialists also were responsible for the many beautiful churches and synagogues in the city. While the Russian Orthodox Cathedral was destroyed during the revolution, the Roman Catholic Church built by Italian merchants still stands, as does the Lutheran Church (the elementary school of which was attended by Leon Trotsky) and the Brody Synagogue, built in 1841, which now houses the Odessa Oblast' Archives.

53 Siniaver, *Arkhitektura staroi Odessy*, 13, with illustrations, 33–35.

54 O. A. Siderenko, *Odessa: Dostoprimechatel'nosti* (Odessa: Maiak, 1971), 35. French names for shopping centers suggesting style seemed to be as popular as British names for hotels indicating comfort.

55 Berdardazzi completed his studies at the Institute of Civil Engineering in St. Petersburg in 1850. He then worked in Bessarabia from 1850 to 1856 and became the city architect of Kishenev from 1856 to 1877. He was briefly a railroad consultant between 1877 and 1878 before going in Odessa where he was first associated with Novorossiia University and then with the Odessa *gradonachal'stvo*. Skinner, "City Planning," 288.

56 During the Soviet period, the bank became the Political Education House. Kotkov, *Arkhitektura Odessy*, 77.

57 Skinner, "City Planning," 289.

58 For an annotated catalogue published by the museum, *Stara Odesa: Arkhitektura Prychornomor'ia* (Odessa: Odes'kyi derzhavnyi khudozhnii muzei, 1927). The preface was written by Alexander de Ribas, a descendant of Joseph, the soldier and town planner in the late eighteenth century.

59 Ibid., 16.

60 *Pamiatniki gradostroitel'stva*, 3:244–64.
61 Herlihy, *Odessa: A History*, 148–49.
62 John O. Norman, "Alexander III as a Patron of Russian Art," in *New Perspectives on Russian and Soviet Artistic Culture*, ed. John O. Norman (New York: St. Martin's Press, 1994), 34.
63 William Craft Brumfield's illuminating essay, "Neoclassical Aestheticism in Pre-revolutionary Russian Architecture," in Norman, *New Perspectives*, 41–53.
64 Ibid., 50.

CHAPTER 11

Port Jews of Odessa and Trieste— A Tale of Two Cities

1. ENLIGHTENMENT: PORT JEWS OF TRIESTE

Trieste, the jewel of the Adriatic, and Odessa, the pearl of the Black Sea, bear comparison.[1] In fact, Lois Dubin in her recent book, *The Port Jews of Habsburg Trieste: Absolutist Politics and Enlightenment*, has invited comparison of the history and status of the port Jews of Trieste with Jews in other ports.[2] She wrote, "the existence of this Jewry in this port city [Trieste] was—like the existence of other port Jewries in places such as Livorno, Bordeaux, London, Amsterdam and later Odessa—predicated on the perception of a Jewish aptitude for commerce that could stimulate trade and cause the city to flourish."[3]

If the term "port Jews" and the specific conditions governing their lives are to have meaning, then the term should be applicable to Jews living and working in other ports in addition to Trieste. The use of the word "port" as an adjective suggests that geography, commerce, and history distinguished the experience of certain Jews from that of other Jews. I will attempt to see to what extent Dubin's model is useful in understanding the history of Odessa's port Jews.

Dubin asserts that the "interplay of economic change, the absolutist state and the Enlightenment" created "new opportunities for European Jews."[4] She describes Trieste as a crossroad between North and South and between West and East. To a certain extent Odessa also, as a southern frontier of the Russian Empire, was an intermediary between Russia's partially industrialized North and her agricultural South. Like Trieste, Odessa traded with the Levant and with Western Mediterranean countries. Dubin's description of Trieste as a "bustling hub for immigrants, a cosmopolitan center" that attracted diverse religious and ethnic minorities is applicable to Odessa as well.[5] In Odessa as in Trieste there was a colorful mixture of costumes, languages, and cultures.[6]

For Dubin, three factors—an absolutist state, commerce and Enlightenment ideas—were the critical elements that shaped the history of Trieste's Jews. To develop commerce, the absolutist Habsburg monarch Maria Theresa issued the initial call for Jews and other non-Catholic merchants to settle in the then tiny port city of Trieste. Although she had little sympathy for Jews, she embarked on this project for pragmatic reasons; she wanted to induce commerce in

---

Originally published as Patricia Herlihy, "Port Jews of Odessa and Trieste: A Tale of Two Cities," *Yearbook 2003*, Simon Dubnow Institute, University of Leipzig: 183–99.

her port city, especially since a rival, Venice, was on the decline.[7] Nonetheless, the privileges she extended to Jews who settled in Trieste were generous.

When Maria Theresa's philosopher son Joseph II issued his Edicts of Toleration, Dubin notes, "the situation of Triestine Jews was so exceptional that they were scarcely affected by Joseph II's toleration edicts that generally expanded the range of economic opportunities open to Habsburg Jews" elsewhere in the empire.[8] By the last quarter of the eighteenth century, therefore, Trieste's port Jews already enjoyed remarkable privileges in recognition of their usefulness. And according to Dubin, usefulness was equated with morality for the Habsburgs. Productive Jews were considered to be good Jews. And so they were needed, wanted, and invited to stimulate trade in that port city. Tullia Catalan in her study on the Jewish community of Trieste also concluded that the Habsburgs had differentiated between "useful" and "non-useful" Jews. Only the former category was welcome in Trieste. Once Trieste became a free port in 1719, all non-Catholics were granted privileges with the goal of inducing a flow of capital to be invested in the commercial and financial activity of the market city.[9]

2. ENLIGHTENMENT: PORT JEWS OF ODESSA

The founder of Odessa, Catherine II, a contemporary of Maria Theresa and Joseph II, was also a self-proclaimed member of the Enlightenment and likewise interested in developing commerce from the Black Sea to the Mediterranean.[10] Unfortunately, she never specifically invited Jews to settle in Odessa, a city only two years old at the time of her death in 1796. Whether she would have invited Jewish merchants to Odessa had she lived is moot. There is plenty of evidence, however, that she made it relatively easy for Jews to move to Novorossiia of which Odessa formed a part.

Catherine, like Maria Theresa, was driven by mercantilist considerations when she allowed Jews to settle where they could benefit the economy. Along with economic considerations, however, Catherine had strategic goals. Catherine's primary concern was to populate the shores of the Black Sea in order to discourage the Ottoman Empire from attempting to reclaim the sparsely settled territory that Russia had acquired as a result of military victories. As the minister of the interior reported in 1804, Catherine II encouraged foreign immigration "from a desire to populate the empty steppes."[11] Her intention was to induce Jews, among others, to settle New Russia.[12]

The empress went to great lengths to do so. She secretly allowed Jews into Riga with the idea that they would then proceed to New Russia. Most of them decided to remain in Riga, however, so she adopted several other measures to lure Jews to New Russia.[13] For example, all the prisoners of war taken in Wallachia during The First Turkish War (1768–74), could settle anywhere in Russia, except for Jews, who were allowed to settle only in New Russia. It is true that Catherine thereby prevented Jews from going to the interior of Russia, but Catherine was more eager to populate newly acquired areas than in imposing restrictions on Jews.[14] In fact, the historian Richard Pipes argued that the reason why Catherine imposed double taxation on Jewish merchants and townsmen living on the old former Polish territory was to drive them to New Russia and the Crimea where they paid no taxes. It was in 1794 that Catherine imposed double taxation on mercantile Jews; that was also the year of the founding of Odessa, when Catherine actually defined (or created) the Pale of Settlement, enlarging it from Lithuania, through Belorus, parts of Ukraine and the Crimea, all the way to the Black Sea shore.

While it might be interpreted cynically that Catherine was only interested in providing bodies to stop the Turks, Pipes also argues cogently that Catherine's record shows "a genuine effort to treat Jews as a religious minority eligible to enjoy the same legal equality and rights as Christians of the same status."[15] She did more for Jews than anyone in Western Europe at that time, he concluded. It would seem Catherine was interested in improving the economic condition of Jews at the same time that she was populating New Russia. The fact that the double taxation was to be on Jewish merchants and townsmen suggests that these were the sorts of productive Jews she hoped to drive to the steppes, to the Black Sea shore (possibly to Odessa) and to the Crimea. Some doubts might be raised, however, whether individual Jews regarded this double taxation as "a favor." But clearly many Jews took advantage of the tax loophole in New Russia and moved there; some eventually found their way to the port of Odessa.

With regard to Odessa, Catherine's intentions are difficult to discern. We do not know if she wanted Jews to move to Odessa since she only specified Novorossiia. But Isabel de Madariaga concluded that exemption from taxes in New Russia "contributed to the development of one of the great cities of Russian Jewry—Odessa."[16] Perhaps Catherine knew she need not specify Odessa and that Jews would eventually settle there.

Catherine's policy was successful in moving Jews into New Russia insofar as one-half million Jews went to live there when the total population of Jews in the Russian Empire was not much more than 600,000.[17] And yet, as we have seen, Catherine never dared to summon Jews expressly to Odessa itself, and only allowed, rather than invited, Jews to New Russia. She permitted Jews into the new territories by indirection, mostly by not excluding them, or bypassing legislation affecting Jews that would make moving to New Russia advantageous to them.

Why was she so indirect and oblique in her legislation regarding Jews? Catherine, a German, rose to power through the assassination of her husband Peter III. As a woman unsure of her right to rule and wanting to curry favor with the Orthodox Church, she was afraid to single out Jews to confer privileges on them. Therefore, she made it possible through rather devious and indirect measures for limited Jewish mobility. As she herself stated, "To begin the reign with a decree permitting free entry to Jews would be a bad means of allaying public excitement; but to declare the free entry of Jews harmful was impossible."[18] Thus, because of her caution, the opportunity was missed during her reign openly to invite experienced Jewish merchants to Odessa.

When her grandson Alexander came to power, his Minister of Commerce N. P. Rumiantsev stated a need to invite foreign merchants and their capital to Odessa in 1803, because "as yet there is none of our own."[19] Once Odessa began to export grain to Europe, the state recruited Armenians, Moldavians, Slavs from Ragusa and Trieste, Italians, French, Germans, Danes, English, and Greeks. Preference was given to maritime merchants. And Jews were not included in that category. Only four years after the founding of Odessa, at least forty-six Greek families lived in Odessa.[20] As early as the 1820s, Greek merchants eclipsed both the French and Italian grain merchants in terms of volume of trade and profits derived from exports. As E. Druzhinina noted, "The role of the Greek merchants in the Black Sea trade was exceptionally great."[21]

In addition to Jews who moved into Odessa from Novorossiia, about 300 Jewish merchants from Galician Brody set up their offices in Odessa because an imperial ukase of 1803 allowed them to store their goods there duty free. Some of these Jews remained and more came from Brody to Odessa in the first quarter of the nineteenth century. Under Austrian rule Brody had the status of a free city so that Jewish merchants engaged in the exchange of goods and products from Leipzig and Breslau to Russia. As Zipperstein noted, "By the 1830s Odessa's Galician Jews had come to dominate the functions of middleman, factor and agent in the grain grade of this *pshenichnyi gorod* (wheat city), although export continued to be monopolized by Greeks and Italians."[22]

By 1815, the population of Odessa was about 35,000 persons, of whom there were about 4,000 Jews. Some of them were Jews who had been settled in agricultural colonies in New Russia in 1809. This experiment proved a failure, largely because the colonists did not receive promised support, and so they moved to towns and cities, including Odessa.[23] To be sure, Jews were present—only about six of them—in 1789 when the Russians captured the Turkish fortress on the site of the future city. As early as 1794, the date of the founding of the city, there were 240 Jews living there or about ten percent of the population.[24] By the middle of the nineteenth century Jews made up nearly nineteen percent of the population.[25] As Zipperstein has pointed out, many of the Jews settled in Odessa were traders in silk, cotton, wool, hardware, iron, shoes, and salt. They engaged in local commerce but also shipped abroad these wares. Still, it would appear their capital did not make them eligible to join merchant guilds in the early days of Odessa's history.[26] Some eventually did amass wealth in commerce, but few in the first half of the century engaged in the lucrative grain trade. Here Greek families with their network around the Mediterranean predominated.

The French consul in Odessa in 1832 stated that Jews served as middlemen in the grain trade.[27] Taking advantage of their experience in the New Russian countryside, Jews were the brokers between the peasants selling the grain and the exporters purchasing the grain.[28] The famous Yiddish actor, Jacob Adler, described his father living in Odessa in the 1850s, "My father, like others in Odessa, dealt in wheat. He sometimes speculated, sometimes acted as a broker, but he seldom had luck either way."[29] Jews would have to bide their time before they became significant exporters of grain. Unlike Jews in Trieste, therefore, Jewish enterprise was not directly associated with the fast growing export of grain abroad.

3. ADMINISTRATION OF PORT JEWS OF ODESSA AND TRIESTE

Meanwhile, as in Trieste, powerful administrators with close connections to the tsars ruled Odessa. Nearly all of them were sympathetic to Jews. It was Catherine who instituted in 1775 the office of governor-general to administer the newer provinces, including that of Novorossiia.[30] The governor-general was appointed directly by the tsar, so his power was great.[31] Catherine's enlightened grandson Alexander created the office of city chief or *gradonachal'nik*. Both the governor of Odessa's province and the chief of Odessa enjoyed a large measure of autonomy, partly because they were delegated much power and practically because they were so distant from the capital.

While Trieste was not a new city, it too was ruled under new administrative laws. As Dubin observes, "because the absolutist state created a wholly new administrative structure for the port city, it could establish things as it saw fit, with relatively little interference or resistance from local elements who might not share the new vision."[32] Not only was Odessa a new city, created ab initio, but it also enjoyed new and peculiar administrative structures. As we shall see, several of these officials supported rights for Jews and enacted measures that might not have suited authorities in the capital.

Both Odessa (indirectly) and Trieste (directly) benefited from the enlightened views of their respective rulers, Catherine II and Joseph II, whose ideas on using minorities to increase the prosperity of the realm might not have been coincidental. When they first met in 1780, the two monarchs engaged in a discussion on urban governance.[33] Later, in 1787, Catherine was eager to show Joseph her new town of Kherson with evident pride during her famous progression down the Dnipro, where the mythical "Potemkin villages" had been erected. As partners in dividing up Poland, Catherine and Joseph no doubt shared ideas on state building and the role of port cities in bolstering the economy.

Not only did Maria Theresa and her son provide liberties to Jews in Trieste, but also for many years enlightened officials administered the city itself. Giuseppe Ricci and later Karl von Zinsendorf endorsed rights for Jews so that there was "virtually no restriction on economic activity. Jews could own real and moveable property and were free to engage in commerce, manufacturing and artisanry on an equal basis of other emigrants."[34] These privileges created a climate favorable to the growth, prosperity, and sense of dignity within the Jewish community.

The early administrators of Odessa were unusual in their friendly relations with Jews. Don Joseph de Ribas, a soldier of fortune born in Naples of Spanish and Irish stock and one of the many adventurers in Catherine II's service, stormed the fortress and helped to secure it in September 1789. He was also one of the chief city planners and became the first city-chief of Odessa. So sympathetic was he to Jews that it was rumored he was Jewish himself.[35] For Odessa, there were also several enlightened governors and city chiefs beginning with the well-known Frenchman, the Duc de Richelieu, who was beloved by the Jews for his kindness and fatherly solicitation for them. Richelieu was invited to rule over Odessa in order to sponsor population growth in the city in general and, in particular, to foster growth of the commercial port.[36] Succeeding governors and city chiefs, such as Mikhail Vorontsov and Alexander Stroganov, also served the Jewish community well.[37] They insisted that Jews participate fully in all aspects of the city's life. For example, in the 1850s, eleven Jews served in city office.[38] In 1870, a special committee of the Ministry of the Interior met to draft a new municipal statute. At the time only one-third of all city council members could be Jews, no matter what percentage of the population Jews formed. The mayor of Odessa, Nikolai A. Novosel'skii, was the only one to argue that there should be no restrictions on the numbers of Jews serving, as long as they passed educational qualifications.[39]

Likewise, Jews in Trieste won for themselves political positions of power. The wholesale merchants of Trieste were organized in a body called the *Borsa*, which acted as an intermediary between the merchants and the local government that consulted it on policy. At the time of the establishment of the *Borsa* in 1774, about fourteen percent of all the commercial houses were Jewish, but at first Jews were excluded from the managing board of the *Borsa*. The heads of the Jewish community, including Marco Levi, one of the wealthiest Jewish merchants, protested. Starting in the 1790s, Jews became members of the *Borsa*'s executive board, although a Jew could never serve as director.[40] It is probably accurate to state that Jews in Trieste enjoyed more privileges than Jews elsewhere in the Habsburg Empire; Jews in Odessa, at least during its first half-century, fared better than Jews in the rest of the Romanov Empire.

4. CULTURAL CONFORMITY IN THE FREE PORTS OF TRIESTE AND ODESSA

It was the primacy of international trade that ascribed value to Jewish wholesale merchants and prompted rulers to grant free port status to both cities. As early as 1719, Charles VI declared Trieste a free port and invited Jews and other merchants to develop the commercial potential of the place. In 1814, the Duc de Richelieu, a disciple of Adam Smith, petitioned Alexander I to confer free port status on Odessa. While it took three years for his request to be granted and another two to be implemented, for forty years Odessa did retain its free port status where normal tariffs did not apply to goods imported or exported by sea.

Free ports were meant to stimulate trade so all merchants, including Jews, were welcome. Thus, free ports attracted foreigners, generated trade, and also diluted somewhat the sense of the inhabitants being tied to the core of the empire. Inhabitants felt freer, more detached from the center partly because of their geographical location, but also because their exempted status made them feel more drawn to other port cities, with which they had much more in common than to the homeland. Eventually, however, both pampered cities became somewhat suspect in the eyes of central authorities; they were felt to be too independent, insufficiently German in the case of Trieste, or not Russian enough in the case of Odessa. Centralizing absolutistic states were in a position to grant favors to port cities, but at the same time, they were also dismayed by exceptionalism if it was perceived that the loyalty of their subjects was compromised. Diversity produced wealth, but it could also promote political dissent.

Theoretically, rationalist Enlightenment ideas acknowledged that people of all religions and ethnicities shared a common humanity, a liberalizing concept that aided Jews in Trieste and Odessa, especially in economic activities. But enlightened monarchs also sought uniformity in practice, and this goal sometimes meant interference in cultural and religious practices. Dubin cites two Habsburg interventions into Jewish life. The first was in the matter of language. In eighteenth-century Trieste most residents spoke Italian, including Jews. Joseph II tried to impose German as the language of administration and commerce in 1789, but the *Borsa* protested, saying, "the local merchant body, composed for the most part of Italian, Greek, Jewish and Armenian traders, conducts their business only in Italian."[41] Jews were likewise told by Joseph to adopt German first and last names, but the Jewish community replied that they had Italian names and only spoke Italian. On this issue Joseph had to back down; he had to be content with the German language being used only for official bureaucratic communications between Trieste and Vienna. The significance of these attempts was not only that they had failed but also that exceptionalism and uniformity could not be reconciled.

If Italian was the lingua franca of Trieste, the same was true for Odessa. It was the language of commerce; all the streets signs were written in Italian as well as Russian, and once Italian opera captured the hearts, souls, and tongues of the city, Italian remained popular. And while many other languages were spoken and foreign languages were taught in school, Russian came to be the dominant language of Odessa even among Jews, although Galicians often retained the German language. Just the same, during the early years of Odessa's history, so few people spoke Russian that the Duc de Richelieu suggested that all the schools teach Russian, almost as if it were a foreign language.

Another attempt by the Habsburgs to impose uniformity was in regulations concerning marriage and divorce. In Trieste, the state allowed religious communities to conduct marriage rites and set regulations concerning who was eligible to marry and to divorce and to keep records of community vital statistics. However, in the 1780s the state issued laws, which stated that religious marriage regulations would be subject to civil law. While the wedding rites themselves would continue to be conducted by religious authorities, certain rules, such as age of marriage and eligibility for divorce, were set by the state. Rather than protest these interfering laws, Jews quietly ignored them, observing their own religious regulations. This subtle method of defiance worked until aggrieved parties either in being refused permission to marry or to divorce by Jewish law, appealed to the state for satisfaction. Even though civil law might favor the parties who appealed to them, ostracism by the Jewish community resulted in the triumph of traditional religious law. On the other hand, the Jewish community adopted some state regulations, such as a ban on clandestine marriages. Jews thus both resisted civil encroachment on their religious practices, and to a minor extent, they redefined their own laws to comply with civil authority.

In Odessa, the situation was similar. Each religion could regulate its own marriage and divorce regulations.[42] But, as in Trieste, this system broke down in the Jewish community "when aggrieved parties seeking divorce, especially women, voluntarily turned to the Russian state to adjudicate the matter."[43] While over the course of the nineteenth century, Jewish rabbis continued to keep the vital statistics of the community (in order to save the state administrative costs), they continued to lose ground in the matter of marriage and especially divorce. As ChaeRan Freeze recently noted, the "growing reliance on secular institutions to resolve private family issues attests to the steady decline in the authority of Jewish rabbis and the breakdown of internal communal discipline in tsarist Russia."[44] It appears that Odessan Jews were less successful in resisting state encroachment in family matters than those in Trieste.

5. TRIESTE AND ODESSA: DIVERGENT PATHS

But in culture Odessa matched Trieste's level. As Steven Zipperstein has pointed out, "Odessa had long been an important center for the institutions of the East European Haskalah, and its modern Jewish schools, synagogues, newspapers and publishers were among the best in the Pale."[45] And yet in the later decades of the nineteenth century, this story of a benign environment for Jews breaks down in Odessa. How can we account for the disillusionment of Jewish intellectuals, the persecution of Jews through several pogroms, the growth of Jewish socialism, and Jewish exodus to other parts of the Russian Empire or abroad? Since the useful Dubin formula of commerce, absolutism, and enlightenment appeared to favor Odessa as much as Trieste, what went awry in Odessa?

To be sure, here I can raise only certain hypotheses or road signs indicating where further research might answer the questions I posed. Let us return to the topic of commerce. We have seen that the Habsburgs invited international Jewish merchants to settle in Trieste. Catherine invited settlers, including Jews, to New Russia, primarily to populate the empty area as a measure of defense, but also in a general way to develop trade. Unlike the case of Trieste, there was no specific call for Jews who were experienced in international trade, and indeed, few, if any, such Jews arrived at Odessa in the first two decades. Jews from Brody were not experienced in maritime trade, and when they arrived in Odessa, most overseas trade was in the hand of the Greeks.

In the early nineteenth century when Greek international traders initially came to Odessa, it was without a special invitation. They simply came. Many Greek family firms became enormously rich, since their arrival coincided with a huge demand for grain from Europe after the Napoleonic Wars. Meanwhile, at best, Jews were acting as brokers and middlemen in the grain trade. For example, midcentury Jewish merchants in Odessa were listed after Greeks, Italians, French, English, and Germans in terms of importance.[46]

The Crimean War was a turning point, not only for the volume of grain exports, which fell to practically nothing, but also because it in effect drove Greeks out of the business in Odessa. When the export of grain resumed, Jewish merchants took up the slack, as it were. At any rate, only after the war do we witness the rise of Jewish international trade in Odessa. This phenomenon is in stark contrast to the situation of Italian Jews, whose wealth was intimately linked with the prosperity of Trieste from its beginning. Jewish maritime merchants, since there were so few of them, for the first half-century of Odessa's existence were not credited with the prosperity of the port city. On the contrary, when they became visible in international trade after the Crimean War, they were perceived as having profited from the ill luck of Greek merchants, or worse yet, for having pushed Greeks out of business.[47]

Certainly, in Odessa the pogrom of 1871, as the one in 1821, partly reflected Greek–Jewish tension.[48] Apparently, no such ethnic tension was evident in Trieste since both the Greeks who dominated trade with the Levant and Jews who enjoyed far-flung commercial success could prosper side by side.

In Trieste, the tightly knit Jewish community at the behest of the absolutist state kept a wary eye out for admitting poor Jews to the city, the "non-useful" ones. According to Dubin, "the authorities instructed the *Capi* (heads of the Jewish community) to submit to the police regular and detailed records of all Jewish arrivals, and to distinguish between those worthy of residence permits and those who ought to be sent away immediately."[49] Despite occasional charitable lapses when poor Jews were admitted, for which Jews were taken to task, Dubin reports, "though there were poor Jews in Trieste, they did not comprise an impoverished mass leading a way of life that appeared distinct and alien from the majority population."[50]

No historian can say the same for Odessa. In the last two or three decades of Odessa's pre-Soviet history, the city was teeming wth poor Jews competing with immigrant Ukrainians and Russians for scarce jobs as workers, day laborers, and stevedores, creating a poisonous brew of resentment that erupted in further pogroms.[51] Jewish smugglers, petty thieves, and schemers in the Moldavanka district have been romanticized in song and story, but the underbelly of such legends reveals a harsh and bitter reality.[52] After 1870 (when Municipal Statutes limited the number of Jews on the city council), only a relatively few Jews were wealthy or held political clout. They were powerless as a Jewish community or as municipal officers, therefore, to stem the tide of poor Jews streaming in from the impoverished hinterland of the Pale.

It is all too evident that enlightened ideals among reforming monarchs and local rulers were a brief phenomenon in Odessa. Kindly liberal governors and city chiefs gave way to military martinets posted there to keep order, not to foster commercial prosperity. After 1870 the city duma, and not liberal governor-generals (the office was abolished in 1874), governed the city. Sometimes anti-Semites were elected to office and the city deteriorated because it lost its powerful connections to the throne.

Instead of being the darling of enlightened despots, Odessa in the 1870s was punished by the tsars for her perceived unruliness, disloyalty, and suspect ethnic composition. Beginning in midcentury Nicholas I and his successors favored other Black Sea ports by investing in their port facilities, granting favorable railroad tariffs to freight directed to them and by withholding improvements of Odessa's port. In Odessa, free port status was withdrawn, the sunshine of Enlightenment was extinguished, and commerce began to wither. It was precisely at this unfavorable time that Jewish merchants were trying to establish themselves in the international maritime trade exporting grain from Odessa.

6. THE MODEL OF TRIESTE AND ODESSA

To return to our tale of two cities with an unhappy ending: nearly all the elements visible in Trieste at the start of its rise to wealth as an international trading port were present in Odessa at its founding as well. Odessa presented a tabula rasa on which enlightened absolutist rulers could plant their imprint. One very important difference, however, was that, with few exceptions, Jews who came to Odessa in the early years were not international merchants. Some Jews ultimately became maritime merchants in Odessa, but never quite on the same scale as the Greeks or even Italians. They were grudgingly accepted as merchants, almost by default, and were not linked to the city as a successful experiment in liberalism. Worse yet, at the time that some Jews became successful merchants, the city was host to many poor Jews who had earned an unsavory reputation. Some disillusioned Jews turned to Zionism, but many others became socialists. In either case, Jews then gave rise to the perception that they were not loyal citizens of the Russian Empire, a myth created as an excuse for unjustifiable pogroms. Even Trieste Jews under French occupation were considered to be disloyal by some jealous of their financial success.[53]

Nonetheless, Jewish culture during Odessa's first half-century matched and even surpassed Trieste in its number of synagogues, schools combining secular and traditional learning, and various other indices of piety, charity, and learning.[54] But perhaps in an attempt to catch up rapidly in the world of trade and material wealth, an increasingly secularized segment of the Jewish population could not sustain a flowering of Jewish religious culture in Odessa.[55] Zipperstein has argued the point that Jews, especially the grain merchants after midcentury, making up for lost time, were all too busy getting and spending to heed their rich cultural heritage.[56] Had Jews been international merchants during the first half-century, perhaps their descendants would have been less interested in commerce and more interested in Jewish culture by the 1880s.

At the turn of the century Hebrew scholars, such as Ahad Ha'am, Haim Bialik, and Mendele Mocher Seforim fled the stultifying intellectual life of Ukrainian villages; they sought Odessa because of its reputed enlightened culture, liberty, and wealth. There they were met with indifference from the Jewish merchants and with superciliousness from the older Russified Jewish intelligentsia. To be regarded as irrelevant by one Jewish sector and as pitiful by another was an intolerable situation for these gifted persons, as Zipperstein has eloquently written.[57] No wonder these "sages," who regarded themselves as a besieged and alienated circle, closed in on themselves and departed Odessa early in the new century.[58]

Again as in the case of the timing of the arrival Jewish merchants, was it not a matter of timing with the arrival of Jewish intellectuals? Had the Hebrew "sages" arrived before the thoroughgoing secularization of many Jews in Odessa, would not their work have been better received? Or, had the Jews been international merchants during the first half-century, perhaps their descendants would have been less interested in commerce and more interested in culture by the 1880s.

This progression from gaining to spending was true in the case of the Greek Grigorii Marazli. A descendant of wealthy Greek grain merchants, he abandoned commerce to devote his life to Odessa's civic life and the promotion of Greek culture in the city. Avram Brodskii, a wealthy Jewish industrialist, also was prominent in civic affairs and contributed much to the city.[59] But there were relatively few such Jewish tycoons in Odessa.

I would suggest that Odessa's Jewish history reflects a pattern familiar in so much of Russia's tragic history. The timing is wrong; many of the essential factors or ingredients for progress and good outcomes can be discerned, but they are not present at the same time or do not often appear in the right sequence. To paraphrase Shakespeare, "the time is out of joint"; we can say developments in Odessa were out of synch compared to those in Trieste.

Dubin's paradigm holds validity, I believe, for Odessa's early years with the singular exception that Jewish merchants were not there from day one, not because they were excluded, but because Catherine, unlike Maria Theresa, did not specifically invite them. After sixty years or so, Odessa's Jews began to make their careers in the grain trade, just as Odessa's commercial position was sinking and antisemitic sentiment was rising. M. Dantsig's poem, written in 1869, as quoted by Zipperstein, expressed the view that "Odessa used to be a good place a few years ago. That was all in another time, all under another star."[60]

Odessa provided some measure of political and economic freedom and scope to Jews in the first half-century of its existence. It also inspired many talented Jewish writers, artists, and musicians; but for a flourishing Jewish culture to survive, Odessa lacked the critical mass of a Jewish population that was not secularized, radicalized, too busy making ends meet, abjectly poor or disillusioned by a crushing regime and by economic disadvantages that stifled even the most promising of beginnings. If Jews in Odessa were not receptive toward the end of the century to Hebrew culture, at least Odessa served as a seedbed for ideas carried off to Tel Aviv, Berlin, and elsewhere.[61]

Odessa's history, however ill-served, ill-stared, and ill-timed, is a record of life itself with its joys, its sorrows, it successes and failures. And as for Jews, many of whom came to love the city, history could have been kinder.

Notes

1. This article is a revised and expanded version of a lecture given at the workshop, "At the Crossroads. Jewish Odessa in the Nineteenth and Twentieth Century," at the Simon Dubnow Institute for Jewish History and Culture at Leipzig University on May 31, 2002.
2. Lois Dubin, *The Port Jews of Habsburg Trieste. Absolutist Politics and Enlightenment* (Stanford, CA: Stanford University Press, 1999). There is no mention of either Trieste or Odessa in Todd M. Endelman ed., *Comparing Jewish Societies* (Ann Arbor: University of Michigan Press, 1997).
3. Dubin, *Port Jews*, 199.
4. Ibid., 3–4.
5. Ibid., 1.
6. Ibid., 15.
7. Tullia Catalan, *La Comunità ebraica di Trieste (1781–1914). Politica, società e cultura* (Trieste: LINT, 2000), 12, relates how Maria Theresa expressly forbade Jews from entering Vienna without her written permission.
8. Ibid., 28.
9. Ibid., 11.
10. Isabel de Madariaga, *Russia in the Age of Catherine the Great* (New Haven, CT: Yale University Press,1981), 504: "As soon as she could, Catherine endeavoured to profit from the permission granted by the Treaty of Kuchuk Kainardzhi to send merchant ships through the Straits into the Mediterranean." For a discussion of Catherine II's plans for her newly created cities along uniform rationalist plans, see Robert E. Jones, "Urban Planning and the Development of Provincial Towns during the Reign of Catherine II," in *The Eighteenth Century in Russia*, ed. John G. Garrard (Oxford: Clarendon Press, 1973), 321–44. Jones called Odessa "the most successful of all Catherine's new towns."
11. Roger P. Bartlett, *Human Capital: The Settlement of Foreigners in Russia 1762–1804* (Cambridge: Cambridge University Press, 1979), 197.
12. Richard Pipes, "Catherine II and the Jews. The Origins of the Pale of Settlement," *Soviet Jewish Affairs* 5, no. 2 (1975): 6.
13. Iulii I. Gessen, *Istoriia evreiskogo naroda v Rossii*, vol. 1 (Leningrad: n.p., 1925), 57–62.
14. Jews in the merchant and artisan class were allowed to live in the countryside and to deal in the sale of spirits, privileges denied Christians of the same status. See Pipes, "Catherine II,"13.
15. Ibid., 19.
16. Madariaga, *Russia*, 508.
17. Pipes, "Catherine II," 17.
18. Bartlett, *Human Capital*, 38.
19. Ibid., 187.

20 A. Orlov, *Istoricheskii ocherk Odessy s 1794 po 1803 god* (Odessa: O. S. Fridman,1885), 104–22.
21 Elena I. Druzhinina, *Iuzhnaia Ukraina 1800–1825* (Moscow: Nauka, 1970), 257.
22 Steven J. Zipperstein, *The Jews of Odessa. A Cultural History, 1794–1881* (Stanford, CA: Stanford University Press, 1985), 42.
23 Saul I. Borovoi, *Evreiskaia zemledel'cheskaia kolonizatsiia v staroi Rossii* (Moscow: Izd. M.i S. Sabashnikovykh, 1928), 45–47.
24 Zipperstein, *Jews of Odessa*, 35.
25 Mikhail Polishchuk, *Evrei Odessy i Novorossii: sotsial'no-politicheskaia istoriia evreev Odessy i drugikh gorodov Novorossii 1881–1904* (Jerusalem: Gesharim, Moscow: Mosty kul'tury, 2002), 22.
26 Zipperstein, *Jews of Odessa*, 36.
27 Patricia Herlihy, *Odessa. A History, 1794–1914* (Cambridge, MA: Harvard University Press, 1986). Druzhinina, *Iuzhnaia Ukraina*, 153, stated that in addition to being artisans, Jews in and near Odessa were needed as middlemen in the export of grain and other agricultural products.
28 Herlihy, *Odessa*, 86.
29 Jacob Adler, *Jacob Adler. A Life on the Stage. A Memoir*, trans. and with commentary by Lulla Rosenfeld (New York: Applause, 2001), 9.
30 Herlihy, *Odessa*, 16.
31 George L. Yaney, *The Systematization of Russian Government* (Urbana: University of Illinois Press, 1973), 72–73.
32 Dubin, *Port Jews*, 4.
33 Madariaga, *Russia*, 293. Catherine is reported to have written Potemkin, the first governor of New Russia about her impression of Joseph II when she first met him in Mogilev, "I think no living sovereign comes near him so far as merit, knowledge and politeness are concerned; I am enchanted to have made his acquaintance." Henri Troyat, *Catherine The Great*, trans. Joan Pinkam (New York: Dutton, 1980), 244–45.
34 Dubin, *Port Jews*, 28.
35 Zipperstein, *Jews*, 38.
36 Bartlett, *Human Capital*, 187.
37 For Vorontsov's demands for equal rights for Jews in Odessa, including a summary of his memoranda to the Ministry of Internal Affairs in 1840, see Oksana I. Zakharova, *Generaly svoikh sudeb. M.S. Vorontsov—general-gubernator Novorossiiskogo kraia* (Moscow: n. p., 1998), 79–80. See also Joachim Tarnopol, *Notices historiques et caracteristiques sur les israelites d'Odessa* (Odessa: A. Braun, 1855), 6.
38 Salo Baron, *The Russian Jew under Tsars and Soviet* (New York: Macmillan, 1964), 18. Catherine II had extended to all Jews the right to participate in municipal government, thus giving Russian Jews as much political power as those given to Tuscan Jews by the Enlightened Habsburg ruler, Grand Duke Leopold.
39 Simon Dubnow, *History of the Jews in Russia and Poland*, vol. 2 (Philadelphia: Jewish Publication Society of America, 1975), 199.
40 Dubin, *Port Jews*, 39.
41 Ibid., 22.
42 ChaeRan Y. Freeze, *Jewish Marriage and Divorce in Imperial Russia* (Hanover, NH: University Press of New England, 2002), 3.
43 Ibid., 4.
44 Ibid., 241.
45 Steven J. Zipperstein, *Elusive Prophet: Ahad Ha'am and the Origins of Zionism* (Berkeley: University of California Press, 1993), 68.

46 Herlihy, *Odessa*, 95. The Jewish firms of Gurovich, Rafalovich, and Efrusi were exceptions, having been established in the 1820s. *Odessa, 1794–1894* (Odessa: Izdaniia gorodskogo obshchestvennogo upravleniia k stoletiiu goroda, Tip. A. Shul'tse, 1895), 206. But the successful Efrusi grain company left Odessa for Europe because of the 1881 pogroms. See Polishchuk, *Evrei Odessy,* 353n21.

47 Erich Haberer, *Jews and Revolution in Nineteenth-Century Russia* (Cambridge: Cambridge University Press, 1995), 57, noted of Odessa that Jewish professional and commercial success by the end of the nineteenth century "made Jews the envy of all other nationalities, in particular the Greeks, who came to blame and victimize them for whatever economic political woes befell the city. This, in turn, stimulated the growth of Jewish nationalism on the one hand, and revolutionary participation on the other."

48 Haim Hillel Ben-Sasson *A History of the Jewish People* (Cambridge, MA: Harvard University Press, 1976), 821. Jacob Adler described violence between Greeks and Jews in his neighborhood in Odessa. Adler, *A Life on Stage,* 6.

49 Dubin, *Port Jews,* 24.

50 Ibid., 200.

51 Robert Weinberg, *The Revolution of 1905 in Odessa. Blood on the Steps* (Bloomington: Indiana University Press, 1993).

52 Boris Briker, "The Underworld of Benia Krik and I. Babel's Odessa Stories," *Canadian Slavonic Papers. Revue canadienne des slavistes* 36, nos. 1–2 (1994): 115–34.

53 Catalan, *Comunità ebraica,* 30: "Nell'emporio adriatico gli ebrei godevano di grande prestigio in campo commerciale e finanziario e la loro concorrenza poteva risultare pericolosa a qualche negoziante o uomo di affari: ciò potrebbe spiegare la tendenza a estendere a tutto la comunità ebraica locale l'imputazione di militare nelle file giacobine."

54 See Zipperstein, *Jews of Odessa,* 41–69.

55 Michael Stanislawski, *Zionism and the Fin de Siècle. Cosmopolitanism and Nationalism from Nordau to Jabotinsky* (Berkeley: University of California Press, 2001), 122, speaking of Vladimir Jabotinsky, "Young Volodya never attended any Jewish school, neither a heder nor a modernist Enlightenment-style establishment of which there many in Odessa." And on page 123 he remarks that it was "typical for an upper middle-class Russian Jew to be born, be bred, and grow into adulthood largely ignorant of Yiddish, Hebrew, and Judaism."

56 Stephen J. Zipperstein, *Imagining Russian Jewry. Memory, History, Identity* (Seattle: University of Washington Press, 1991), 63–86.

57 Zipperstein, *Elusive Prophet,* 27, and Zipperstein, *Imagining Russian Jewry,* 63–86.

58 See Adam Michael Rubin, "From Torah to Tarbut. Hayim Nahman Bialik and the Nationalization of Judaism" (PhD diss., University of California, Los Angeles 2000), 64, in which Rubin quotes Natan Goren, 'That Odessa of grace and ease, provocative and enchanting, its intoxicating evenings filled with the scent of fruit blossoms on the shore with its villas and resorts, gardens and orchards, taverns like caves in the earth, warmfaced maidens, the sparks of the south in their joyful, laughing eyes how far this was from Mendel's sarcastic satire, the severe anger of Ahad Ha'am, the inspired sorrow of Bialik."

59 Patricia Herlihy, "Commerce and Architecture in Odessa in Late Imperial Russia," in *Commerce in Russian Urban Culture, 1861–1914,* edited by William Craft Brumfield, Boris V. Anan'ich et al. (Washington, DC: Woodrow Wilson Center Press; Baltimore: Johns Hopkins University Press, 2001), 188.

60 Zipperstein, *Jews of Odessa,* 118.

61 Rubin, *From Torah,* 45. Also 52n32, "Odessa and its sages created a great historical epoch whose influences transcended the boundaries of Russian Judaism for the world of Judaism."

CHAPTER 12

Russian Wheat and the Port of Livorno 1794–1865

From the late eighteenth century, one of the most important changes in the foreign commerce of European nations was the growth of a massive importation of wheat. This wheat, needed to feed the ever more populous and more urbanized Western lands, was sought in ever more distant areas. Among its principal suppliers was the fertile steppe region of southern Russia. From the period of the Napoleonic wars, wheat from the South-Russian steppes flowed in large quantities to Western consumers, primarily through the new port city of Odessa, founded on the shores of the Black Sea by the Russian empress Catherine II, in 1794.[1]

The organization of this cereal trade has considerable interest, and profoundly affected the history of many European ports. Until the development of rapid communications (primarily through the telegraph) and of big, fast ships (primarily using steam power), a large element of speculation was inevitably present in this export trade. Even as they bore grain away from the port of Odessa, the shippers often remained ignorant of the latest prices and strongest markets in the West, and did not know the ultimate destination of the cereals they carried. The tariff policies of the Western states heightened this uncertainty. Between 1828 and the abolition of the "corn laws" in 1846, one principal Western consumer, England, applied a sliding scale of tariffs upon imported wheat, which made the volume of imports inversely dependent upon the abundance of the annual harvests. Most other Western states followed a similar policy. But the abundance of the annual local harvest was often difficult to predict, and so also were the level of tariffs and the strength of the demand for imported cereals. These conditions favored the use, in the sea transport of cereals of intermediary, or deposit ports. These were ports, close to the large population centers of Western Europe, where wheat imported from distant areas could be deposited or stored, while its owners determined where it could most profitably be sold.

In the transport of Russian wheat, the chief of these deposit ports were found in the Western Mediterranean—Malta, Trieste, Genoa, Marseille, and others. One of these ports we shall single out for particular study here, as its role in the deposit trade was especially important, if not always typical: Livorno.

The port of Livorno rose to the status of a major Mediterranean harbor in the sixteenth century. According to the most recent historians of Livorno's sixteenth-century

---

Originally published as Patricia Herlihy, "Russian Wheat and the Port of Livorno, 1794–1865," *The Journal of European Economic History* V (1976): 45–68.

commerce, the grain trade played a fundamental role in its meteoric rise, but this grain came from the north and not the east.[2] In the late 1500s, Tuscany was visited by repeated famines. In 1590 and 1591, Riccardo Riccardi, scion of a great Florentine family and agent of the Grand Duke Ferdinand I, traveled to Danzig, Hamburg, and Lübeck specifically to purchase grain.[3] Over the years 1590–93, 202 ships from northern Europe (exclusive of England) put into Livorno, and almost all were loaded with grain.[4]

Livorno achieved prominence as a cereal port not only because the Tuscan hinterland it served suffered frequent famines. The port also held a central position within the Mediterranean region, and its merchants and ships could take advantage of commercial opportunities over an extensive area. The growing international trade in grain presented Livorno with an exceptional opportunity. By the late sixteenth century, great grain deposits were being constructed near the port. There grain, much of it from the north, could be deposited and kept in expectation of large profits if famine or wars should strike accessible areas. A description of the port written in 1839 mentions how, in what was vaguely called the old days, the ditches (*fosse*) into which the grain was put numbered 543, and had a capacity of 250,000 sacks.[5] Average per capita consumption of grain in Tuscany at that time seems to have been about four sacks (twelve *staia*); the ditches, in other words, could have held enough grain to support for one year about 62,500 persons.[6]

By the early nineteenth century, the number of ditches seems to have fallen slightly to 499, and their capacity to 210,000 sacks.[7] In spite of this small decline, Livorno remained, by virtue of its position and facilities for storage, what one nineteenth-century writer called the greatest "grain deposit in the Mediterranean."[8]

Since its rise to the status of a major port in the sixteenth century, Livorno also maintained vigorous trade relations with the lands of the eastern Mediterranean. As early as 1727, it imported 90,000 sacks of wheat from the Morea.[9] By the early nineteenth century, substantial colonies of Tuscan merchants had grown up in many cities of Greece and Turkey. By 1847 there were enough resident Tuscans in Salonika to make necessary a school for their children.[10] A consular report from Constantinople in 1831 lists the names of twelve Tuscan Jewish merchants who resided there.[11] In that city there were also sixty-seven artisans and workers from Tuscany.[12] Sixteen years later, the Tuscan colony at Constantinople was numerous and prosperous enough to purchase a cannon for a military regiment, the Fifth Guard, at Livorno.[13] In 1848, when the Italian subjects of the Austrian Empire revolted in Lombardy, their conationals at Constantinople were fighting in the streets with Austrian residents of the same city. Italians to the number of 168, residents of Constantinople, signed a petition to the Turkish government protesting the actions of the Austrian consul.[14] By virtue of the size of their communities and the vigor of their commercial ties with the Porte, the Tuscans in 1831 were allowed consular representation within the Turkish Empire.[15] By 1841, Tuscany had consular representatives at Smyrna, Alexandria, Aleppo, Beirut, Salonika, Rhodes, Dardanelles, Adrianople, and Trebizond.

The list of goods, which Livorno sent "in quantity" to the Ottoman Empire in 1836 was large: alum, red fezzes from Livorno itself, coffee probably re-exported from South America, white paper, chestnuts, cured leather, silk cloth, cotton manufactures, worked marble, chairs, pepper, and sugar, which were again probably reexported colonial products.[16]

In 1818, a traveler lists the chief Italian exports to Odessa; we may assume that some of them passed through the port of Livorno, "Italy sends large quantities of common Sicilian wine, liqueurs, syrups, Lucchese oil, preserved citron, oranges, lemons, citrons, shelled almonds, comfits, different kinds of cheese, particularly parmesan, choice wines such as Lacryma Christi and others in bottles, quantities of refined sulphur, brimstone in mass and in rolls, the silks and other manufactures of Florence and Genoa, biscuits, pictures, marble ornaments, statuary and jewelry."[17]

The Spanish consul at Odessa wrote about the same time that, "On reçoit d'Italie des vins de Messine, des liqueurs; de l'huile de Lucques, de Gênes; des pâtes de divers sortes, du soufre, du fromage de Parmesan, des marbres."[18]

When, in the late eighteenth century, Russian ships penetrated into the Mediterranean, they elected Livorno as a favorite port of call.[19] In 1765, the *Nadezhda Blagopoluchiia* (Hope of Prosperity), out of Kronstadt on the Baltic, put into Livorno. She brought iron, linen, rope and skins, and took out sandalwood, macaroni, and lead. Russian warships appeared off Livorno in 1770, during Catherine's first Turkish War. In 1772, Johann Wolfgang Goethe, travelling in Italy, saw at Livorno a reenactment of the Russian naval victory at Chesma (1770), done with fireworks, and was much impressed by the show. The officers of a Russian naval squadron under Admiral Chichagov spent freely at Livorno, and sailed away leaving 4,121 rubles of unpaid debts.[20] In 1786, the Tuscans were entering representations of protest at the Imperial Russian court.

Russian grain followed Russian sailors to Livorno. Already in 1803, Livorno imported a large quantity of grain from Odessa, and still more in 1817.[21] The Austrian consul did not exaggerate when he wrote in 1830, "Commercial relations between Livorno and Russian ports of the Black Sea have been very important for several years."[22] Odessa itself attracted a community of Tuscans—merchants, hairdressers, and musicians who served in the city's theater, a music teacher, a bank clerk, and a worker in the medical inspection service; in 1853, Tuscans at Odessa numbered at least twenty-three persons, as that many contributed to a charitable collection.[23] Other Tuscans penetrated to even more remote areas of the Russian Empire; Francesco Gherardi from Arezzo, father of nine children, was the chief doctor for the imperial troops stationed in Georgia and received many decorations in recognition of his services.[24]

The commercial history of Livorno in the nineteenth century has yet to be satisfactorily written. Historians, almost by profession inclined to be *laudatores temporis acti*, have tended to glorify the city's great years of the sixteenth or seventeenth century, while dismissing the nineteenth century as, in comparison, a period of decadence.[25] This is an exaggeration. A more balanced evaluation has been made by G. Mori, who remarked concerning the present state of research on the history of Livorno in the nineteenth century, "Studies on this period of Livorno's history are so few and so full of gaps that whatever conclusions we might reach must be considered partial and uncertain."[26]

We know at least that Livorno in the early nineteenth century was a growing town—a fact not easily reconciled with the assumption that its commercial importance was waning. Table 1 illustrates its growth from 1790 to 1848.

Table 1 The Population of Livorno, 1790–1848

Year	Population	Year	Population
1790	50,000	1828	70,353
1800	59,000	1830	72,000
1807	64,000	1835	76,000
1812	45,000	1838	77,941
1818	59,098	1848	82,648
1825	67,000		

Source: *Giornale del Commercio* [of Livorno], July 1839; G. Baldasseroni, *Leopoldo II, Granduca di Toscana e i suoi tempi*, 1871, 111.

To support this growing population, Livorno depended primarily upon its commerce. It is, to be sure, true that Livorno in the early nineteenth century was not the biggest Mediterranean, or even Italian port. Baruchello reckons that by measure of total port traffic Livorno was the fifth port in the region after Marseille, Trieste, Constantinople, and Genoa.[27] Its inability to overtake its rivals during a period of general growth seems understandable enough. For most of these booming ports served a populous, prosperous, and productive hinterland, hungry for goods and rich with commodities to sell, while Tuscany in comparison remained a backward land. Still, Baruchello ranks Livorno first in the number of ships coming from the Black Sea, surpassing Marseille, Genoa, and the English ports.[28] For in one item of trade Livorno's importance was unquestionable. And that item was wheat.

To be sure, even in the shipping of wheat Livorno had initially faced strenuous competition. The earliest records of the Russian cereal trade indicate that Trieste consistently held first place in the volumes received, and Genoa too shows an early advantage.[29] A traveler to Odessa in 1829 reported, "Three or four hundred Genoese vessels annually come to Odessa for corn—for corn!—while Sardinia, one of ancient Rome's granaries, within a day's sail of Genoa, lies uncultivated."[30] As Table 2 illustrates, Livorno, comparatively a late starter, by the late 1830s was holding its own, and more than its own, as a port of destination for Russian wheat:

Table 2 Destinations of Wheat Exported from Odessa, 1838

Livorno	446,842	chetvert's	Holland	28,914	chetvert's
Genoa	177,099	"	Belgium	16,909	"
Marseilles	93,758	"	Gibraltar	4,348	"
England	82,453	"	Ionian Islands	3,829	"
Trieste	58,326	"	Greece	2,215	"
Malta	44,486	"	Austria	1,230	"
Constantinople	30,455	"			

Source: Archivio di Stato di Firenze (ASF), Affari Esteri, Filza 2528, Feb. 29, 1839.

From both Livorno and Genoa, the wheat was shipped principally to Spain and France.[31] By 1838, Livorno ranked among the most important grain ports of the Mediterranean. And most of the grain she handled came from the Black Sea, as Table 3 illustrates.

Table 3 Provenance of Wheat Imported from Livorno, 1835–38

Year	Black Sea	Other	Total
1835	305,762	514,950	820,712
1836	501,714	427,658	929,372
1837	1,362,030	504,239	1,867,169
1838	1,701,042	332,170	2,033,212
Total:	3,871,448	1,779,017	5,650,465

Source: ASF. RR Rendite, Uffizio dei Grani, June 11, 1839.

There were many factors that promoted Livorno's late but strong rise as a deposit port in the grain trade. One was the distinctively advantageous status it enjoyed as a free port; the governmental regulations regarding imports and exports were remarkably liberal for the epoch. In 1834 even the small charges on stored grain were lifted; this marked a culmination of the long-standing policy of the Granducal government, which warmly favored the liberalization of trade through Livorno. In 1847, the government removed all tariffs on grain imported into the Grand Duchy.[32] Four years later, when it was proposed to place a charge of 8 soldi per sack on the entry of wheat, the Customs Office wrote in protest:

> Suppose a load of thirty, fifty or one hundred thousand sacks of wheat were coming into the Mediterranean from the Black Sea, and suppose there was a choice of a free port or one where you had to pay 8 soldi a sack. Where would the merchant unload his goods?[33]

Clearly, competition was keen among deposit ports, and a few soldi per sack of wheat would not compensate for the risk of jeopardizing trade.

This Tuscan liberalism contrasted greatly with the protectionism prevailing in the Kingdom of Sardinia, under the laws of which Genoa had to seek prosperity. In an effort to favor her own merchant marine, Sardinia imposed dues and other restrictions on foreign carriers using her ports. Non-Sardinian ships carrying grain sought more hospitable ports, and many sought Livorno. Shortsighted protectionism of this sort did not escape the criticism of those interested in the commercial growth of Genoa, and in the 1830s this more than any other factor was singled out in explanation of Livorno's hot and successful pursuit of Genoa as the principal grain depository in the Western Mediterranean.[34]

A liberal trade statute rendered other advantages too. The grain deposit facilities at Livorno, always large, were still remarkable in the early nineteenth century for their size and quality. Genoa herself, in 1839, made use of them, so marked was their superiority.[35] The enlargement of port space from 1833 to 1840 and again in 1851, as well as the expansion of grain storage facilities in 1848, indicate that Livorno's commerce was far from languishing in the first half of the nineteenth century.[36]

Freedom to import and export grain and facilities to store it were vital considerations for the commercial houses, which traded in wheat, and these advantages prompted many of them to locate their principal offices at Livorno. The presence of large and prosperous foreign firms at Livorno excited the jealousy and protests of the local merchants, who demanded greater participation in the lucrative trade. These complaints paradoxically echoed similar protests voiced at Odessa. There too, it was alleged that "foreigners" were dominating overseas trade to their own profit. The complaints in the Russian port were indeed leveled at the same kind of men as at Livorno—often at the same men, chiefly Greeks or Jews. Nothing shows the tenuous basis of the accusation that the grain trade profited only foreigners more than to hear it raised from both ends of the Mediterranean. Foreigners perhaps, but foreigners in the West as well as the East, these great merchant families often had members, sons or brothers, present in many Mediterranean ports, who were in turn citizens of many lands. Highly skilled in the commercial arts, successful in maintaining the fortunes of their families over decades and generations, these Greek and Jewish merchants might well be regarded as citizens of the Mediterranean.

A report prepared by a Tuscan official, Count L. Serristori, in 1839, provides an interesting perspective into the composition of the commercial classes at Livorno.[37] According to this report, in times past, only a few large commercial houses, no more than eight to ten in number, had dominated Livorno's overseas trade, and these houses were all foreign. Most Tuscan merchants had no direct dealings with buyers or sellers in ports abroad; they were in consequence only petty dealers, whose volume of business was discouragingly small in comparison with that of the great commercial houses. Serristori, however, enthusiastically assured his readers that times were changing. He proudly counted 280 wholesale merchants and bankers, most of whom now had direct dealings abroad and many of whom were Tuscan nationals. He mentioned that several commercial houses (though significantly, Greek or Jewish) had established branches in London, and could handle on their own the profitable business of international exchange. Perhaps it was some of these merchants, or their descendants, whom Karl Marx observed in England in 1853:

> How important . . . the Black Sea trade generally is becoming, may be seen at the Manchester Exchange, where dark-complexioned Greek buyers are increasing in numbers and importance, and where Greek and South Slavonian dialects are heard along with German and English.[38]

Serristori's optimistic hopes concerning the bright future of the native merchants were never fully realized. In 1842, another report complained, "Few are the number of native merchants, and if one discounts some Jews, they are not the richest."[39] The report includes a particularly virulent condemnation of the foreigners: "they come to Livorno, speculate, enrich themselves, and commonly carry back to their fatherland the fruit of their speculation." The protest again only echoes the reception that many of the same merchants were receiving from native Russians, because of their leadership in the commerce of Odessa.

At Livorno, as indeed also at Odessa, the small size of the merchant marine under local ownership excited further dissatisfaction. Tuscan ships carried only a minute portion of the total

Russian grain brought to port. Despite some official attempts to encourage the construction or acquisition of ships, Tuscany never acquired a sizable merchant fleet, and was slow to take advantage of that decisive technological advance—the use of steam power in the propulsion of ships.[40]

The Grand Duchy of Tuscany had better success in securing consular representation in the important ports of the eastern Mediterranean. This diplomatic effort was partially inspired by hostility toward Austria. Tuscany had traditionally been represented at the Porte and in Odessa by the Austrian consul, but in the 1830s, Florence was receiving numerous complaints from Tuscan captains, concerning the difficulties of clearing cargoes, or other obstructions encountered, at the Black Sea ports.[41] And Tuscan officials also suspected that the Austrian consul was purposely delaying in arranging for a commercial treaty between the Grand Duchy and the Ottoman power. The stirrings of Risorgimento sentiments doubtlessly reinforced, or were reinforced by, both public and private suspicions that the Habsburg Empire was doing its utmost to promote trade through its own port of Trieste, at the expense of Livorno.[42] To protect the interests of its own merchant marine, the Grand Duchy appointed its own consuls at Constantinople (1831) and Odessa (1837); after the Crimean War, consuls were also named for Taganrog, Mariupol', and Berdians'k.[43]

Not a large, locally owned merchant marine, but free movement of ships, a good port, spacious storage facilities, and a commercial class of experienced if rarely "native" merchants helped give Livorno its late but large importance in the deposit trade. Wheat taken to a deposit port was frequently re-exported, but at Livorno, a significant market for grain was developing at no further distance than the Tuscan Grand Duchy itself. Tuscany's own need for grain made Livorno not only a port of deposit and re-export, but also a port of entry into a growing market for wheat. Tuscany contained only about 1.5 million people in 1839–40, not including the 78,000 inhabitants of Livorno itself.[44]

But what the region lacked in numbers it made up in demand. In the five-year period 1835–39, the amount of foreign wheat entering Livorno totaled 7,772,451 sacks, and of this amount more than one-half—4,082,854 sacks—was shipped into the Grand Duchy.[45] Tuscan consumers particularly favored Russian grain. Egyptian wheat, for example, which was also ordered in large quantities by Tuscan purchasers, sometimes never arrived, as the temperamental Egyptian government imposed sporadic export restrictions.[46] And the quality of Egyptian wheat was at all events inferior to that of the Russian. Except during wars against Turkey and the Crimean War, the Russian government never cut off the supply of wheat for western markets, and the Mediterranean merchants were eager to carry it. Even in years of poor harvests in Russia, wheat flowed to the West.

Tuscan purchasers rated Russian grain as unsurpassed in quality. Russian wheat was prized for its richness of gluten, and the quality of the flour produced from it.[47] Hard wheat was the kind most suitable—rather we should say indispensable—for manufacturing that great staple of the Italian diet, pasta. Hard wheat could not be raised in volume in Tuscany, and consumers of pasta and the millers who served them had to seek it in Sicily. But Sicilian production did not keep pace with demand, and Sicily too was subject to changeable restrictions on grain export.[48] Russian wheat was even better in quality and more readily available. The pasta produced from it was tastier and also more nutritious, as the protein count of Russian hard wheat was relatively high. The pasta makers of Tuscany came in surprisingly large measure to base their business on imported Russian grain, much of which was ground into flour at the mill near Livorno. When the government of the Grand Duchy attempted to impose a tariff on such flour taken from Livorno into the duchy, the manufacturers of pasta in the hinterland raised a chorus of protests, "because the wheat of which the pasta makers have need is hard wheat from Taganroc [sic] and Odessa."[49] Utilizing Russian wheat in abundant quantities, the manufacturers of pasta not only sold their products within Tuscany, but also exported spaghetti and biscuits made of the flour of hard wheat (semolino) to purchasers abroad.[50]

The Tuscan market for Russian soft wheat was also strong. By weight it excelled the Egyptian. Tuscany's own, locally produced soft wheat seems to have been as good if not better than the Russian, but it was in short supply and much demanded abroad, notably in England, where it was used both for seeds and in the manufacture of quality bread.[51] Russian wheat, moreover, traveled better than the Egyptian; the latter appears to have been subject to weevils and deterioration if exposed to dampness. Russian wheat was more durable, and, according to Anthoine de Saint-Joseph, a process for treating Russian wheat was discovered in Odessa in 1803, which protected its quality over long sea voyages.[52] This process seems to have been based on partially drying the wheat before shipment. Along the Mediterranean route, the hot and humid conditions on board ship frequently caused wheat to rot and turn sour. An English grain merchant, Samuel Drewe, described the advantages of this preheating process as it was used in Poland:

> They kiln-dry it [wheat] abroad, and it will lie three years without injury, and do for the foreign market; the old wheat they cannot ship for this country; when it is beginning to be foul, they kiln-dry and ship it for the Mediterranean; because if they were to ship fresh wheat for the Mediterranean, it would heat in the vessels; this does not heat in the vessels, and therefore does better.[53]

At Livorno the storage ditches (*fosse* or *buche*) were needed primarily to protect Egyptian wheat. A description of the ditches, dated 1850, explains:

> It is known that all wheat has need for storage ditches. That wheat which comes from Egypt is susceptible to warming up quickly and to the development of worms called "pinnachio" which quickly spoil it. That wheat which comes from the Black Sea on the other hand... is able to withstand quite a long trip and still remain in storehouses above ground without fear of deterioration, if it had not been kept too long at the point of origin, or had not suffered in deposit or in loading, in which case it too must be stored in ditches.[54]

But the most important reason for the growing Tuscan demand for Russian wheat was that, like Italy generally, the Grand Duchy could not produce enough grain to feed its people. This had not always been true. In the eighteenth century, Tuscany imported wheat only in years of famine, and in good years even exported it. In 1782 and 1783, for example, which were years of dearth, Tuscany consumed an average of 184,301 sacks of grain more than its farmers produced, but over the span of good harvest years from 1787 to 1791, it had enough surplus to sell small quantities to foreign consumers.[55]

The situation changed after the Napoleonic wars. The war itself had disrupted production. Conscription drew the young men from farming, many never to return, whether from battle deaths or the discovery of a better life. Even in the first years of peace, bad weather hampered recovery.[56] The terrible crop failures of 1816 and 1817 struck Tuscany hard, and Tuscans joined the general European rush to the ports of the Black Sea, in search of wheat.[57] After these disastrous years, recovery in local production seemed to be progressing well, when in 1823 the price of wheat registered a substantial decline, and remained at low levels for an extended period.[58] These low prices drove peasants from the land and from the cultivation of wheat—not a crop, which, at all events, can be raised with much competitive success on the inhospitable Tuscan hills. Faced with stagnant or diminishing local production but with a growing population, Tuscany had to trade for wheat. This was a fate reluctantly acknowledged by contemporary observers—even by those who advocated a policy of economic autarchy within the Grand Duchy. "Let us not forget," one writer reminded the Tuscans in 1840, "that Tuscany is still very far from producing what is necessary for the sustenance of her inhabitants; so much so that every year the import of not small quantities of foreign grain is necessary."[59]

This "not small quantity" in the five years ending with 1839 was averaging 1,554,490 Tuscan sacks per year, or 518,163 Russian *chetvert's*. In 1851, the quantity was 1,589,438 sacks; in 1852, it reached 1,591,072 sacks. In 1853, it attained 2,161,672 and in 1854, 2,034,827 sacks.[60] And Russian grain constituted an ever-larger proportion of the imported wheat, as it was cheap and obtainable. When harvests were poor in Tuscany, they were usually also poor in neighboring states, which characteristically responded to their own shortages by raising barriers against the exportation of wheat. "Thus, it often happens," relates a Tuscan report, dated 1856, "that when our harvests are scarce and our needs greater in consequence, export of grains is prohibited by the Estense and Pontifical states."[61] Tuscany thus sought its needed wheat at the ports of the Black Sea, and, inevitably, commercial bonds of growing strength were established between Russia and the Grand Duchy. In 1838 Odessa exported 990,511 *chetvert's* of wheat and in the same year Livorno imported 567,014 *chetvert's* from the Black Sea ports and from Odessa principally.[62] Clearly, the trade between Odessa and Livorno was already substantial. Moreover, consular reports from Odessa reveal increasing awareness of the importance of the Russian trade for the tables and the prosperity of Tuscany. In 1844 the Tuscan consul at Odessa, T. Rodokanaki, who was a member of a great Greek mercantile family established at Livorno, wrote to his superiors in the Grand Duchy, and advised them of the wisdom of conferring an honorary title on Count Vorontsov, the governor-general of New Russia and Bessarabia. The stated reason for so honoring Count Vorontsov was not his great merits, but the need to cultivate good relations with men of authority and influence in South Russia, "since the trade with the Black Sea and with Azov is regarded, as it is in fact, an object of no slight consequence to the commercial prosperity of the royal state [Tuscany]."[63] "No care," the letter continues, "should seem superfluous in order to capture the benevolent protection of those superior authorities which have a direct and immediate influence on the better progress of commerce…"

In 1847 Russia and Tuscany signed a new commercial treaty by which the ships of each would be treated equally in the ports of both the states.[64]

The dependency of Tuscany on Russian wheat was never more obvious than during the Crimean War, which spread consternation through Tuscany's commercial and governmental circles. Emperor Nicholas I forbade all export of wheat from the Russian Empire. The reasons given unofficially were that this grain was needed for the troops, and that English warships were not likely to respect the neutrality of grain carriers. There was risk, in other words, that Russian grain might eventually feed the enemy. As of March 1, 1854, even neutrals were forbidden to purchase Russian wheat.[65]

In this, many Livornese merchants saw their ruin. They bombarded their government with mournful letters, begging for intercession at the court of the tsar. The following letter, sent by one Giorgio Pieruzzini, in May 1854, is typical of many:

> The subscribed Tuscan subject, trader in Livorno, engaged in the commerce of cereals and oil seed which are exported from the markets of the Mediterranean and the Russian Ocean where he has agents, has the honour to humbly explain to your Excellency that on account of the prohibition against export of cereals from the ports of the Black Sea and Azov decreed by His Majesty the Emperor of all the Russias, he has been hard hit financially because of the quantity of wheat which for some time past he had purchased in Russia, to the amount of 5,000 chetverts of hard and soft wheat, all in the ports of the Sea of Azov, ready to be exported. Not only will the weather damage this cereal, but there will be incalculable sacrifices because of the ship rents paid, the expenses of storing and maintaining the wheat already purchased and the daily devaluation of that wheat. Moved by such considerations which sorrowfully worry me, I see no other recourse than to supplicate your Excellency to intercede for me with the Imperial Russian Government in order to obtain some modification in regard to Tuscany of the measures taken against the export of cereals, or at least to accord to Tuscany the right to resell the cereals which has been accorded to other nations so that the damages may be avoided.[66]

In June of the same year, Tuscany officially asked for permission to resell the wheat in Odessa, and in November of the same year the Russian consul at Rome notified Florence that Tuscany would enjoy the same privilege accorded to all neutrals, that is, that those cereals purchased at Odessa before March 12, 1854, would be repurchased by the Russian government.[67]

With the closing of the Russian ports to commerce in grains, Tuscany had to find alternative sources of wheat. The Florentine *mercuriali* (official reports, published three times a week, of the prices of basic foodstuffs sold in the city) record the sudden appearance of Spanish wheat on January 20, 1855, and the variety sold was, not surprisingly, hard wheat.[68] *Il Corriere Italiano*, a commercial newspaper published in Vienna, observed, rather casually, that the closing of the Russian ports would mean only that the grain trade would take new directions. Generous supplies of grain, the *Corriere* affirmed, were available in Turkey, along the coast of Africa, and in the two Americas.[69] During the first three months of 1855, when the

Russian ports were completely blocked, Genoa imported most of her wheat from Spain; other shipments came from France, Tuscany, the Barbary coast, Sardinia, and elsewhere.[70] Despite the confidence of the *Corriere*, the supply of wheat fell, and prices inevitably rose. The fear of runaway wheat prices prompted P. Rodokanaki to advise the grand duke, that he should, if possible, keep full the deposits at Livorno; the known existence of large quantities of available wheat would discourage local speculators from bidding up prices.[71]

Not only Tuscany but most of Western Europe showed concern in regard to the supplies of wheat and its price as the Crimean War continued. In the midst of the war, in September 1855, the Tuscan consul at Hamburg wrote with alarm:

> Here and in all north Germany food prices have increased in an extraordinary manner because of the lack of shipments of wheat from Russia and also because of a failure of the potato crop, which forms the principal food item in the diet of workers, and then too because of the series of purchases made of wheat, meat, etc. for the Anglo-French armies and navies.[72]

In answer to an anxious query from the French consul in Tuscany, concerning the available stocks of cereals, the Florentine authorities replied that the last harvest had fortunately been fairly abundant, and that prices of wheat in July were somewhat below the peak prices of May and June, but they were still quite high. As for the future, prices could be expected to reflect the facility with which wheat could be imported from Egypt and the Black Sea

> from whence Tuscany draws the greatest part of her wheat for her consumption needs. Who then, in fact, does not know that Tuscan production, even in the years of greatest abundance is never enough to suffice for the needs of this country.[73]

However, the shortage of wheat was eased somewhat the following year. Tuscany applied to the imperial Russian court for the same concession accorded Austria: that of purchasing wheat at the Danubian ports, Galați in particular. The applications, sent from the foreign minister in Tuscany to the Russian chargé d'affaires in Rome, tactfully reminded him of the close ties binding Russia and Tuscany. The Russian government responded favorably to the request, on condition that the Tuscan purchasers solemnly declare that such wheat would be consumed only within Tuscany and not exported to the enemy. Almost at once we have notice of five Tuscan captains in Galați, purchasing wheat and applying for the necessary export licenses. Rodokanaki was among the first to take advantage of the newly opened market at Galați, and his purchases of wheat were substantial—amounting to 5,500 kilos or 33,000 Tuscan sacks.[74]

The export of Danubian grain helped relieve the shortage of wheat in Tuscany, but Tuscan diplomats still pressed for greater concessions. The Russian envoy in Rome assured the Florentine officials that he had written to Count Nesselrode himself, the imperial chancellor, urging him to reopen the south Russian ports. For a short time there seemed to be hope that neutrals would be allowed to export cereals from the Russian ports of the Black Sea. A letter from Vienna to Florence, dated December 12, 1855, carried news that the emperor had permitted the commercial house of Gopsewich of Trieste to take wheat from a port on the Azov sea.[75] The reasons for this favor were not explained, and given the excited times, the story may have been based more in rumor than in fact. Still according to the reports reaching Tuscany, Gopsewich had won this lucrative concession because he had intimate ties with the leading bankers of St. Petersburg.[76] Meanwhile, the Tuscans gained assurance that England and France would permit any neutral ship (if unloaded) to enter the Sea of Azov to purchase wheat, as long as that wheat was destined for a neutral or for a country friendly to the Allies.[77] But in spite of these hopes, the emperor did not permit the export of cereals until peace.[78] To make matters worse, in November 1855, the Ottoman government forbade export of grain from the lands it ruled, in order to assure abundant supplies of cereals for the armed forces.[79]

The disturbing experience of the Crimean War made Tuscany acutely conscious of her dependence upon grain imported from the ports of the Black Sea. With peace, she hurried to appoint consuls at new posts in South Russia: Mariupol', Kerch, Taganrog, and Berdians'k. Vice-consulates dependent on Odessa were also established in Kherson and Eupatoria (June 1856).

The volumes of Russian wheat imported into Tuscany and Italy continued to increase after Italian unification (1861). Before the First World War, Italy was one of imperial Russia's chief trading partners, and a principal consumer of the most characteristic Russian export of the epoch—wheat.[80] But we must restrict our attention here to the period before 1861, and to the history of the port of Livorno.

Concerning Livorno and its history, this significant pattern of development emerges from our study. Livorno was important both as a port of deposit and as a port of entry into the growing market of Tuscany. Its central position in the Mediterranean; the liberal trading statute which governed its commerce; good facilities for handling ships and for loading, unloading, or depositing their cargoes; and the presence there of experienced merchants who had excellent knowledge of Mediterranean markets—all these factors helped assure Livorno's importance as a deposit port for cereals in the early nineteenth century. For a period in the late 1830s, Livorno seems to have served as the most important deposit port in the Mediterranean, serving an essential function in the flow of Russian wheat to the West. But the prosperity which the deposit trade in cereals engendered depended on factors beyond the control of a single port. As we have already stated, this deposit trade basically reflected several factors: the tariff policy of the sliding scale, maintained by most Western governments, which prevented merchants from knowing well in advance what terms they would receive for imported cereals; the limited capacity, speed and range of sailing ships; and slow communications concerning markets before the advent of the telegraph. After 1850, the new policy of free trade in grain, and the technical improvements in ships and in communications, made possible and profitable direct trade between the nations which produced and consumed wheat. The fate of the deposit ports in the cereal trade was thus sealed, and Livorno too lost its previous importance. In 1853 Tuscan authorities observed that not even Tuscan ships put into the port of Livorno as frequently as in the past; England's new and liberal trading policy kept them at sea, seeking to reach as rapidly as possible this newly opened and lucrative market:

> Some ships which leave from here for the Black Sea go directly from there for England, and some of these sail again directly from England for the Black Sea, since some of them are bound by contract for two or three voyages. Among these ships are some belonging to the commercial firms established here [Livorno] which find it profitable to send their ships directly from the Black Sea for England and vice versa. All of this is a consequence of Great Britain's commercial reform, which has promoted direct commerce, and thus has diminished the resources in this market place, which used to come from the deposit of cereals especially.[81]

As other European nations liberalized their policy toward grain imports, Livorno suffered still more. Ironically, Tuscany, one of the first European champions of free trade, declined as a commercial entrepôt, because the liberal policy in the cereal commerce which she had so long espoused was at last adopted widely across Europe.

The new and efficient means of transportation and communication also served to undermine Livorno as a deposit port, set between producers and purchasers. The implications of the new technology were described by the captain of the Port of Livorno in 1858:

> Our port has felt the general consequences of the new commercial transformations caused by steamships and the telegraph. Since large deposits were made impossible after the almost universal adoption of free trade, traffic had to be limited to consumption, especially after speculation disappeared because of the rapidity with which the telegraph carries the news of prices of goods.[82]

The decline of the deposit trade was a severe blow to the commercial importance of the port of Livorno. There were, to be sure, some compensations. Tuscany was becoming an ever-better customer for Russian grain, and Livorno was Tuscany's chief port of entry. But the grain importers of Western Europe who had formerly purchased their wheat at Livorno or other deposit ports now negotiated directly with the producers. In this transition to a new organization in the cereal trade, Livorno lost its position as a chief intermediary between Russia and Europe.

Notes

1 For accounts of the grain trade between South Russia and Western Europe, see Mikhail Vol'skii, *Ocherk istorii khlebnoi torgovli*; V. A. Zolotov, *Vneshniaia torgovlia Iuzhnoi Rossii v pervoi polovine XIX veka* (Rostov: Rostovskii gosudarstvennyi universitet, 1963); V. Giura, *Russia, Stati Uniti d'America e Regno di Napoli nell'età del Risorgimento* (Naples: Istituto universitario navale di Napoli, 1967); and Patricia Herlihy, "Odessa: Staple Trade and Urbanization in New Russia," *Jahrbücher für Geschichte Osteuropas* 21 (1973): 184–95.

2. F. Braudel and R. Romano, *Navires et marchandises à l'entrée du port de Livourne (1547–1611)* (Paris: A. Colin, 1951), 52. "C'est le blé qui oeuvre largement le port à un large commerce international qu'il n'abandonnera plus de longtemps."
3. G. Mori, "Linee e momenti dello sviluppo della città, del porto e dei traffici di Livorno," *La Regione* 3 (1956): 11.
4. Braudel and Romano, *Navires*, 51.
5. Archivio di Stato di Firenze (henceforth ASF). RR Rendite, Year 1839, No. 842, May 7, 1839. ASF. Affari Doganali, Year 1850, No. 1364, Aug. 4, 1850, for another description of the grain storage facilities of Livorno.
6. For the consumption of grain in Tuscany, see P. Colletta, "Alcuni pensieri sulla economia agraria della Toscana," *Antologia* 49 (1825): 11.
7. ASF. RR Rendite, Year 1839, No. 842, May 7, 1839.
8. ASF. Affari Doganali, No. 1364, Year 1850. Letter dated July 22, 1850, from Sevastopulo, president of the Camera di Commercia, to Primo Ronchivecchi: "L'esperienza ha dimostrato che la piazza di Livorno è considerata come il principale deposito del Mediterraneo sul rapporto dei cereali, appunto per la fama giustamente acquistata de' suoi comodi di conservazione, che, anche nello stato presente sono superiori a quelli di tutte le altre piazze."
9. M. Baruchello, *Livorno e il suo porto: origini, caratteristiche e vicende dei traffici livornesi* (Livorno: Soc. An. editrice Riviste techniche, 1932), 443.
10. ASF. Affari Esteri, Filza 2480, March 7, 1847.
11. ASF. Affari Esteri, Protocollo 207, No. 7, Dec. 16, 1831. The report also names two Christian Tuscan merchants, Paul (Paolo) Rodokanaki and Pietro Parini.
12. Ibid.
13. ASF. Affari Esteri, Filza 2480, Dec. 7, 1847.
14. ASF. Affari Esteri, Filza 2480, April 9, 1848.
15. ASF. Affari Esteri, Filza 2475, June 7, 1841.
16. ASF. Affari Esteri, Protocollo 257, No. 23, Jan. 1836.
17. Henry S. Dearborn, *A Memoir on the Commerce and Navigation of the Black Sea and the Trade and Maritime Geography of Turkey and Egypt*, vol. 1 (Boston: Wells and Lilly, 1819), 243. Later Count Serristori, a Tuscan official interested in promoting Tuscan trade with the ports of the Black Sea, proposed the following list as suitable articles of export, "Vari oggetti dell'industria toscana sarebbero esportati con lucro nei porti russi del Mar Nero, per esempio: i vini dell'Isola dell'Elba, i marmi, le pietre lavorate per costruzioni di fabbriche ad uso di scale, porte e finestre, coppe da olio, mattoni, tegoli, i carboni del littorale per quanta può contenere la stiva del bastimento; quest'ultimo articolo costando in giornata a Odessa non meno di franchi *cento la soma*." ASF. Affari Esteri, Protocollo 191, June 19, 1829.
18. G. De Castelnau, *Essai sur l'histoire de la Nouvelle Russie*, vol. 3 (Paris: Rey et Gravier, 1820), 54. E. Repetti, the famous nineteenth-century Tuscan geographer, listed the major Tuscan exports to Russia as carved coral, oil, salted meats, straw hats (undoubtedly the famous Leghorn hats), marble, alabaster, and sulphur. *Dizionario geografico, fisico, storico della Toscana*, vol. 2 (Florence: Gio. Mazzoni, 1835), 764.
19. The following examples of Russian ships putting in at Livorno are taken from Hans Halm, *Oesterreich und Neurussland* (Breslau: Thiel & Hintermeier, 1943), vol. 1; *Habsburgischer Osthandel im 18. Jahrhundert. Donauhandel und -schiffahrt 1781–1787*, vol. 2 (Munich: Osteuropa Institut, 1954), 54n236.
20. ASF. Affari Esteri, Filza 2206, October 14,1785.
21. Anthoine de Saint-Joseph, *Essai historique sur le commerce de la Mer-Noire* (Paris, 1805), 204; J. von Hagemeister, *Report on the Commerce of the Ports of New Russia, Moldavia and Wallachia Made to the Russian Government in 1835* (London: E. Wilson, 1836), Appendix, Table 2. According to these authors, 1,112,000 *chetvert's* (2,203,600 hectolitres) of grain were exported in 1803, and 1,200,000 in 1817, the next peak year.

22 ASF. Affari Esteri, Protocollo 292, Jan. 11, 1830.
23 ASF. Affari Esteri, Protocollo 30.5.63, Nov. 1839; ASF. Affari Esteri, Filza 2473, April 15, 1835; ASF. Affari Esteri, Protocollo 494.36, Feb. 1856; ASF. Affari Esteri, Protocollo 509.81, June 1857. The Tuscan consul at Odessa reported home in 1847 that a larger Catholic church was needed "in una città ove si noverano moltissimi sudditi toscani," ASF. Filza 2544, March 1,1847.
24 ASF. Protocollo 371.21, July 1845.
25 Baruchello, *Livorno*, 662ff.
26 Mori, "Linee e momenti," 25.
27 Baruchello, *Livorno*, 591.
28 Ibid.
29 Anthoine de Saint-Joseph, *Essai*, 204; ASF. Ministero delle Finanze, Miscellanea "A," 1819–1845; ASF. Capi Rotti 16, 1824. Hagemeister, *Report*, 99, gives by port the average annual imports of Russian wheat for the several years preceding 1835. The figures, in *chetvert's*, are the following: Turkish ports, 500,000; Genoa, 275,000; Livorno, 220,000; Marseille, 200,000; Malta and others, 150,000; Trieste, 75,000. In 1845, the French consul at Odessa noted that most of France's imported wheat arrived indirectly from deposit ports. He also stated that the wheat sent to Genoa was in large part consumed locally, but "l'entrepôt du Livourne réexporte la plus grande partie de ce qu'il reçoit," Archives du Ministère des Affaires Étrangères, Paris (henceforth, AMAE), Odessa, vol. 6, July 12, 1845.
30 *Records of Travels in Turkey, Greece, etc. and of a Cruise in the Black Sea with the* Captain Pasha *in the Years 1829, 1830 and 1831*, vol. 1 (Philadelphia and Baltimore: Saunders and Otley, 1833), 251.
31 Hagemeister, *Report*, 6. However, the ultimate destination of the wheat was often England. The French consul in Odessa noted in 1843, "As always, England took most of the exports from Odessa." He went on to explain that a substantial part of the exported wheat was first sent to Marseille or Livorno and then re-exported to England. In his estimation, France was the second largest importer of Russian wheat. AMAE, Odessa, vol. 6, May 29, 1843.
32 ASF. Affari Doganali, No. 190, Jan. 15, 1847.
33 ASF. Affari Doganali, No. 190, April 1850.
34 E. Guglielmino, *Genova dal 1814 al 1849: gli sviluppi economici e l'opinione pubblica* (Genoa: Nella sedia della R. Deputazione di storia patria per la Liguria, 1939), 237.
35 Ibid., 131.
36 ASF. Affari Doganali, Filza 1225, Aug. 8, 1848.
37 "Livorno e i suoi traffic," *Giornale del Commercio*, June 24, 1839.
38 Karl Marx, *The Eastern Question* (London: Swan Sonnenschein and Co., 1897), 15.
39 ASF. RR Rendite. Filza 1842, No. 541, March 22, 1840.
40 Between the years 1837 and 1853, sixteen Tuscan ships on the average put into the port of Odessa each year, whereas an average of 171 Sardinian (chiefly Genoese) ships came yearly during the same period. See the Tuscan consul reports in ASF. Affari Esteri, and Archivio di Stato di Livorno (henceforth ASL), Governatore. For an interesting discussion on the cost of building steamships in Tuscany, see ASF. Affari Esteri, Protocollo 263, No. 49, July 1833.
41 ASF. Affari Esteri, Filza 2473, July 1, 1835, Quaglia to Fossombroni, "Il Capitano Cassovich, commandante la nave con bandiera toscana nominata *Venere* partito pochi giorni fa per Livorno, proveniendo da Odessa, mi porto lagnanza che aveva incontrato le maggiori difficoltà in quest'ultimo porto per far vidimare e porre in regola le sue carte di bordo dal console austriaco, che asseriva non esser munito d'istruzioni per prestar visi."
42 ASF. Affari Esteri, Protocollo 207, No. 7, Dec. 24, 1830, in which the Council of State reported to the grand duke concerning Austria. "Si è evidentemente preso a promuovere i vantaggi di Trieste contrariando Livorno."

Later the council warned, "Ma la predilezione per Trieste, la gelosia verso Livorno sono le molle che animano gli agenti austriaci in Turchia." ASF. Affari Esteri, Protocollo 207, No. 7, Sept. 7, 1831.

43 ASF. Affari Esteri, Protocollo 207, No. 7, Dec. 10, 1831; ASF. Affari Esteri, Filza 2474, April 19, 1837; *Almanacco della Toscana* (Florence: n.p., 1858); G. Baldasseroni, *Leopoldo II, Granduca di Toscana e i suoi tempi* (Florence: Tipografia all'insegna di S. Antonio 1871), 506.

44 ASF. RR Rendite, No. 916, Year 1842, undated letter marked "A."

45 ASF. RR Rendite, No. 411, Year 1842, report entitled "Grani forestieri giunti a Livorno, estratti per il territorio e per fuori."

46 ASF. Affari Doganali, No. 1364, Year 1850, July 30, 1850.

47 L. Borasi, *Grano duro e paste alimentari* (Vercelli: Tiop. Gallardi, 1939), 9.

48 ASF. Affari Esteri, Filza 2538, July 24, 1844; ASF, Affari Esteri. Filza 2544, Feb. 5, 1847; ASF. Affari Esteri, Protocollo 498.13, April 30, 1856.

49 ASF. RR Rendite, Year 1834, No. 1779, undated petition from "I fabbricanti di paste di Livorno."

50 ASF. RR Rendite, Year 1838, No.1123. O. Forni, Director of Customs at Livorno wrote to A. Humbourg, administrator of the revenue department at Livorno, saying that until the next increment in the tax on flour, pasta makers of Livorno should be able to compete successfully with those of Marseille, Genoa, Naples, and other Mediterranean ports in exports of semolina, pasta and biscuits. These foods were shipped to America, the African coast, Gibraltar and Lisbon, chiefly.

51 ASF. RR Rendite, Year 1842, No. 411, March 29, 1842. The Grain Office at Livorno listed the following kinds of wheat according to weight per sack: from Taganrog, from 170 to 180 Tuscan pounds; from Odessa, from 164 to 168 pounds; from Alexandria in Egypt, from 152 to 156 pounds. Heavier wheat was considered to be of superior quality. See Borasi, *Grano,* 17. Tuscany exported annually about 225,000 sacks of locally grown wheat, which was especially sought after for seeding or for making particularly fine bread. See ASF. Ministero delle Finanze, No. 1447, May 18, 1856.

52 Saint-Joseph, *Essai,* 58.

53 *First and Second Reports from the Committees of the House of Lords Appointed to Inquire into the State of Growth, Commerce and Consumption of Grain* (London, 1814), 123.

54 ASF. Affari Doganali, Year 1850, No. 1354, July 30, 1850.

55 ASF. RR Rendite, Year 1842, No. 541, March 18,1842.

56 A. Zobi, *Manuale storico di economia toscana* (Florence: 1847), 357.

57 C. Di Nola, *Politica economica e agricoltura in Toscana nei secoli XV–XIX* (Città di Castello, 1948), 51, and Dearborn, *Memoir,* vol. 1, 240.

58 Archivio Comunale di Firenze (henceforth, ACF), Mercuriali, Series 45, No. 6. A complete series of these *mercuriali* from 1809 to 1861 are located in the Archivio Comunale di Firenze.

59 ASF. RR Rendite, Year 1841, No. 454, Dec. 1, 1841.

60 ASF. RR Rendite, Year 1840, "Grani forestieri giunti a Livorno." ASF. Ministero delle Finanze, No. 1447, May 18,1856. ASF. Affari Esteri, Protocollo 571.46. Feb. 1854.

61 ASF. Ministero delle Finanze, No. 1447, May 18, 1856.

62 ASF. Affari Esteri, Filza 2530, March 13, 1840. Also ASF. RR Rendite, Year 1840, "Dimostrazione dei cereali stati introdotti nel Porto di Livorno dal dì primo gennaio a tutto il dì 31 dicembre 1839."

63 ASF. Affari Esteri, Filza 2538, April 12, 1844.

64 ASF. Affari Esteri, Protocollo 394.59, May 14, 1847. In Tuscany the Council of State recommended that honors be distributed to all the Russians who were instrumental in getting the new treaty signed and suggested that titles should go to Karl Nesselrode as Minister for Foreign Affairs, and Ivan Butenev who had been in charge of the negotiations. An honorary title should also be conferred upon "the first official and secretary for foreign

affairs of St. Petersburg whose name at the moment is not known." ASF. Affari Esteri, Protocollo 394.59, June 7, 1847.

65 National Archives, Washington, DC (henceforth, NA) Odessa, Consular Report, March 1,1854.
66 ASF. Affari Esteri, Protocollo No. 474.19, May 2, 1854; ASF. Affari Esteri, Protocollo No. 474.19, May 4, 1854.
67 ASF. Affari Esteri, Protocollo 475, June 23,1854; ASF. Affari Esteri, Protocollo 480.13, Nov. 13,1854.
68 ACF. Mercuriali, Series 45, No. 22.
69 *Il Corriere Italiano*, Feb. 15, 1856.
70 Ibid.
71 ASF. Affari Esteri, Protocollo 482.101, Nov. 8, 1855.
72 ASF. Filza 2554, Sept. 25, 1855.
73 ASF. Protocollo 416.84. July 24, 1854.
74 Ibid.
75 Ibid., Protocollo 493.49, Dec. 15, 1855.
76 Ibid., Protocollo 491.24, Sept. 24, 1855.
77 Ibid.
78 NA. Odessa, Consular Report, April 7,1856. The American consul reported that on April 5 exports of all articles were permitted from Odessa.
79 ASF. Affari Esteri, Protocollo 493.33, Nov. 20, 1855.
80 For discussions of Italo-Russian trade relations after 1860, see Ugo Caprara, *Il commercio del grano*, 2 vols. (Milan: Istituto editoriale scientifico, 1928–1928); Vincenzo Cacciapuoti, *Relazioni commerciali tra l'Italia e la Russia, 1878–92* (Naples: N. Jovene, 1928); and C. Morandi. *Le relazioni tra l'Italia e la Russia dal 1900 al 1917* (Florence: n.p., 1949).
81 ASF. Ministero delle Finanze, Capi Rotti 101, May 10, 1853. See also Vol'skii, *Ocherk*, 131 who notes that after the abolition of the Corn Laws, many more ships sailed from Odessa directly to England.
82 ASF. Ministero delle Finanze, Capi Rotti 101, Aug. 27, 1858.

CHAPTER 13

South Ukraine as an Economic Region in the Nineteenth Century

My purpose in this chapter is to examine the economic integration of South Ukraine in the nineteenth century, and to review the commercial relationship of the region with other parts of Ukraine, the Russian Empire, and the outside world. To do this, I must initially describe the region of our interest, characterize in general terms economic developments in our period, and state what I understand by the governing concept, "economic region."

In administrative terms, South Ukraine consists of the three guberniias of Kherson, Katerynoslav, and Tavriia or Taurida (the Crimea) (see Map 1). These administrative borders enclose the core, but do not circumscribe the limits, of the economic region I examine.[1]

In ca. 1800, when our inquiry begins, this region had only recently been incorporated into the Russian Empire. In 1774 the Treaty of Kiuchuk-Kainardzhi with the Ottomans confirmed the imperial domination of the northern littoral of the Black Sea.[2] The lands that the Turks surrendered were predominantly *chornozem* steppe, very fertile but still very thinly settled. This "new Ukraine," as it is sometimes called, thus contrasted with the "old Ukraine" to the north, which was one of the most densely settled regions of the empire.

The new Ukraine remained very much a frontier region during the opening decades of the nineteenth century. For example, in Kherson guberniia, one out of seven males was in military service in 1827, and the ratio remained constant until the 1850s.[3] The population was, however, growing rapidly and the area of cultivation extending. A principal stimulus to growth was the opening of a voracious market for wheat in Western Europe and for other products, such as wool and tallow, easily produced from animals raised on the South Ukrainian steppes. The export of wheat to Western Europe first boomed during the Napoleonic Wars, but slackened in the immediate postwar decades, as western states imposed barriers ("corn laws") against wheat imports. But the abolition of the corn laws in western countries (from the 1840s), their soaring populations and industrialization and urbanization sustained a steady growth in wheat exports, which continued over the second half of the century. Even the Crimean War (1853–56) represented only a temporary interruption.

What exactly defines an economic region? I understand by the term a geographic area, in which local markets show similar price levels and price movements in regard to certain key

---

Originally published as Patricia Herlihy, "South Ukraine as an Economic Region in the Nineteenth Century," in *Ukrainian Economic History: Interpretative Essays*, ed. I. S. Koropeckyi (Cambridge, MA: Harvard University Press, 1991), 310–38.

South Ukraine as an Economic Region in the Nineteenth Century • CHAPTER 13 | 227

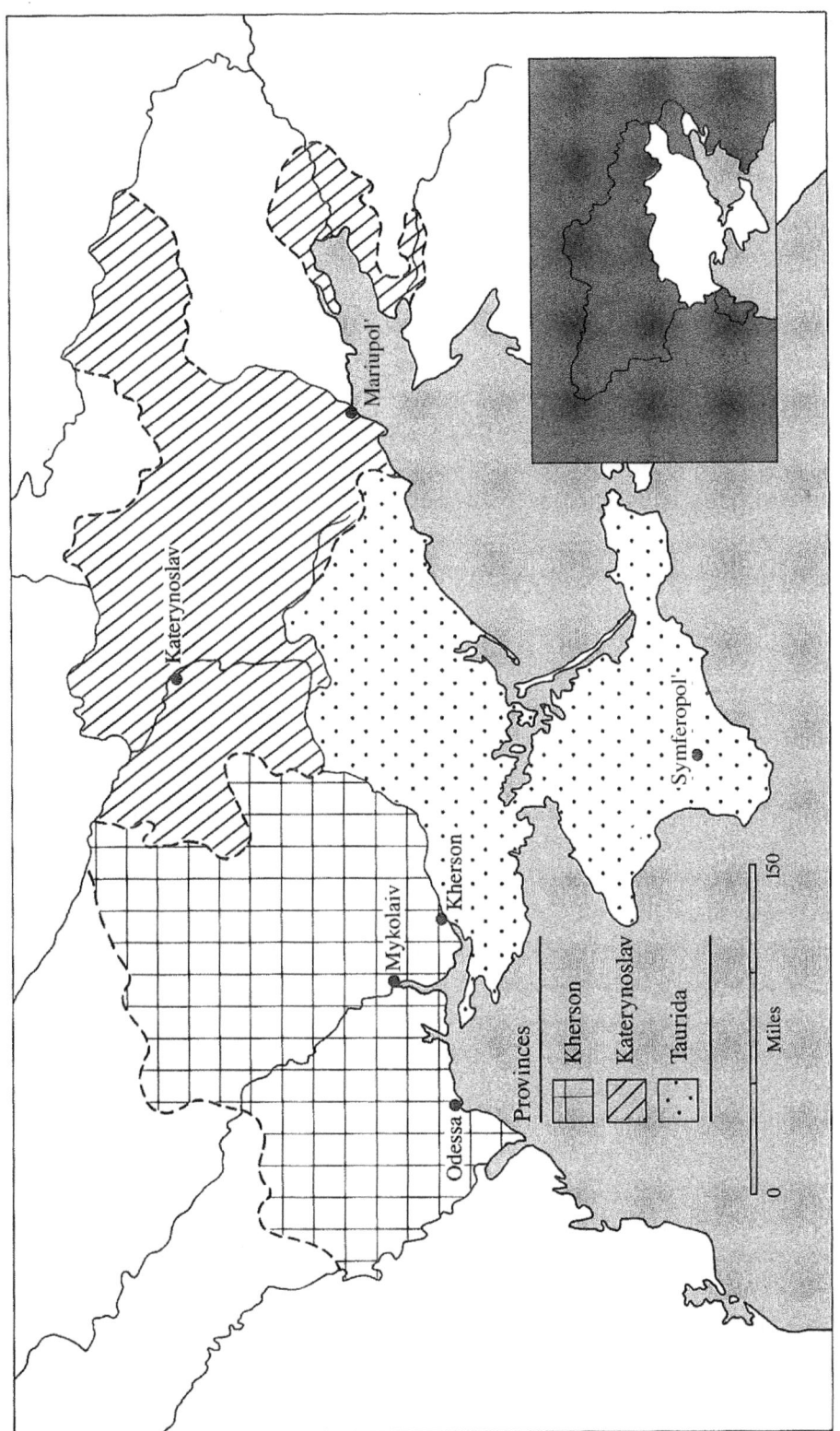

Map 1 South Ukraine. Reprinted from Patricia Herlihy, *Odessa: A History, 1794–1914* (Cambridge, MA: Harvard University Press, 1987).

commodities.[4] This area is "the whole of any region in which buyers and sellers are in such free intercourse with one another that the prices of the same goods tend to equality easily and quickly."[5] In other words, purchasers anywhere in the region pay approximately the same price for the same goods at the same time. Of course, if the region is large, "allowance must be made for the expense of delivering the goods to different purchasers."[6] But if prices test the degree of regional integration, they are obviously not its cause. A high degree of regional integration requires the support of a substructure that facilitates the exchange of information and the transport of goods. Elements in the substructure are entrepôts or fairs, where both information and commodities are exchanged, and a suitably efficient system of communications and of transport. In an economically integrated region, goods move readily from areas of abundance to areas of scarcity. Goods are therefore distributed more evenly over space, and their prices everywhere tend to converge. Regional integration of this kind encourages specialization in production; the local areas produce what best they can on the basis of their differing factor endowments, and they use their surpluses to trade for their other needs.

It should, however, be noted that local markets may not be integrated to the same extent in regard to all commodities. The commodities most likely to be traded within the region are those that are widely consumed, are of predictable quality, and are relatively durable. Cereals, wheat in particular, are often used in testing for the integration of markets.[7] Through a kind of "free rider" phenomenon, integration of regional markets in regard to one commodity aids integration in regard to others. Nonetheless, differences are likely to remain.

In examining the complex and changing economic situation of South Ukraine in the nineteenth century, I shall first look at the substructure and then at the evidence of regional integration as revealed by prices. It must be admitted that the supporting data is not entirely satisfactory. My principal sources yielding price information are three. The first are the price schedules for rye, wheat, and oats, published between the years 1846 and 1859 in the *Zhurnal* of the Ministry of Internal Affairs.[8] Unfortunately, the series given for the southern provinces contain many gaps. The first part of the series (up to 1856) gives prices by guberniia and the second (1856–59) by city, thus impeding consistent analysis. The series is nonetheless valuable, and we also make use of official government publications to compile data for the last years of the nineteenth century.[9]

The second principal source is the prices collected by a Russian economist, Iulii Eduardovich Ianson, during a tour through South Ukraine in 1867 and 1868. He published the results of his research in 1870. Ianson studied markets both in the Odessa region and in the Crimea, and gathered price citations from a variety of private sources, chiefly account books kept by estate owners, merchants, and millers.[10] His price series extends from 1860 to 1867.

Finally, in their study of the emergence of what they call an "All Russian agrarian market," I. D. Koval'chenko and L. V. Milov compiled much information about prices from the entire empire out of archival records and published data.[11] Unfortunately for our purposes, with rare exceptions they present the data in already processed form, chiefly through coefficients of correlation across guberniias. Moreover, the items used as the principal tests for integration are rye or rye flour and oats for the earlier period (to 1855). For the late nineteenth and early twentieth centuries (to 1914), they analyze the prices of draft horses, cattle, and real estate and also salaries. But they do not include in their analysis the prices of wheat.[12] Wheat prices are frequently cited in the series they exploit, at least from 1846, and wheat was a particularly important commodity of trade in *chornozem* regions. Their failure to consider this the most commercial of cereals is perplexing, in a book expressly devoted to the formation of the agrarian market. They do not explain why wheat was dropped or never included in the analysis. Why?

Although the book is not as useful for this study as it might have been, it nonetheless contains unique information not available outside of archives. I shall make much use of its data in this paper and shall also offer additional comment about its methods and content.

THE SUBSTRUCTURE

A. Fairs

It is well known that annual or seasonal fairs played a major role in the internal commerce of the Russian Empire.[13] For example, it was largely through fairs that the manufactures of the more industrialized, chiefly central guberniias were marketed in the predominantly agricultural regions, such as Ukraine itself.[14] In the mid-nineteenth century, the value of Russian-made goods sold in Ukrainian fairs exceeded that of agricultural products purchased by Russian buyers, although the value of foreign manufactures allegedly exceeded that of the Russian by twenty times.[15] An economist writing in 1858 recognized the role fairs played in integrating markets when he stated, "There is no doubt that with the advent of the railroad from Moscow to the Black Sea all fairs along the route will diminish gradually, except perhaps the wool [fairs]."[16]

The principal Ukrainian fairs were at Kharkiv (some four major fairs a year, each lasting about a month), Poltava, Chernihiv, and Romny—all of which are in North Ukraine. The locally produced commodities traded at the fairs were primarily wheat, rye, millet, maize, animals, wool, tallow, sheepskins and leather.[17] Because of its importance in foreign export, wheat enjoyed a special status. In South Ukraine, however, fairs had only a limited importance. As shown on Map 2, the three southern guberniias contained only one important fair, that of Ielysavethrad (Kirovohrad). Its value of sales earned it tenth position among the eleven principal Ukrainian fairs.[18] The port cities (primarily Odessa) cast a shadow extending far into the hinterland, within which the fairs typical of the rest of the empire could not grow. Most purchases were made not at inland fairs but at the ports themselves. Or else, the purchasers at the ports went themselves or dispatched agents to buy these products, wheat especially, directly from the inland producers. Conversely too, the port cities were the foci by which foreign luxury products and manufactures were made available to inland purchasers.

In regions distant from the ports, agricultural commodities were purchased and gathered into large batches for shipment to Odessa. Principal towns serving this function were Kremenchuk and Katerynoslav (Dnipropetrovsk) on the Dnipro River, and Mohyliv-on-the-Dnister (Mohyliv-Podil's'kyi in today's Ukraine). There were also other locales, not so much true markets as staging areas, where cereals were accumulated for shipment to the ports. Among

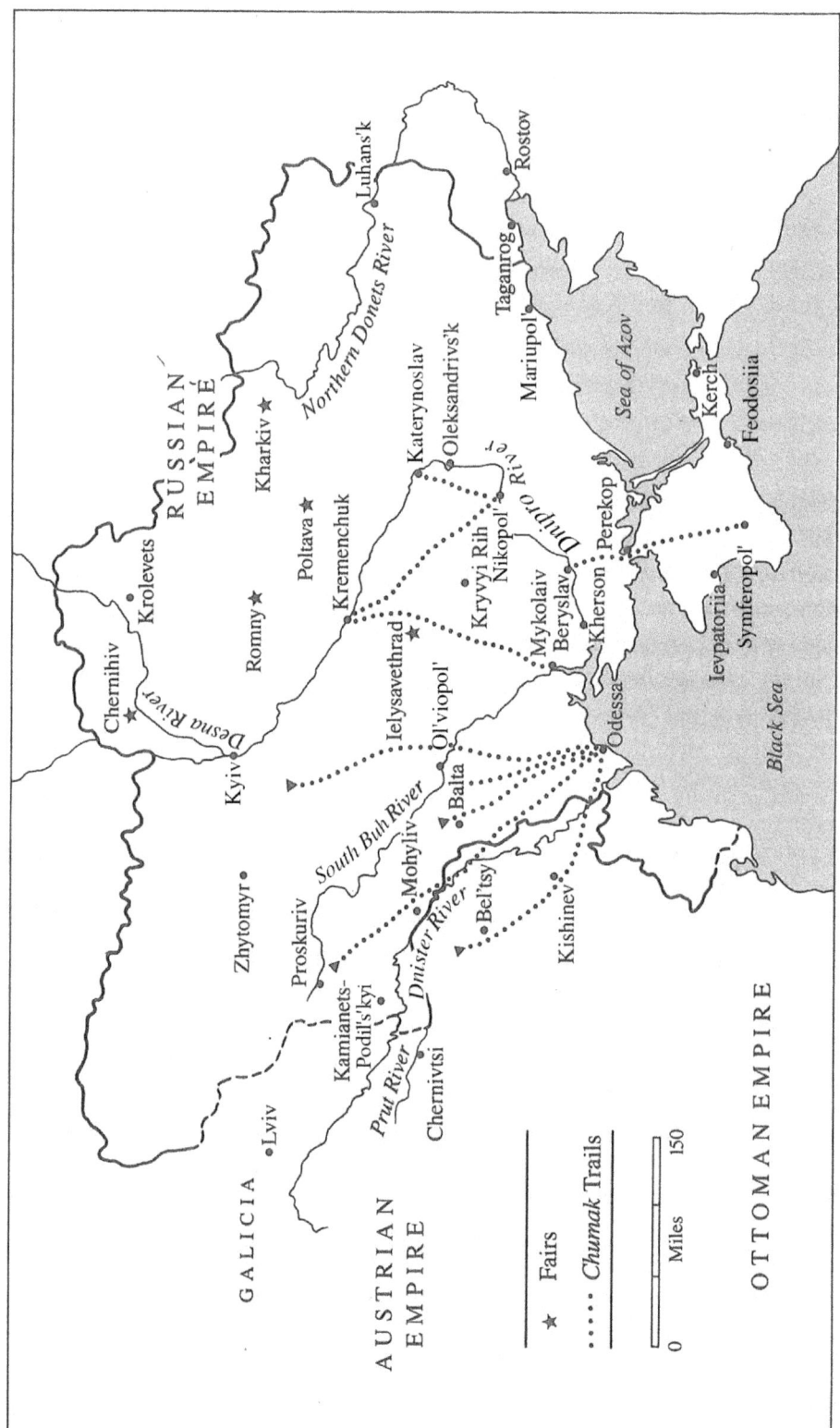

Map 2 Fairs and *Chumak* Trails. Reprinted from Patricia Herlihy, *Odessa: A History, 1794–1914* (Cambridge, MA: Harvard University Press, 1987).

the more important were Oleksandrivs'k (Zaporizhzhia) and Nikopol' on the Dnipro. Located just below the Dnipro rapids, Oleksandrivs'k and then Nikopol' gathered the wheat carried by land around the rapids and placed it on barges, to complete its journey by water to the Black Sea ports. Of importance too was Proskuriv (Khmel'nyts'kyi) in the basin of the Volhynian rivers; it marked the northern limit of Odessa's region in the middle nineteenth century.[19]

B. Water Transport

The importance of the ports for the inland economy indicates that very early in the development of the region bulky commodities, such as wheat, could be carried over considerable distances at acceptable costs. The flat and treeless steppe was fairly easily traversed, both by riverboats and by carts.

The rivers emptying into the Black Sea were natural highways across the steppe, but they were also very circuitous. Moreover, the chief of them, the Dnipro, was also obstructed in its course by its well-known series of rapids. Cargoes had to be unloaded and taken by cart around them, and, as mentioned, Oleksandrivs'k marked the spot where the river became navigable again. The Dnipro and the upper Dnister largely defined the interior regions, which could be served by water transport.

Cabotage, or coastal shipping, played a role of considerable importance in linking together the Black Sea ports one with the others. For example, between 1858 and 1867, the number of boat arrivals at the port of Eupatoriia in the Crimea averaged 355 per year, and the average yearly departures 347. Approximately one-half of this coastal trade out of the Crimea was with Odessa. The number of foreign ship arrivals at the same port of Eupatoriia was half as many. The port of Kherson, at the mouth of the Buh, which eventually became Odessa's great rival, was initially a satellite port, receiving and combining smaller cargoes for transshipment to Odessa, the region's great entrepôt for international commerce. In this function, it resembles Oleksandrivs'k and Nikopol' on the Dnipro.

Unlike the ships in international trade, all those engaged in coastal traffic were required by law to be of Russian ownership. Traffic on the coastal waters intensified considerably in the nineteenth century. Table 1 shows the number of arrivals of cabotage ships at the port of Odessa in the middle and late decades.

Table 1 Arrivals of Cabotage Ships at Odessa, 1842–92

Year	Arrivals
1842	431
1852	1,209
1862	1,365
1872	2,777
1882	2,693
1892	3,401

Source: *Odessa 1794–1894* (Odessa: Izdaniia gorodskogo obshchestvennogo upravleniia k stoletiiu goroda, Tip. A. Shul'tse, 1895), 217.

At first, most of the boats came from Kherson, but later, they also came from Akkerman (Bilhorod-Dnistrovs'kyi), Ochakiv, Mykolaiv, and Crimean ports, primarily Eupatoriia. By the end of the nineteenth century, cabotage ships from Kherson carried grain, flour, wool, and coal; from Mariupol', coal; from Akkerman, grain and wine; and from Eupatoriia, salt. Like threads, these coastal voyages sewed together the region's maritime fringes.

C. The Chumaky

The vast inland region between the Dnister and Dnipro rivers was not adequately served by water transport, but it was the largest and most productive part of the economic region. To bring agricultural products to port required the use of great carts or wagons, pulled by oxen, and driven by teamsters known as *chumaky*. Their services remained important over the entire course of the nineteenth century. Map 2 shows the principal routes taken by the *chumaky* in the mid-part of the century. These routes show rather well the depth to which the pull of the ports extended into the hinterland. By 1870 five major *chumaky* grain trails terminated in Odessa, only one in Mykolaiv, and none in Kherson. The *chumaky* routes originating in Kremenchuk terminated in Beryslav and Nikopol'. Nikopol' was also the chief terminus of the *chumaky* trail from Katerynoslav. Another *chumaky* trail led to the Crimea; it was especially important for the salt trade.

The range of the *chumaky* and their wagons is astounding, and is a principal reason why fairs were not needed in the near vicinity of the ports. For example, at the time of the Uspen'skyi Fair in Kharkiv (August 15 to September 1 or later), the *chumaky* set forth from Kharkiv with empty carts for the Crimea; they purchased goods along the way. If the weather was good (that is, dry) and if the *chumaky* gathered sufficient wares, they traveled on as far as Odessa and Bessarabia. There, they sold their goods and passed the winter. Early in the spring those in the Crimea loaded up with salt and dried fish at Perekop for the return trip. Some 100,000 wagons a year carried salt from Perekop to Kharkiv. While horse-drawn wagons could move winter and summer, the *chumaky* drove their oxen and carts only during summer, when the roads were dried out and the oxen could graze on the growing grass. Each wagon could hold forty to fifty *pudy* (ca. 1,440–1,800 pounds) of wheat. Its best speed was thirty *versty* (ca. twenty miles) per day and only ten to fifteen *versty* when the roads were muddy. The oxen had to take shelter when it rained.[20] Since the grass that the oxen consumed cost nothing and the *chumaky* slept in the open air, this was a fairly economical method of land transport. But the costs of moving wheat from hinterland to port remained high in relative terms, as we shall see.

D. Railroads

Railroads came late into South Ukraine, the first being constructed in 1865 (from Balta to Odessa). Map 3 shows the railroads in Ukraine in 1906. It seems too that strategic rather than commercial considerations dictated their routes. Some of the lines, however, followed the north-west, south-east direction of the Dnister and Buh rivers, but more markedly, they paralleled the *chumaky* trails. The length of the railroad lines increased in South Ukraine (including the Don Military District) from 2,623 *versty* in 1870 to 4,789 in 1894. In 1880 trains brought in 79 percent of all grain to Odessa. The advent of the railroad significantly reduced the costs of shipping wheat to Odessa, as we shall see.

Nonetheless, the railroads did not replace the river barges, or even the *chumaky* carts, as the principal means of bringing cereals to port.[21] After 1880, the portion of wheat carried to port by train was actually declining. By 1892 the percentage of grain carried to Odessa by rail slipped to 32.2 percent.[22] This surprising trend partially resulted from high railroad tariffs (water transport was generally cheaper). Then too, contrary to all expectations, barges and carts could serve more economically the distant areas of cereal production, recently brought under cultivation.[23] It seems that, unlike the experience of India, the coming of railroads to South Ukraine was not the decisive factor in integrating cereal markets within the region.[24]

The late construction and disappointing contribution of the railroads were one reason why South Ukraine, in spite of growing exports, was unable to compete successfully against other world suppliers of wheat, the United States, Canada, Argentina, and others. In the late nineteenth century, beset by problems of transport and control of quality, the region progressively lost position among the world suppliers of wheat, to the United States, Canada, Argentina, and other lands. Efficient inland transport in these latter countries gave them the competitive edge.

THE INTEGRATION OF SOUTH-UKRAINIAN MARKETS

A. The Early Evidence, 1809–19

The earlier price data available to us that include South Ukrainian towns date from 1809 to 1819 and were published by Koval'chenko and Milov (Prilozhenie 3 and 4, with ten observations each, as the years 1812 and 1813 are combined). The two tables they provide cite prices by year for rye, rye flour, and oats. I have taken their data for nine Ukrainian towns and, to gain added perspective, for one town located beyond Ukraine's northern border, Mahiliou-on-the-Dnipro. Mahiliou was old-settled and densely settled, and lay outside the *chornozem* region. Its data help place the Ukrainian experience within a larger context.

The first schedule given by the Soviet authors mix together prices of rye (by *chetvert'*; 1 *chetvert'* = 0.108 tons) and of rye flour (by *kul'*; 1 *kul'* = 96.5 kg.). Although Koval'chenko and Milov do use this table to calculate coefficients of correlation, I did not think it worthwhile (nor did I have the data) to replicate the elaborate procedures by which they estimated the price of rye from that of rye flour.[25] Moreover, their resulting matrix of correlations gives some impossible values. In Table 2, the correlation of Arkhangel'sk with Chernihiv is .62, and of Chernihiv with Arkhangel'sk is .67; they should, of course, be the same. The correlation of Arkhangel'sk with Ufa is either .86 or .66, depending on what corner of the matrix one is reading. There are other indications of a rather careless proofreading. Given these difficulties, I decided not to examine the prices they give for rye and rye flour, nor the correlations derived from them.

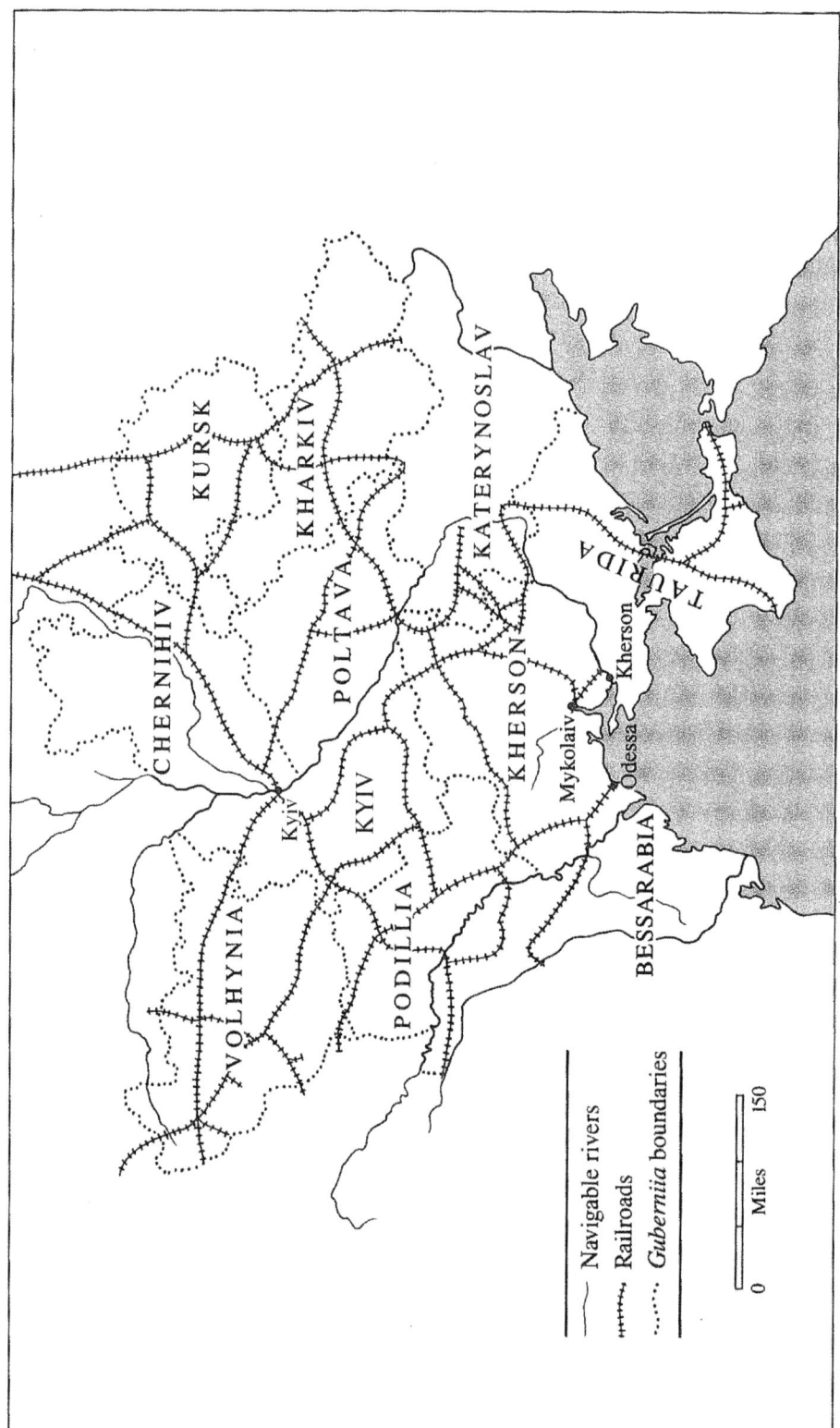

Map 3 Railroads in South Ukraine, ca. 1907. (Reprinted from Patricia Herlihy, *Odessa: A History 1794–1914*, Cambridge, MA, 1987).

Table 2 Correlation Matrix Prices of Oats at Ukrainian and South Russian Towns 1809–19

	Katrv	Zhtmr	Km-Pd	Kyiv	Mhl	Pltva	Smfpl	Khrkv	Khrsn	Chrnh
Katerynoslav		−.138	−.058	−.078	.745	.879	.649	.941	.384	.345
Zhytomyr	−.138		.849	.860	−.181	−.095	.347	−.243	.457	.128
Kamianets'-Podil's'kyi	−.058	.849		.833	−.074	−.134	.512	−.120	.553	.442
Kyiv	.078	.860	.833		−.131	−.055	.410	−.166	.626	.381
Mahiliou	.745	−.181	−.074	−.131		.770	.752	.848	.137	.463
Poltava	.879	−.095	−.134	−.055	.770		.523	.914	.314	.338
Symferopol'	.649	.347	.512	.410	.752	.523		.648	.437	.552
Kharkiv	.941	−.243	−.120	−.166	.848	.914	.648		.226	.437
Kherson	.384	.457	.553	.626	.137	.314	.437	.226		.646
Chernihiv	.345	.128	.442	.381	.463	.338	.552	.437	.654	

Source: Based on prices cited in Koval'chenko and Milov, *Vserossiiskii agrarnyi rynok*, Prilozhenie 4. Prices are in paper rubles per *chetvert'*.

The analysis here is thus limited to prices for oats—not an ideal commodity, as oats were less actively traded than other cereals. The average price for oats over the decade shows a large spread, ranging from 367 paper rubles per *chetvert'* at Kharkiv to 810 at Symferopol'. The schedules identify a region of very low prices in Northeast Ukraine (385.8 at Poltava, 364 at Kharkiv), though similar growing conditions in these close and contiguous provinces may be the principal reason. Two areas of high prices are found: in the Crimea (810.4 rubles at Symferopol') and Mahiliou beyond the northern border (800.1 rubles). These are the only clearly delineated regions in these early years. Especially notable for our purposes are the big price differences in the three New Russian towns (411.3 at Katerynoslav, 669.4 at Kherson, and 810.4 at Symferopol'). There was as yet no unified market for oats.

Table 2 gives the coefficients of correlations, which we recalculated on the basis of the data supplied by Koval'chenko and Milov. The figures agree with their own results.

The number of negative correlations (12 out of 45, or more than a fourth) shows that the areas surveyed were still weakly integrated in the early nineteenth century. The correlations of Kherson with Katerynoslav (.384) and with Symferopol' (.437) are positive but very weak, showing little trade in oats in New Russia. Katerynoslav seems much more oriented toward Poltava (.879) and toward Kharkiv (.941) and to form part of a northeast Ukrainian sector marked by very low oat and perhaps wheat prices. There is, in sum, by 1809–19, still no evidence that South Ukraine had coalesced as an economic region.

B. Midcentury

The next available set of data is the prices collected by the Ministry of Internal Affairs for rye, rye flour, wheat, oats, and hay, from August 1846 to September 1856.[26] The unit of observation was the guberniia, and the intent was to collect prices twice every month. The complete series ought to have included forty-one observations, but no one of the southern guberniias I surveyed showed all citations. From Kherson, for example, there are only eleven citations for rye flour and for wheat, respectively. Moreover, the price series shows strong seasonal swings. Because the prices collected do not necessarily represent the same season of the year, correlations obviously become difficult.

I first calculated average prices for the three commodities for ten guberniias, eight in Ukraine and two, Bessarabia and Mahiliou, just beyond its borders. I then matched prices of each guberniia with those of the other nine for each commodity, in order to determine which of the two areas showed the higher price. The highest possible score that a guberniia could attain was 27 (comparisons with nine other guberniias for three commodities). The comparisons identified two regions of consistently high prices and one in which they were quite low. The region of highest prices was Mahiliou, which scored 24 out of the possible 27. Only oats were slightly cheaper in Bessarabia, Taurida, and Kherson. At Mahiliou the price of wheat was 43.5 percent higher than at Chernihiv just to its south, 43.3 percent higher than at Kyiv, 47 percent above prices at Kharkiv, and 52.6 percent above those of Poltava. Mahiliou with its large population and poor soil was clearly a region where food was very expensive. It stands very much apart from the other guberniias we included.

By middle century, the second region of high cereal prices, on the other side of Ukraine, had gained in visibility. It included Taurida, which also scores 24 out of 27 but with much smaller differentials than those registered at Mahiliou; Bessarabia, with a score of 23; Kherson, with 19; and Podillia, with 15. These guberniias had ready access to ports and to the sea, and the influence of the ports seems apparent. For example, the price of wheat was 25.8 percent higher at Kherson than at Poltava; in Taurida it was 34.6 percent higher. The period includes the record years of cereal exports from Ukraine when crops failed in the West in 1846 and 1847. It is not unlikely that these areas close to the ports were responding to foreign demand and beginning to lure with high prices shipments of cereals from the deeper hinterland.

The averages also identify an area of very low cereal costs, the outlines of which we already saw in the early years of the century. The guberniias of low prices were Katerynoslav with a score of 10, Chernihiv (9), Kyiv (8), Kharkiv (5), and Poltava (0). The price of oats, for example, was 1.87 rubles at Poltava, and 3.32 at Taurida—almost double. The region of very cheap cereal prices now was extended to include the guberniias of Kyiv and Chernihiv, which it did not clearly encompass in 1809–19. The data, in sum, indicate much clearer differentiation of regions within Ukraine and immediately beyond its borders.

I also calculated coefficients of correlation for the three sets of prices and the nine guberniias. Here, the different dates of the citations were a problem. To offset this, I inserted dummy values. When a citation was missing, I entered the closest previous true price into the series. But I did not want to manipulate the data too vigorously, and therefore did not calculate correlations for series in which, out of the forty-one observations, fewer than twenty-one were real. Even so, the results were disappointing, particularly since at Kherson, the center of our interest, the citations for rye and for wheat were only eleven. Because the table is large and cumbersome, I do not reprint it here. Nonetheless, some conclusions seem appropriate.

The number of negative correlations for the ten guberniias collapse to only 12 out of the 234 calculated values—an indication that cereal prices in most places were responding to the same market forces. Given the need to insert dummy data, high correlations are not to be expected. Still, Kherson shows a reasonably strong correlation with Bessarabia for oats (.760) and with Taurida (.802), but slightly weaker with Katerynoslav (.671), weak with Kyiv (.521); and almost no correlation with Kharkiv (.298) and Chernihiv (.270). This suggests that in the 1840s and 1850s, distance remained a powerful factor in obstructing the integration of markets.

From November 1856 the Ministry of Internal Affairs adopted cities, and no longer guberniias, as the units of observation, and continued to publish twice every month prices for rye flour, wheat, and oats. The practice was discontinued in September 1859. The complete series consists of seventeen citations. Again, however, gaps are frequent. For example, no prices at all are given for wheat at Kyiv or Poltava. The short duration of the series and the strong seasonal fluctuation of prices also obstruct correlational analysis. On the other hand this set includes cities such as Odessa, Feodosiia, Berdians'k, Taganrog, and others, which are not represented in any earlier collection.

I selected sixteen Ukrainian cities, and also Kishinev in Bessarabia and Mahiliou-on-the-Dnipro, for analysis. As wheat was the most expensive and the most traded cereal, its prices are doubtlessly the best indicators of market structure. The average prices for wheat between November 1856 and September 1859 show a clear division into three groups or clusters. Wheat prices range from a low of 5.65 rubles per *chetvert'* at Kamianets'-Podil's'kyi to a high of 9.61 at Feodosiia in the Crimea. But no town shows a price in the range of six rubles, and only one, Berdians'k on the Sea of Azov, has a value between eight and nine rubles. We thus have clusters of cities showing cheap prices (less than 6 rubles) intermediate prices (seven rubles), and high prices (nine rubles).

To look first at the last cluster, Mahiliou (9.56 rubles per *chetvert'*) again emerges as a city with very high cereal costs. The other towns with high prices are all found on or close to the sea: Feodosiia (9.61) and Symferopol' (9.01) in the Crimea; Odessa (9.02); and perhaps Berdians'k (8.24). The cluster of cheapest markets includes Zhytomyr to the west of Kyiv (5.83), Kamianets'-Podil's'kyi in Podillia (5.65), Kremenchuk (5.72), and Kharkiv (5.8). (Kyiv and Poltava doubtlessly fall into this category, but for them wheat prices are not given.) These towns form a band distant from the sea. The third cluster of moderate-price markets consists of Kishinev in Bessarabia (7.21); Balta in Ukraine (7.34), a principal supplier to the Odessa market; Katerynoslav (7.66); and Rostov-on-the-Don (7.80). Two seaports are also found in this category, Kherson (7.66) and Taganrog (7.66). Most are inland cities but within moderate distances of ports. The two ports of Kherson and Taganrog still were not principal overseas shippers.

The novelty revealed in the data is the clear appearance of this intermediate tier of towns, which are showing the influence of the high prices for wheat offered on the seaboard but still sell their grain at a substantially lower price (approximately in the range of seven rubles, as distinct from nine at portside). Notable too is the reorientation of Katerynoslav, which earlier seemed turned toward the cheap-price zone of the deep hinterland, but now is fully in the zone of intermediate prices. The evidence, in sum, indicates that the pull of the ports was affecting ever more distant areas of South Ukraine.

I calculated the coefficients of mutual correlation among all eighteen towns, which resulted in a huge table of nearly 900 cells. It confirmed some obvious expectations. Prices for wheat at Feodosiia show a high correlation with those at Symferopol' (.921) and also Kherson (.915). But the most surprising result was the low correlations registered by Odessa. Its strongest match was with Kishinev in Bessarabia (.780), a close supplier of its port. It registered comparable scores with nearby Balta (.731) and with Kamianets'-Podil's'kyi further along on the same *chumaky* trail (.726). It showed only moderately strong correlations with its sister ports of Rostov (.721), Feodosiia (.699), and Kherson (.664). None of these scores are very impressive. I take this to mean that the Odessa market was not primarily reflecting seasonal variations in cereal prices but the level of overseas demand. These variations still strongly affected prices at inland markets. The short duration of this series magnifies the importance of seasonal variations, and Odessa's prices seem less subject to them than those of inland cities.

C. The 1860s

We now can make use of the data collected by the economist Ianson, who exploited private sources and claimed that he spared no pains to assure its accuracy. The town of Mogilev, which he included in his research, is Mohyliv-on-the-Dnister, falls within Odessa's region even as Mahiliou-on-the-Dnipro does not. Ianson's data also enlarges the number of Ukrainian towns that we can include in our analysis. Table 3 shows price movements at Odessa and at towns that were the principal inland suppliers to its port.

Table 3 Price in Rubles for a *Chetvert'* of Wheat in the Odessa Region, 1860–67

	Odessa	Nikopol'	Ielyzavethrad	Mohyliv	Bel'tsy	Proskuriv
1860	8.75	6.25	5.75	5.45	4.90	
1861	8.50	5.50	5.25	5.40	4.70	
1862	7.60	5.50	5.20	4.62	4.64	
1863	7.25	6.00	5.90	4.15	5.20	
1864	7.10	4.25	4.20	4.39	3.40	4.40
1865	7.68	7.20	4.80	6.00	5.90	3.80
1866	10.50	8.25	6.95	6.23	7.00	5.20
1867	11.75	11.00	8.00	8.52	10.00	8.40
Ave	8.64	6.74	5.75	5.59	5.71	5.45
Index	100	78	67	65	66	63

Source: Ianson, *Statisticheskoe issledovanie*, 277.

Table 3 shows that the wide divergence between the price of a *chetvert'* of wheat at portside and in the hinterland persisted through the 1860s. About one-third of its price at Odessa is attributable to transport costs. By this measure, the region remained weakly integrated in the 1860s. On the other hand, the movement of prices at all these observation points was becoming very close. Table 4 presents the correlations.

In spite of the continuing large price differential between Odessa and the hinterland towns, the markets at all of them were responding to the same shifts in demand, radiating out of Odessa itself.

Table 4 measures the extension of Odessa's economic region into the hinterland. Its harbor also could take advantage of coastal shipping to extend its influence to other Black Sea ports. The indefatigable Ianson collected data from the Crimea, and this allows us to examine how well, in the 1860s, seacoast shipping, or cabotage, was integrating the coastal zones of the region. Table 5 shows monthly wheat prices at Feodosiia and Odessa from 1866 to 1868.

In all previous series, prices in the Crimea had surpassed those of Odessa. This was no longer the situation in 1866–68. Moreover, correlations in prices between the two ports had not been noticeably strong in previous tests. Now, the high correlation of .968 shows that prices in both ports were moving very much to the same rhythm, which was doubtlessly set by overseas demand.

Table 6 shows price movements at Odessa and the second Crimean port of Eupatoriia.

Table 4 Correlation Matrix: Movements of Wheat Prices in Six Ukrainian Towns

	Odessa	Nikopol'	Ielyzavethrad	Mohyliv	Bel'tsy	Proskuriv
Odessa		.943	.978	.968	.923	.949
Nikopol'	.943		.949	.971	.995	.939
Ielyzavethrad	.978	.949		.931	.937	.956
Mohyliv	.968	.971	.931		.957	.953
Bel'tsy	.923	.995	.937	.957		.947
Proskuriv	.949	.939	.956	.953	.974	

Source: Data in Table 3.

Table 5 Prices of Wheat at Feodosiia and Odessa, Monthly Averages, 1866–68

		Feodosiia	Odessa
1866	April	8.75	8.925
	August	9.5	10.68
	September	11.32	10.90
1867	July	9.0	11.00
	August	10.0	11.56
	September	11.0	12.87
	November	11.5	12.94
	December	12.12	11.12
1868	June	10.0	11.0
Average		10.35	11.22
Correlation		.968	

Source: Ianson, *Krim*, 70.

Table 6 Autumn Wheat Prices at Eupatoriia and Odessa, 1863–68

	Eupatoriia	Odessa
1863	7.5	8.5
1864	6.5	8.25
1865	7.0	8.62
1866	8.5	12.25
1867	10.5	14.0
1868	9.5 (summer)	11.5
Average	8.25	10.52
Correlation	.984	

Source: Ianson, *Krim*, 70.

In effect, the comparison with Eupatoriia supports the same conclusions as that with Feodosiia. The Crimea was no longer the area of South Ukraine where wheat prices were highest. Odessa, riding the ever expanding demand of foreign purchasers, now claimed that distinction. But the price movements in the two ports show closer coordination than we found when we compared prices at Feodosiia and Odessa.

Table 7 compares the two Crimean ports of Eupatoriia and Feodosiia, and extends the comparison to barley and oats.

Table 7 Indices of Autumn Cereal Prices at Eupatoriia and Feodosiia, 1865–68

	Eupatoriia			Feodosiia		
	Barley	Oats	Wheat	Barley	Oats	Wheat
1865	100	100	100	100	100	100
1866	142	125	121	138	166	135
1867	166	125	150	152	147	170
1868	150	161	125	180	166	156
Average	139.5	127.75	124	142.5	144.75	140.25
Correlation	.972	.972	.990			

Source: Ianson, *Krim*, 75.

The correlations are again very strong. The greater average costs of these cereals at Feodosiia primarily reflect the importance of the latter as an international exporter of grain.

The ports of South Ukraine gained renown on international markets primarily through the sale of wheat. Wheat flour was a relatively new item of export in the 1860s. Table 8 shows how prices of flour compared at Odessa and Feodosiia.

Table 8 Prices of Wheat Flour at Feodosiia and Odessa, 1865–67

		Feodosiia	Odessa
1865	Feb.	6.625	7.19
	March	7.0	7.19
	Nov.	6.75	8.16
1866	Feb.	6.875	8.12
	May	7.25	8.60
	Nov.	8.37	10.23
	Dec.	9.0	9.86
1867	April	8.875	9.64
	Oct.	8.75	10.9
	Nov.	9.0	9.86
	April	9.25	10.37
Average		7.97	9.13
Correlation		.984	

Source: Ianson, *Krim*, 71.

Here, the price advantage that Odessa was offering is even more substantial than with wheat—again a change from the earlier pattern. But the correlation of the two price lists is again very high, confirming the strength of the ties between them and with their common overseas purchasers.

D. The Turn of the Century

Connected whether by *chumaky* trails, by railroad, or by barge or coastal vessel, the cities of South Ukraine show clearly the primary characteristic of an integrated market already by the 1860s—the prices of the principal commodities show high correlations. But price levels also differed, reflecting the continuing high costs of transport. Table 9 shows us the pattern of wheat prices prevailing forty years later, at the turn of the nineteenth century, for the principal southern ports.

Table 9 Prices for a *Pud* of Winter Wheat, 1890–1909

	Rostov-on-the-Don	Taganrog	Mykolaiv	Odessa
1890–99	81.1	86.7	85.7	
1900–1904	84.4	88.4	88.4	102.0
1905	89.1	99.1	96.1	101.2
1906	94.9	95.1	90.9	95.2
1907	117.4	116.6	110.5	114.7
1908	136.4	129.0	125.6	132.8
1909	126.1	121.9	128.9	131.9
1910	109.1	108.1	97.8	110.7
Average	104.81	104.61	102.98	112.64
Index	93	93	92	100

Source: *Sbornik statistiko-ekonomicheskikh svedenii po sel'sknomu khoziaistvu Rossii i inostrannykh gosudarstv* (St. Petersburg, 1910 and 1912), 336, 420.

Table 10 Correlation Matrix: Wheat Prices

	Rostov-on-the-Don	Taganrog	Mykolaiv	Odessa
Rostov-on the Don		.996	.986	.984
Taganrog	.996		.976	.990
Mykolaiv	.986	.990		.994
Odessa	.984	.990	.994	

Source: Preceding table.

Table 11 compares the three guberniias of New Russia and two immediate neighbors.

Table 11 Prices for a *Pud* of Winter Wheat, 1901–1910

	Bessarabia	Kherson	Taurida	Katerynoslav	Don Cossack Territory
1901–1905	75	77	85	77	78
1906	67	74	77	79	106
1907	123	128	128	124	117
1908	120	123	123	120	116
1909	126	108	118	109	97
1910	80	88	90	88	90
Average	98.5	99.67	103.5	99.5	100.67

Source: Same as Table 2, 432.

Table 12 Correlation Matrix Prices of Winter Wheat, 1901–10

	Bessarabia	Kherson	Taurida	Katerynoslav	Don Cossack Territory
Bessarabia		.980	.989	.980	.890
Kherson	.980		.996	.998	.940
Taurida	.989	.996		.997	.935
Katerynoslav	.980	.998	.997		.955
Don Cossack Territory	.890	.940	.935	.955	

Source: Same as preceding table.

Price levels among these large regions had diminished to a maximum differential of 5 percent. And only the territory of the Don Cossacks shows less than maximum correlation in its price movements with its neighbors. The market for wheat in South Ukraine was now strongly integrated.

SUMMARY AND CONCLUSION

Over the course of the nineteenth century, South Ukraine gradually was integrated into a true economic region. The earliest data, dating from 1809–19, show a region of high cereal prices beyond the Ukrainian border to the north, in the Belarusian guberniia of Mahiliou; one of very cheap prices in the northeast Ukraine (Kharkiv and Poltava); and again one of expensive prices in the extreme south, in the Crimea. Apart from the Crimea, the guberniias of the southern and western Ukraine fall into no consistent pattern and certainly did not form a unified market.

By the 1850s, this pattern had been modified but not erased. The southern littoral had become unified as a zone of high wheat prices, and an intermediate zone of moderately priced markets had coalesced just to its north, and just below the zone where prices remained very low. To the far north beyond the Ukrainian borders, the guberniia of Mahiliou retained its now traditional status as a zone of costly food. In creating this pattern, the burgeoning demand for wheat emanating from the ports seems to have played the crucial role. The influence of the ports is especially manifest in the inflationary effects it had on prices at Katerynoslav. Formerly oriented toward the cheap markets of the northeast Ukraine, Katerynoslav by the late 1850s had been drawn into the zone of moderately priced markets supplying the port cities.

By the 1860s, the more detailed data that become available show that for a large region extending inland from the sea as far as Proskuriv and Mohyliv-on-the-Dnister the movements of wheat prices were highly correlated. The same region of like price movements extended along the Black Sea coast and through the Crimea. Price levels, however, in the various towns show considerable differences, reflecting the continuing high cost of carrying the wheat from inland areas to the ports serving the international trade. By the turn of the century, these differences were much reduced. Still, some differential remained, and the territory of the Don Cossacks was not tightly joined economically with the other South Ukrainian provinces.

The systems of transport and communications uniting the region still left room for substantial improvements. Nonetheless, it should be apparent that the nineteenth century was a period of remarkable growth and change in the markets of South Ukraine.

Notes

1. As Holland Hunter stated in the volume reporting on the first of these conferences, "Defining the boundaries of the economy is . . . a basic political question—one that economists usually assume has been settled before their analysis begins." I. S. Koropeckyj, ed., *Ukraine within the USSR: An Economic Balance Sheet* (New York: Praeger Publishers, 1977), 4.
2. E. I. Druzhinina, *Kiuchuk-Kainardzhiiskii mir: ego podgotovka i zakliuchenie* (Moscow: Akademiia nauk SSSR, 1955).
3. E. I. Druzhinina, *Iuzhnaia Ukraina v period krizisa feodalizma 1825–1860 gg.* (Moscow: Nauka, 1981), 15. For statistics concerning the percentage of Ukrainians in the total population of South Ukraine, see Myron Kordouba, *Le territoire et la population de l'Ukraine* (Berne: R. Suter, 1919), 27–32, 73–94.
4. Alfred Marshall, *Principles of Economics*, 8th ed. (New York and London: Macmillan, 1961), 324.
5. Ibid.
6. Marshall, *Principles*, 325.
7. For the use of grain prices in the measuring of market integration, see R. W. Unger, "Integration of Baltic and Low Countries Grain Markets, 1400–1800," in *The Interactions of Amsterdam and Antwerp with the Baltic Region, 1400–1800*, edited by J. M. van Winter (Leiden: M. Nijhoff, 1983), 1–10. Unger uses wheat and rye prices to test for the emergence of an integrated cereal market in the Baltic region and the Low Countries. See also John Hurd II, "Railways and the Expansion of Markets in India, 1861–1921," *Explorations in Economic History* 12 (1975): 263–88. Hurd uses wheat and rice prices to measure integration.
8. *Zhurnal Ministerstva vnutrennikh del*, vols. 15–38 (St. Petersburg, 1846–59).
9. *Sbornik statistiko-ekonomicheskikh svedenii po sel'skonomu khoziaistvu Rossii i inostrannykh gosudarstv* (St. Petersburg: Otdel sel'skoi ekonomii i sel'skokhoziaistvennoi statistiki, 1910–12).
10. Iu. Ianson, *Statisticheskoe issledovanie o khlebnoi torgovle v odesskom raione* (St. Petersburg, 1870), and his *Krim: ego khlebopashestvo i khlebnaia torgovliia* (St. Petersburg: V. Bezobrazov, 1870). For bibliography on grain and other prices, see T. F. Izmest'eva, "Istochniki po istorii tsen XIX–nachala XX veka," in *Massovye istochniki po sotsial'no-ekonomicheskoi istorii Rossii perioda kapitalizma* (Moscow: Nauka, 1979), 381–411.
11. I. D. Koval'chenko and L. V. Milov, *Vserossiiskii agrarnyi rynok XVIII–nachalo XX veka* (Moscow: Nauka, 1974). Also Boris Mironov, "Le mouvement des prix des céréales en Russie du XVIIIe siècle au debut du XXe siècle," *Annales: Economies, sociétés, civilisations* 41 (1986): 217–51. Mironov's work appeared after I had finished my own research. His analysis, emphasizing the importance of the foreign demand for wheat, differs quite sharply from that of Koval'chenko and Milov, and both his method and conclusions, while referring to the entire empire, are very similar to my own analysis of cereal prices in South Ukraine.
12. Koval'chenko and Milov, *Vserossiiskii agrarnyi rynok*, 219, note that the most important commercial cereal at Zhytomyr, Kamianets'-Podil's'kyi, Poltava, Kharkiv, and Kyiv was wheat, and that the export of wheat had been growing since the 1790s. The raising of wheat as a commercial crop in the *chornozem* regions in fact obstructed the development of the market for rye. "Only the powerful commercialization of wheat evidently overwhelmed the development of the market for rye." But should not this factor be given detailed examination in a study of the agrarian market?
13. On fairs in the Russian Empire, V. I. Denisov, *Iarmarki* (St. Petersburg: V. O. Kirschbaum, 1911); on Ukrainian fairs, I. Aksakov, *Issledovanie o torgovle na Ukrainskikh iarmarkakh* (St. Petersburg: Imp. Akademii nauk, 1858); on fairs in South Ukraine, Druzhinina, *Iuzhnaia Ukraina*, 177–80.

14 Denisov, *Iarmarki*, 5. By 1910 there were some 2,200 fairs in Ukraine, mostly minor ones of short duration.
15 Aksakov, *Issledovanie*, 47.
16 Ibid.
17 I. O. Hurzhii, *Ukraina v systemi vserosiis'koho rynku 60–90kh rokiv XIX st.* (Kyiv: Naukova dumka, 1968), 76.
18 Aksakov, *Issledovanie*, 48.
19 Ianson, *Statisticheskoe issledovanie*, i–iv.
20 Aksakov, *Issledovanie*, 40–42.
21 As late as 1917 no grain reached Kherson as railway freight. Some grain was handled by carts, but more than 40 percent of all grain arriving at Kherson was shipped from the river port of Oleksandrivs'k. Guy Michael, *Russian Experience, 1910–1917* (Privately published by Pauline M. D. Michael, 1979), 142.
22 V. A. Zolotov, *Khlebnyi eksport Rossii cherez porty Chernogo i Azovskogo morei v 60–90 gody XIX veka* (Rostov: Rostovskii gosudarstvennyi universitet, 1966), 49.
23 Ibid. For details on the railroads in South Ukraine, A. M. Solov'eva, *Zheleznodorozhnyi transport Rossii vo vtoroi polovine XIX v.* (Moscow: Nauka, 1975), 90–93; and 188–92. Also *Istoriia narodnoho hospodarstva Ukrains'koi RSR, Ekonomika dosotsialistychnykh formatsii*, vol. 1 (Kyiv: Naukova dumka, 1983): 265. For discussion of the inadequacies of railway transport to Odessa in this period, Lewis Siegelbaum, "The Odessa Grain Trade: A Case Study in Urban Growth and Development in Tsarist Russia," *The Journal of European Economic History* 9, no. 1 (1980): 129–30.
24 John Hurd II, "Railways," 263–88.
25 Koval'chenko and Milov, *Vserossiiskii agrarnyi rynok*, 71–72; the authors note that the procedure does not always yield satisfactory results.
26 These data are also partially used by Koval'chenko and Milov; see their comments on the quality of the reporting in *Vserossiiskii agrarnyi rynok*, 75–76. But they omit, as we have mentioned, all the references to wheat prices, which were items of great interest to those who collected the data. Their methods also invite some criticisms. To establish the yearly price for rye and oats, they took the prices for the three spring months and for the three autumn months, and averaged them together, to arrive at a "spring-autumn" price, which they argue best represents the true value of the respective cereals for the given year. When spring or autumn prices were missing, as unfortunately is often the case, they substituted the prices from contiguous summer or winter months. The procedure effectively reduces the number of observations from the full forty-one (though this is rarely found) to only ten, one per year. The chief criticisms that can be made about the procedure are two. First, it sacrifices data, as the observations for the summer and winter months enter only as substitutes, when they probably distort more than they supplement. The series is already very lacunose, and observations ought not to be wasted. Secondly, the wisdom of averaging elements within a time series before analyzing the series as a whole is very questionable. It has the result of smoothing the variations from one element to another—smoothing out the very fluctuations that the coefficient is supposed to be measuring. The argument they advance for this dubious strategy is that they need to remove seasonal fluctuations. This they do, but what about the most powerful fluctuation of all—the abundance of the yearly harvests? In other words, a high correlation of yearly prices may show not integrated markets but the fact that the weather was the same, and harvests comparable over large areas of the empire.

For these reasons, I believed it necessary to use these observations, including, of course, those bearing on wheat. The methods I used to adjust for seasonal fluctuations will be explained presently. The results of this effort to utilize the data were coefficients lower than those achieved by Koval'chenko and Milov. Still, researchers ought not to be beguiled by correlations in the .900s, and should not transform their data with that goal primarily in mind. Weak associations can be as interesting as strong.

Index

Note: Page numbers followed by 'n' refer to notes.

A

Abaza, A., 11, 31, 187, 189
Abramovitch, S. Y., *see* Mendele Moykher Sforim
Adler, Yacob, 199, 207n29, 208n48
Adrianople, 210
Adriatic, 196
Afghanistan War, 23
Africa, 218
Ahad Ha'am, 83–86, 88, 89, 95n2, 96, 205, 207n45, 208n58
    Al parashat derakhim (At the Crossroads), 88
Aivazovsky, Ivan K., 61
Akhmatova (Gorenko), Anna
    Requiem, 54
Akkerman, 232
Albanians, 2, 138
Aleppo, 210
Alexander I, 33, 124, 138, 147, 171, 180n27, 183, 184, 193n24, 201
Alexander II, 57, 68, 104
Alexander III, 125, 126, 195n62
Alexandria, viii, 2, 164, 210, 224n51
Alexandrovsky Palace, 38
All-Russian Imperial Census, 118
Altalena, *see* Jabotinsky, Vladimir
Amati, Caterina, 43
American South, 174
Amsterdam, 196, 244n7
Anatra, Anzhzelo, 11
Andreyev, Leonid, 53
Androsov, 184
Ansel'm, I. A., 11
Anselmi, Giuseppe, 43
An-sky, S., 89
    Dybbuk, The (Between Two Worlds), 89
Anthoine, Antoine Ignace, 135n54, 150n3
antirevolutionary, 53
antisemitism, 90, 93, 94
Aphrodite, 29, 182
Aprilov, Vasil, 55, 120, 132n9
Arab Cultural Center, 15, 18
Archangel Michael women's monastery, 14
Archeological Museum, 32, 33, 187, 194n42
Arensky, Anton, 43
Arezzo, 211
Argenti, Philip, 147, 151n35, 151n42, 152n54, 152n58, 152n60, 152n70, 159, 160, 164, 167n5
Argentina, 155, 233
Arkhangel'sk, 233
Armenian Apostolic Church of Saint Gregory the Teacher, 14, 17
Armenians, 24n5, 34, 37, 44, 57, 61, 130, 131, 134n18, 171, 198, 201
Arsh, Gregory, 132n8, 147, 150n2, 150n5, 150n7, 151n11, 151n16, 151n17, 151n18, 151n22, 151n24, 151n25, 152n80, 154, 166n2
Ashkenazi, 11, 26n21
Australia, 175
Austria-Hungary, 34
Austrian Empire, 210
Austrian Galicia, 14
Avierino family, 141, 160
Azov, Sea of, 51, 127, 137, 155, 160, 172, 218, 220, 238

B

Babel', Isaak (Isaac), 5, 25n11, 29, 42, 43, 45, 47–52, 57, 61, 62, 64, 64n6, 65n21, 65n29, 65n39, 65n42, 65n46, 65n53, 66n73, 66n80, 66n82, 66n84, 66n86, 66n90, 66n91, 83, 85, 90–94, 97, 114, 127, 135n45
    Konarmiia (The Red Cavalry), 92
    Odesskie rasskazy (Odessa Tales, Odessa Stories), 92
    Zakat (Sunset), 92
Babyi Yar, 75
Bagritsky (Dziubin), Eduard, 52, 91, 92, 94, 96
    Duma pro Opanasa (Lay of Opanas), 92
    Fevral' (February), 92
    Proiskhozhdenie (Origin), 92
Baiul, Oksana, 62
Bakhtin, Mikhail, 13, 52, 66n63
Baldasseroni, G., 152n43, 224n43
Balkovs'ka Street, 15

Balta, 114n37, 180n33, 232, 238
Baltic Sea, 182
Barkai (The Morning Star), 87
Baroque style, 39, 171, 186, 189, 190
Baruchello, M., 135n50, 152n61, 212, 222n9, 223n25, 223n27
Batiushkov, Konstantin, 5, 41
Battistini, Mattia, 43
Bay of Odessa, 7
Bazarna Street, 189
Beethoven, Ludwig van, 52
Beirut, 210
Belarus, 89, 243
Belarusians, 34, 118, 123
Bel'tsy, 239, 240
Ben-Ami, 85
Ben-Tsiyon, S., 86
Berdians'k, 215, 220
Berlin, 89, 132n3, 178n5, 193n29, 206
Bernardazzi, Alexander, 12, 60, 186, 190, 192n19
Bessarabia, 30, 187, 194n55, 217, 232, 236–238, 242, 243
Bialik, Haim Nahman, 85, 86, 88, 89, 91, 205, 208n58
 Be'ir Hahareigah (City of Slaughter), 89
 El Hatzipor (To the Bird), 89
Bilaniuk, Laada, 79, 81n17, 81n20, 82n38
Bilhorod-Dnistrovs'kyi, *see* Akkerman
Binshteyn, Arkady, *see* Lvov, Arkady
Black Sea, viii, ix, 5, 16, 23, 25n6, 25n10, 25n16, 27, 29, 32, 33, 37, 41, 54, 55, 57, 61, 83, 100, 119, 121, 127, 132n4, 133n14, 135n44, 137, 144, 145, 150, 153n87, 154, 155, 160, 165, 166, 166n1, 170, 172, 173, 178n3, 180n35, 182, 184, 186, 192n1, 192n9, 196–199, 204, 209, 211–221, 222n17, 223n30, 226, 229, 231, 239, 243
Black Sea Cossack Host, 23
Blackwell, William L., 171, 179n10, 180n32
Boffo, Francesco, 6, 7, 37–39, 184, 185, 192n15, 192n19, 193n19, 193n25, 193n26
Bolsheviks, 6, 12, 19, 33, 46, 48, 52, 53, 60, 74, 87, 160, 161, 166
Bombay, 150
Bordeaux, 196
Borinevich, A. S., 188
Borinevich, S., 178
Borsa (of Trieste), 200, 201
Boston, viii, 25, 65n17, 103, 104, 108, 110, 114n22, 114n40, 115n68, 180n35, 222n17
Braila, 127, 148
Breslau, 150n4, 178n3, 199, 222n19
Bristol Hotel, 190
Brodskii, Avram, 189, 205
Brody, 13, 56, 85, 199, 203
Brody Synagogue, 194n52
Brussels, 101
Brzezinski, A., 189, 194n42
Buber, Martin, 88
Buchanan, James, 144
Bucharest, viii, ix, 25n6, 108

Budapest, 108
Buh, 107, 137, 231, 232
Building Committee of Odessa, 184, 185
Bulgarians, 2, 15, 56, 120, 123, 132n9, 171
Bul'varnyi (neighborhood), 109, 157
Bund, 56, 57
Bunin, Ivan, 53
Buonavoglia, Luigi, 41
Butenev, Ivan, 224n64
Butyrskii, K., 184
Byron, George Gordon, 89

C
Cairo, 2
Calcutta, 128, 150
Cambiaggio, Luigi, 7
Cambridge (United Kingdom), 101
Canada, 155, 172, 233
Candelis, George, 187
Caruso, Enrico, 43
Catalan, Tullia, 197, 206n7, 208n53
Cathedral of the Transfiguration, 14, 15
Cathedral Square, 14, 33, 38
Catherine II, 2, 3, 18, 19, 27, 28, 33, 52, 74, 75, 80n6, 80n8, 100, 124, 130, 137, 170, 180n27, 182, 197, 200, 206n10, 206n12, 206n14, 206n17, 207n38, 209
Catherine Square, 19
Caucasus, 24, 25n6, 46, 47, 113n18, 114n28
Central Asia, 47
Cervantes, Miguel de, 89
Chaliapin, Fedor, 43, 49
Chapayev, V. I., 46
Chapman, S. D., 146, 151n41, 152n64, 153n88
Charles VI, 201
Chekhov, Anton, 51, 53
Cherkunov, F., 192n19
Chernihiv, 229, 233, 235, 237
Chernivtsi, 13
Chernoivanenko, Oleg, 19
Chesma (1770), 211
Chichagov, Vasilii, 211
Children of the Age, 47
Chios, 48, 127, 141, 142, 145, 146, 160, 161, 164, 193n34
Chizhov, N., 2, 24n5
Chornobyl (Chernobyl), 23
Chudak, 52
Church of Saints Adrian and Natalia, 14
Church of Saint Gregory the Illuminator, 14
Church of Saint Gregory the Theologian, 14
Church of Sturdza Charitable Community, 14
Church of the Holy Trinity, 163
Church of the Presentation of Christ, 193n19
Civil War, Russian, 13, 46–48, 50–54, 91
Classical style, 39, 183, 185
Clemens, Samuel, 129
Club of the Merry and Witty (KVN), 6
Cologne, 101

Constantinople, 25n6, 48, 140, 143, 160, 167n5, 210, 212, 215
Continental Blockade, 3
Corinthian columns, 38, 184
Corriere Italiano, Il, 181n46, 218, 225n69
Crimea, ix, 25, 47, 113n4, 113n10, 113n15, 113n18, 115n53, 133n14, 137, 170, 179n6, 179n9, 179n14, 197, 198, 226, 228, 231, 232, 236, 238–240, 243
Crimean War, 11, 124, 127, 144, 147, 148, 155, 160, 173–175, 187, 193n35, 203, 215, 218–220, 226
Curtis, William E. 132n4, 153n87

D

Dall'Aqua (Dalakva), Gaetano, 7, 192n19
Dal'nyts'kyi neighborhood, 157
Dante
  Inferno, 91
Dantsig, M., 205
Danzig, 13, 108, 210
Dardanelles, 210
De Ribas, Alexander, 30, 64n9, 135n55, 192n6, 194n58
De Ribas, Felix, 11
De Ribas, Joseph (Jose), 7, 21, 22, 28, 182, 200
De Ribas, Michele, 64n8
De Wollant, François, 7, 19, 20, 25n15, 29, 64n4, 80n1, 182–184
Dearborn, Henry S., 25n6, 180n35, 222n17
Decembrist revolt, 55
Déjà vu, 48
Dement'ev, 11
Demidoff San Donato, *see* Demidov, P. P.
Demidov, P. P., 125, 140
Den' (The Day), 87
Denmark, 34
Derybasivs'ka Street, 11, 21, 22, 53, 148, 162, 193n19, 194n42
Detskoe Selo, 184
Di Grasso, 43
Di Yidishe Folksbibliotek, 90
Diment, Galya, 64
Dimo, Egor, 149
Dimo, Sotiri, 149
Dimo, Vladimir, 149
Dlugach, Mikhail, 61
Dmytrenko, Iu. M., 32, 188, 190
Dnipro (Dnieper), 137, 200, 229, 231, 232
DniproHES, 5
Dnipropetrovsk, 229
Dnister, 107, 108, 231, 232
Dobroe Delo, 95
Don Cossacks territory, 242, 243
Donetsk, 172
Doric columns, 11, 38, 184, 190
Drewe, Samuel, 216
Druzhinina, E. I., 135n56, 141, 150n1, 151n34, 178n3, 179n16, 192n3, 199, 207n21, 244n2, 244n3
Dubin, Lois, 196, 197, 200, 201, 203, 205, 206n2, 206n3, 207n32, 207n34, 207n40, 208n49

Dubnow, Simon, 84, 85, 206n1, 207n39
Duc de Richelieu, Armand Emmanuel, 22, 32–34, 105, 107, 114n33, 114n34, 128, 139, 179n6, 183, 188, 200, 201
Dziubin, Eduard Godelevich, *see* Bagritsky (Dziubin), Eduard

E

Earle, Hobart, 16, 82n40
East Indies, 142, 144
Edda, 89
Edicts of Toleration, 197
Edison Company, 40, 186
Efrusi company, 11, 208n46
Egyptian, 171, 215, 216
Eisenstein, Sergei
  Battleship Potemkin, The, 39, 47, 74, 185
Elman, Mischa, 42, 43
Emigrants, 2, 121, 155, 200
English, 2, 30, 33, 89, 102, 107, 108, 110, 120, 127, 129, 130, 132n2, 139, 140, 143, 144, 148, 160, 171, 176, 184, 189, 190, 193n19, 198, 203, 212, 214, 216, 218
English Club, 184, 190, 193n19
Enikale, 139
Ethnic diversity, 2
Eupatoria, 220
Europe, 2, 7, 11–13, 23, 39, 52, 54, 59, 64n2, 81n10, 82n32, 86, 100, 103, 104, 106, 114n32, 115n43, 128, 134n41, 136n67, 138, 143–146, 148, 154, 160, 166, 171, 176, 182, 183, 186, 192n10, 198, 203, 208n46, 209, 210, 219, 221, 226
Evangelical Lutheran Church, 15
Exchange Square, 31, 187

F

Fainzilberg, Ilya, *see* Il'f, Ilya
Fal'ts-Fein family, 11
Fedor, Thomas S., 103
Fellner, Ferdinand, 39, 186, 189
Feodosiia, 61, 237–241
Ferdinand I, Grand Duke, 210
Filiki Eteria, 18, 54, 160
Finkel', M. I., 111, 115n42, 134n40
First Turkish War (1768–74), 197, 211
First World War, *see* World War I
Fishel', T. L., 190
Five-Year Plan, 48
Flaubert, Gustave, 92
Florence, 171, 175, 179n14, 211, 215, 218, 219
Florentine mosaics, 188
Fontana, 163
Forni, O., 224n50
Fournier, Anna, 77, 81n10, 81n23
France, 9, 32, 34, 103, 113n11, 135n56, 136n58, 144, 145, 163, 179n6, 183, 192n13, 213, 219, 220, 223n29, 223n31
Franko, Ivan, 76
Frantsuz'kyi Boulevard, 11

Frapolli, Francesco, 7, 184
Frapolli, Giovanni, 7
Freeze, ChaeRan, 202, 207n42
French, 2, 15, 24n5, 29–32, 34, 37, 41, 47, 48, 50, 54–56, 62, 82n40, 84, 89, 92, 93, 102, 107, 120, 125, 128, 129, 131, 132n2, 135n58, 136n60, 137, 139, 140, 141, 143, 146, 148, 151n29, 151n31, 165, 171, 175, 176, 179n6, 181n48, 181n51, 183, 187, 194n54, 198, 199, 203, 204, 219, 223n29, 223n31
French Benevolent Society, 129
Frey & Co., 186

G

Galați, 148, 219
Galicia, 2, 14, 56, 84, 124
Garibaldi, Giuseppe, 55, 129
Gąsiorowski, Felix, 12, 31, 194n42
Geneva, 54, 86
Gentile, 56, 59, 116n90, 119, 126
Georgians, 34, 130
Germans, 2, 24n5, 119, 123, 131, 135n53, 157–159, 193n30, 198, 203
Germany, 13, 34, 110, 125, 143, 147, 219
Gerschenkron, Alexander, 191
Gherardi, Francesco, 211
Gibraltar, 212, 224n50
Gilgamesh, 89
Ginzburg, Asher Zvi, *see* Ahad Ha'am
Gladkov, M. R., 189
Glazunov, 43
Glinka, Mikhail, 40, 186
Goethe, Johann Wolfgang, 89, 211
Gogol, Nikolai
    Dead Souls, 122, 134n19
Gogol Street, viii, 184
Golden Child, 23
Golden Duke Film Festival, 6
Gopsewich commercial house, 220
Gorbachev, Mikhail, 12, 13
Goren, Natan, 208n58
Gorky, A. M., 188
Gourfinkel, Nina, 186, 192n11, 193n31
Great Patriotic War, *see* World War II
Greek, 2, 7, 8, 11, 15, 18, 24n5, 25n16, 26n17, 27, 30, 32, 34, 36, 48, 50, 54, 56, 57, 64, 82n40, 84, 85, 89, 119, 120, 124, 127–129, 131, 134n18, 135n53, 137–167, 170, 171, 176, 182, 187, 188, 193n38, 198, 199, 201, 203–205, 208n47, 208n48, 214, 217
Greek Bazaar, 8
Greek revival style, 32, 188
Griboyedov, Alexander
    Woe from Wit, 40, 186
Guadalquivir, 3
Gubar', Oleg, *see* Hubar, Oleh
Gudok (The Whistle), 92
Gurovich firm, 208n46
Gut Morgn, 87
Gypsies, 44

H

Habsburg Empire, 201, 215
Hamburg, 210, 219
Ha'melitz, 86, 90
Hanseatic League, 13
Ha'Olam (This World), 86
Happy-Go-Lucky Guys, 5, 45
Harris, Edmund G., 30, 187
Ha'Shiloach, 86
Haskalah (Jewish Enlightenment), 56, 57, 84–86, 89, 196–199, 201–204, 206n2, 208n55
Hebrew, 47, 83, 85–92, 124, 134n32, 205, 206, 208n55
Heine, Heinrich, 89
Helmer, Hermann, 39, 186
Helmer and Fellner, 39, 186, 189
Herzen, Alexander, 121
Hitler, Adolf, 75
Holderness, Mary, 25n6, 103, 179n7, 179n9, 180n28
Holovatyi, Otaman Antin, 23
Holy Brotherhood, 58
Horace, 89
House of Culture, 189
House of
    Camo, 193n19
    De Ribas, F., 11
    Julien, 193n19
    Khorvt, 193n19
    Kramarev, M., 11
Hovevei Zion (Lovers of Zion), 86, 87, 89
Hrets'ka Street, 11
Hromada, 54
Hrytsak, Yaroslav, 79
Hubar, Oleh, vii, ix, 64, 25n13, 26n18, 26n19, 26n24, 26n26, 66n93, 80n2
Humbourg, A., 224n50

I

Iakovlev, Ia. A., 153n80, 153n86, 153n89, 188
Iannopulo, Vasilii, 30, 138
Ianson, Iuli E., 228, 239, 244n10, 245n19
Iatsenko, I. F., 188
Ielysavethrad (Kirovohrad), 229
Il'f, Ilya
    Golden Calf, 52, 61, 66n85, 93
    Odnoetazhnaia Amerika (One-Storied America), 93
    "Trip to Odessa," ix, 52
    Twelve Chairs, 22, 52, 92
Imperial Horticultural Society, 32, 164, 188
Imperial Hotel, 194n42
Inber, Vera
    Almost Three Years, 54
India, 57, 110, 150, 160, 233, 244n7
Inglesi, Dimitrios, 30, 138, 148, 149
International Club of Odessites, 6
Irish, 28, 182, 200
Italian Renaissance, 16, 39, 186, 190

Italians, 2, 9, 15, 20, 24n5, 27, 29, 30, 32, 34, 37, 40, 41, 43, 44, 55–57, 61, 82n40, 84, 101, 102, 120, 129, 136n62, 138, 139, 140, 145, 146, 162, 165, 171, 175, 176, 179n14, 179n17, 183, 186, 188, 189, 194n42, 194n52, 198, 199, 201–204, 210–212, 220
Italy, 9, 34, 41, 129, 136n61, 163, 171, 179n14, 211, 216, 220
Ivano-Frankivs'k, 13

J

Jabotinsky, Vladimir, 27, 35–37, 56, 58, 62, 64, 64n2, 64n13, 64n14, 66n71, 66n89, 83, 84, 91, 208n55
    Five, The (Piatero), 83, 91
    Samson Nazarei, 91
Jewish Cemetery, 23, 124
Jewish Hospital, 189
Jewish Legion, 91
Jewish orphanage, 189
Jews, 2, 5, 13, 15, 23, 32–34, 36, 40, 42, 44, 46, 56–59, 64, 64n15, 65n19, 66n69, 66n72, 82n40, 83–87, 89–94, 118, 119, 124–127, 131, 132n7, 133n11, 133n16, 134n23, 134n37, 134n41, 135n42, 139, 140, 149, 150, 153n85, 153n86, 153n87, 156–158, 176, 177, 189, 196–208, 214
Joseph II, Habsburg, 197, 200, 201, 207n33
Journal de St. Pétersbourg, 147, 152n75
Journal d'Odessa, 30, 115n56, 115n72, 128, 134n27, 134n28, 135n49, 135n55, 151n15, 151n36, 152n66, 153n83, 172, 178n5, 179n15, 180n24

K

Kabiol'skii, Vil'gel'm, 12
Kadima (Forward), 88
Kalevala, 89
Kamianets'-Podil's'kyi, 238, 244n12
Kandinsky, Wassily, 61
Kankrin, E. F., 173
Kartamyshevs'ka Street, 15
Kataev, Valentin
    White Sails Gleam, 22, 60
Katayev, Evgenii, *see* Petrov, Evgenii
Katerynoslav, 30, 62, 187, 226, 229, 232, 235–238, 242, 243
Katerynyns'ka Square, 9, 20
Katerynyns'ka Street, 14, 39, 185, 193n23
Kaufman, Bel, 42
Kaulbars, W., 41
Kaveret (Beehive), 86
Kazik, Anatolii, 5
Kerch, 139, 220
Khadzhibei, 29, 75, 83, 170, 178n2
Kharkiv, 13, 76, 78, 229, 232, 235–238, 243, 244n12
Kherson, 30, 78, 109, 118, 128, 137, 157, 187, 200, 220, 226, 231, 232, 235–238, 242, 243, 245n21
Khersons'ka Square, 8, 15
Khersons'kyi neighborhood, 109, 157
Kholodna, Vira, 22, 23, 47

Khrushchev, Nikita, 25n10
Kivan, Adnan, 15
Klausner, Joseph, 83, 86
Klein, Roman, 188
klezmorim, 44
Kniazyk, Oleksandr, 21, 23
Koble, 7
Kol mevasser (The Herald), 87, 90
Kolokol, 121, 133n12, 133n14
Königsberg, 108
Konsta, Lysander, 164, 167n24
Korolenko Street, *see* Sofiivs'ka Street
Kotsebu, Pavel E., 33
Koval'chenko, I. D., 228, 233, 235, 236, 244n11, 244n12, 245n25, 245n26
Kozachinsky, Alexander, 19
Kozak, Anatolii, 25n9, 45, 65n27
Kozlov, E., 192n19
Krakhmalnikov, Abram Wolf, 60
Krakhmalnikov Brothers, 60
Kramarev, M., 11
Krastov, Oleksandr
    Mikhail Vorontsov, 33, 122, 172, 184, 200
Krayzelburg, Lenny, 62
Kremenchuk, 229, 232, 238
Kronstadt, 211
Kryvyi Rih, 78, 172, 177
Kumbaris, Alexander, 138
Kuprin, Alexander, 41, 51, 61, 62, 65n17, 65n54, 66n83
    "Ballroom Piano Player, The," 51
    "Gambrinus," 41, 51
    "Miraculous Doctor," 51
    "My Flight," 51
    Yama (The Pit), 51
Kuzio, Taras, 77, 81n25
Kyiv, 6, 13, 47, 54, 75, 76, 79, 80n4, 81n22, 82n36, 108, 121, 125, 145, 163, 235–238, 244n12

L

Lakhnenko, 123
Langada, Mikhail, 160
Langada Sutsos, Helen, 160, 166, 167n8
Langeron, de, Louis Alexandre (Alexander F.), 7, 32, 33, 128, 139, 183, 192n19
Laocoön, 20
Large Fountain, 23
Lashkarev, L., 11
Last Tango, The, 47
Latin, 89
Latti, 184
Lavrov, Sergei, 75
Le Havre, 108
Leipzig, 8, 196, 199, 201n1
Levinsky, Elhanan, 85–87
    A Trip to the Land of Israel in the 800th Year of the Sixth Millennium, 86
Liban, 11

Libman, 12
Life for Life, 47
Lilienblum, Moshe, 57, 85
Linder, Max, 47
Lisbon, 61, 224n50
Literary Museum, 6, 19, 80n1, 187
Liverpool, 108
Livorno, 30, 127–129, 135n50, 136n65, 140, 143–148, 152n61, 162, 196, 209–225
Lobanov-Rostovskii, Alexander, 144
London, 33, 51, 54, 60, 104, 107, 114n39, 121, 128, 134n32, 135n48, 142, 143, 151n30, 152n76, 153n85, 160, 161, 179n17, 180n25, 190, 196, 214
London Hotel, The, 51, 190
Louis XVI style, 40, 186
Low Countries, 34, 244n7
Lübeck, 210
Luhansk, 78
Lustdorf, 54
L'viv, 13, 14, 76
Lvov, Arkady
    Dvor, 60, 93

M

Madariaga, Isabel de, 198, 206n10, 206n16, 207n33
Madonna with Child, 44
Magnitogorsk, 5
Mahiliou (Mahiliou-on-the-Dnipro), 233, 235–237, 239, 243
Mahs (Maas), A. E., 188, 194n45
Mahs Section (of almshouse), 188
Main Synagogue, 14, 95
Maiorov, A. I., 11
Mala Arnauts'ka Street, 15
Malta, 140, 209, 212, 223n29
Manchester, 108, 135n41, 143, 214
Marazli, Grigorii (Gregory), 18, 30–32, 138, 141, 162, 163, 187, 188, 193n35, 193n38, 205
Maria Carolina of Sicily, 29
Maria Theodorovna Orphanage, 32, 188
Maria Theresa of Habsburg, 196, 197, 200, 205, 206n7
Marini, house of, 12
Mariupol', 137, 160, 215, 220, 232
Mark Twain, *see* Clemens, Samuel
Marseille, 30, 64, 140, 142, 143, 146, 160, 179, 209, 212, 223n29, 223n31, 224n50
Martos, I. P., 37, 39, 185, 192n19, 193n22
Marx, Karl, 74, 214, 223n38
Marxism–Leninism, 84, 175
Maupassant, Guy de, 47, 92
Mavrokordato, Catherine, 147, 161
Mavrokordato, Constantine, 161
Mavrokordato, Dmitri, 160
Mavrokordato, Erato, 162
Mavrokordato family, 160
Mavrokordato, George, 161
Mavrokordato, John, 161
Mavrokordato, Laurenzi, 160
Mavrokordato, Matthew, 161
Mavros, Alexander, 30, 138
May Laws (1882), 125, 134n37
Mayakovsky, Vladimir, 52
McKay, John P., 136n60, 177, 181n57
Mechnikov, I. I., 32, 188
Mediterranean, viii, 3, 7, 30, 59, 127, 128, 142, 143, 146, 148, 150, 176, 177, 178n3, 186, 196, 197, 199, 206n10, 209–216, 218, 220, 224n50
Medvedev, Dmitry, 75, 94
Mel'nikov, A. I., 37, 184, 185
Mendele Moykher Sforim, 48, 85, 88, 89, 94
    Di Klyatshe, 94
    Dos Kleyne Mentshele (The Little Man), 90
    Fishke der Krumer (Fiske the Lame), 90
    Funem yarid (Back from the Fair), 90
    Ha'avot vehabanim (Fathers and Sons), 88
    Kol kitve Mendele Mokher Sefarim, 88
    Limdu hetev (Learn to Do Good), 88
Mendelevich, 11
Mendelssohn, Felix, 41
Mensheviks, 59
Mesner, Eduard, 12
Messager, 128
Mickiewicz, Adam, 18, 41
Mikhalkov, Nikita
    Slave of Love, 47
Milan, 101
Milov, L. V., 228, 233, 235, 236, 244n11, 244n12, 245n25, 245n26
Minkovskii, Pinkhas, 40
Miron, Dan, 65n16, 83
Mironov, Boris, 244n11
Mohyliv (Mohyliv-on-the-Dnister), 229, 239, 240, 243
Moldavanka, 32, 43, 45–49, 59, 60, 85, 92, 188, 204
Molière, 89
Montferrand, Auguste, 37
Montovani, Giovanni, 43
Monument to the Reader, 19
Morandi, Francesco, 7, 38, 39, 184, 186
Mordvinians, 34
Mori, G., 211, 222n3, 223n26
Moriconi, Adelaide, 43
Moscow, 34, 41, 46, 51–53, 55, 60–62, 75, 76, 81n11, 91, 92, 94, 101, 104, 108, 112, 118–121, 124, 132n2, 132n3, 132n6, 145, 171, 193n22, 229
Moskvich, Grigorii, 103, 113n8
Municipal Theater, 186
Museum of Western and Eastern Art, 189
Mussorgsky, Modest
    Boris Godunov, 40, 186
Mykhailivs'kyi Cathedral, 193n19
Mykhailivs'kyi neighborhood, 157
Mykolaiv, 78, 132n4, 137, 160, 161, 171, 232, 242

N

Naples, 28–30, 182, 200, 224n50
Napoleonic Wars, 103, 138, 146, 203, 209, 217, 226

Napravnik, E., 43
Naryshkin, Lev Aleksandrovich, 31
Naryshkina, M. A., 39, 185, 193n24
NATO, 14, 80
Nebolsin, G. P., 175
Negri, Cesare, 41
Negroponte family, 142, 160, 164
Neizvestny, Ernst, 23
Neoclassical style
　French neoclassical style, 31, 187
Nesselrode, Karl, 219, 224n64
Nesturkh, F. P., 10, 188
Netherlands, 110, 116n74
New Bazaar, 8
New Economic Policy (NEP), 46, 48, 92, 93
New Exchange (Bourse), 38, 184, 190, 191
New Orleans, 44, 107, 108, 115n69, 178n1
New Russia, *see* Novorossiia
New York City, 90, 110, 135n41
Nicholas I, 33, 39, 55, 90, 92, 121, 177, 185, 189, 204, 218
Nicholas I Commercial School, 92, 194n42
Nicholas II, 59, 164
Nikopol', 231, 232, 239, 240
Nogai Tatars, 32
Norman, John, 191, 195n62
North Ukraine, 229
Norway, 3, 34
Novgorod, 62
Novorossiia (New Russia), ix, 25n6, 25n7, 29, 33, 103, 114n35, 120, 122, 124, 128, 130, 132n1, 133n14, 135n48, 140, 145, 149, 151n26, 151n28, 170–182, 192n3, 194n55, 197–199, 203, 207n33, 217, 221n1, 222n21, 236, 242
Novorossiiskii kalendar' (*New Russian Calendar*), 33, 164
Novosel'skii, Nikolai A., 200
Novosel's'koho Street, 15
Nusah, 88
Nusah Odesa, 88

O

Odessa-Brody pipeline, 13
Odessa Circle, 55
Odessa Conservatory, 42, 43
Odessa Discount Bank, 145, 149, 161
Odessa (English) Club, 184
Odessa Greek commercial school, 30, 139, 164
Odessa Herald (*Odesskii vestnik*), 33, 85, 121
Odessa Literary Museum, 187
Odessa Municipal Credit Society, 187
Odessa Opera, 39, 43, 185
Odessa Philharmonic Orchestra, 16, 42, 190
Odessa Studio, 47
Odessa University, 32, 163, 188
Odesskii listok, 91
Odysseus, 27, 170
Oistrakh, David, 42

Old Bazaar, 8, 43, 63
Oleksandrivs'k (Zaporizhzhia), 231, 245n21
Olesha, Yuri, 30, 46, 51–54, 59, 61, 62, 64n10, 65n38, 65n56, 65n57, 65n58, 66n60, 66n65, 66n67, 66n77, 66n88
　Envy, 51, 61, 62
Ol'via, 11
Opera House (City Theater), 37, 39–41, 44, 186, 193n29, 193n31
　First Opera House, 39, 147, 185, 190
Orange That Saved Odessa, The, 19
Orlov, 135n47, 150n10, 167n10, 178n2, 184, 192n5, 207n20
Ottoman Empire, 182, 197, 210
Otton, L., 187, 189

P

Palace of
　Brzezinski, 194n42
　Mochevski, 194n42
　Rzewuski, 194n42
　Sabanski, 194n42
Palace of Sailors, 7
Palais-Royale, 190
Pale of Settlement, 56, 58, 84, 94, 198
Paleologos, Dimitrios, 30, 138
Palestine, 57, 84, 87–89, 91
Palladian, 32, 187
Panama Railroad Company, 143
Pantikapea, 11
Papahajis, Kyriakos, 138
Papudov, 11, 30, 162, 167n13
Pardes, 86
Parini, Pietro, 222n11
Paris, 32, 44, 45, 54, 55, 60, 91, 101, 114n29, 121, 134n31, 136n58, 144, 147, 151n27, 160, 161, 165, 166, 179n17, 180n35, 223n29
Passage, 27, 41, 190
Passage Hotel, 190
Pastera Street (Kherson's'ka), 15, 32, 38, 185, 188
Pasternak, Boris, 61
Pasternak, Leonid, 61
Paul I, 18, 29, 138
Paustovskii, Konstantin, 5, 25n11, 46, 48, 50, 52, 54, 61
People's Will, 54, 55
Perekop, 232
Persia, 25, 34, 142, 144
Persian Revolution (1909), 189
Peter I (Peter the Great), 137, 182
Peter III, 198
Petrenko, Victor, 62
Petrocochino family, 161
Petropavlovs'kyi neighborhood, 109, 157
Petrov, Evgenii
　Golden Calf, 52, 61, 66n85, 93
　Twelve Chairs, 22, 52, 92
Piatigorsk, 190
Pieruzzini, Giorgio, 218

Pinsker, Lev (Leon), 57, 86, 87
    Autoemancipation, 57
Pipes, Richard, 197, 206n12
Plock, 13
Podillia, 30, 145, 187, 237, 238
Pogrom, ix, 28, 35, 48, 57, 58, 85–87, 89, 91, 94, 125, 203, 204, 208n46
Poland, 2, 13, 26n20, 51, 56, 84, 136n68, 151n39, 170, 194n42, 200, 207n39, 216
Polish, 18, 29, 41, 44, 47, 51, 54, 80n2, 85, 120, 123, 124, 131, 133n14, 134n18, 174, 189, 197
    landlords, 2, 11, 134n21, 172–175, 181n43
    uprising, 54, 120, 189
Poltava, 229, 235–238, 243, 244n12
Port Jews, 196–208
Port neighborhood, 157
porto-franco, 13
Potapov, 184
Potemkin (battleship), 59
Potemkin, Grigorii, 19, 80n1, 207n33
Potemkin mutiny, 74, 121
Potemkin Steps, 12, 39, 185, 186, 191
"Potemkin villages," 200
Potier, K. I., 183
Potocki, Stanislav-Felix, 187
Prague, 104
Preobrazhens'ka Street, 11, 22, 23, 162
Proskuriv (Khmel'nyts'kyi), 231, 239, 240, 243
Prosvita, 54
Provence, 3
Prymors'kyi Boulevard, 6, 20, 32, 37–40, 51, 59, 183–186, 189–191
Pseudo-gothic style, 39, 185, 189
Pushkin, Alexander
    Eugene Onegin, 41, 101, 105, 113n13, 171, 179n13
Pushkin Street, 20, 164, 187, 189, 190
Putin, Vladimir, 75, 76

Q
Quarenghi, Giacomo, 37

R
Rabelaisian model, 13, 52, 92
Rabinovich, Mark, *see* Ben-Ami
Rabinovich, Osip, 87, 90
    Istoriia o tom, kak reb Khaim-Shulim Feiges puteshestvoval iz Kishineva v Odessu, i chto s nim sluchilos' (The History of How Reb Khaim-Shulim Feiges Traveled from Kishinev to Odessa and What Happened with Him), 90
    Kaleidoscope, 90
    Shtrafnoi (Penal Recruit), 90
Rafalovich, A., 11, 104, 105, 111, 113n6, 208n46
Raftopoulos family, 161
Raikin, Arkady, 93
Ralli, Ambrose, 143
Ralli family, 128, 135n52, 142–145, 160
Ralli, John (Zannis), 142
Ralli, Lucas Eustratius, 143
Ralli, Paul, 135n52, 145, 149, 161
Ralli, Stephen, 135n52, 162, 174
Rape of Europe, The, 23
Rassvet (Dawn), 87
Ravnitsky, Y. H., 85, 86, 90
Reformed Church, 15
Remisnycha Street, 14
Renaissance style, 16, 190
Ressel, Demian von, 41
Revolution of 1905, 38, 66n76, 208n51
Revolution of 1917, 54, 94, 176, 191
Rhind, Charles, 143
Rhodes, 210
Riabchyns'ka, Yuliia, 62
Riccardi, Riccardo, 210
Ricci, Giuseppe, 200
Richelieu, Duc de, 7, 10, 11, 20, 22, 32–34, 38, 39, 52, 103–105, 107, 114n33, 114n34, 128, 135n56, 137–139, 170, 179n6, 183, 185, 188, 200–202
Richelieu Lyceum, 104, 139, 170, *see also* University of Novorossiia
Richter, Svyatoslav, 43
Riga, 25, 179n7, 197
Rimsky-Korsakov, Nikolai Andreevich, 43
Rinaldi, Adelanda, 43
Risheliеvs'ka Street, 14, 15, 18, 58
Risorgimento, 129, 136n61, 178n5, 215, 221n1
Rodokanaki family, 127, 135n50, 145–147, 152n61
Rodokanaki, Fedor, 162
Rodokanaki, Michael, 127, 145
Rodokanaki, Paul, 146
Rodokanaki, Pericles, 147, 164
Roman Catholic Church, 194n52
Romania, 34, 48
Romny, 229
Roosevelt, Theodore, 193n38
Rossini, Gioachino, 41
    Barber of Seville, 129
Rostov-on-the-Don, 60, 62, 103, 125, 142, 144, 151n19, 160, 161, 238, 242
Rothstein, Robert A., 25n8, 47, 64n1, 65n24, 65n26, 65n30, 65n35, 65n41, 65n50, 66n90
Rotterdam, 110
Rozenkern, Peter, 45
Rubin, Julius, 174, 180n39
Rubinstein, Anton, 41–43
Ruffo, Titta, 43
Rumiantsev, P., 198
Russell, J. C., 172, 174, 179n18
Russia, 2, 3, 7, 11, 18, 25n5, 25n6, 28, 29, 33, 34, 37, 41, 44, 52, 53, 56–58, 61, 64n1, 75, 76, 82n32, 82n37, 82n40, 82n42, 83–85, 89, 91, 105, 113n3, 114n23, 117, 121, 122, 130, 132n1, 132n5, 133n14, 136n61, 137, 141, 144, 153n85, 154, 155, 161, 164, 165, 170, 171, 174, 176, 177, 178n5, 179n14, 180n27, 182–195, 197, 202, 206n10, 209, 215, 217–221, 221n1, 222n18

Russian Empire, 29, 34, 47, 57, 74, 83, 84, 87, 88, 103, 104, 117, 118, 120, 127, 137, 138, 142, 144, 147, 150, 153n87, 154, 155, 160, 182, 186, 196, 198, 201, 203, 204, 211, 218, 226, 229, 244n13
Russians, viii, 2, 7, 11, 13, 20, 23, 24, 24n5, 27–30, 32–34, 36, 37, 39, 40, 41, 43, 44, 47–50, 52, 54–57, 59, 62, 64, 65n28, 65n33, 65n36, 65n44, 66n62, 66n66, 74–80, 81n10, 81n11, 81n12, 81n16, 81n18, 81n20, 81n22, 82n26, 82n30, 82n32, 82n34, 82n35, 82n37, 83-96, 104, 107, 108, 114n25, 115n43, 115n46, 115n64, 115n66, 118-131, 133n14, 134n18, 134n20, 134n38, 136n60, 137, 138, 139, 140, 141, 142, 144, 147-150, 151n28, 153n80, 153n87, 154, 155, 157-160, 163-166, 167n15, 170, 171, 173-177, 178n5, 179n10, 179n17, 180n27, 180n32, 181n48, 181n50, 181n57, 182-186, 189, 191, 193n39, 194n42, 194n52, 195n62, 195n63, 196, 198, 199, 201-204, 207n31, 207n38, 208n55, 208n56, 208n57, 208n59, 208n61, 209–225, 226, 228, 229, 231, 235, 236, 244n13, 245n21
Russian Society of Shipping and Trade, 11
Russian Steam Navigation and Trading Company, 33
Russian Technical Society, Odessa branch, 7
Russian Theater, 11, 52
Russov, Alexander, 11

S
Sabanievski bridge, 193n19
Sabanski, Isador, 11, 189, 194n42
Sahara Desert, 62
Sailor from the Kometa, A, 25n10
Saint-Joseph, Antoine de, 128, 137, 216, 222n21, 223n29, 224n52
Saint Nicholas Mirlikiiskii Church, 14
Salonika, 210
Sankte-Campioni, 43
Santorini, 160
Sardinia, 212, 213, 219, 223n40
Sauron, François, 140
Scaramanga family, 140, 187
School of Commerce, *see* Nicholas I Commercial School
Schulz, Jürgen, 191
Schumann, Robert, 41
Scudieri, Giovanni, 7
Sculpture Garden of the Literary Museum, 19
Scylla and Charybdis, 13
Seaman's Club, 39, 185
Sea of Azov, *see* Azov, Sea of
semi-secluded (family space), 59
Serafino, Theodore, 138
Serristori, L., 214
Sevastopol, 13, 78
Sevastopulo family, 11, 148
Sevastopulo, John, 165, 166, 167n9, 167n26
Sevastopulo, Marco, 162, 165
Sevastopulo, Marie, 149

Sewage (system), 103, 104, 108, 156, 157
Shaevich, K., 56
Shakespeare, 89, 186, 205
  King Lear, 43
  Othello, 43
Shapoval, Yurii, 74
Shchepkin'ska Street, 11
Shelley, Percy Bysshe, 89
Shevchenko, Taras, 74, 76
Shevrembrandt, G., 189
Shidlovsky, M. N., 39
Shmidt, Valer'ian, 12
Sholem Aleichem, 24n4, 47, 49, 60, 87, 93
  Cantor's Son, The, 90
  Letters of Menakhem-Mendl, The, 90
  Sheyne-Sheyndl, 90
  Tevye der Milkhiker (Tevye the Dairyman), 90
Shomrey Shabos, 95
Sicard, Charles, 102, 114n34, 128, 135n54
Sicily, 3, 29, 215
Silver Age, 91
Siniaver, M. M., 184, 185, 192n14, 192n16, 193n27, 194n53
Sion' (Zion), 87
Skal'kovs'kyi, A. O., 141
Skinner, Frederick W., 114n23, 114n25, 192n3, 193n33
Slavs, 92, 120, 121, 124, 198
Slobidka-Romanivka neighborhood, 32, 109, 188
Smith, Timothy, 144
Social Democratic Party, 56, 59
Social Democratic Workers' Party, 55
Society for the Promotion of Enlightenment (OPE), 85
Society of Engineers and Architects, 194n42
Sofiivs'ka Street, 187
Sophocles, 89
South Ukraine, 81n9, 154, 159, 226–245
Southwestern School, 83
Soviet Ukrainian Republic, 191
Spain, 34, 213, 219
Spanish, 28, 30, 47, 82n40, 117, 139, 140, 176, 182, 200, 211, 218
St. Petersburg, 25, 29, 33, 34, 37–39, 43, 47, 49, 62, 86, 88, 101, 103, 108, 112, 113n9, 114n33, 118–121, 124, 125, 132n2, 132n3, 132n6, 135n54, 135n56, 136n62, 140, 145, 147, 151n13, 153n84, 166n3, 171, 178n5, 179n6, 179n14, 180n35, 182, 184, 191, 192n19, 193n23, 194n55, 220, 225n64, 242, 244n8, 244n9, 244n10, 244n13
Stalin, Iosif, 54, 66n81, 77, 82n35, 89, 92, 93
Stanford University, 24n3, 64n15, 162, 206n2, 207n22
Stanislawski, Michael, 56, 66n71, 66n92, 208n55
Staroportofrankivs'ka Street, 188
State Museum of Art, 190
State Stock Exchange, 11
Steiglitz family, 140

Stenbock-Fermor, Elizabeth, 162, 164–166
Stepanov, Nikolai, 23
Stephens, John, 136n68, 143, 151n39, 152n44, 152n48
Stites, Richard, 45, 46, 65n28, 65n33, 65n36, 65n44
Stolyarsky, P. S., 42, 43
Storehouse, 11, 170, 171, 216
Strassburg, 101
Stroganov, Alexander G., 33, 200
Sturdza almshouse for children, 32, 188
Sturdza, Mikhail Dmitri, 159, 164, 167n5
Strudza, Zoe Theodorovna, 188
Sud'ina, Taisia, 23
Sutsos, 160, 165, 166, 167n8
Sweden, 34
Swiss, 2, 57, 139, 140, 171, 180n28
Switzerland, 34, 86, 89, 190, 192n19
Sylvester, Roshanna P., 49, 65n48
Symferopol', 235, 236, 238
Symyrenko, 123
synagogue, 14, 42, 95, 124, 125, 194n52, 202, 204

T

Taganrog, 51, 136n69, 137, 140–142, 144, 160, 161, 165, 166, 172, 173, 180n25, 187, 215, 220, 224n51, 237, 238, 242
Talmud-Torah, 86, 189
Tarnopol, Joachim, 87, 207n37
Tatars, 2, 32, 34, 128, 137
Taurida, 30, 187, 226, 236, 237, 242, 243
Tchaikovsky, Pyotr Illych, 43
Tchernichovsky, Shaul, 86, 89
  Beleyl Hanukah (On Hanukah Night), 89
  Seu nes tziyonah (Carry the Banner to Zion), 89
Teatral'na Square, 190
Technological Society of Odessa, 194n42
Tedesco, A. A., 41
Tel Aviv, 89, 134n32, 181n54, 206
Ternopil', 13
Theater of Opera and Ballet, 7
Thomas de Thomon, 37, 38, 183–185
T'homi, Abraham, 193n31
Todorov, A. D., 188
Tokarev, Oleksandr, 19, 20, 22, 23
Tolli, I. A., 163
Tolstoi, Mikhail Dmitrievich, 189
Tołwiński, M., 188, 192n19
Tomasini, 184
Torhova (Trade) Street, 189
Toricelli, Giordano, 7, 11, 37, 184, 190, 192n19
Tower of Babel, 27
Trading Hall, 190
Transnistria, 50
Traskov, Vladimir, 23
Treaty of Jassy, 28, 137, 182
Treaty of Kiuchuk-Kainardzhi, 226
Trebizond, 210

Trieste, 24n3, 30, 106, 129, 136n65, 140, 142, 143, 160, 179n17, 196–208, 209, 212, 215, 220, 223n29, 223n42
Trotsky, Leon, 194n52
Troubadour d'Odessa, 41, 128
Trubetskaya (wife of Langeron), 33
Tsarskoe Selo, 38
Tsederbaum, Alexander, 86, 87
Tsifer & Co., 186
Tsomakion, Marfa Viktorovna, 135n52, 145, 152n53
Tumanskii, V. I., 5, 25n11
Turgenev, Ivan
  Fathers and Sons, 88
Turin, 43, 136n61
Turkey, 25, 34, 103, 133n14, 136n68, 144, 151n39, 166, 166n1, 180n35, 210, 215, 218, 222n17, 223n30
Turkish Empire, 54, 155, 210
Turkmenistan, 51
Tuscany, 135n50, 136n65, 146, 147, 210, 212, 215–221, 222n6, 223n40, 224n51, 224n664
Two Soldiers, 5, 19
Tyraspil's'ka Square, 193n19

U

Udovenko, Hennadii, 76, 77, 79, 81n19, 82n35
Ufa, 233
Ukrainians, 2, 13, 24n5, 34, 36, 44, 54–57, 59, 64, 76–80, 81n15, 82n34, 84, 118, 119, 123, 126, 131, 134n18, 134n21, 204, 244n3
Ukrainka, Lesya (Larysa Petrivna Kosach), 76
  On the Wings of Song, 53
Unger, R. W., 244n7
United States, vii, 2, 34, 46, 57, 59, 62, 93, 94, 104, 111, 114n29, 116n90, 125, 134n41, 142–144, 155, 161, 166, 172, 175, 186, 233
University of Novorossiia, 120, 149, *see also* Richelieu Lyceum
Uspen'skyi Fair, 232
Utesov, Leonid, 4, 22, 44–46
Utochkin, Serhii, 22, 26n26, 61, 62

V

Vaisbein, L. I., *see* Utesov, Leonid
Val'b, 184
Vanini, A., 188
Venice, 30, 197
Venizelos, Eleutherios, 165
Vienna, 32, 45, 101, 104, 139, 147, 175, 202, 206n7, 218, 219
Vilna, 84, 87
Viollet-le-Duc, Eugène, 193n26
Vitrychenko, Olena, 62
Vlodek, L. L., 12, 190
Volga, 2
Volokhov, D. K., 185
Voluntary Fleet, 11
Vorontsov, Mikhail S., 33, 122, 172, 185, 200

Vorontsov Palace, 6, 7, 9, 11
Vorontsovs'kyi Lane, 188
Vreto, 138
Vsevolozhskii, N. S., 24n5
Vysotsky, Vladimir, 46

W

Wallachia, 151n28, 179n9, 197, 222n21
Warsaw, 26n20, 33, 48, 54, 83, 84, 86, 89, 117, 121, 194n42
Watkins, Melville H., 172, 180n20
Wegelin, Daniel, 117
Weinryb, D., 135n41
Weizmann, Haim, 88
Western and Eastern Arts Museum, 31, 187
Western European, 89, 105, 120, 171, 179n17
Western Ukraine, 14, 75, 79, 243
Winslow, C. E., 112, 113n7, 116n89
Witte, S. Yu., 176
World Union of Zionist Revisionists, 91
World War I, 39, 46, 48, 54, 64, 126, 127, 161–166, 186, 220
World War II, 5, 23, 39, 50, 51, 80n1, 93, 185, 193n30
World Zionist Organization, 86
Wright Brothers, 62

Y

Yadov, Yakov
    "Bublichki" (Bagels), 46
Yalta, 78
Yaponchik, Mishka (Mykhailo Vinnyts'kyi), 48
Yeames, James, 136n69, 140
Yeames, William, 136n69
Yelenin, Vladimir, 75, 80n7
Yeni-Dünya, 29, 83, 182
Yermakova, Natasha, 79
Yiddish, 27, 45, 47, 48, 83–92
Yiddishisms, 48, 92, 93
Ypsilanti, Alexander, 138
Yushchenko, Viktor, 19, 79, 81n16
Yushkevich, Semyon, 91

Z

Zahorodniuk, Vyacheslav, 62
Zagoruiko, V., 134n18, 134n21, 135n55, 152n55, 171, 178n3, 179n11, 180n33
Zamboni, Giacomo, 43
Zaporozhian Sich, 74
Zarifi, 30
Zhdanov, see Mariupol'
Zhurnal of the Ministry of Internal Affairs, 228
Zhvanetsky, Mikhail, 20, 83, 93
    Moia Odessa (My Odessa), 94, 95n4
    Odesskie dachi (Odessan Dachas), 94
Zhytomyr, 235, 238, 244n12
Zinger, Mark, 42
Zinsendorf, Karl von, 200
Zipperstein, Steven J., vii, 24n3, 42, 56, 64n15, 65n19, 66n69, 66n72, 95n2, 199, 202, 205, 207n22, 207n24, 207n26, 207n35, 207n45, 208n54, 208n56, 208n57, 208n60
Zolotov, V. A., 114n26, 141, 151n19, 151n21, 151n33, 178n3, 179n17, 180n30, 180n31, 181n53, 221n1, 245n22
Zubov, Platon, 19, 29, 80n1